AUSTRONESIAN
PATHS AND
JOURNEYS

AUSTRONESIAN
PATHS AND
JOURNEYS

EDITED BY JAMES J. FOX

Australian
National
University

PRESS

TO THE MEMORY OF MARSHALL D. SAHLINS

We would like to dedicate this volume to the memory of Marshall Sahlins who was a brilliantly productive and remarkably insightful 'Austronesianist'. His *Social Stratification in Polynesia* was an early, important and provocative comparative study (1958); his *Moala: Culture and Nature on a Fijian Island* (1962) was a major ethnographic monograph of lasting value; and his *Islands of History* (1985) was an interpretive analysis that gave global significance to events in the history of the Pacific. His influence was profound on both students and colleagues. We have all learned much from him and his work.

ANU PRESS

Published by ANU Press
The Australian National University
Acton ACT 2601, Australia
Email: anupress@anu.edu.au

Available to download for free at press.anu.edu.au

ISBN (print): 9781760464325
ISBN (online): 9781760464332

WorldCat (print): 1247151070
WorldCat (online): 1247150967

DOI: 10.22459/APJ.2021

Cover design and layout by ANU Press. Cover photograph: A gathering of members of the clan Nabuasa in the village of Lasi in the mountains of West Timor to hear the recitation of the journey of their ancestral name. Photo by James J. Fox.

Contents

Abbreviations

BP//MT	Bula Pe//Mapo Tena
BS//BT	Buna Sepe//Boa Timu
DK//SB	Dela Kolik ma Seko Bunak
ENSO	El Niño–Southern Oscillation
IA//ML	Iu Ai//Maka Lopo
KF//BT	Koli Faenama ma Bunak Tunulama
KL//LB	Kea Lenga//Lona Bala
LD//KK	Leli Deak//Kona Kek
LL//KP	Lo Luli//Kalu Palu
LL//PD	Loma-Loma Langa//Pele-Pele Dulu
LP//MS	Liu Pota//Menge Solu
MK//TN	Manu Kama//Tepa Nilu
ML//BS	Malungi Lai//Balokama Sina
NE//FN	Ndao Eli-Sama//Folo No-Do'o
NL//LE	Ndi Lonama//Laki Elokama
PAN	Proto-Austronesian
PB//BL	Pau Balo ma Bola Lungi
PMP	Proto-Malayo-Polynesian
PP//SL	Pinga Pasa ma So'e Leli
TT//BL	Tetema Taenama and Balapua Loni

List of illustrations

Figures

Maps

Plates

Tables

1

Towards a comparative ethnography of Austronesian 'paths' and 'journeys'

James J. Fox

Introduction

The expansion and dispersal of Austronesian languages from Taiwan to Timor and across the Indian Ocean and through the Pacific, stretching from Madagascar to Easter Island, demonstrate a remarkable social mobility. Exploration of this mobility has been the implicit theme in the majority of the various volumes of the Comparative Austronesian series. This exploration has included not just the delineation of the distribution of Austronesian languages and the examination of the archaeological evidence for the spread of plants, people and their products, but also the consideration of the social factors underlying this mobility: technologies of travel, systems of exchange, forms of subsistence and their implications, trade patterns, demographic pressures on small islands, the reception of distant strangers, the role of status systems that propel individuals outward, the prestige of founder status and the recognition and celebration of multiple ancestral origins. This volume is a further, explicit exploration of this critical idea of mobility focusing on the concepts of the journeying and the paths this journeying implies. In addressing this topic, each of the individual chapters in this volume opens a path or paths to a wide range of other comparative issues.

The focus in this volume is as much on actual journeying on specific paths as it is on spiritual journeys in the realm of memory and imagination. Some of the most locally established Austronesian populations embrace the idea of distant journeying and may indeed perform such journeys in their ritual celebrations, as in practice, such journeys tend to be path specific and are often highly embellished in their details.

There may even be an underlying basis for this path specificity. In a stimulating paper that examines motion events in several Austronesian languages, the linguists Shuanfan Huang and Michael Tanangkingsing argue that 'path salience in the encoding of motion clauses appears to exhibit a strong diachronic stability, suggesting that Proto-Austronesian was probably also a path-salient language' (2005: 307).[1] Essentially, this argument provides a semantic-typological predilection for the prevalence of attention to path information in motion events.

Of more general relevance is recent research on cognitive mapping. Based on the foundational identification of place and grid cells, Bellmund et al. have, in a recent paper in *Science* (2018: 8), titled 'Navigating cognitions: Spatial codes for human thinking', proposed 'cognitive spaces as a primary format for information processing in the brain'. In this model, 'cognitive spaces enable generalization and can reveal novel trajectories via the representation of positions along defined dimensions' (Bellmund et al. 2018: 7). Replaying such trajectories involves evaluating 'previous paths' and may extend to the simulation of 'future paths' so that the 'replay of both correct and incorrect future trajectories supports learning and planning' (Bellmund et al. 2018: 6).

Whatever direct relevance this basic research may have, it points to the idea of the path as a mechanism for the encoding and critical differentiation of information—information that can be retrieved, re-evaluated and reused. In the cases considered in this volume, paths and the rehearsal of journeys along them encode specific cultural information. The patterning of this information is the subject of this volume.

---

1   The idea of path saliency began with Leonard Talmy's topological distinction regarding motion events according to whether path or manner is coded as the head of a verb phrase (1991) and has been developed by Dan Slobin (2004) in terms of a further distinction between satellite-framed languages ('S-languages') and verb-framed ('V-languages'). As Huang and Tanangkingsing, who use their own typology, note: '[T]here is a great diversity across languages in the level of salience and granularity in path or manner expression, in type of semantic components employed, and in the balance in the different parts of the language system in expressing spatial motions' (2005: 311).

Specific Austronesian paths

Among Austronesians, the metaphor of the path is a recurrent socially defining metaphor. It offers a means of understanding—a vehicle for identifying and tracing relationships between specific nodes of knowledge. It can also be a record of former engagements and an evocation of origins, thus providing an enactment of the past. Just as readily, such metaphors may envision future directions and open expectations to as yet unknown realms of possibility. The journeys defined by such paths are generally oriented and often directed. Their significance requires critical attention and interpretation. This volume examines the use of such metaphors in specific Austronesian contexts.

The 10 chapters in this volume explore multiple metaphors of paths drawn from societies across the Austronesian-speaking world, ranging from Taiwan to Timor, from Borneo to Madagascar and from Flores into the Pacific. The paths examined in these chapters define a diverse combination of physical and spiritual journeys. A majority of the chapters rely on reflexes of the Proto-Austronesian construct for 'path or road': *zalan.

For the Bunun of Taiwan, the term for path is *dan*. 'To traverse a path' is *mu-dan*; 'walking' is *mudadaan*, while 'finding one's way' is *kilim dan*. The specific Bunun paths that Wen-ling Lin discusses are part of a major collective effort at 'wayfinding'—the rediscovery of lost paths in a concerted campaign to reclaim what was once traditional land. For the Amis of Taiwan, paths are *lalan*. While *lalan* can refer to structures in the mundane world, Yi-tze Lee discusses the invisible thread-paths that Amis shamans call forth to journey to the world of the spirits and the need for a constant checking of these paths to avoid dangerous diversions.

For the Betsileo of Madagascar, paths are *lalana*. The paths that Denis Regnier describes are a network of laterite paths that criss-cross Betsileo territory and must be traversed in searching out ancestral origins to ensure proper marriages. For the Kelabit, the term for path is *dalan* and in Monika Janowski's chapter it is used to refer to heroic journeys in the quest for power. For the Iban, the term *jalai* can refer to the paths or journeys of life and death. Clifford Sather in his chapter discusses the interdependency of these paths: the *jalai mati*, the 'journey of death', as a continuation of the *jalai idup*, the 'journey of life'.

A similar idea—perhaps a basic general Austronesian idea linking the journey of life to the journey into death—lies at the heart of fundamental conceptions of the Rotenese of the Timor area. The repertoire of Rotenese mortuary chants celebrates a variety of possible 'life-courses'. Life-courses in their variety, as indeed the passage to the afterlife, were regarded as journeys on specifically marked paths (*dalan*).

For the Lamaholot of Flores, paths are referred to as *laran*. These can refer to physical roads but also ritual paths. In her chapter, Dana Rappoport focuses on the long song path (*opak moran laran Tono Wujo*) that recounts the journey of the rice maiden eastward—a narrative song sung to enact this path.

In areas of Melanesia, there are local lexical terms for path, as is the case for the populations of two islands, Dobu and Muyuw, in the Milne Bay Province of Papua New Guinea. For the Dobu, the term for 'path' is *'eda*; for Muyuw, the term for 'path' is *ked*; yet the idea of the path and its metaphorical usages are bound up in similar Austronesian conceptions. In her chapter on Dobu, Susanne Kuehling presents a wideranging examination of the complex network of relations involved in contemporary *kula* exchange, where journeying follows an oriented pattern of cyclical activities linked to the winds, the sea and, significantly, the pattern of yam gardening. Her analysis of this 'pulse' of exchange across an extensive array of named places provides a stunning re-examination of the interconnected dynamics of *kula* relations. For the Muyuw, as Fred Damon—who has, like Susanne Kuehling, sailed with *kula* traders—explains, the idea of *ked* embraces a manifold range of meanings, from *kula* exchange to the proper manner and performance of reciprocity. As such, it is a key social concept to understanding Muyuw social life.

Yu-chien Huang's chapter provides an appropriate conclusion to this collection by traversing the Austronesian world in its comparison between specific paths among the Yami of Taiwan and the population of Yap in Micronesia.

These chapters, as a whole, offer an explicit discussion of a general theme—one that pervades the ethnographic discussion of Austronesian populations but has not been given the formal attention it deserves. Moreover, the examination of this key metaphor opens 'paths' in different directions, leading to the examination of other critical comparative issues.

In considering earlier discussions of Austronesian paths and journeys by previous ethnographers, one can, at best, present a strategic selection of observations from among a wealth of ethnographic accounts.

Ancestral paths

In his monumental *The Work of the Gods in Tikopia*, originally drafted in 1929–30 after his return from the field, but only published in 1940, Raymond Firth (1967) describes in detail the rituals of the sacred canoes, which are (or once were) the first and foremost of an entire cycle of celebration. This focus on canoes as the primary vehicles of Tikopian fishing and voyaging is critical to these commemorative ceremonies, but Firth also examines a pertinent adjunct ritual that occurs in conjunction with these ceremonies. This ritual the Tikopians describe as the 'path of the ancestor' (*te ara o pu*)—the ritual enactment of an initial exchange between the ancestors of the chiefly lineages of Kafika and Taumako. This 'path' (*ara*) is not of great length—particularly on a tiny island like Tikopia—but its significance requires regular renewal. It commemorates the marriage of the 'Great Ancestor' of Taumako, Pu Lasi, son of Te Atafu of Tonga, with the daughter of the Ariki Kafika. As Firth makes clear, in this context, 'path' defines a relationship that demands the carrying of a great load of foodstuffs including shark meat from Taumako to Kafika. As he states: 'The *ara* is the most formal occasion on which this relationship is expressed' (Firth 1967: 131). It is a prime example of the use of path as a metaphor of multiple significance and, in particular, of a continuing relationship established by an ancient marriage.

This use of path to define relations among kin is common in the region and more generally throughout the Austronesian-speaking world. Judith Huntsman and Antony Hooper in the historical ethnography *Tokelau* discuss this explicitly:

> Pedigree relationships are expressed in terms of *ala* (or *auala*) 'paths' … Such 'paths' are traced to a pair of siblings rather than an ancestral couple … By tracing to siblings, it is established *how* two people are related; that they *are* related is assumed. In fact, in many instances, people may be linked by two or even more 'paths' of this kind, relating them in different ways and increasing the closeness of their relationship. (1996: 117; emphasis in original)

Interestingly, from an Austronesian perspective, this tracing of paths is distinguished from the tracing of genealogies (*gafa*) that begin with either a single individual or an ancestral pair and recount lines of descendants in a set and orderly fashion.

Among ethnographies of Oceania, Richard J. Parmentier's *The Sacred Remains* (1987) provides the most diverse litany of the use of metaphors of 'path'. On Palau/Belau, 'paths' (*rael*) present a powerful image. Parmentier brilliantly summarises their use and significance:

> A path is a method, technique, patterns, or strategy—in short, a way of doing something. Warfare strategies, fishing techniques, oratorical skills, and patterns of exchange are called 'paths'. But paths are also established linkages, relationships, and associations among persons, groups, and political units which were created by some precedent-setting action in the past, and which imply the possibility, as well as the obligation, for following the path in marriage, exchange, cooperation and competition. (1987: 109)

There are various sorts of paths: ancient paths (*mechut el rael*), distantly linked paths (*ngamekechui rael*) and newly created paths (*beches el rael*). Ancient paths are those instituted by gods or ancestors and possess great significance; others are more contemporary, of lesser worth and thus less travelled. Each path is defined by its origin (*uchul*: 'beginning, base, trunk') and its end point (*rsel*: 'tip'). It can consist of a linear progression that may be either limited or extended. Parmentier clearly recognises the importance of paths as a means of establishing an order of precedence:

> [L]inked elements can be viewed in terms of sequential precedence, with the origin point outranking all other points, according to a logic which stipulates that priority in time implies seniority in ceremonial precedence. (1987: 109)

Paths link villages and titled houses in a complex network. So, too, is the entire Belau archipelago joined in a path that extends from its southern islands—where fire was discovered and where the techniques of measurement, carving and carpentry were obtained from the sea— in a progression towards the north. These archaic ancestral connections define a critical path of origin with its 'trunk' (*uchul*) at Lukes or Mekaeb and its 'tip' (*rsel*) at Oikuli on the main island of Babeldaob.

This conceptual scheme is narrated as a journey. As Parmentier explains:

> Rather than having separate schemes for space and time, traditional Belauan culture unites these two Western categories through the notion of a journey (*omerael*, from the verb *merael*, 'to walk, to travel' itself derived from the notion, *rael*, 'path, road, way' [PAN *dalan*]). The journey of a god, person, group, or mythological creature provides a basic space-time for conceptualization and discourse. (1987: 133–34)

Parmentier's discussion offers an excellent exemplification of a common feature of many Austronesian societies: a journey whose path provides a fundamental 'origin structure' for the society (see Fox 1992). This is a point that is made repeatedly in the chapters in this volume.

Defining journeys of origin

As Parmentier recognised, the paths recounted in these journeys are replete with specific nodes. Each carries specific information. The nodes in these socially defining ancestral journeys can be places, thus making the journey a topology—a recitation of placenames or named ancestors—and giving the journey a genealogical cast or, as is most common, a combination of both. As Dana Rappoport indicates in her chapter on the journey of the rice maiden in east Flores, new elements may be added as improvised nodes to make such recitations more current and relevant. Examples of similar defining journeys abound in the Austronesian literature.

One of the best examples of this kind of defining journey has been highlighted by Elizabeth Traube in her ethnography of the Mambai of Timor-Leste produced over decades. She has noted:

> The idea of a journey comprehends both the sequence of past events that is presented in a narrative account of origins and also the very activity of telling. Narrative discourse, as much as the events it relates, is thought of as a trip or a journey across space and time. Tellers endeavour to 'follow a path' or 'track an ancestor,' that is to retrace verbally the movements of the tale's protagonists. (Traube 1989: 331–32)

In the case of the Mambai, this journey or 'walk of the flag' focuses on a sibling set of three ancestors, one of whom, Au Sa, is accorded little attention; another, Ki Sa, who is central to the narrative and the 'planting of the flag of the interior'; and a third, Loer Sa, who leaves, only to return from overseas as a 'familiar stranger', in the form of the Portuguese colonial flagbearers. This narrative admits of various retellings that allow it to be made contemporary. In a version after the 1975 invasion of East Timor, Au Sa comes to be recognised as the dark ancestor of the Indonesians in contrast to Loer Sa, who is considered traditionally to have given rise to the Portuguese (Traube 2011).

In a similar vein, Susana Barnes has aptly emphasised the importance of the narrative of key ancestral itineraries in the Uatolari area of Timor-Leste:

> Ancestral itineraries and histories serve not only to reinforce the emplaced nature of claims to authority, but also to reaffirm the order of arrival and settlement of various descent groups living within these territories. At the same time, these narratives provide a guide in understanding the dynamics and processes whereby subsidiary groups were formed and in-migrant groups were incorporated into the social order. (2011: 30)

A key founding narrative, recounted by Barnes, centres on the relationship between an elder–younger brother pair: the elder brother fails in his ritual duties and is exiled, leaving his younger brother in place as 'lord of the land'. In describing Uatolari narrative journeys as 'histories of incorporation and accommodation', Barnes cites E. Douglas Lewis, whose ethnography of the Tana Ai population of central eastern Flores, *People of the Source* (1988), offers a model examination of an ancestral journey and analyses its implications as an origin structure. This journey features a set of three ancestors: two brothers who journey together, arrive at an auspicious site and thus found the domain of Wai Brama, with a third ancestor, who travels by a different route and eventually joins the domain as its final clan member.

These journeys, identifiable by their genealogical underpinnings, contrast with similar founding journeys among the Atoni Pah Meto of west Timor. The nodes that mark the recitations of the journeying of the clans of the Meto are made up primarily of placenames. As Andrew McWilliam explains:

> West Timor is mapped conceptually by a bewildering array of named places ... Recounting the origins of the clans in West Timor is perhaps better described as tracing the path of the name. This is because all individuals in Meto society are affiliated to agnatically-related kin groups called *kanaf*, a Timorese word

meaning name or name group. Thus, when a speaker recounts the history of his group he is, in effect, mapping the journey of the name along a spatial and temporal trajectory which is punctuated by significant events or settlement sites (one notion of the gate) along the way ... In other words, the reproduction of the group name is measured or recorded in terms of sequential places rather than a sequence of people. (1997: 104–5)

As McWilliam astutely notes, whether the specific place nodes on these journeys are poetically described as 'gates', 'fences', 'rocks' or 'trees', there is a great deal of additional cultural information attached to them. The recitation of these topologies provides an outline schema of a fuller history.

In his account of the formation of the domain of Amanuban whose centre at Tumbesi is defined by its 'rock and tree'—its sacrificial altars and raised wooden posts—McWilliam offers this example of a ritual assertion by a *kanaf* to set the boundary of its rule from its ceremonial centre (1997: 109):

> Take the head wrap and axe
> And take the hair comb and silver coin
> To tie in the roof spar
> At the path of Teas
> The platform of Teas
> To become the guardians of
> The flowers of the *hue* tree
> The flowers of the *usaip* tree
> At the outside fence
> And the outside boundary.

McWilliam's ethnography *Paths of Origin, Gates of Life: A study of place and precedence* (2002) offers a superb historical examination of how such Meto paths come together in a local political formation.

In his ethnography of the Banda Eli population, who have been displaced from their home island of Banda to the island of Kei in eastern Indonesia, *Songs of Travel, Stories of Place* (2010), Timo Kaartinen presents a rich analysis of the recitations of sad memories of places lost and never regained. Among various oral genres that Kaartinen considers, he offers an extended examination of an *onotani* lament that recounts an ancestral sea journey—carried by the wind, drifting like flotsam—from Banda via a string of islands, Kur, Uf and Rumadan, to Greater Kei, with its distinguishing mountain tops. This topogeny, coupled with its poignant commentary and recurrent refrains, sets out the foundations of the Banda Eli's journey into social exile. Excerpts from this lament give a hint of its expressive performative power (Kaartinen 2010: 112–16):

> They search in the Banda islands …
> for your nest, our navel …
> gust of wind, log of driftwood
> gust of wind, log of driftwood
> thus we land on the tall island of Kur
> the island of Kur, rising to the skies
> there is no faith in you island
> no blessing, we retreat …
> we land inside the reef of the Ujuf Island …
> at sea we speak Bandanese
> at sea we speak Bandanese
> pearls of wisdom
> the nutmegs have died
> there is no faith, and you keep drifting
> there is no blessing inside this island
> no blessing left in the whole world!

Kaartinen's exegesis of this text, his discussion of what he refers to as 'songs of history' and 'the poetics of travel' and, in particular, his observation of the importance of 'the concretization of mythic-historical pasts in named places and their topographies through ancestral activities, especially travel' (2010: 122) have broad Austronesian relevance.

Dana Rappoport's chapter in this volume, 'The long journey of the rice maiden from Lio to Tanjung Bunga, eastern Flores: A Lamaholot sung narrative', offers a critical comparative perspective on fundamental Austronesian ideas. Lamaholot narratives of the rice maiden take two forms. A 'short' form, known as the 'road song', is sung by participants on the way to the ceremony. This song is intended to alert the spirits to the participants' presence as they pass specific points on their journey. The 'long' form of these narratives, consisting of thousands of lines and referred to as the 'narrative of the road', constitutes the core of ceremonial performances sung and danced through the night until dawn on repeated occasions during the agricultural cycle. The ceremony recounts the story of Noga Ema' (also known as Tonu Wojo), her killing and transformation into rice and her beneficent journey as the female personification of rice (and as an 'ancestral sister') from the Lio area of central Flores to Tanjung Bunga in the Lamaholot region at the eastern end of Flores. The musical and linguistic complexity of these narratives is remarkable. So, too, is the variation in these narratives among the villages of the Lamaholot regions (see Graham 1991; Kohl 1998).

This long 'narrative of the road' consists of a number of embedded journeys, the last of which recounts the mysterious journey of the rice maiden, her successive impregnations and progeny and the ever-present possibility of the loss of the precious gift that she bears. The narrative is set in the past and re-enacting the journey brings it into the present. Spatial succession defines a temporal succession. The chief narrator (*opak*) is referred to as the 'drum' (*bawa*) or the one who 'beats the drum continuously'. Although no drum is used to accompany the chant, this naming of the chief narrator creates an analogy between his voice and that of the drum. The narrator is accompanied by an embellisher (*nukun opak*) plus paired singers (*hode' ana*) as well as a soloist, who, in concert with one another, offer a succession of narrative sequences, punctuated by duet singing and a variety of choreographed dancing.

As Rappoport pointedly notes: 'Two criteria govern the singing of the journey: continuity and correct naming.' Such enunciation requires an extraordinary knowledge of particular nodes of specific information about persons, places and events, set in succession and recited in proper order without omissions. The complementarity of lexical items—the parallelism of the narrative's presentation—contributes to the stability of this coding. Only a well-ordered path constitutes a proper performance. A performative error is dangerous and is believed to be potentially fatal to the narrator.

The performance evokes comparisons with ritual journeying elsewhere in eastern Indonesia. The drum is a crucial instrument that opens contact with the spirit world and marks the steps of a variety of narrative journeys.[2] Joel Kuipers has described in fine detail the divinatory and spirit placation ceremonies (*zaizo*) of the Weyewa of Sumba in which drums provide the accompaniment for singers. In these ceremonies, the spirits are called to return along familiar paths to their former village (Kuipers 1990: 135):

> do not be slow in descending
> do not be late in departing ...
> the tracks that were followed e-e-e
> the path that was travelled e-e-e

---

2   See Needham (1967) on the significance of percussion as a mechanism in ritual.

as you gaze at the village gate
as you look at the house ladder
if you are Mbili
if you are Koni
truly
and you come straight down
along the soaring house tower
along the Kamberan center rafters
and you come down to the ground.

Similarly, in Kodi on Sumba, the drum is at the centre of spirit communication. Janet Hoskins describes it as a:

crucial nonhuman intermediary … sent on a journey up through the seven layers of the heavens and six layers of the earth (*pitu ndani cana, nomo ndani awango*) to the upperworld on the eighth level to ask for blessings. (1993: 227)

As at funeral ceremonies, so, too, in divination rituals, the role of the drum is to convey the words of humans to the divinity. The drum is addressed and given offerings and, as it is about to begin its long journey, it is told, as Hoskins (1988: 45) reports:

You are the bird we set singing
You are the butterfly we set flying
So let us walk down the same path together
So let us ride astride the same horse together

Dana Rappoport, in her account of the Maro rituals of Sa'dan Toraja, provides a stunning example of the use of the drum in trance-journeying. In the midst of a chaotic succession of ceremonial activities—the 'madness' of the Maro—the spirits are called on to empower the knife held by an officiant, in trance, who cuts his forehead and lets forth his blood to rub on those around him. A chorus of women, dishevelled with their hair in disarray, chant in unison. One of their number demands a drum, circles it and then steps on top of it, as the chorus recounts the journey of the trancer (Rappoport 2009: 145):

I'm already on top of the drum
On the peak of the zither
On the point of the glorious knife.

A truly beautiful heavenly village
A wonderful house indeed
The glorious ritual grounds.

> I'm almost at peace up there
> I'm almost not returning
> I'm almost not returning

Eventually, the chorus of women recounts the reluctant return of the trancer—transformed 'with the energy of gold'—who descends, 'bathed by the sound of the drum, rinsed by zithers and washed by flutes' (Rappoport 2006: 96–97).

As in the case of the Toraja trancer, journeys can be productive and life-giving. The journey of the rice maiden and the germination of rice from her body, as told in the Lamaholot region of Flores, form one of a variety of recurrent myths of the origin of rice and other foods. In eastern Indonesia, this narrative more often relates to the origins of a full suite of plants. The island of Rote, for example, has several different origin myths. The most prominent is one that tells of the origin of rice and millet from sea creatures who are planted and then ceremonially transferred around the island by women whose personal names are the personification of places—often irrigated fields. The narrative constitutes a topogeny—a recitation of placenames that describes a journey clockwise around the island (Fox 2014a: 265–66). Another myth tells of the origin of millet and maize from the blood of a heavenly being. The figure Lakimola Bulan//Kaibake Ledo pierces his little finger and little toe and then walks through the dry land: wherever his blood drops, red millet and red rice spring forth (Fox 2014b: 277–82). Yet another telling blends elements of the other two versions to create a new telling: the woman Seku Tine//Rele Hade scoops the seeds from the sea and plants them on the slopes of a site called Lakamola//Kaibaka, an upland area with a small lake in eastern Rote. When 'the nine grains and eight seeds' (*pule sio*//*poka falu*) spread throughout the island, they are collectively referred to as the 'children of Lakamola'.

More striking a comparison is that of the Tetun origin of domestic plants as told in Wehali, in south central Timor (Therik 2004: 257–59). This tells of a time when there was no food in Wehali and one of the six ruling *liurai*, the Liurai Berechi, offered his body to become food for the people. From his head came red and green coconuts, from his right hand came *fuan* bananas, from his left hand came mung beans, from his guts and intestines, vines and pumpkins. His blood flowed into the sea and became the *nase* fish and from inside the head of this fish, when it was caught, came special sorghum seeds (*batar tasi*) that can only be grown in the gardens of Wehali. Finally, when the legs of the *liurai* were burned, their ashes became gunpowder.

The critically interesting feature of this narrative is the complex network of paths that trace the transfer of these plants into and out of Wehali. Green coconuts were sent to Fatumea Takolo in the land of the rising sun, red coconuts to Fatumea Talama in the land of the setting sun, while the people of Wehali took only young green coconuts to sprinkle on and cool their gardens. Mung beans, which are the staples of Tetun subsistence, were brought from Akani, planted in Wehali and then taken back by Akani to be planted more widely. Each of the plants in this recitation has its distinctive pathway. The whole of this narrative is a recitation of interwoven paths linked to Wehali as a sacred centre.[3]

Journey as a quest

The full narrative of the journey of the rice maiden is more than just a narrative of the transference of rice. It begins as a foundation myth and proceeds to recount the search by the ancestral figure Pati Sogén for a wife. This is a journey as quest and thus belongs to a rich genre of diverse Austronesian narratives, many of epic proportions, focusing on the adventures of cultural heroes. Monika Janowski's chapter, 'Journeys in quest of cosmic power (*lalud*): Highland heroes in Borneo', provides an excellent illustration of this genre—an example from the Kelabit of Borneo, featuring the journey and martial adventures of Tuked Rini and his companions (see also Janowski 2014).

These narratives contrast male mobility with female stability in place.[4] The acquired spiritual power and magical endowments of these wandering males are paramount and their journeying advances the narrative as it

---

3   I have now held two recording sessions in Bali with the Mako'an Piet Tahu Nahak, Tom Therik's chief informant, who first revealed this origin narrative to him. I have recorded two further versions of it, but I have not yet managed to understand all its complexities. After recording one longer version and spending time trying to map out the sites mentioned in the narrative, Piet Tahu decided to recite another version, which was longer, more elaborate and more difficult to comprehend fully. My efforts remain a work-in-progress.

4   This pattern of male mobility and female stability in place highlights the special ritual significance of the journey of the rice maiden among the Lamaholot.

moves the hero-figure from adventure to adventure. Kichapi, the young hero in William Geddes's *Nine Dayak Nights* (1957: 81), voices his efforts in journeying:

> Walking on, forever walking on
> Uphill I go, and downhill
> On hills of a thousand different kinds;
> Each stream at its mouth flows into a second,
> Each lake at its end joins another …

In the end, after many struggles and near-death escapes, Kichapi succeeds in triumphing over his final opponent and gaining his beloved Gumiloh; so, this tale of wandering ends in the attainment of a bride and residence with her in her village.

In a rich and varied genre, the Kichapi narrative can be compared with a variety of similar male-journey narratives: the Saribas Iban narrative of Sugi Sakit recorded and analysed by Clifford Sather in *A Borneo Healing Romance* (2017); the ritual song of the double-named Nias noble Situo Mäli Itô//Situo Mäli Ndewâ, who wanders for years to find a wife, as recorded by W.L. Steinhart in *Niasse Teksten* (1954: 5–42);[5] the long Tiruray narrative featuring Laqei Lengkuos's journey and eventual obtainment of his bride, Menfelabu (see Wein 1989); or the Palawan narrative that recounts Mämiminbin's journeying to the realms of the Master of Thunder and Lady of the Fishes and eventual marriage to the Äriq ni Labit, the sister of Labit whose steadfastness in place is maintained throughout the entire narrative to the point that she never leaves her house (Revel and Intaray 2000).

The different name changes of the hero that occur in the various episodes of some of these narratives suggest that they may be an amalgam of tales of several different heroes whose exploits have been creatively joined as one. Particularly important, as Janowski indicates, are the status and spiritual qualities of both males and females: their consequent beauty, lustrous appearance and their rich and striking apparel. These are generally narratives that exalt a social elite.

---

5   Steinhart's Nias corpus, produced between 1934 and 1954, is a monumental collection of Austronesian texts in strict canonical parallelism with detailed notes on the language of the texts, but it provides frustratingly little information on their social and ritual context.

The journeys of these heroes can also be seen as a trial. The prize is often a change in power and status. Frequently, the hero is assisted by helpers—human, animal or spirit-advisors. The hero is told to take the difficult path—'the narrow road'—the difficulty of which tests the capacities of the hero and thus serves as evidence of his inherent worth. Like specific placenames that mark a journey, the creatures encountered on the journey serve as nodes that inform, direct and advance the narrative.

One of the longest and most elaborate oral narratives in this genre is the *Guritan of Radin Suane* from the Besemah of south Sumatra. This monumental recitation, recorded by William A. Collins and eventually published (1998) after years of effort to transcribe, decipher and understand its formulaic high language, is a long quest by Radin Suane to search for and eventually win a bride. Collins describes this *guritan* as 'a prince's quest for a wife and a princess' choice of a husband' (1998: 19).[6] In its details, it is a portrait of a Besemah past.

The recitation is formulaic in structure and in language. It takes 20 cantos—more than 1,100 lines—for Radin Suane to prepare his weapons, jewellery, clothes and other accoutrements ready for his departure. Embedded in this departure sequence is a long recitation of almost 200 lines of a formulaic topogeny that names and describes the surrounding lands and their ruling dynasties (Collins 1998: 93–94):

Wan itu jalan ke Bengkulu	That is the way to Bengkulu
Tunak kundu Mentiring Sakti …	The place of the soul of Mentiring Sakti …
Wan itu jalan ke Jagat Aceh	That is the way to Jagat Aceh
Tunak kundu Pangeran Dunang …	The place of the soul of Pangran Dunang …
Wan itu jalan Kisam Tinggi	That is the way to Kisam Tinggi
Tunak kundu Radin Bambayan	The place of the soul of Radin Bambayan

---

6   In the Borneo narrative summarised by Janowski, Tuked Rini is already married to Aruring when he sets off on his journey. He returns with two lost relatives who have heroically helped him. One of the men tries to persuade Aruring to sleep with him, but she refuses and declares she wants only Tuked Rini. This resembles the convention in other narratives such as the *Guritan of Radin Suane*, in which the princess rejects other suitors and, instead, chooses her hero husband.

This topogeny identifies 37 realms, from Aceh at the northern end of Sumatra to Semarang, Demak and beyond along the coast of Java, each with its named local aristocrats.

When Radin Suane finally sets sail following an invitation to a three-month-long cockfight in preparation for a wedding, he directs the ship on a straight, unswerving path as if on land (Collins 1998: 118):

Tumpak tuju di Remban Tinggi	Our destination is Remban Tinggi
Nyimpang ke kiri dibenupkan	Deviate to the left and be sunk,
Nyimpang ke kanan dipelebur …	Deviate to the right and be smashed …

As the distinguished Finnish scholar Aarne A. Koskinen noted in his study of the symbolism of the path in Polynesia (1968), among Austronesians, any deviation from a set path is regarded as an error and, for Christians in Polynesia, could be defined as sin. Koskinen was particularly struck by the folk etymological implications of the two similar sounding terms *(h)ara* for 'path' from **zalan* and *hara* for 'error, sin' from **salaq*, and he drew on this connection to consider the critical significance of the idea of keeping to the path. His observations have a wide applicability among Austronesian speakers, especially, as he indicates, because paths also refer to relations among kin.

An explicit example of such symbolic associations occurs among the Rotenese, who link the word for 'error, sin or lack' (*sala*) with the word for 'deviation' from a path (*singok*) as a formal ritual language pair. Thus, a frequent refrain is the ritual expression at funerals:

Au ana-ma ma-salak	I am an orphan wronged
Ma au falu-ina ma-singok.	And I am a widow off-course.

In grand metaphorical terms, this expression for bereavement is extended to describe the human condition in the world.

Journey to the afterworld

For the Iban, as Clifford Sather expounds in his chapter, 'Life, death and journeys of regeneration in Saribas Iban funerary rituals', the journey to another world after death is a stage in a life-giving regenerative process. The initial funerary journey continues through multiple transformations—a series of rebirths and deaths—until finally the *antu*, which Sather describes as the 'postmortal self', returns to the world 'as dew, which, through the medium of rice, is re-embodied in a new generation of humans'. This path charts an immanence of all life that transforms death into a life-giving potency—a conception that is widespread among Austronesians (Fox 1987).

Sather draws on the Lamaholot ethnography of Penelope Graham for similar notions (1991). Another expression of similar ideas can be found among the Mambai. The spirits of death go through a series of transformations, moving from land to sea, where 'they sleep inside the waters, sleep inside the sea'. From there, they become nourishing rains or, as the Mambai phrase it, they 'walk with the rains' and come 'to descend into the white corn and yellow corn, to descend into the white bean and yam' (Traube 1986: 194).

The journey into the afterworld is a topic so widely and so copiously examined that it might well be considered a defining theme in the Austronesian ethnography. Classic monographs on this topic—often with extended narrative documentation—include Hans Schärer's massive two-volume compendium, *Der Totenkult der Ngadju Dajak in Süd-Borneo* [*The Death Cult of the Ngadju Dajak in Southern Borneo*] (1966), Peter Metcalf's *A Borneo Journey into Death* (1982), Jeannine Koubi's *Rambu Solo' 'la Fumée Descend' le culte des morts chez les Toradja du Sud* [*Rambu Solo', 'The Smoke Descends': The cult of the dead among the South Toradja*] (1982), H. van der Veen's *The Sa'dan Toradja Chant for the Deceased* (1966), P. Middelkoop's *Een Studie van het Timoreesche Doodenritueel* [*A Study of the Timorese Death Ritual*] (1949), Maurice Bloch's *Placing the Dead* (1971) and, along with an exceptional array of specific papers, they provide one of the most extensive fields of comparison among Austronesian populations.[7]

---

7   As Sather discusses in his chapter, Robert Hertz's 1907 essay (Hertz 1960) has had a substantial influence on comparative research on this topic. His stimulating ideas have had their influence in Austronesian studies, as for example, in Hans Joachim Sell's *Der schlimme Tod bei den Völkern Indonesiens* [*The Concept of Bad Death among the People of Indonesia*] (1955) or Pascal Couderc and Kenneth Sillander's superb collection of papers, *Ancestors in Borneo Societies: Death, transformation and social immortality* (2012); Henri Chambert-Loir and Anthony Reid's *The Potent Dead: Ancestors, saints and heroes in contemporary Indonesia* (2002); or more broadly, in Richard Huntington and Peter Metcalf's *Celebrations of Death: The anthropology of mortuary ritual* (1979).

Clifford Sather's chapter on Saribas Iban death rituals is one of the clearest and most concise descriptions of the performance and eschatology of complex celebrations. By contrast, Fox's chapter, 'Rotenese life-courses and the journey to the afterworld', deals with a population whose rulers began to embrace Christianity in the early eighteenth century. The slow spread of Christian ideas about life after death have eliminated any coherence in traditional eschatology. As among the Iban, the rituals allude to the spectral dissolution of the person in the journey westward to the afterworld, but the pathways of this world are unclear. What have become elaborated are formulaic ritual narratives of different possible 'life-courses'. Whereas the Iban confine the discussion of the deceased's life to the earliest stages of their rituals, the recitation of a formulaic 'life-course' assigned to the deceased is—or was until recently—central to the Rotenese funeral ceremony. These 'life-courses' are described as 'paths' and many of them comprise further embedded 'paths' within them, including journeys in search of a wife.

Paths and journeys in practice

Sather notes the Iban term *jalai*, which means both 'path' and 'journey', 'has a normative connotation and inscribes a linear and/or temporal dimension to whatever activity it refers'. In a similar vein, writing about the Muyuw term for path, *ked*, Frederick Damon writes:

> People often speak as if the *ked* determines their action; they are just doing what the way prescribes ... the *ked* is the agent; people are just the means by which its action is accomplished.

By such understandings, a straight path implies good intentions; by contrast, a crooked, wandering path indicates deviousness. Such normative evaluations apply widely among Austronesians.

Rituals can be performed to open a path to facilitate the flow of life, to straighten a path to avoid deviation or, critically, to remove hindrances on an intended path. As an example, Sather writes that:

> before a new longhouse is constructed, its site must first be measured out and ritually constituted as a *jalai*. This is done through a rite called *ngerembang jalai*—literally, 'to clear' or 'trod down a path'. The purpose of the rite is to remove obstructions.

In his chapter, 'On the word *ked*: The "way" of being and becoming in Muyuw', Frederick Damon exemplifies the idea of the *ked* by reference to a Muyuw death ritual:

> A death is likened to a tree falling, blocking paths among the living who are connected by lines of affinity or *kula*. People should ignore one another until they have performed a small clearing ritual.

Paths may set out a trajectory, but they also demand physical action in the journeys they define. This physical component—the actions involved in stepping, striding, walking, riding and sailing—is also a key focus of the chapters in this volume. The second chapter in the volume, Wen-ling Lin's 'From paths to traditional territory: Wayfinding and the materialisation of an ancestral homeland', highlights the actions of walking as a long multigenerational rediscovery process in reclaiming ancestral land. This is part of an ongoing struggle by the Austronesian-speaking populations of Taiwan to revive, reassert and regain distinct local identities and national recognition. This specific case involves the Bunun of the Laipunuk region in the Central Mountain Range of Taiwan and constitutes a return to a 'homeland' from which these Bunun were displaced. As Lin beautifully phrases it, 'the path was born of walking, and this walking shaped the landscape'. Equally interesting, though subtly more difficult to appreciate, is the process of redefining the boundaries of the village by Amis shamans who hold invisible threads that link them to the spirit world. As Yi-tze Lee describes in his chapter, 'Testing paths in shamanic performances among the northern Amis of Taiwan', the first and most dangerous task for Amis shamans is to find the correct path that will link them to the spirit world and only when this path has been found can they use it in their public procession through the village to define social and spatial boundaries. No less significant is the emphasis that Denis Regnier, in his chapter, 'Funerary speeches and marital investigations in highland Madagascar', places on the trekking that occurs among scattered groups of Betsileo to determine the intimate details of ancestry that will ensure proper marriage arrangements. The mobility of the populations of Madagascar makes the island an area of subtle but complex diversity in which one's journey towards social identity is ultimately determined by placement in a specific local tomb.

In his book *Iban Bejalai* (1993), Peter Kedit presents an extended discussion of Iban journeying that includes not just ritual journeys, but also a great variety of undertakings intended to seek experience, wealth and renown. Institutionalised as the regular practice of young men to leave the longhouse for a period to gain a living, new skills and enhanced respect, the practice of *bejalai* supported Iban expansion and migration. It is similar to the practice of Malay and Minangkabau *merantau* ('to leave home, to go abroad') or Javanese *lelono* ('to go wandering, travelling') and what is described by all manner of iterant workers and most fishermen in present-day Indonesia as *cari hidup* ('to seek a livelihood').

In her chapter, 'Winds and seas: Exploring the pulses of place in *kula* exchange and yam gardening', Susanne Kuehling examines one of the best-known practices of traditional Austronesian trading: the *kula* exchange network linking numerous island populations in southeastern Papua New Guinea who are involved in trade associated with the circulation of shell valuables. This remarkable trading complex was first examined in Bronisław Malinowski's classic ethnography *Argonauts of the Western Pacific* (1922). Based on long fieldwork on Dobu and on her own journeys among *kula* traders, Kuehling provides a further perspective on these seaborne activities.

For most traders, this is a journey conceived of as upwards or downwards in line with the rising or setting sun and across a series of specific named spaces (*mwatui*). *Mwali* shells enter the trading network from the north and west while *bagi* shells enter from the eastern part of the network. What Kuehling calls the 'pulse' of this trade consists of the countercirculation of these individual shells whose number she estimates as more than 1,000 of each kind. As she writes:

> The pulse of *kula* and the rhythm of the winds combine to create windows of opportunity and adventure, giving men a chance to prove themselves and to escape the daily grind of subsistence work.

As she notes, the stability of the household—wives and children, who remain on land—constitutes support to the men who venture to sea. Gardening is linked to these *kula* activities and, in Kuehling's assessment, 'both activities are of equal importance'.

The final chapter in this volume, Yu-chien Huang's 'Walking on the village paths: *Kanaawoq* in Yap and *rarahan* in Yami', links two Austronesian populations on islands a considerable distance from one another: the Yami of Orchid Island off the coast of Taiwan and the population of Yap in Micronesia in the Pacific. Her chapter poses an interesting comparative question about the different nature of paths and of 'pathing' in these two societies. Among the Yami, path-making is improvised and open to change and paths are meandering and changeable, whereas on Yap, paths are wide, flat and carefully tended; they are interconnected and politically and socially endowed with meaning and there is an etiquette and protocol for walking on them. Huang develops this comparison of paths brilliantly and points to the way an ethnography of paths can illuminate differences in Austronesian societies. The question is whether her idea of different modalities in path and 'pathing' can be further generalised: can one detect a more pronounced individual modality in the defining of paths among societies in western Austronesian and a more notable collective modality in paths among societies in eastern Austronesia; or, more specifically, under what conditions do these varying modalities arise? It is useful to conclude this volume by posing new questions for further research.

Pathways through the Austronesian-speaking world

The dispersal of Austronesian languages has created innumerable pathways. Tracing these pathways is one of the preoccupations in the study of the Austronesians. Similarities across the Austronesian-speaking world are notable but equally so are the differences among Austronesian societies. The social use of metaphors of the 'path' is apparent in some of the chapters in this volume and implicit in others. The development of comparative Austronesian studies has highlighted both these continuities and these regional differences.

Virtually everywhere, except in the remote Pacific, Austronesian speakers—or more specifically, Malayo-Polynesian speakers—spread into areas inhabited by earlier populations whose languages and existing patterns of local adaptation had varying but significant influences on Austronesian social and cultural practices. Austro-Asiatic and even pre–Austro-Asiatic influences are evident in western Austronesia as are the non-Austronesian—often referred to, loosely and indeterminately, as 'Papuan'—influences in eastern Austronesia. The diversity of this expansion, its many migratory pathways and the millennia-long multilingual social interaction of mixed communities have created what is today a complex Austronesian-speaking world.[8]

---

8   Innovative research by Owen Edwards (2018) on substrate retention from pre-Austronesian languages has begun to provide new insights into historical linguistic relationships in the Timor area and has wider methodological and theoretical implications for an understanding of the Austronesian-speaking world. Marian Klamer (2019) provides an excellent summary discussion of current findings and debates on the dispersal of Austronesian languages in island Southeast Asia.

Traces of these influences are evident, for example, in the relational terminologies of the Austronesians. The formal complexities of these terminologies that define and distinguish kin and affine—sorting them by generation, gender, relative age, seniority, sex-of-speaker, relational distance and marriage connection—show fundamental continuity as well as considerable variation across the Austronesian world. There is evident continuity between the cognatic terminologies of the Austronesians of Taiwan and those of the Malayo-Polynesian speakers of western Austronesia to the island of Sumbawa where significant differences begin to appear roughly coincident with the Central-Eastern Malayo-Polynesian subgroup. Key affinal relational categories common throughout western Austronesia disappear and differing patterns of relative age and sibling relations emerge and are combined with tendencies towards category-directed marriage.

Eastern Indonesia is a transition zone but is by no means uniform. Many of the relationship patterns notable in societies in Oceania first emerge in eastern Indonesia and are carried into the Pacific. Societies on either side of New Guinea, in particular, share distinctive relational patterns, whereas Polynesian societies share patterns more in common with those that occur in the area of transition from western to eastern Indonesia. This would certainly be in keeping with a migration through eastern Indonesia and into Oceania marked by a distinct movement into the Pacific that had relatively little influence from local non-Austronesian-speaking populations (for specific details on these various patterns, see Fox 2015, 2019).

In this complex cultural world, it remains possible to recognise a considerable continuity in the nature of Austronesian paths and the journeying that takes place on them. Whether broad or narrow, straight or winding, all journeys—however difficult—are both instructive and transformative. This volume with its 10 chapters describing distinctive paths, each discussed in its cultural context, offers a journey into a wide and fascinating Austronesian-speaking world.

References

Barnes, Susana. 2011. 'Origins, precedence and social order in the domain of Ina Ama Beli Darlari.' In Andrew McWilliam and Elizabeth G. Traube, eds, *Land and Life in Timor-Leste: Ethnographic essays*, pp. 23–46. Canberra: ANU Press. doi.org/10.22459/LLTL.12.2011.02.

Bellmund, Jacob L.S., Peter Gärdenfors, Edward L. Moser and Christian Doeller. 2018. 'Navigating cognition: Spatial codes for human thinking.' *Science* 362(6415): eaat6766. doi.org/10.1126/science.aat6766.

Bloch, Maurice. 1971. *Placing the Dead: Tombs, ancestral villages and kinship organization in Madagascar*. London: Seminar Press.

Chambert-Loir, Henri and Anthony Reid, eds. 2002. *The Potent Dead: Ancestors, saints and heroes in contemporary Indonesia*. Sydney and Honolulu: Allen & Unwin and University of Hawai`i Press.

Collins, William A. 1998. *The Guritan of Radin Suane: A study of the Besemah oral epic from South Sumatra*. Leiden: KITLV Press.

Couderc, Pascal and Kenneth Sillander, eds. 2012. *Ancestors in Borneo Societies: Death, transformation and social immortality*. Copenhagen: NIAS Press.

Edwards, Owen. 2018. 'Parallel histories in Rote-Meto.' *Oceanic Linguistics* 57(2): 359–409. doi.org/10.1353/ol.2018.0016.

Firth, Raymond. 1967 [1940]. *The Work of the Gods in Tikopia*. Reprint. London: The Athlone Press.

Fox, James J. 1987. 'Southeast Asian religions: Insular cultures.' In Mircea Eliade, ed., *The Encyclopedia of Religion. Volume 13*, pp. 520–30. New York: Macmillan.

Fox, James J. 1992. 'Origin and order in a Micronesian society: A comparative assessment of two books on Palau.' *Canberra Anthropology* 15(1): 75–86. doi.org/10.1080/03149099209508460.

Fox, James J. 2014a [2006]. 'Genealogy and topogeny.' In James J. Fox, *Explorations in Semantic Parallelism*, pp. 265–76. Canberra: ANU Press. dx.doi.org/10.22459/ESP.07.2014. [Reprinted from 'Genealogy and topogeny: Toward an ethnography of Rotinese ritual place names', in James J. Fox, ed., *The Poetic Power of Place: Comparative perspectives on Austronesian ideas of locality*, pp. 91–102. Canberra: ANU E Press, 2006. doi.org/10.22459/PPP.09.2006].

Fox, James J. 2014b. 'Blood-red millet: An origin narrative.' In James J. Fox, *Explorations in Semantic Parallelism*, pp. 277–82. Canberra: ANU Press. doi.org/10.22459/ESP.07.2014.

Fox, James J. 2015. 'Eastern Indonesia in Austronesian perspective: The evidence of relational terminologies.' *Archipel* 90: 189–216. doi.org/10.4000/archipel.375.

Fox, James J. 2019. 'A research note regarding Trobriand *tabu* and its comparative significance.' *Oceania*: 89(3): 336–42. doi.org/10.1002/ocea.5230.

Geddes, William A. 1957. *Nine Dayak Nights*. Melbourne: Oxford University Press.

Graham, Penelope. 1991. 'To follow the blood: The path of life in a domain of eastern Flores, Indonesia.' PhD thesis, The Australian National University, Canberra. doi.org/10.25911/5d74e27794d86.

Hertz, Robert. 1960. *Death and the Right Hand*. Trans. by R. Needham and C. Needham. London: Cohen & West.

Hoskins, Janet. 1988. 'Etiquette in Kodi spirit communication: The lips told to pronounce, the mouth told to speak.' In James J. Fox, ed., *To Speak in Pairs: Essays on the ritual languages of eastern Indonesia*, pp. 29–63. Cambridge: Cambridge University Press. doi.org/10.1017/CBO9780511551369.002.

Hoskins, Janet. 1993. *The Play of Time: Kodi perspectives on calendars, history and exchange*. Berkeley, CA: University of California Press.

Huang, Shuanfan and Michael Tanangkingsing. 2005. 'Reference to motion events in six western Austronesian languages: Toward a semantic typology.' *Oceanic Linguistics* 44(2): 307–40. doi.org/10.1353/ol.2005.0035.

Huntington, Richard and Peter Metcalf. 1979. *Celebrations of Death: The anthropology of mortuary ritual*. Cambridge: Cambridge University Press.

Huntsman, Judith and Antony Hooper. 1996. *Tokelau: A historical ethnography*. Auckland: Auckland University Press.

Janowski, Monica. 2014. *Tuked Rini, Cosmic Traveller: Life and legend in the heart of Borneo*. Copenhagen: NIAS Press.

Kaartinen, Timo. 2010. *Songs of Travel, Stories of Place: Poetics of absence in an eastern Indonesian society*. Helsinki: Academia Scientiarum Fennica.

Kedit, Peter M. 1993. *Iban Bejalai*. Kuala Lumpur: Ampang Press.

Klamer, Marian. 2019. 'The dispersal of Austronesian languages in island South East Asia: Current findings and debates.' *Language and Linguistics Compass* 13(4): 1–26. doi.org/10.1111/lnc3.12325.

Kohl, Karl-Heinz. 1998. *Der Tod der Reisjungfrau: Mythen, Kulte und Allianzen in einer ostindonesischen Lokalkultur* [*The Death of the Rice Maiden: Myths, cults and alliances in an east Indonesian local culture*]. Stuttgart: Verlag W. Kohlhammer.

Koskinen, Aarne A. 1968. 'On the symbolism of the "path" in Polynesian thinking.' In Aarne A. Koskinen, *Linking of Symbols: Polynesian patterns 1*, pp. 57–70. Helsinki: Soumen Lähetystieteellinen Seura R.Y.

Koubi, Jeannine. 1982. *Rambu Solo' 'la fumée descend' le culte des morts chez les Toradja du Sud* [*Rambu Solo', 'The Smoke Descends': The cult of the dead among the South Toradja*]. Paris: Editions Du Centre National De La Recherche Scientifique.

Kuipers, Joel C. 1990. *Power in Performance: The creation of textual authority in Wejewa ritual speech*. Philadelphia: University of Pennsylvania Press. doi.org/10.9783/9781512803341.

Lewis, E. Douglas. 1988. *People of the Source: The social and ceremonial order of Tana Wai Brama on Flores*. Dordrecht: Foris Publications.

McWilliam, Andrew. 1997. 'Mapping with metaphor: Cultural topographies in West Timor.' In James J. Fox, ed., *The Poetic Power of Place: Comparative perspectives on Austronesian ideas of locality*, pp. 103–15. Canberra: Department of Anthropology, Comparative Austronesian Project, Research School of Pacific and Asian Studies, The Australian National University.

McWilliam, Andrew. 2002. *Paths of Origin, Gates of Life: A study of place and precedence*. Leiden: KITLV Press.

Malinowski, Bronisław. 1922. *Argonauts of the Western Pacific: An account of native enterprise and adventure in the archipelagoes of Melanesian New Guinea*. London: Routledge & Kegan Paul.

Metcalf, Peter. 1982. *A Borneo Journey into Death: Berawan eschatology from its rituals*. Philadelphia: University of Pennsylvania Press. doi.org/10.9783/9781512818079.

Middelkoop, P. 1949. *Een Studie van het Timoreesche Doodenritueel. Verhandeling KBGKW: LXXVI* [*A Study of the Timorese Death Ritual. Royal Batavian Society of Arts and Sciences Treatise No. 76*]. Bandoeng: A.C. Nix & Co.

Needham, Rodney. 1967. 'Percussion and transition.' *Man* (NS)2: 606–14. doi.org/10.2307/2799343.

Parmentier, Richard J. 1987. *The Sacred Remains: Myth, history and polity in Belau*. Chicago: University of Chicago Press.

Rappoport, Dana. 2006. '"De retour de mon bain de tambours": Chants de transe de ritual maro chez les Toraja Sa'adan de l'ile Sulawesi (Indonésie) ["Back from my drum bath": Trance songs of the maro ritual among the Toraja Sa'adan of the island of Sulawesi (Indonesia)].' *Cahiers de Musique Traditionnelles* [*Traditional Music Notebooks*] 19: 93–116. doi.org/10.2307/40240636.

Rappoport, Dana. 2009. *Songs of the Thrice-Blooded Land: Ritual music of the Toraja (Sulawesi, Indonesia)*. Trans. by Elizabeth Coville. 2 vols + DVD. Paris: Éditions de la Maison des Sciences de l'Homme: Éditions Épistème.

Revel, Nicole and Mäsinu Intaray. 2000. *La quête en épouse/The Quest for a Wife: Mämimbin, a Palawan epic sung by Mäsinu*. [Trilingue Palawan-Français-Anglais]. Paris: Éditions Unesco.

Sather, Clifford. 2017. *A Borneo Healing Romance: Ritual storytelling and the Sugi Sakit*. Kuching: Borneo Research Council.

Schärer, Hans. 1966. *Der Totenkult der Ngadju Dajak in Süd-Borneo* [*The Death Cult of the Ngadju Dajak in Southern Borneo*]. 2 vols. 's-Gravenhage: Martinus Nijhoff. doi.org/10.26530/OAPEN_613419.

Sell, Hans Joachim. 1955. *Der schlimme Tod bei den Völkern Indonesiens* [*The Terrible Death among the People of Indonesia*]. 's-Gravenhage: Mouton & Co.

Slobin, Dan. 2004. 'The many ways to search for a frog: Linguistic typology and the expression of motion events.' In Sven Strömqvist and Ludo Verhoeven, eds, *Relating Events in Narrative: Typology and contextual perspectives*, pp. 219–57. Mahwah, NJ: Lawrence Erlbaum Associates.

Steinhart, W.L. 1954. *Niasse Teksten* [*The Niasse Text*]. KITLV [Royal Netherlands Institute of Southeast Asian and Caribbean Studies]. 's-Gravenhage: Martinus Nijhoff.

Talmy, Leonard. 1991. 'Path to realization: A typology of event conflation.' *Berkeley Linguistics Society* 17: 480–519. doi.org/10.3765/bls.v17i0.1620.

Therik, Tom. 2004. *Wehali: The female land—Traditions of a Timorese ritual centre*. Canberra: Pandanus Books.

Traube, Elizabeth G. 1986. *Cosmology and Social Life: Ritual exchange among the Mambai of East Timor*. Chicago: University of Chicago Press.

Traube, Elizabeth G. 1989. 'Obligations to the source.' In David Maybury-Lewis and Uri Almagor, eds, *The Attraction of Opposites: Thought and society in a dualistc mode*, pp. 321–44. Ann Arbor: University of Michigan Press.

Traube, Elizabeth G. 2011. 'Planting the flag.' In Andrew McWilliam and Elizabeth G. Traube, eds, *Land and Life in Timor-Leste: Ethnographic essays*, pp. 117–40. Canberra: ANU Press. doi.org/10.22459/LLTL.12.2011.06.

Veen, H. van der. 1966. *The Sa'dan Toradja Chant for the Deceased.* The Hague: Martinus Nijhoff.

Wein, Clemens. 1989. *Berinareu: The religious epic of the Tirurais*. Manila: Divine Word Publications.

2

From paths to traditional territory: Wayfinding and the materialisation of an ancestral homeland

Wen-ling Lin

Introduction

The concepts of an 'ancestral home', 'old tribe' and 'traditional territory' have often been the main concerns at various Taiwanese indigenous social and cultural events. Every 'return to the old site' or 'exploration for an old tribe' implies, more or less, the loss or disappearance of an original habitat. Following the instructions of their elders, younger generations search through the mountains for the sites where their ancestors used to live and work. Wayfinding while walking to a certain place has become a common theme of these activities. The trajectories of such movements circumscribe the possible scope of a traditional territory. By walking, indigenous peoples make repeated visits to their ancestral home, giving form to their 'ancestral homeland' as conceived by their elders. The concept of a 'homeland' comes into being during the process of searching and a relationship is formed between people and the land. This differs drastically in terms of feelings and expression from the dematerialisation of space in contemporary social life.

Laipunuk is a region in the southeastern section of Taiwan's Central Mountain Range, including the upper and middle reaches of the Luye River, a tributary of the Beinan River. It encompasses the present-day townships of Yanping and Haiduan in Taitung County, the western parts of the Maolin and Taoyuan districts of Kaohsiung City and the border between Wutai Township and Pingtung County. According to the literature, in the early days, it was where the Ngerarukai Rukai ('Oponoho' or Wanshan in Chinese), the East Rukai Danan community, the Southern Tsou and the Puyuma lived. The original meaning of 'Laipunuk' in Bunun is 'area originally belonging to the Rukai people', referring to the land of the Wanshan people.

In 1941, the Japanese forced those Bunun who were still living in the Laipunuk area to move down from the mountains. Since then, Laipunuk has been uninhabited and has become a 'blank spot' on the map.

Sixty years later, at the end of 2001, the Bunun descendants of Laipunuk initiated an expedition to find a way home. These expeditions continued for 18 years. In the first three years of this period, expeditions were undertaken as a collective action by the descendants of the Laipunuk people living in Yanping and Haiduan townships in Taitung County. After 2004, it became an annual settlement-seeking journey of the Husungan family. In 2006, two members of the Husungan family, Tama Nabu and Nas Tama Biung,[1] believed the action of 'going home' to Laipunuk could not stop. These two then joined Dahu to begin rebuilding the Husungan family's house. In 2008, with the idea of using the 'mountain as a school', the creation of a Laipunuk elementary school was promoted.[2] A virtual elementary school centred on the mountains was opened, later renamed the Laipunuk Pasnanavan ('Laipunuk Place of Learning').[3] Liu Man-Yi, one of the founders of the Laipunuk Pasnanavan, proposed that 'the ancient paths and the residual wall is the classroom, and the tribe's *Tama* is the teacher'. This school in the mountains incorporated the theme of 'going home' into its curriculum.

---

1   *Tama* ('father') is the honorary name given to a male elder. *Nas* is a Bunun title for a deceased person.

2   Adhering to the educational philosophy of the 'mountain as a school', the entire tribal area of Laipunuk is a rich school with no walls, in which nature provides endless learning materials.

3   The tribal elders said *pasnanavan* in Bunun has the meaning not just of 'learning' but also of a 'place of learning'.

Map 2.1 Map of Laipunuk
Source: mapstalk.blogspot.com/.

This chapter will focus on the initial stage of the *Laipunuk: kulumah*[4] ('Laipunuk: Going Home') from 2001 to 2004, and, based on two documentary films recorded during this period, it explores the origins of the Bunun descendants' efforts to find their way home and retrace their roots. This involves an examination of the ideas and meanings of paths and the way they lead to a home.

Tahai Binkinuaz (Chinese name: Tsai San-Shen), one of the Bunun descendants of Laipunuk, participated in the 'root-seeking' (*kilim mai-asang*) activity of the first period. He filmed, directed and edited *Open the Window of Taiwanese History: Return to Laipunuk* (2002) and *Back to the Land Where the Navel is Buried* (2003). These two documentaries recorded the 10 'going home activities' between the winter of 2001 and April 2003.

The Bunun descendants' physical activities of 'root-seeking' generally involved a small group of tribal people walking into the depths of the mountains—activities through which they experienced and recognised the environment and natural sites where their ancestors had led their daily lives. Walking as a group defined the interaction between these people and their material space. Through this process, individuals gained access to traditional knowledge of the ecology, animals and plants that had provided an existence on the land. They followed a variety of paths

---

4   *Kulumah* means 'going home' in the Bunun language.

that formed a network allowing them to comprehend their ancestors' traditional life. Here the path became the object and the medium for a flow of ideas, meanings and memories.

Dan is the Bunun term for a 'path' and *mu-dan* means 'to walk' or 'to go'. *Mudadaan* means 'walking', and Bunun people often use this term when discussing which way to go. What is special is the expression *kilim daan* ('find the way'). There is no expression for 'opening a path', but the closest is *kan-anak kilim daan* ('I am looking for a way'), and this was often used because there are no paths in many places and people need to find their own way (Valis Ishahavut, Personal communication, 2019).

According to Aliman (2006: 47), the traditional Bunun paths of Laipunuk were divided into *hanupan dan* ('hunting trails') and *huma dan* ('agricultural paths'), which had different uses. The main focus was on the routes from an *asang* ('settlement')[5] that were used for hunting and when transporting harvested crops, to arrange marriages and alliances, sell products or fight with foreigners. It was only during the Japanese occupation that a cross-ridge trail was made through the Laipunuk; it was only 1.5 metres wide and was called the 'crossroad'. It followed the contours of the ridge and was convenient for transporting Japanese mountain cannons. The grass beside the trail was cut for 20 metres on either side to defend against the Bunun, who were good at ambush.

Wayfinding and walking as a theme became intertwined with issues of traditional territory, tribal mapping and traditional knowledge of the ecology linking people to the land. This chapter discusses the significance of these activities to investigate and respond to three theoretical questions: 1) How does the act of walking define a traditional cultural territory and its boundaries? 2) What discourse is expressed through such bodily actions that differs from a literal, geometric, panoramic and state-oriented discourse? 3) What kind of unnamed objects and unexpressed relationships does a path mediate?

---

5   *Asang* is the term for a settlement consisting of one or several families.

Research approach: Walking, mapping and mediations

Christopher Tilley (1994), in his book *A Phenomenology of Landscape: Places, paths, and monuments*, adopts a phenomenological approach and suggests that archaeologists can use the sensory experience of phenomenology to explore and explain a cultural landscape and how people in a particular location interact with the environment and landscape in which they live. Tilley's research on sensory experience suggests that people who understand the world of experience are key to phenomenological methods (1994: 11). The understanding and description involved in phenomenology lie in the subject's experience of things—that is, the relationship between being and being-in-the-world. 'Being-in-the-world' means that, in the process of objectification, people 'separate themselves' from the objective world and make the world an object that can be understood and grasped. Such a process is based on a certain 'gap'. Only with such a 'gap' and distance can people initiate perception—seeing, listening, touching—for physical action, intentionality and matters such as belief, memory and evaluation. These perceptions allow an understanding of the world of phenomena (Tilley 1994: 12).

'Being-in-the-world' implies that the human subject is a mediator in the world and becomes physically oriented towards the world's original openness. The relationship between the individual and space is a lived space or, in Merleau-Ponty's view, a phenomenal space (2014). It is different from objective space. Objective space is a homogeneous space of geometry and science. In this objective space, all positions are outside other positions and each can be replaced with another.[6] Phenomenal space is derived from activity, and life's relationship in this space produces the ability for bodily movement and the intentional relationships formed by such movement (Young 1980: 149).

This meaning of place is closely related to human activities, narratives or depictions. Michel de Certeau (1984: 115–36) believes that each space has a 'spatial story' that belongs to a locality. The uniqueness of a space can be understood through a spatial story. The emotional sharing of stories between individuals can establish collective awareness and identity. Participating individuals can also find their own positioning and orientation in history.

---

6   Objective space can be defined by pure externality. In this space, the body becomes an objective object that does not differ from other objects.

Christopher Tilley's (1994) discussion of spatial stories begins with paths, movements, landscapes and narratives, in addition to highlighting humans as the subject of experience with their perceptions of the surrounding environment. The discussion, telling and description of this have an important influence on the formation of meaning.

Tim Ingold (2000) also observed the influence of 'narrative' on environmental perception. The discourse and images embedded in the environment enable people to reorganise the environment in their own memories. In Ingold's view, the story reveals the storyteller's perception of the environment and of himself. Therefore, through a story, the environment and the storyteller are organised in a developing, interrelated relationship. In addition to the discussion of the relationship between stories, narratives, subjective dynamics and local construction, Ingold clearly highlights the key role played by walking in understanding the environment and a lived-in world. He argues that research on walking will bring a change of perception (Ingold 2004: 315). On different occasions, Ingold (see 2004, 2010, 2011a, 2011b) has elaborated on the epistemological meaning of 'the human body as a moving active subject in space', arguing that researchers need to be sensitive to the skill of the footsteps (embodied skills of footwork) and the subsequent transformation of learning, empathy, perception and consciousness.

Walking as embodiment—as a social and imaginative practice—can be a way of telling, commenting on, performing and creating stories and places. This requires attention to imagination in generating understanding, connections and questions (Elliott and Culhane 2017: 95). A walk itself is not just following a path from one place to another; a walk is a performance that fosters active participation in the environment (O'Neill and Hubbard 2010: 56). Walking is an art, but also an act of consciousness, habit and practice. It is shaped by both local conditions and the landscape. 'Walking is the medium and outcome of a spatial practice, a mode of existence in the world. The analogy can be taken further in the consideration of paths' (Tilley 1994: 29).

A path as the outcome of spatial practice allows the passage of people, ideas and memories. According to Arjun Appadurai (2015), a path has two interrelated dimensions—mediation and materiality—which work together.[7]

---

7   Mediation is a concrete practice and materiality is the place of mediation.

A path is also a medium for storage. A path leads people to construct a database, a process that makes the path itself a rich source of cultural knowledge. As a medium, a path promotes communication. It belongs to (at least) two parties who are engaged in communication and negotiation (Herzogenrath 2015: 1).

Moving the body, drawing the living region of the ancestors

Among the various tactics adopted by the Japanese against Taiwan's aborigines, the process of resettlement through collective migration had the most profound impact. In 1919, the Japanese colonial government trialled moving groups in various parts of Taiwan. The first trial move of the Bunun people began in 1922.

The Japanese Government spent two full years (1924–26) constructing a 64-kilometre Laipunuk garrison road, which ran through Kaohsiung and Taitung.[8]

A year after the Da Guan Shan Event in 1932,[9] the Japanese began a large-scale relocation of the Bunun people in this area to better control them (Haisul Palalavi 2006: 197). In 1941, when the Japanese colonial government moved the last three Bunun households from Siusui,[10] the Laipunuk group removal was completed (Aliman 2006: 92; Tahai Binkinuaz 2004: 108). The Bunun of Laipunuk were forced to migrate from deep in the mountains to the villages of Hongye, Taoyuan, Wuling, Yongkang and Lushan in Yanping Township.[11] 'Laipunuk' as a location has since disappeared from the map.

---

8   The road rises from the western branch of the mountains, climbs over the Central Mountain Range and descends to the Luye River, before turning east to the northern silk village (now Taoyuan Village in Yanping Township). Along this section of the Laipunuk police road, there are various police stations at named sites: Dah Dah (Hong Ye), Siusui (Qing Shui), Kaili (Feng), Kakaiyu (Jiajiadai), Tavilin (Tao Lin), Takibana (Ju), Pisbadan (Shou), Takibadan (Chang Pan), Zhao Ri and Sakaivan (Chu Yun).

9   The Da Guan Shan Event occurred in the Shibuya station of the Taitung Hall in Taiwan, where Lamataxinxin Husangan Istanda and his Bunun followers launched a raid against the ruling authorities. Lamataxinxin and others attacked three police officers stationed in Shibuya, causing two deaths and one serious injury. At the end of that year, Lamataxinxin and others were arrested and executed by the Japanese police.

10   Siusui: Qing Shui in Chinese; Clear Water in English.

11   The residents of five villages in Yanping Township, Taitung County, are the Bunun who have been displaced from Laipunuk (see Haisul Palalavi 2006: 204, 207–09; Li Minhui 1997: 58–60; Huang Ying-Kuei 2001: 151, 181, 195, 208; Ye Jia-Ning 2002: 96).

Around 2001, after 60 years away from their homeland, the Bunun descendants of Laipunuk began the effort to go home. Based on the oral histories of tribal elders and the cartographic skills of the townspeople of Yanping, the descendants of Laipunuk ventured into the mountains to explore their homeland. They recorded the distribution of the tribes of Laipunuk and the usage of familial landholdings, hunting fields and other traditional sites. Ecological knowledge, historical events and the interactions among these tribes were recorded.

1. From *kilim maiasang* ('settlement-seeking') to *kulumah* ('going home')[12]

In 1988, after the abolition of martial law, representatives of Taiwan's indigenous peoples took the opportunity to fight for their land rights and demonstrated on the streets to promote the 'returning my land movement'. Between 1997 and 2004, the Executive Yuan Aboriginal Committee (Aboriginal National Council of the Executive Yuan) began the first wave of surveys of indigenous peoples' traditional territories and tribal mapping. As part of this, the Bunun people of Yanping and Haiduan townships in Taitung County initiated the process of *kilim maiasang* ('settlement-seeking').[13] They launched 10 Laipunuk exploration efforts beginning in the winter of 2001 and continuing to April 2003.

These Laipunuk exploration activities tried to find ways of returning to their ancestors' homelands. This attempt to return to the Laipunuk had a forerunner. According to Nabu, a member of the Husungan family, Haisul was one of the first individuals to return to the area. Haisul was the initiator of the rebellion of Laipunuk against the Japanese on 9 March 1941. The story of the Laipunuk rebellion sparked the emotions of future generations and set the tone for the Laipunuk events 60 years later.

According to Nabu Husungan Istanda:

> *Katu sisivung sia tasa tu asang a sat u mulushulushu. Katu tahaz takisingsing tan tu dalah, asang, haimangsut, mais nihai naka, madaz iswuka.* [Don't fall in love with the land, don't fall in love

---

12   *Asang* means 'a settlement'. The prefix *mai* refers to the 'past' or a 'former time'. *Mai-asang* thus refers to a former home or old tribal settlement.

13   These activities were mainly organised and promoted by the Bunun Cultural and Education Foundation.

with the flat land, settlements, and appliances. Keep moving and migrating. If you are stranded in a place for too long, you will die and disappear].[14]

After 60 years, the descendants of Laipunuk who lived on the plains below the mountains began to respond to the exhortations of their elders. Their exploration efforts were similar to those in earlier times. Instead of migrating to new places to open up wild land, sow seeds and settle down, as in the old days, the Bunun descendants of Laipunuk sought their roots and attempted to re-establish the sites that had long disappeared from the map.

Because the move down from the mountains had occurred long ago, the 'way' to return to Laipunuk required repeated surveys. From different starting points and paths, the Bunun descendants of Laipunuk struggled to find the homeland of their elders' memories on the blank space on the map—a nameless place—and gradually allowed its location and boundaries to emerge with each footstep they took.

Tahai Binkinuaz, one of the Bunun descendants of Laipunuk, filmed, edited and directed *Open the Window of Taiwanese History: Return to Laipunuk*, which records 10 of the exploration efforts in detail. The film is in Bunun language with Chinese subtitles. The gist of the film—the motif of the excursions, the core concept and the central activities—is clearly stated:

> In order to retrieve the history and culture of Laipunuk and to seek the traces left behind by our ancestors, at the end of [the] year 2001, the descendants of Laipunuk started returning to their native place. We asked the elders for help and interviewed them. We also searched for historical documents and materials. In the end, we used our feet to explore and feel our native home. (Tahai Binkinuaz 2002)

This statement clearly expresses the necessity of seeking 'the traces left behind by the ancestors' to retrieve 'the history and culture of Laipunuk'. Their determination to find the roots of their history and culture thus stimulated the Bunun to launch their efforts to return home. 'Finding a way home' is achieved through continuing cycles of intention and realisation.

---

14   Nabu extended the words of the elders; the Bunun were a migratory people and the elders believe the survival of their culture depends on their constant movement (Nabu Husungan Istanda, Interview, 2016). Also see Liu Man-Yi (2017).

On 10 December 2002, Human Rights Day, the Bunun elders were taken back to the previous location of Laipunuk by helicopter. This project was sponsored by the Council of Cultural Affairs of the Executive Yuan and was named 'Na Kulumahin Kata' ('We Are Going Home'). This return to Laipunuk—the elders' first helicopter flight—was made possible only by the efforts of their descendants who explored the location and built a temporary landing pad for the helicopter. Before setting off, the elders told their ancestors:

> Ancestors! We are going to visit you tomorrow. Do not be scared, because we will take a helicopter, a machine that you have never seen before. We are not there to shoot you. We are there to visit you. So please do not be frightened when you see us. Please bless us. Your descendants will go back to pay you a visit from now on. So, ancestors, please take care of your offspring! This time, we are going home to do the things we have to do.

For the Laipunuk-born elders who had been unable to return to their homeland for more than half a century, the trip was more than just a homecoming, allowing them to walk on their homeland and 'meet' their deceased family. The elders also wanted to see the place where they had 'buried their navels'—the place from which they had come. In the film, we see a closeup of the elders' faces, showing the emotions of homecoming. For this scene, the narrator says:[15]

> In the past, when we were born, we Bunun people would bury our navels in our homes. But our elders haven't seen the remains of their umbilical cord for a long time. They haven't returned to their homeland for a long time.[16]

The first six minutes of *Open the Window of Taiwanese History: Return to Laipunuk* presents the elders' return to their homeland by helicopter and the core idea behind this return. Later scenes focus on the many other explorations in the mountains. Near the end of the film, the 'We Are Going Home' project and the Bunun elders' return to Laipunuk by helicopter are presented again. At this point, three major phases of the film can be recognised:

---

15 This passage was reported widely in the media at the time.
16 The Bunun traditionally bury the umbilical cord of a newborn under the house. The umbilical cord is the link between the new life and the mother; the house is regarded as the birthplace of the mother's culture. Therefore, burying the umbilical cord under the house symbolises the connection between the newborn and the family.

1. The elders board the helicopter, see their long-lost homeland from above and then disembark to physically stand on their land, welcomed by the younger generation.
2. The younger generation explores the mountains, trying different routes to search for their former tribal locations.
3. The elders, once disembarked from the helicopter, together walk on their homeland.

With its continuous inscription of 'walking into the forests to look for their original land', the film portrays the Bunun's persistence in searching and the physical labour involved. Through the arrangement of these images, the elders express their previously repressed emotions. In the third section of the film, while walking on the path with others, one elder says:

> This is my path. This is my path and so I am crying. I cannot stop myself from crying. When I was here, I was about 13 or 14 years old … 65 years have passed, and now I am 80 years old. I have come back again to walk on this land.[17]

Another elder finds the site where he buried his navel. He squats on the ground, plants a tree and says:

> Orange tree! You have to grow up well here alone in the mountain. You were brought here by me, from the low country to the place I was born. Keep watch on my navel for me. It is fortunate that you are here. You have to grow well.

The middle section of the film records the descendants of Laipunuk walking into and among the forests and mountains. They use their feet to search for their former tribal land. In every effort of exploration, events and memories change as a result of the judgement of and choices made by the descendants. During the first return trip, a narrator says:

> In the winter of 2001, we explored Laipunuk for the first time. Because it was the first time, only five people participated in the activity. We walked along the previous Japanese paths since they were easier for us. We started from Siusui police station and arrived at the Mamahav tribal site. We saw the drawbridge that was severed by Haisul in the Laipunuk event. When the Japanese paths were no longer available, we walked down into the river valley and

---

17 Nabu Husunggan Istanda mentioned several times on different occasions that when his mother saw her long-lost hometown, she was overcome by emotion.

waded across the stream to get to Kaili[18] station. At Kaili station, there were the remains of Japanese temples. We honoured the children who were mistakenly killed by Haisul during the conflict between the Japanese and the Bunun people. We found close by there was a thriving community of Taitung cycads. We only spent four days and three nights and we came home.

For the Bunun who participated in this excursion, walking on the Japanese paths was a particularly touching experience. They saw the sites where historic events had taken place and thus remembered the tragic incidents narrated by the elders. Through the narrator's commentary and the scenes presented, we witness how the people waded across streams and climbed precipices. We also experience the mist deep in the mountains and the plants that grow there. The narratives and images give concrete expression to the native place and its living conditions as described by the elder man in the film. The film thus becomes like a texture than can be 'touched' by the younger generation.

With the hope of representing the original tribes, the descendants describe the places they finally 'saw' after their painstaking walks:

Mamahav: A tribe that has many chillies.

Masuvanu: A tribe that has lots of honey.

Halimudun: A tribe that is full of weeds.

Halipusung: A tribe that has limestone.

Masudala: A tribe that has many maple trees.

Tavilin: A tribe of peach trees.

Bacingul: A tribe that grows many ring-cupped oaks.

Takivahlas: The tribe of the Takivahlas family, a tribe by the river.

Takisayan: The tribe of the Takisayan family, a tribe beside a great rock.

Kailisahan: A tribe that has smooth slate covers.[19]

Madaipulan: A tribe where the river is muddy.

These visual details and the recognition of placenames create an identity with the land, infusing the places with emotion and memory (see Basso 1996).[20]

---

18   Kaili: Feng in Chinese; Maple in English.
19   This tribe is named after a large, smooth slate-covered house.
20   In the Bunun tradition, each tribe or family had a different name depending on its hunting trail or tribal path. Therefore, different families and tribes have their own names for paths.

2. A tribal map made through wayfinding (by walking)

In 2002, those born in Laipunuk returned to their old tribal lands by helicopter. This was named 'Laipunuk first year'. The first exploration team that was sent out set up a white house in front of the Takivahlas house to open the land and to plant millet. In the sixth year of Laipunuk, the Takishusungan (Husungan family) returned to reconstruct their house. They have since returned every year between December and January, continuing into the eighteenth year of Laipunuk.

Plate 2.1 Bunun raise the banner of the first year of Laipunuk in 2002 in an old settlement
Photo: Bunun tu Asang (Bunun Cultural and Educational Foundation).

The younger generation of Laipunuk did not base their search for the mountain locations of former tribes on any readily available map; nor did they use advanced navigation techniques. Instead, these descendants carried out a process of 'wayfinding' to return to their native land. They invariably encountered significant 'objects' that were not indicated on any map but were nevertheless meaningful to them. These 'objects' could be a 'sign' of the environment, a change in the weather or various traces left by humans. The 'archives' to which this younger generation referred were their own experiences and the stories they had heard from the elders. In this context, the meaning of 'wayfinding' for these descendants was not simply bodily movement through space. Rather, their physical labour was a process of experiencing and understanding how they related to their excursion and the environment, and the significance it produced.

As a result of the many possibilities of each excursion, the routes taken differed. Twenty-four people participated in the second trip to Laipunuk. This trip was full of unexpected events and uncertainty. During the section of the film that covers this second trip, the voiceover in Bunun slowly and calmly describes the journey:

> We entered the mountain from Sakusaku[21] of Kaohsiung County and headed for the tribes near the Pisbadan[22] police station. But we got lost in the mountains. When we waded across the stream, we encountered a great canyon. For two days, we did not discover the source of its water. It was really difficult. On the sixth night, we communicated with our ancestors' spirits. On the seventh morning, our leader, Aliman, told us: 'An old tribe was located here. It is right above where we camped.' In this way, we found the place where the elder Chen Sheng-yuan buried his navel, *mazaibulan*.[23]

Each time an expedition was held, the Bunun tried to explore the mountains using a different route. Sometimes they took the forest paths of Yanping; other times they left Sakaivan[24] station from Kaohsiung; and still other times they waded across the Luye River looking for possible paths. Step by step, these Bunun followed their ancestors' paths, travelling further and further. Sometimes their route overlapped with a previous one and sometimes they found new routes. Without the guidance of a map, they moved by 'wayfinding' (in contrast to the way people who use maps move in a linear manner from one point to another). The conditions of the ancestors' living spaces became clearer and clearer. The 'wayfinding' activity of the return to Laipunuk thus became a mapping of the former tribes (see Ingold 2000). The particularities of this map were produced through walking. The tools for making this map were the people and their movement, their interactions and their experiences in the region,

---

21 Sakusaku: Liu Kuei in Chinese; Six Turtles in English.
22 Pisbadan: Shou in Chinese; Long Life in English.
23 See Liu Man-Yi (2017).
24 Sakaivan: Chu Yun.

and the map was marked out by spoken memories of specific names, stories and events. The map had a uniqueness, with its own temporal depth and significance.

When these placenames were drawn, one by one, Laipunuk became a storytelling tribal map. This map specifically reproduced the distribution of households, fields and environmental features—the family profiles of the local tribes at the time, as well as their hunting grounds, traditional lands and associated historical events—restoring the life and history of the Laipunuk people, connecting them with the land and prompting memories and homesickness among the elders.

The search through the mountains for Laipunuk was intended not to verify its existence as a place on a map, but to entitle Laipunuk, which had been concealed, and to open it to further reproduction of meaning: 'We explore with our feet', drawing the route of 'uncovering'.[25] The traces left by the people's footprints defined the scope within which historical conjunctures were to be found. These conjunctures outlined a region of the 'old tribe'—a significant place to their Bunun descendants.[26] Laipunuk, which had become a 'blank' on the map, offered these Bunun descendants a specific space in which to form social relationships within which each individual could create an identity as a Bunun Laipunuk. In this way, they developed a discourse of spatial politics through which they could claim their rights politically (Massey 2005: 195).

Because 'wayfinding' was a recurrent process, mapping could not be concluded after just one excursion and needed to be an ongoing process. This activity had several layers of meaning. The actor-perceiver in this process of 'wayfinding, had to become immersed in the texture of the environment, and based on these experiences and observations, had constantly to adjust perceptions and judgments to a path that would lead toward a destination' (Ingold 2000: 20). Such immersion in the environment and constant searching coloured the 'mapping' of the return to Laipunuk with what Robert Rundstrom (1991: 6) has called a 'process

---

25   Starting from the sixth minute of the film, the voiceover states: 'Till now, we have been to our homeland to site-investigate 10 times. We took the route from Linben to enter the mountain, as well as the route from Mount Chuyun in Kaohsiung. Sometimes we go upstream along the river. The old route no longer exists now. We have to find our own route back home.'

26   John Gray (2003: 228), in his ethnographic research in the Scottish Borders, proposes that a boundary is drawn in accordance with the activities of the subjects, and describes a circle as a way to differ the 'we' from others.

cartography' whereby the 'charting of the map (wayfinding/mapping) is situated both within the culture (communication between generations and ancestors) and in the longer context of trans-cultural conversation', endowing it with the possibility of communication within the tribe and with non-tribal people. Furthermore, since 'wayfinding' was an ongoing process, the charting of a map was never a once-and-for-all act. The map could be redrawn as different people participated in the journey and brought divergent levels of mobility. The flexibility of and communication during mapping led to the next mapping process and the appearance of yet another map (Rundstrom 1993: 21). This pattern of work enabled 'the charting of the tribal map to gain more and more details and to re-connect the histories between the tribes' (*Bunun Blog*).[27]

The different routes of the excursions uncovered divergent scenes and traces of memory. As a result, the terrain of the ancestors' lives became intertwined with the bodies of those searching and their experience and understanding of the environment and the words of the elders. This understanding was embodied in the exercise of walking: observing, touching, listening, feeling and climbing. The things learned from this experience could be considered embodied knowledge that was produced through the functioning and cooperation of multiple sensory organs.

The key phrase, 'Return to Laipunuk', became the core concern of the Bunun's claim for their right to revive their traditional territory. The action taken by the descendants of Bunun Laipunuk to realise such a goal was walking—an action that is highlighted in their documentaries. An interaction between the Bunun and their land was rebuilt each time they walked along ancient routes (see Massey 2005: 130). When the Bunun returned to their abandoned tribal lands, their history of 'displacement' under successive governments unfolded. From a historical viewpoint, a resistant force was released at the sites of historical events (see Keith and Pile 1993: 3).

---

27 www.bunun.org.tw/tw/index.asp?au_id=56&sub_id=160.

3. The path reconnecting the Bunun people and Bunun Laipunuk

Returning to the former tribal sites brought the elders, the youth, children and all men and women together. To learn more about and become closer to their past, the younger generations would constantly ask the elders for help and clarification. The younger generations contacted the elders during fieldwork to learn more about their homeland at Laipunuk.[28] This fieldwork created an active process of communication that conveyed different generations' ideas about their tribal history, experiences and knowledge. The process of 'going home' involved the experiences of generations and the exchange of inherited knowledge and also an active sharing of emotions and connections between different generations.

This communication between generations was not limited to the living. Every time the tribespeople undertook a trip home, they held rituals to tell their ancestors of their approach and to plead for their blessings for a safe return from the depth of the forests. Their journey implied a reconnection through time and space, a return to a symbiosis of the heavens and the earth. As a result, 'Returning to Laipunuk' was not merely a journey of 'settlement-seeking' (*kilim mai-asang*), but also an attempt to reconstruct the historical relationship of the Bunun with Bunun Laipunuk.

'Returning to Laipunuk' was also a social event that brought about interaction and reconnection among the Bunun while calling for an awareness of Bunun cultural identity and ethnic self-determination. According to the *Bunun Blog*, 'Returning to Laipunuk' was seen as an action that:

> not only unifies the ethnic identity and awareness of the Bunun of Yanping county, but also restores the Bunun subjectivity and the correctness of an historical interpretation from a Bunun viewpoint. Furthermore, as a base of taking charge of *Laipunuk*, this action aims to rehabilitate the traditional territory of Bunun, which will be the foundation of resource management and land attribution.[29]

---

28 Preparations for 'Returning to Laipunuk' included interviews with older Bunun, a literature review, site investigation and other data compilation.

29 www.bunun.org.tw/tw/index.asp?au_id=56&sub_id=160.

Plate 2.2 Sacrifice to the ancestors
Photo: Bunun tu Asang (Bunun Cultural and Educational Foundation).

In other words, 'Returning to Laipunuk' is the Bunun descendants 'walking on the way home'. These paths carry various flows of and communication between people, things, ideas, meanings and memories. Therefore, the path is a medium that carries and reveals various relationships and mediates between them.

According to this statement, the activities of finding the way home over a complex area, clarifying a possible path and maintaining it by continuing to walk on it give the path meaning. Through its substance, the path allows people to continue to walk back and forth; goals appear, are realised and maintained. This gradual formation of paths allowed the former tribal locations to be identified, helped reveal the ancestors' way of living and then led to the reconstruction of houses. It opened the way for a journey of learning from the forest. It was an attempt at re-linking, and a lesson for the Bunun. The path clarified ideas. It offered not so much a spatial continuity of points as the connectivity of the group through time. As such, the path offers 'mediation'. It mediates various 'force fields' through negotiation, arbitration, connection and assembly. This path is a basis for relearning and becomes a cultural creation of the contemporary Bunun people.[30]

As people walked into the mountains and outlined the scope of the old tribes, the process of historicising was documented on film. The 'Returning to Laipunuk' and the trails followed on the way home were recorded in at least two mediums: the bodies of those walking and the images recorded on video. These two different mediums preserve a historical document of 'walking back to the homeland', serving an intermediary role through time and space to extend the significance of bodily action in different contexts.

'Through images, we hope to bring back the memories of the elders and remind the Bunun offspring of their affection toward *Laipunuk*. Therefore, a *Laipunuk* identity will be formed.' This paragraph was written in May 2002 in the proposal for the filming of *Back to the Land Where the Navel is Buried*.[31] The director was one member of the site investigation team. His documentary *Open the Window of Taiwanese History: Return to Laipunuk* combines images and narration to create a specific narrative style. The film is framed around the site-investigation process, during which people walked into the mountains many times; yet the camera mostly focuses on the natural environment—the climate and plants— rather than on the people moving about. The director has tried to let the Bunun elders and the audience view the natural environment of the

---

30   The Bunun people left the forest and broke their connection with the land, making it difficult to be Bunun. The contemporary people who have a sense of identity with Bunun culture more or less experience the process of *min Bunun* ('recircling Bunun'). See also: laipunuk.blogspot.com/p/bunun-min-bunun-tama-nabu-min-bunun-min.html.

31   www.bunun.org.tw/tw/index.asp?au_id=56&sub_id=160.

homeland directly through the camera, as if they were there with the site investigation team and could see and feel the place where their ancestors once lived.

The director presents his site investigation through images that show the audience both the physical and the psychic labour he expended during the journey. Although, compared with people's firsthand experience, the video itself was not necessary for the search process, as a recording tool, it does not function until the site investigation team arrives at a specific destination. The director sees and feels on behalf of those who could not be at the spot personally and transfers his experience through visual images, while presenting what he knows through stories told by the elders. The eyes of the director are internalised in the video, while his visual perception of the surroundings is embedded in the memories and knowledge passed down from the ancestors of Bunun. In other words, the flow of Bunun memories and affections toward the place are contained and transferred within this vision.

As MacDougall (1998) has pointed out: 'Image, as a way of representation, is something to be seen and touched.' Laura Marks, a film scholar, notes the connections between 'vision' and 'touch' through image representation: '[I]f seeing is considered a way of embodiment, then touch, as well as other sensory perceptions, play[s] a necessary role in such seeing' (Marks 2000: 22). Through the director and the sensory images he presents, the Bunun people saw and remembered the old tribe. The key to rekindling memories lies in multiple sensory perceptions. Images in a film can make direct contact, reviving people's memory and demanding their sensory participation. As the audience identifies the subject of these actions, they participate in the meaning and experience signified in the narration.

According to the *Bunun Blog*: 'When the recorded images of site-investigation were played to the elders, they were moved to tears.'[32] The idea of a homeland came into being as their offspring climbed through the mountains. On their way to the site, their offspring experienced the change in climate and saw living things in their natural landscape. The journey to the homeland demanded that people walk back and forth, and images of this walking could be played and replayed afterwards. Watching this walking provided access to the experience of physical labour involved in the production of possible meanings (Lee and Ingold 2006: 68).

---

32   www.bunun.org.tw/tw/index.asp?au_id=56&sub_id=160.

Conclusion

'*Wukan mas maidudu tu dan, kaupa mas maza na kandapanan su* [There is no easy way but to look where you choose to walk].' Nabu said this in a thoughtful way as he was going home: 'The road is still very long; [I encourage] everyone to go slowly!' This 'slow walking' allowed people of different generations to take different paths but meet each other on the way home. The path home was the way people emerged as Bunun ('the real humans', in Bunun language). For those who walked on this path, it was not just a way of moving, but a way to bring forth a cultural inheritance. The path was born of walking, and this walking shaped the landscape. Over time, the landscape became a repository of common knowledge and symbolic meaning. This path home became a means of linking tradition and generating new knowledge. By this means, people drew forth different relations and put forward issues of the existence, survival and maintenance of culture. Through this path, a contemporary chain of identity was negotiated and transformed, and given cultural rejuvenation.

References

Aliman (Wang, Tu-Shui). 2006. Exploring the history of the Bunun ISDAZA (Laipunuk) from a local perspective. [In Chinese]. Masters thesis, Institute of Ethnic Relations and Culture, National Donghua University, Hualien, Taiwan.

Appadurai, Arjun. 2015. 'Mediants, materiality, normativity.' *Public Culture* 27(2): 221–37. doi.org/10.1215/08992363-2841832.

Basso, Keith. 1996. *Wisdom Sits in Places: Landscape and language among the western Apache*. Albuquerque, NM: University of New Mexico Press.

de Certeau, Michel. 1984. *The Practice of Everyday Life*. Trans. by Steven Rendall. Berkeley, CA: University of California Press.

Elliott, Denielle and Dara Culhane. 2017. *A Different Kind of Ethnography: Imaginative practices and creative methodologies*. Toronto: University of Toronto Press.

Gray, John. 2003. 'Open spaces and dwelling places: Being at home on hill farms in the Scottish Borders.' In Setha M. Low and Denise Lawrence-Zuniga, eds, *The Anthropology of Space and Place: Locating culture*, pp. 224–44. Oxford: Blackwell.

Haisul Palalavi. 2006. *The Origin of Bunun Tribes and History of Tribal Migration.* [In Chinese]. Taipei: The Executive Yuan Aboriginal Committee.

Herzogenrath, Bernd, ed. 2015. *Media Matter: The materiality of media, matter as medium.* New York: Bloomsbury. doi.org/10.5040/9781501304835.

Huang, Ying-Kuei. 2001. *Taitung County History: Bunun Zu.* [In Chinese]. Taitung County: Taitung County Government.

Ingold, Tim. 2000. *The Perception of the Environment: Essays on livelihood, dwelling and skill.* New York: Routledge.

Ingold, Tim. 2004. 'Culture on the ground: The world perceived through the feet.' *Journal of Material Culture* 9(3): 315–40. doi.org/10.1177/1359183504046896.

Ingold, Tim. 2010. 'Footprints through the weather-world: Walking, breathing, knowing.' *Journal of the Royal Anthropological Institute* 16: 121–39. doi.org/10.1111/j.1467-9655.2010.01613.x.

Ingold, Tim. 2011a. *Being Alive: Essays on movement, knowledge and description.* London: Routledge. doi.org/10.4324/9780203818336.

Ingold, Tim. 2011b. *Redrawing Anthropology: Materials, movements, lines.* Farnham, UK: Ashgate.

Keith, Michael and Steve Pile, eds. 1993. *Place and the Politics of Identity.* London: Routledge.

Lee, Jo and Tim Ingold. 2006. 'Fieldwork on foot: Perceiving, routing, socializing.' In Simon M. Coleman and Peter Collins, eds, *Locating the Field: Space, place and context in anthropology*, pp. 67–86. Oxford: Berg.

Li Minhui. 1997. The group migration policy and social reconstruction of Taiwanese mountain tribes during Japanese rule: Bunun River Basin family as an example. [In Chinese]. Masters thesis, Department of Geography, National Normal University, Taipei.

Liu, Man-Yi. 2017. *Kulumah Laipunuk: Finding the roots and going home.* [In Chinese]. New Taipei City: Walkers Cultural Enterprises.

MacDougall, David. 1998. Transcultural Cinema. Princeton, NJ: Princeton University Press.

Marks, Laura. 2000. *The Skin of the Film: Intercultural cinema, embodiment, and the senses.* Durham, NC: Duke University Press. doi.org/10.1215/9780822381372.

Massey, Doreen B. 2005. *For Space*. London: Sage.

Merleau-Ponty, Maurice. 2014. *Phenomenology of Perception*. Donald A. Landes, trans. New York: Routledge.

O'Neill, Maggie and Phil Hubbard. 2010. 'Walking, sensing, belonging: Ethno-mimesis as performative praxis.' *Visual Studies* 25(1): 46–58. doi.org/10.1080/14725861003606878.

Rundstrom, Robert. 1991. 'Mapping, postmodernism, indigenous people and the changing direction of North American cartography.' *Cartographica* 28(2): 1–12. doi.org/10.3138/5J46-51T2-7M42-316G.

Rundstrom, Robert. 1993. 'The role of ethics, mapping, and the meaning of place in relations between Indians and whites in the United States.' *Cartographica* 30(1): 21–28. doi.org/10.3138/2362-P365-2G88-1P65.

Tahai Binkinuaz (Tsai San-Shen), dir. 2002. *Open the Window of Taiwanese History: Return to Laipunuk*. [In Chinese]. Documentary, 60 mins.

Tahai Binkinuaz (Tsai San-Shen), dir. 2003. *Back to the Land Where the Navel is Buried*. [In Chinese]. Documentary, 10 mins.

Tahai Binkinuaz (Tsai San-Shen). 2004. Laipunuk Bunun tribal migration before 1942. [In Chinese]. Masters thesis, National Chengchi University, Taipei.

Tilley, Christopher. 1994. *A Phenomenology of Landscape: Places, paths, and monuments*. Oxford: Berg.

Ye, Jia-Ning. 2002. *The History of Taiwan's Indigenous Peoples: A history of Bunun*. [In Chinese]. Nantou, Taiwan: Taiwan Historica.

Young, Iris Marion. 1980. 'Throwing like a girl: A phenomenology of feminine body comportment motility and spatiality.' *Human Studies* 3: 137–56. doi.org/10.1007/BF02331805.

3

Testing paths in shamanic performances among the northern Amis of Taiwan

Yi-tze Lee

Introduction

The Amis people are the single largest group of indigenous people in Taiwan. With a population of roughly 250,000 people living mostly in the eastern part of Taiwan, the Amis are famous for their agricultural rituals led by groups of shamans. These rituals include millet sowing, weeding, field cleaning, pest control, harvesting, storage and, finally, fishing activities that conclude the rice cycle. While rituals give meaning to the daily lives of the Amis, changes have occurred in these rituals owing to three main causes: 1) because of migration and the relocation of animals related to ritual activities, 2) because of changes in subsistence strategies, and 3) because of urbanisation that limits ritual access and agricultural use on traditional territory. Together, these three factors have brought about a 'deterritorialisation' of the Amis people on their own land and so have reshaped their ritual landscape.[1] The most prominent yearly rituals include *Midiwai*, the ritual to announce millet sowing at the end of December; *Misatuligun*, the ritual for field cleaning in March; *Mivava*,

---

1 By legal definition of the Taiwan Government, there is no 'traditional territory reservation area' for the Amis since they lived with Han people during the Japanese colonial period.

the pest-control ritual in April; and *Miladis*, the fishing ritual that ends the rice cultivation cycle in June (see Table 3.1). These rituals reflect the significant relationship between people and animals in the landscape.

The seasonal cycle is based on the millet-planting schedule. In early February, a ritual is carried out after millet plants start to shoot. This weeding ritual called *Mivalidas* is carried out when every household has finished preparing its farming tools. During the process of ritual weeding, villagers tie weeds into stacks and make the collective work in the field mimic a game of 'tug-of-war'. The next farming ritual is called *Mivava*, in April. '*Vava*' is a broom made from the leaves and stems of the areca palm. A leaf stem is tied with betel nuts wrapped in it. Villagers line up to follow the shamans, who throw betel nuts and rice wine into the air for ritual cleansing and to chase away pests and hungry spirits. *Mivava* is an important ritual for environmental protection of the growing millet while the ritual process identifies both sparrows (*ciruciru*) and hungry ghosts (*tagenawan*) as pests. Millet needs to be harvested around May and the ritual for post-harvest storage is called *Mianan* (*anan* is a ritual term for 'granary' in Amis). When *Mianan* is carried out, the deceased ancestors of a family are summoned to enjoy and bless the harvest and to protect the harvest in storage. Nowadays, *Mianan* is held in mid-June when the rice crop is harvested and husked for storage.

Table 3.1 Yearly ritual cycle of Nangshi[2] Amis

Month	December	January	February	March	April	
Season	*Kasi'nawan* (Cold season)			*Ka'Oladan* (Rainy season)		
Ritual event	*Midiwai*		*Misatuligun*		*Mivava*	
Activities	Millet planting		Weeding, growing yams		Dispelling pests and ghosts	
Month	May	June	July	August	September	October	November
Season	*Kacidalan* (Dry and sunny)		*Kabaliusan* (Typhoon)		*Kafaliwan* (Windy)	
Ritual event	*Mianan*	*Miladis*	*Miadop*		*Malalikid*	*Mirecuk*
Activities	Harvest millet and restore	Fishing ritual	Hunting		Harvest festival	Shamanic rituals

---

2 'Nangshi' is the geographic term for the area where the northern Amis people live. It covers the current administrative regions of Huaien City, Chian County and Shinchen County.

Plate 3.1 Two shamans prepare a male bird trap for the Misatuligun ritual

Photo: Yi-tze Lee.

Plate 3.2 During the *Mivava* ritual, elders and shamans symbolically sweep away filth to reorder the main border path of the village. One shaman holds an invisible *calai* thread

Photo: Yi-tze Lee.

Women are thought to be the origin of the family and they inherit the natal family's property. One linguistic expression reinforces the notion that a woman is the core element of a family. The Amis word *maran-ina-ai*, which refers to members of the same family, comes from the root *ina*, which means 'mother'. A man marries out of his natal family but retains greater rights in its affairs than in the family into which he marries. This is also reflected in the spiritual world: the guardian spirits to whom Amis shamans turn are a group of female spirits called *dongi*. *Dongi* are the guides for the *sikawasai* shamans. The *duas* ('ancestors and deceased family members') can only be summoned home if the *dongi* are pleased and the *calai* (the invisible threads they provide) are tested. Although there are both male and female shamans in Amis tradition, as a result of changes in modern life, male shamans are no longer considered as powerful as their female counterparts. At present, there are no male shamans in Dongchang village, where I conducted my fieldwork.

Contemporary Amis ritual activities have become a new arena for cultural revitalisation: the format of rituals still follows the traditional cycle, but rituals now combine the worship of Chinese deities using incense and firecrackers with new sources of community solidarity promoted by government political mobilisation efforts. Through repeated ritual practice, symbolic paths in the ritual landscape are constantly reshaped and reconstructed, drawing new boundaries. In contemporary activities, the dialectic meaning of paths and the way they are tested via the use of symbolic threads can shed light on how ritual landscapes are constructed through memories of physical performances, but also through the incorporation of a political agenda. This transition occurring in the ritual landscape and the changing meanings of paths whose authenticity is tested are a consequence of Amis–Han historical interaction, connected to an understanding of the colonial legacy of ethnic relationships.

This chapter reflects on how symbolic indicators of paths and path-testing illustrate the dialectic relationship that exists in Amis ritual between authority and authenticity. The invisible threads known as *calai*—symbolising authentic paths to the spirit world—serve as embedded vectors of bodily orientation in rituals as well as a means to resolve conflict and bring about restoration of both spiritual and ethnic boundaries. In a tentative and cautious ritual process, invisible threads of *calai* are sought from the *dongi* and then carefully protected by shaman leaders. This process also reflects the Amis view that women represent the inner core of the household while men are actors in the outside world of mountains and rivers. To provide a background understanding of the use of paths and their testing in rituals, I will start with the historical transition and migration of Amis people.

Amis migration routes and livelihood transition

Among Taiwanese indigenous people, Amis are the ones who undertake gardening and farming as their subsistence strategy, living most closely to the settler regions of Han Chinese. For a long time, the Amis sustained themselves by hunting, fishing, gathering wild vegetables and cultivating millet as their major food sources. They developed a sophisticated cycle of ritual practices in harmony with seasonal rhythms. This traditional lifestyle changed greatly during the Japanese colonial period (1895–1945), when the Amis were forced to adopt rice cultivation and work as coolies. A major change in the colonial period was the introduction of Japonica rice and other crops. A change to two harvests each year provided a more secure food supply. At the same time, the Amis were mobilised into a wartime supply system, which demanded more efficient planting, forced labour to build railways and harbours and heavy taxation (Ka 1995; Tsurumi 1977). The Amis also faced conflicts over religion and modern formal education. Traditional connections with the natural world began to dissolve and subsequent generations of Amis were gradually alienated from their forefathers' connections with nature. Rituals, however, continue to impart the wisdom handed down from the elders.

The gendered conception of space

The traditional spatial conception of the Amis is represented by the different corners of a house and is based on the division of labour among men and women. Different productive tools are placed in different corners of the house depending on gender associations. The Amis also believe some dominant spirits dwell in particular directions. They are all represented in Figure 3.1.

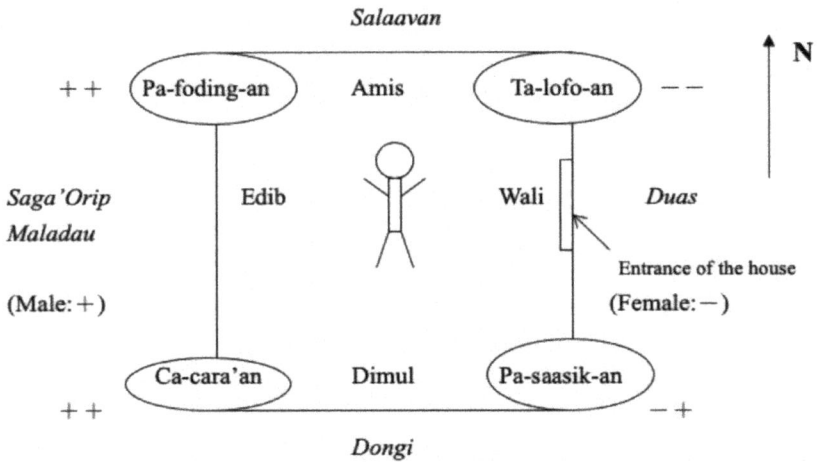

Figure 3.1 The Amis's spatial conception of the house and the location of spirits
Source: Drawn by the author.

Ritual directions

Amis, Dimul, Edib and *Wali* define the directions north, south, west and east.

- East is the direction of *Duas* (ancestors). According to the village origin legend, the ancestors took a boat and came from the east by sea.
- The *Dongi* in the south is the guardian goddess of the human body. The Amis sleep and sit facing the south during a period of healing to receive the blessing from the *Dongi*.
- *Saga'orip* in the west is the spirit of crop growth. *Maladau*, who dwells in the west, is the god that men worship for hunting; to the west side of the village are mountains.
- *Salaavan* in the north indicates the place where the souls of the villagers who die a bad death or die outside the village go. This direction is also where Amis people came from historically because Dongchang is the northernmost tribe among the Amis.

Four special corners

- *Pa-foding-an*: This corner is the place in the house where men put their fishing net (from *foding*: 'fish'). Women are forbidden to touch the fishing net and cannot come into this corner during critical phases of farm work.

- *Ca-cara'an*: *Cala* (or *Cara*) refers to the mandible of the mountain pig. This is the traditional place where males put the mandibles of wild animals and worship the spirits of animals after hunting. The clay pot for men's worship, called *dewas*, is stored here. The taboo against women entering this corner is even stricter than the taboo for the corner in which the fishing net is hung. This is a prime male locality.

- *Pa-saasik-an*: *Saasik* means a bunch of straw and refers to the broom made from straw. This is the place where the broom, dustpan and farming tools are stored. This is also the place where some clans in the village honoured heads taken in headhunting when that practice was still conducted. In ritual activities, it signifies 'exiting or sweeping out'. The corner is ambiguous in regard to gender because both women's (farming and cleaning) tools and men's worship activity (for the head) are associated with this corner.

- *Pa-lofo-an*: *Lofo* means 'granary'. It can refer to the female clay pot for worship, which is called *sivanohai*. Women's pottery and the utensils used for family rituals are stored in this corner. The family granary is built in the northeast and grain is stored there after the harvest. Men are not allowed to do such work. This is a prime female locality.

According to the symbolic arrangements, men are associated with the west and women with the east. Besides this east–west dichotomy, there is another distinction: men are associated with uncultivated fields, forest land and coastal areas and women are associated with the house. Hunting and fishing are conducted far away from the house and are usually carried out by men of the same age set; women are forbidden to touch or get close to the western corners of the house where male implements are kept. In contrast, the east side of the house primarily represents female activities, such as farming, grain storage and house sweeping.

This spatial concept is an 'uneven' opposition: women are not allowed to enter men's corners of the house while men can sometimes enter a women's corner if women are not available—a superiority of 'maleness' in a ritual sense, but later changed since male shamans are not available nowadays. From the evidence of the arrangement of tools in the house, this spatial conception endows rituals with meaning: shamans turn to a specific direction for particular rituals as well in the practice of healing. This spatial conception is also critical in the use and arrangement of symbolic *calai* on ritual occasions. I will now examine the functional meaning of *calai* in Amis rituals.

Calai: A road offered and tested before being taken

For Amis shamans, the *calai* is a critical tool in conducting rituals. *Calai* is the ritual term used for a road or path. It can be transformed into a healing tool and a means of demarcating boundaries. It is described as a shining string that resembles the thread of a spider's web. The *calai* is an invisible but important tool used by Amis shamans in rituals to create a connection between themselves and the spiritual world.

There are three senses of the term *calai* that need to be explored. First, *calai* refers to an invisible thread that a shaman holds in her hand while engaged in rituals. When shamans call upon the ancestors, the *calai* represents a symbolic thread that links the mundane with the sacred world. A shaman requests the *calai*, which is given by the female guardian *dongi* spirits who dwell in the southern world. A typical daily ritual, for example, the healing practice called *badevu* (literally, 'searching for the soul'), starts with the shaman offering rice liquor as she prays to the ancestors; she then turns to the south, chanting to the *dongi* spirits to obtain their blessings and a precious *calai*. Once the leading shaman has successfully acquired a *calai* from the south, she will take care of the sacred thread and use this invisible *calai* as a tool to access locations where the patient's soul has been hidden. The whole process is performed in a mime-like drama with the recitation of names revealing to the patient's family the presence of deities and guardian goddesses. Here the *calai* serves as a compass directing the shaman to different places in the spiritual world.

Second, *calai* can also refer to a 'path' and is used interchangeably with the Amis word for 'path', *lalan*. A path or road is part of the infrastructure of the mundane world but may be disguised in the Amis spiritual world. In the latter, access to a path cannot be taken for granted and needs to be tested over and over again to ensure its authenticity. This takes the form of an extended verbal exchange known as *baceva*—an articulated quest to determine the genuineness of the path. The *calai* is a path leading to the spiritual world, but the ancestors may provide misleading directions, forcing the shamans to test their authenticity. A shaman needs to examine the *calai* whenever she receives a 'spiritual road' from the guardian spirit, *dongi*. This examination is to ensure the safety of the shaman who must walk this path, thus demonstrating her spiritual power in public. Here the *calai* is a probe for power and authenticity.

Third, a *calai* can be transformed during a ritual from the symbol of a road to that of a border. In testing the authenticity of a *calai* during a ritual performance, the presence of a clear border and a clean body is constantly stressed. Shamans and ritual participants have to be cautious when transitioning between spiritual and earthly activities. At a critical moment, the *calai* can be transformed from a path to a cleansing tool to assess the boundaries of the body and the village. The *calai* thus offers a remedy for distorted or broken boundaries that occur after contacts with non-Amis or in living a contemporary lifestyle in which traditions are no longer observed. Here the *calai* is an indicator of, and possible remedy for, boundary transgressions.

In these three aspects of *calai*, we see its transformative nature and multiple functions. Feelings toward the spiritual are ambivalent, requiring delicacy, respect, awe, caution and fear—all at the same time. *Calai* in ritual represents paths for the Amis, whether or not, after scrutiny, these are taken. It shows how the Amis interpret their ethical relations and the boundaries they create in daily experience. I want to delve now into examples of this ritual landscape as well as the environmental changes that have occurred in it.

In the case of the Amis, an awareness of 'filth' is emphasised in the process of dealing with the 'spiritual body' of the dead[3] and the repetitive self-cleaning actions of the shaman. The symbolic cleansing therefore prevents

---

3   Thomas Csordas (1990: 5) directs attention to the primacy of the body by stressing that the 'body is not an *object* to be studied in relation to culture but is to be considered as the *subject* of culture, or in other words as the existential ground of culture' (italics in the original). Csordas also notes that to collapse the dualities of perception and practice, the body itself has to be a unitary concept, not opposed to the principle of mind. Body is thus the hinge of the notion of *preobjective* and *habitus* (Csordas 1990: 8).

any feelings of danger and unease.[4] While filth is dealt with by a process of knife-cutting or *calai*-healing, a sense of potential harm is created by the shaman's actions. This sense of a contaminable body and wandering soul hence becomes the background of the whole funeral, embodied in the shaman's performances.

Baceva: Testing and healing

A notion that links the use of *calai* with spiritual power and healing is *baceva*. *Baceva* can mean either 'to test' or 'to deceive' (for the sake of self-protection).[5]

The importance of *baceva* is related to the shamanic use of *calai*. On ritual occasions, in requesting a spiritual road, shamans invariably take the first *calai* given to them by the *dongi*, but then return the threads to them with symbolic gestures. They again request a *calai* and examine the spiritual thread carefully. Usually it takes at least two or three tests to find the correct *calai*. By their performance, they show to the public and to family members that what they have finally received is the correct *calai* for the event. This is the *baceva* process in requesting spiritual tools.

On the occasion of a funeral, experienced shamans enter the yard of the house of the bereaved family 'to call back the soul of the dead'. The shamans who do soul-calling are also the leaders of the feast for spirits. They cannot be lineal relatives of the dead person. According to the Amis, if a shaman officiated at the funeral of one of her lineal relatives, the *kawas*[6] ('spirits') would laugh at her or cheat her (in Amis: *a baceva du kawas*) for the ceremony. Moreover, the spirit of the dead would 'feel

---

4   In the funeral ritual, after the spiritual feast for the dead and ancestors, shamans repetitively cleanse the materials used for worship before they are stored by family members; even the ground on which they have been standing has to be cleaned several times with hand gestures.

5   I can provide an example of the notion of *baceva* from my personal experience in the field. While I was staying in the village, I asked many times about the exact date of the biannual ancestor-visiting ritual (*tala duas*; literally, 'going to the place of ancestors'), so I could prepare in advance. After being bothered by my repeated questions, my brother-in-law said to me: 'Well, the time is up so we can go catch fish soon!' I was totally perplexed by his answer, since I knew that catching fish referred to the end of a ritual, but the actual ritual had not yet happened! Several days later, I returned to his house and asked my brother-in-law why he had mentioned catching fish when the *tala duas* ritual had not occurred. He looked at me as if I had not understood him and replied: 'You know, we cannot speak of the date too early even if we have decided on it since the *kawas*-spirits may be listening! The *kawas* and our ancestors will laugh at us for our foolishness and arrogance. We need to give them the wrong answer for our own protection. *Baceva du kawas*, remember?' I then realised that I did not practise *baceva* as well as the locals even though I knew the process of the ritual.

6   In Amis, *kawas* is a general term for spirits.

shame' (*mangudu*) and not show up during the feast. Notably, a funeral is a ritual that mediates between the impurity of the deceased and the sacredness of the ancestors. Thus, a shaman whose lineal relative has recently died, and who is therefore tinged with impurity, cannot serve to call the dead nor can a shaman who has just undergone his or her *bafafui* ritual (re-initiation rite) officiate in the soul-calling ritual because the impurity of the funeral will make the shaman sick.[7]

In performing a search for the soul, the shaman tosses out an invisible *calai* to guide the dead and to keep the shaman herself away from the *kawas* and avoid contamination from direct contact. After finding the soul, the shaman tears off a piece of banana leaf attached to the *calai* in her hand and throws it in the direction of the place where she found the soul. This act is meant to 'reinstate the boundaries' separating the human and spiritual worlds after the shaman's intrusion in search of the soul. Before letting the soul reunite with the body, the shaman has to shave the filth off the soul with a knife and, literally, 'cut off' the ill part of the soul and throw it back to the spiritual world.

On the one hand, the *calai* represents the road to the spiritual world, but it needs repeated testing to provide reassurance before it can be used to lead to power and perform authentic healing. On the other hand, the *calai* provides a precarious connection between the human and spiritual worlds, as well as establishing the boundaries of the family and the village and between life and death.

---

7   An incident during my fieldwork demonstrates the ambivalence of Amis shamans towards the dead. One of the only two male shamans of the village died. Unfortunately, the most experienced and powerful shaman had just lost her adopted daughter, so she could not lead the ritual although other shamans really thought she should: 'Her voice is the clearest and most powerful one.' On the day of the burial, the shamans gathered to pay their respects to the dead. A senior shaman walked out immediately after the indoor blessing for the soul-calling ritual, trying to avoid being selected as the leader of the ritual. The most experienced shaman ran out after the first shaman and tried to convince her to be the leader. Later I realised that the senior shaman also worshipped Taiwanese Daoist gods in her family. According to her, leading the funeral ritual would have broken her fast for the worship and lowered her ability to connect with the Taiwanese gods. But, in the end, she agreed to lead the soul-calling ritual.

Changes in ritual landscapes: Environmental shifts in contemporary settings

For Taiwan's indigenous peoples, there have been changes in rituals and their relationship with particular species in the construction of particular paths. Environmental shifts in the paths have included changes in subsistence activities, increasing urbanisation and investment in political initiatives. Liu (2007) has discussed the meaning of rice and deer as representations of gender divisions among the Kavalan and Amis people. The ritual pair is an emblem of reproductive dynamics: deer resemble men and rice resembles women. Hunting took place after harvest and shamans provided the symbolic path for Amis men when they returned from their hunting activities. When lowland deer were exterminated through commercial hunting, the ritual species shifted to a rooster since a white rooster is sacrificed to Maladaw, the protective deity of men, who is said to ride on a white pheasant. This was an 'environmental shift' in a ritual path. Commercial farming and the animal trade have brought about other important environmental shifts. Hu (2007) has discussed how the giant Magellan birdwing butterfly (*Troides magellanus*) of Orchid Island was commercialised and became an economic trophy product. Similarly, Lo (2010) has discussed the way Atolan Amis women have taken action to protect their clam-gathering grounds as a protest against the illegal construction of a tourist resort on their traditional territory. Actions with ritual meaning have been used in a struggle for political rights and economic wellbeing. Relationships between species and the ritual landscape have consequences for historical discourse, symbolic boundaries and action networks.

I examine three cases of the use of the idea of a path in different Amis ritual settings and consider the symbolic meanings of these practices as changes in power relationships and struggles for recognition. These cases will focus on the *Mivava* pest-dispelling ritual, the *Miasik* house-cleansing ritual and the *Mirecuk* shamanic power rejuvenation ritual. I intend to demonstrate how vital ritual actions are linked to 'path-finding', 'border-making' and 'infrastructure renewal' in Amis religious practice. The inner meaning of Amis cultural heritage has been sustained even though the original physical locations and materials have gradually become unavailable. In all these performances, the *calai* as a symbolic path is the focus of a continuous struggle for power.

Plate 3.3 During the *Mirecuk* ritual, shamans help a crippled man hop over the fire stack to cure his problem leg

Photo: Yi-tze Lee.

Mivava: Sacred thread to distinct species of birds in the rice field

The Amis believe that various spirits (*kawas*) dwell in different places in the world. When a person dies, he or she will go to a territory belonging to the ancestral spirits (*duas*). From here, the spirits of the dead regularly visit the living. Amis shamans are responsible for making possible communication between the living and the spirits of the dead. Lidaw village has the most comprehensive ritual practices among the Amis. There are about 200 days in the year that come under conditions of *paising* ('taboo'). Every household also intermittently needs a *sikawasai* for dealing with illness (*badevu*), giving offerings to the ancestors (*ba-nanom*), cleansing newly built houses (*miasik*) or hosting funeral rituals (*misa-pangcah*). Before a ritual can be carried out, villagers need to prepare a standard set of offerings: sticky rice or millet cake (*toron*), betel nut (*icep*), betel pepper (*fila*) and rice liquor (*epa'*). Depending on the purpose of the ritual, additional plants must also be prepared. A shaman sometimes even specifies the location and the direction from which these plants are collected. When everything is prepared, the shaman will rely on the power of these plants to ensure the effectiveness of the ritual. The *calai*—the symbolic road—is attached to the leaves of these plants.

A most important public ritual pair is *Misatuligun* (worship to the land deity) and *Mivava* (cleansing the field for rice cultivation) (see Table 3.2 for a comparison of private and public ritual settings). In these rituals, the *calai* shows its capacity to act as a path as well as a means of testing paths. In the past, Amis women cultivated open fields after the sowing of millet or rice. The shamans would perform a *Misatuligun* ritual to keep wild birds away and protect the rice seedlings and a *Mivava* ritual to dispel unruly pests. During the *Misatuligun* ritual, they would take the pieces of a *taker* from a linen bag and put them together. A *taker* is a hunter's bird trap made of bamboo sticks and a long linen circle. In the ritual, the shaman faces southward to pray to the *dongi* to obtain a *calai*. Once she has the *calai*, she knows the correct ways to the animal spirits and then aligns the symbolic *calai* on ginger leaves to each of their *taker* before attaching them at the southern ridge of the rice field. After a while, each shaman retrieves the *taker* and offers rice liquor because the *kawas* (spirits) of wild birds have been caught on the *taker*. After this, each shaman takes a piece of ginger leaf and throws it into the air to release the 'captured spirits'.

A proper *calai* helps the *sikawasai* to specify possible wild birds during the ritual: sparrow (*cirociro*), drongo (*tatacio*), red-necked pheasant (*trok*), duck (*koakoa*) or brown shrike (*cicale'*).

Table 3.2 Comparisons of items in family and tribal rituals

Item	Family rituals (private)	Tribal rituals (public)
Plants as ritual platform	Banana leaves	Silver-tail miscanthus
Ritual vessels	*Sifanohay* (female ritual vessel)	*Diwas* (male ritual vessel)
Ritual offerings	Betel nut, betel pepper, rice liquor, sticky rice cake	All the elements for family rituals, plus a rooster
Spiritual protector	*Dongi* (female spirits) to provide calai	*Malataw* in the mountains and wild areas
Ancestors in rituals	*Duas* (ancestor spirits) of the household	Famous tribal leader, chiefs, shamans

This shamanic performance is called *Tala-omah* and is an activity to draw spiritual power from *loma'* ('the household') to *omah* ('the field'), using ginger leaves linked to specific birds to catch them and prevent them eating the rice seedlings. The ritual space is transformed by driving bird spirits from the rice field. This in effect drives these birds from the rice field, which belongs to the female sphere, to the outside male sphere. This action of *Tala-omah* beautifully effects a transition from inner to outer, from plant to animal and from female to male (as ginger leaves are for female and birds are for male). The *calai* is the symbolic connection between these two worlds, where a path from the inner world leads to the outer world—a path channelled by the shaman's embodied action. During the ritual chanting of *Mivava*, the *calai* is used to distinguish migrant from resident birds. Only migrant birds are symbolically caught before releasing them again since these birds are a menace from the other world. Resident birds, especially pheasants or quails, are symbols of male age groups and therefore need to be protected from harm while in custody.[8] The *calai* not only provides the path from the mundane environment to a sacred space; it also has the capacity to distinguish between different species in the Amis life world. The *calai* held by shamans are constantly tossed out and drawn back during the *Mivava* ritual to cleanse the territory and remake the boundary of the village. Through the active bodily movement of shamans, the *calai* are transformed from a healing and discriminating tool to a powerful symbol of protection.

---

8   Gender difference is a constant theme in shamans' creation of boundaries (Strathern and Stewart 2003) and is entangled in a multispecies agenda (Kirksey and Helmreich 2010).

Miasik: Path-finding negotiations and testing for authenticity

Another ritual in which the *calai* serves as a path that must be tested is *Miasik*. The main purpose of the *Miasik* ritual is to cleanse a newly built or renovated house and to put away remaining construction materials to obtain good luck. In this ritual, a shaman requests a *calai* from the *dongi* spirits, holds the sacred *calai* in her hand and uses this invisible thread to 'scan' the whole house from inside to outside. For an Amis shaman, authenticity in ritual is critical. The correctness and quality of the *calai* from a guardian *dongi* need to be constantly examined in response to possible threats.

According to the *sikawasai*, the *dongi* are guardian deities in daily life, but they also guard and keep intact the purity of the ancestral world. A *calai* creates a mutual connection to both the mundane and the sacred worlds. After each ritual occasion, the *calai* has to be returned to the *dongi* and they have to be thanked for their generosity. There is a sense of care and cautiousness in dealing with each *calai*; it is the path between two worlds. The purity of the road is essential at both ends.

When the *calai* is transformed from a path to a cleansing tool, the authenticity and purity of the *calai* are doubly important. When a shaman acquires an invisible *calai*, it cannot be used directly. The ancestors can be mischievous towards their offspring and play jokes on their family if they have not carried out worship properly, but also the Han people, who have taught the Amis modern techniques for building houses, may have disguised the correct means of construction and inserted malicious spells into the house. In this case, the *calai* for the *Miasik* ritual will indicate the proper path to connect to the household ancestors, but also to connect with the non-indigenous Han technician deities. The *calai* thus embodies ambivalent relationships and historical memories between the colonised and the settlers' technological worlds.

During the *Miasik*, a shaman attaches the acquired *calai* to a place very different to the leaves used in a public ritual such as the *Mivava*. In this house-cleansing ritual, the right leg of a domestic pig is used as the means for cleansing as well as for blessing. The pig sacrificed in the ritual is shared with the participants, but only the shaman can consume the right leg since it is used as an embodiment of the *calai*. The use of a pig's leg as a *calai*'s vessel boosts the power of cleansing and blessing. 'Wrong or bad' *calai*-paths are also sought and questioned in case they are hidden in the construction materials such as nails, wire or wood blocks—items that need to be thrown out of the house at the end of the *Miasik* ritual. The test of a *calai*'s authenticity is performed by the shaman, who carries the leg to touch different parts of the house in the *baceva* process. As another example of *baceva*, when used in everyday bargaining conversations, the term means 'to check by cheating' or 'bluffing'. *Baceva* involves validating the genuineness of an expression or the authenticity of information. Calling someone *baceva* does not mean that he or she is a cheater, but rather seeks reassurance of the sincerity of the interlocutor as well as the moderation/mediation of someone who asks for help.[9] *Baceva* during the *Miasik* ritual reflects the possibility of harm either from dissatisfied ancestors or from the colonisers' technological influences.

Mirecuk: Body politics in the making of Amis orientations

According to Amis traditional subsistence strategies, gender differentiation is embodied in household living spaces and the way in which the different tools used for daily activities are arranged in their respective spaces. The northeastern corner of a house is called the *talofoan* and is where pottery, cooking utensils and, especially, female ritual vessels or *sifanohay* are placed. This is an assigned female space. Diagonally opposite the *talofoan* is the *cacara'an* corner, at the southwestern side of the house. *Cara* refers to animals' mandibles and is applied to the corner of the house where men display their glorious hunting trophies. It is also the corner where men put their hunting tools and ritual vessels known as *diwas*. The northwestern corner is called the *pafotingan* and is where fishing nets and tools are placed. This is also a male corner. The southeastern corner is called *pasaasikan* and is where women's farming tools are stored. This household geomancy of sides and corners has latent rules that reflect male and female distinctions: the male sphere is at the western and northern corners of the house, while the female sphere is at the eastern and southern corners.

---

9   In Korean shamanic performance, the authenticity of a ritual practice also needs to be examined over and over again to prevent financial fraud and ensure the reliability of information flow (Kendall 2009).

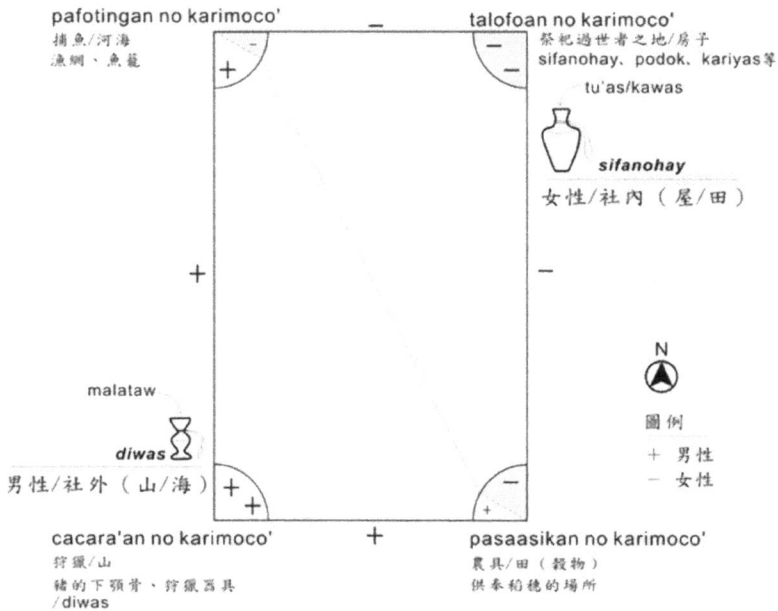

Figure 3.2 Household orientations for the Nangshi Amis
Source: Drawn by the author.

The directional opposition that associates males with the south and females with the north can be found in the funeral ritual as well as the *Mirecuk* ritual. Both rituals involve a process of regeneration and reunion with the *kawas/duas* ('spirits'/'ancestors'). The essential directions of this male–female spatial opposition are the southwestern corner for males (where the mandibles of wild pigs are hung) and the northeastern corner for females (where the granary is placed). *Mirecuk* is the time for the rejuvenation of shamanic power. It takes place in late September when all harvest work has been finished. The main purpose of *Mirecuk* is to let shamans worship the spirits related to the illness that makes them shamans, and in this way to renew their spiritual power and connections. Each shaman who is based in a particular lineage and family traces an inherited connection to particular spirits. The whole of the day's ritual of *Mirecuk* is devoted to the history-laden and life-generating path to the realm of spirits. To journey to the realm of spirits, shamans have to ask for a *calai* as their *lalan* from their guardian *dongi*. This will guarantee the correct path to the spiritual world. Only by following the correct ancestral path is the connection to the benevolent spirits guaranteed. A misleading path can result in missing the spiritual realm and not returning to life in the mundane world. On this ritual occasion, the testing of the authenticity of the thread leading to the spiritual road is different from that in the *Miasik* ritual. In the house-cleansing ritual, the testing of authenticity is done through the shaman's dialogue with the spirit. The result is visible to those attending when the correct *calai* is tied to the right leg of the pig to bring forth the blessing. In *Mirecuk*, the shaman tests the authenticity of the path by constantly checking contact with the *calai*. The shaman who receives a *calai* from a spirit checks this contact not only by verbal assurances, but also by various movements in receiving and returning invisible threads. By waving and padding lightly on her body and by expelling signs of spiritual contact through coughing, crying and jumping up and down in a small circle, the shaman indicates that the *calai* is attached only to her hands and not to other parts of her body. Every entry into and exit from the invisible path requires a bodily examination to show the separation from the potentially harmful spirits.

Healing is a major activity practised during the *Mirecuk* ritual, aiming to boost the ritual power of individual shamans, and the 'patients' are the *sikawasai* shamans of the host and her family members, who are usually women. The other shamans will be the healers who request and test *calai* from different deities. The ritual is performed publicly and villagers can be guests to witness the ritual power. Since women are leaders of the Amis household and of their families, healing during this ritual of spiritual rejuvenation is focused mainly on women's bodies and their condition. In such cases, healing is carried out through the benign power of the *calai*. The process is called *badevu*, meaning 'to stitch and mend the body'. In the prayer before the healing action, the power of the *dongi* is invoked and the condition of the person is described:

> *Ato haw Haidan haw fayi haw!*
>
> Here, my great aunty![10]
>
> *Sasurian dongi, Matiting dongi, Kakumudan dongi, Lalicayan dongi, Afuduay dongi!*
>
> You are the healer, person-maker, protector, gatherer, listener, with soft steps!
>
> *Saw anini sakirami haw a misuri hatini safadongi namo!*
>
> Yes, today there is a person who needs your healing power!
>
> *Haw ira suri satu kirami haw kamo matia tuni hulakan!*
>
> Please take away the pain and heal, just as you take off our clothes.
>
> *Aka baceva a lalan do kamay namo aka baceva bilimakimay.*

---

10   *Fayi* means 'old lady' or 'aunt' in Amis, and *faki* means 'old man' or 'uncle'. *Fayi* is a term of daily address to older women. However, during ritual chanting, shamans use *fayi* to convey intimacy with the *dongi* spirits.

Please do not give us the wrong path to tread, please guide our hand on the right location.

Haw pakalemeden miso kami maluina lemed tini acay kirami haw na misuri namo to kalimakimay ku maidama.

The one we need to heal is like a mother and child to you. Please cure her and let us benefit from your power by doing so.

Sa'hini sahanaca i tamuan minaor tu lingalawa, yia!

Please take this spirit/offering first so we can share later!

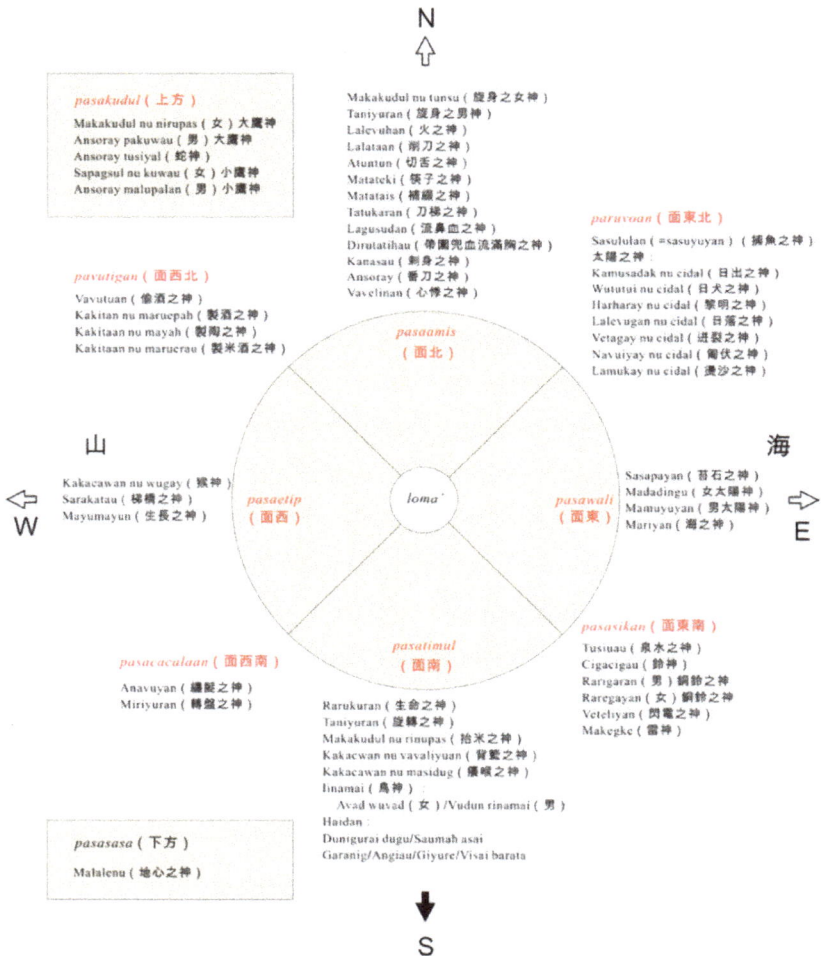

Figure 3.3 The major spirits (*kawas*) Amis shamans encounter during the *Mirecuk* ritual. As well as the eight directions on the plane, there is also a *pasakudol* (upper level) and a *pasasaan* (underground level)

Source: Butal et al. (2009: 112).

In the process of praying and chanting, Amis shamans use special terms to ask the guardian *dongi* spirits not to direct them on a wrong path or lead them to the wrong destination. The shamans repeatedly check and clear the *calai* while they remind and reassure the spirits about their faith in them and their need to obtain the right tool and set out on the right path. In some cases, this constant need for reassurance may seem strange since the *dongi* are guardian spirits. In most cases, however, these requests are a constant reminder that the Amis who have migrated along traditional routes and live in an ever-changing environment are conscious of their need for symbolic healing. Like the conflicts and conundrums revealed in modernised magic (Meyer and Pels 2003), the *Miasik* ritual reveals the caution the Amis have regarding the construction techniques they have learned from other ethnic groups; it also reflects the constant tension between requests directed to the guardian spirits and the possible loss of their protection without warning.

The banter involved in *baceva* is expressed modestly to prevent the spirit becoming jealous. The same attitude is adopted towards family members as well. During the final session of the *Mirecuk*, the eldest son of a *sikawasai* told me:

> During the ritual session, every conversation and action is monitored by the ancestors, and if we talked about the exact time of doing something, the ancestors would mock our pride and send malicious tricks to us. *Baceva* is to let the spiritual beings think that we don't know the correct way and need to be taught again in our ritual preparation.

This comment shows the importance of *baceva* to the shamans and ritual participants. *Baceva* reflects a human–spirit connection in a restrained way: knowing the correct practice in a ritual process is one thing, but showing the right timing is another. *Baceva* creates a space for authenticity testing of both belief and behaviour. Verbally, shamans comply with the rules of *baceva* to show their discipline. Physically, they need to check all the *calai* that are given from the spiritual world, using these magical threads to cleanse, sweep, pad, expel and carry out other actions to distinguish good from evil. By so doing, shamans deploy their bodies within the symbolic boundaries set by the *calai*. This constitutes the ritual politics of the body.

Path and testing: The embodiment of changing ritual relations

In the rituals of *Mivava*, *Miasik* and especially *Mirecuk*, the importance of the *calai* as a symbolic path whose authenticity requires testing evokes a ritual landscape that is substantially represented in embodied experiences (Csordas 2002). This is the environment in which Amis elders still live. Through their bodily performances, shamans carry out various processes of negotiation in acquiring and examining paths. The shaman's body, the ginger leaves the shamans hold and the pig's leg all become vessels for the symbolic *calai*-path that is given by the spirit. Only a physical body can provide substance for the path that is created.[11] My argument is that the authenticity of a path can only be recognised through this embodiment. Through the shamanic bodily performances of constant checking, examining and verbally providing assurances, a *calai* is transformed from an imaginary thread to a powerful tool of ritual efficacy.

A *calai* represents the 'road' or 'path' that is signified. The signifying process is by no means simple. There may be misleading ways, unsuitable materials and mistaken actions. As a consequence, each symbolic road needs to be examined and the objects found along it interrogated over and over again during the ritual process. While the rituals led by Amis shamans may reveal the basic infrastructure of the spiritual world, the movements and actions in this ritual space are still negotiated via bodily gestures and cautious steps along this symbolic *calai*-path. It is said that, in the past, male shamans were more aggressive. They negotiated forcefully and tried to persuade the *dongi* to give a better *calai* sooner. Nowadays, only female shamans perform these rituals, using their negotiating skills and bodily movements to gain the right path. Today, no male shamans practice in the Nangshi area. Instead, men work outside the village and cannot (or will not) observe the necessary dietary restrictions; men are also in contact with more unreliable and potentially dangerous outsiders in their daily activities than are women. Male villagers have abandoned more of their traditional activities than women, and therefore are less capable than

---

11   Scheper-Hugh and Lock (1987) use the idea of the 'mindful body' in their exploration of medical anthropology and delve into the issues of bodily phenomena as the arena of ideological power struggles. This concept also resonates in the realm of religion where the body is the locale of power relations between humans and spirits.

before of 'arguing' a case in the rituals. Women's negotiation style with the *dongi* spirits for the correct *calai* reflects the feminising of participation in contemporary Amis society.

In this chapter, I have tried to indicate the sustainable adaptation of ritual activities. These activities create local memories and an appreciation of paths defined by *calai*. External forces have affected the performance of Amis rituals. Changing subsistence strategies have affected the shaman's field ritual of catching symbolic birds in *Mivava*. Urbanisation and modernity have led to contested ways of living and have changed key elements in house construction that require purification by groups of shamans in *Miasik*. Verbal and bodily performance require tentative examination of the ritual pathway and boundaries for ancestral recognition in *Mirecuk*. Ritual is where memories are created and Amis society is reshaped.

References

Butal, Aits, Gene-Sheng Tung and Yi-tze Lee. 2009. *Pangcah Miaraw: The ethnobotany of Amis in Eastern Formosa.* Taipei: Forestry Bureau, Council of Agriculture, Taiwan.

Csordas, Thomas. 1990. 'Embodiment as a Paradigm for Anthropology.' *Ethos* 18(1): 5–47. doi.org/10.1525/eth.1990.18.1.02a00010.

Csordas, Thomas. 2002. *Body/Meaning/Healing.* Contemporary Anthropology of Religion series. New York: Palgrave Macmillan. doi.org/10.1007/978-1-137-08286-2.

Hu, Jackson. 2007. 'The articulation of modern fetishisms and indigenous species.' *Taiwan Journal of Anthropology* 5(1): 1962.

Ka, Chi-Ming. 1995. *Japanese Colonialism in Taiwan: Land tenure, development, and dependency, 1895–1945.* Boulder, CO: Westview Press.

Kendall, Laurel. 2009. *Shamans, Nostalgias, and IMF: South Korean popular religion in motion.* Honolulu: University of Hawai`i Press. doi.org/10.21313/hawaii/9780824833435.001.0001.

Kirksey, Eben and Stefan Helmreich. 2010. 'The emergence of multispecies ethnography.' *Cultural Anthropology* 25(4): 545–76. doi.org/10.1111/j.1548-1360.2010.01069.x.

Liu, Pi-chen. 2007. 'Rice, deer and rooster: Foods, power and gender symbols among the Kavalan of Taiwan.' [In Chinese]. *Taiwan Journal of Anthropology* 67: 43–70.

Lo, Su-mei. 2010. 'Cultural identity, ecological conflict, and ethnic relations: On the discourses of traditional territory of Atolan Amis.' [In Chinese]. *Journal of Archaeology and Anthropology* [Taiwan] 72: 1–34.

Meyer, Birgit and Peter Pels. 2003. *Magic and Modernity: Interfaces of revelation and concealment.* Stanford, CA: Stanford University Press.

Scheper-Hugh, Nancy and Margaret M. Lock. 1987. 'The mindful body: A prolegomenon to future work in medical anthropology.' *Medical Anthropology Quarterly* 1(1)(NS): 6–41. doi.org/10.1525/maq.1987.1.1.02a00020.

Strathern, Andrew and Pamela Stewart, eds. 2003. *Landscape, Memory and History: Anthropological perspectives.* London: Pluto Press.

Tsurumi, E.P. 1977. *Japanese Colonial Education in Taiwan, 1895–1945.* Cambridge, MA: Harvard University Press. doi.org/10.4159/harvard.978067 4434080.

4

Funerary speeches and marital investigations in highland Madagascar

Denis Regnier

Introduction

The Betsileo are tireless walkers. In the countryside of the southern Malagasy highlands, walks are an essential part of daily activities. Men walk to the rice fields or to the forest, women walk to the garden or to the river and children walk to school or with the cattle they tend. And, of course, all of them walk to visit friends and relatives in other villages or to church, the grocery shop and the weekly market. The Betsileo countryside, as a result of myriad walks over generations, is crisscrossed with a striking network of laterite paths (*lalana*) and narrow bridges across rivers.

The ubiquity of paths and the frequency of walks are crucial aspects of the Betsileo landscape, but they are equally crucial to their culture and social organisation. In this chapter, I focus on two specific kinds of 'walks' (*fandehana-tongotra*, from *mandeha an-tongotra*: 'to go by foot') or 'journeys' (*dia*) among the Betsileo: funerary speeches (*tetiharana*) and (pre)marital investigations (*famotorana*). Funerary speeches are walks only in a metaphorical sense, whereas marital investigations often require 'real' travelling on foot over long distances. Yet both cultural practices are conceptualised as journeys that have to be undertaken in particular situations. They are so closely connected they can be seen as the two faces of the same coin.

My starting point is research I first conducted for my PhD (Regnier 2012) and during several years of postdoctoral work (Regnier In press). It concerns the widespread discrimination against slave descendants among the southern Betsileo. A key aspect of the problem, as I have analysed it, is a strong pattern of marriage avoidance: Betsileo free descendants strictly refuse to marry slave descendants. I begin the chapter with background information on this avoidance of marriage with slave descendants among the southern Betsileo. I then explain what I mean by 'vigilance about origins', before describing funerary speeches as journeys in the context of Betsileo funerals and marital investigations as journeys in the context of customary marriage.

Avoiding marriage with slave descendants

Slave descendants in the southern highlands of Madagascar are viewed as inferior people and free descendants strictly refuse to marry them. Although other factors might also be important, the slave descendants' actual socioeconomic condition depends much on whether they own agricultural land (Regnier 2012, In press), work as sharecroppers for their former masters (Kottak 1980; Freeman 2013) or lead a semi-itinerant life (as described by Evers 2002), looking for *karama* (wage labour) in Betsileo country or beyond. In Beparasy, a region of the southern Betsileo highlands where I conducted fieldwork, the local slave descent group is rather fortunate: they own good rice lands and a significant number of zebus, and they also enjoy some prestige derived from the role of one of their ancestors in the settlement of the region (Regnier 2019).

The reasons for the discrimination against slave descendants among the southern Betsileo appear to be quite complex but, at the risk of oversimplifying, they can be summarised as follows. First, free descendants view slave descendants as irredeemably unclean (*tsy madio*) or dirty (*maloto*). They contend that marrying them will lead to mixing clean and unclean ancestries (*raza*), so both their ancestors and the descendants of the 'mixed' couple will become unclean because of this. The children of a mixed couple will necessarily be unclean because the southern Betsileo apply a principle of hypodescent in the case of non-isogamous marriage. In consequence, if they bury unclean children in their tombs, free people will pollute these tombs and render the tombs' ancestors dirty.

The views I have just summarised constitute the most important emic reason for the marriage avoidance; this is how free descendants explained to me the problem they have with marrying slave descendants. But I have also sought to analyse the problem from an etic perspective and suggested that the discrimination and marriage avoidance can be further explained by a combination of historical and cognitive factors. I have argued that the colonial abolition of 1896 did not have the effects of a cleansing ritual, which was traditionally performed in the region when slaves were liberated (Regnier 2015). The Betsileo therefore continued to view the slaves liberated in 1896 as ritually unclean and, as a result, they avoided marrying them. I contend that, because of this early pattern of marriage avoidance in the aftermath of abolition, the free descendants have come to strongly essentialise—in the sense of psychological essentialism (Gelman 2003)—slave descendants, to the point that they now think that slave descendants cannot become clean persons again. Since cleansing unclean people was possible in the precolonial past and the condition of being unclean was thus considered transient, this would mean that a 'cognitive shift' occurred in the aftermath of the abolition (Regnier 2015). This is an etic standpoint insofar as the southern Betsileo do not see any shift in the way they view slave descendants; they seem to consider that they have 'simply' inherited views that existed in the precolonial past.

The essentialist construal of the categories of 'clean' and 'unclean' people, as well as the rule of hypodescent, is not easy to reconcile with the fluidity, performativity and optative nature of Malagasy kinship, identity and personhood as has been described during several decades by ethnographers such as Astuti (1995), Bloch (1993), Huntington (1988), Southall (1986), Wilson (1992) and others. The case of Betsileo slave descendants, whose social identity as 'unclean people' is ascribed at birth by free descendants, provides an alternative to this model. This competing model of social identity appeared in the southern highlands as a direct consequence of colonialism and colonial abolition.

In the southern Betsileo postcolonial context, it is therefore crucial for free descendants to check the ancestry (*raza*), origins (*fiaviana*) or roots (*fototse*) of their marriage partners. I called this culturally specific attitude a permanent 'vigilance about origins' because it pervades everyday encounters and forms of communication (Regnier 2019). I have already mentioned the two cultural practices that stand out as particularly effective ways of checking origins: funerary speeches and marital investigations.

Funerary speeches

Funerals are central events in the social life of the small rural community of Beparasy. The Betsileo had elaborate funerals in the past, especially for their 'nobles' (*hova*), whose bodies underwent ritual transformations, but the combined influences of colonisation and Christianisation have considerably altered these customs. Today's funerals are shorter than they were in the past—they usually last for only a few days—yet they remain socially important events and every Beparasy adult who is related to the deceased's family should pay a visit, participate in the several-day-long vigil in the village, attend the burial, eat a communal meal and listen to the funerary speeches.

In a nutshell, funerals in Beparasy can be described as follows: when a person dies, senior members of their family—ideally, on both parental sides—meet up to decide where (that is, in which village) the funeral will take place and where (that is, in which tomb) the deceased will be buried (Parker Pearson and Regnier 2018). The deceased is then brought to the village and the body is washed in a house by relatives, following specific rules and ancestral customs. The deceased is dressed up and placed in a room on the ground floor of a house, on a bed and inside a *trano vorona*—that is, a kind of 'house' placed over the bed and made of thin white cloth. This room is called the *tranom-bavy* (women's house) and that is where the family, mostly women, will keep a vigil over the dead person, praying and singing during several days and nights. When they arrive, visitors will go to the *tranon-dahy* (men's house)—usually a room upstairs in another house, very close to the house where the *tranom-bavy* is located. In this room, senior family members (mostly men) greet visitors, thank them for their arrival and explain the circumstances of the death. The visitors then announce the gifts they have brought to the bereaved family to participate in the funeral. Usually these gifts consist of rice, cloth (*lamba*), mats, cattle or a small amount of money. The gifts are recorded in notebooks so the family can reciprocate them in the future. If they have come from afar, the visitors are allocated a house in the village where they will be hosted and fed during the several days of the funeral.

It is compulsory for the family organising the funeral to slaughter one or more cattle, since they have to feed their guests with rice and boiled meat. Cattle meat at funerals is called *hena ratsy* ('bad meat') and at the end of the event the remaining meat is distributed to the guests, who will take it home and consume it with their family.

Tetiharana are speeches that are pronounced on the *kianja ratsy* ('bad court'—that is, the open space or clearing close to the village that is used for funerals), where all the deceased's relatives and their guests gather after the burial, for what is called the *fiefana* ('completion'), which marks the end of the several-day-long funeral. During the *fiefana*, people sit on the ground and listen to the various speeches by family representatives, who recall the circumstances of the death and explain how the funeral was accomplished, stressing that everything was done according to traditional customs and, notably, that relatives and the 'government' (*fanjakana*— that is, the state) were informed of the death and the taxes for holding a funeral were paid. They also thank all the guests and families involved, citing the names of those who have brought substantial gifts to the organiser of the funeral. If the deceased was a Christian, religious songs are sung and a catechist may also read passages from the Bible. Then come the *tetiharana* speeches, which are often the most eagerly awaited moment of the concluding stage of a funeral.

During the days preceding the burial, *tetiharana* speakers will have memorised the accounts of family history that are written in the notebooks kept by the heads of the local descent groups. If the speakers found gaps in these accounts, they would have questioned their family elders. The *tetiharana* starts with a telling of how the first male ancestor of the deceased's patrilineal group is said to have arrived in Beparasy, after having alluded to previous ancestors and their regions of origin. The name of this first local ancestor is mentioned, and so is his descent group name. Then his wife is named, as well as her descent group and her village of origin. The name of the village they founded, or where they originally settled, is recalled, followed by the names of their children. The speech goes on with the offspring of the couple's children over generations, always providing the same information until it reaches the deceased. Once the *tetihara* of the patrilineal founding ancestor is over, another speaker, on the side of the deceased's mother, should follow. At least two *tetihara* speeches should be given (one on the paternal side and one on the maternal side) but sometimes other *tetihara* are added—for example, those of the deceased's FM's or MM's groups. The structure of the *tetihara* speech is of particular interest because its narrative recalls not only the names of the descendants of an ancestral couple, but also their geographical dispersion, mentioning migration and postmarital residence. Importantly, it also gives information about the marriages of the apical ancestor's descendants, since it names their spouses, their descent group and the villages from which they come. The *tetiharana* is therefore much more than a recounting of the members of a local descent group to which the dead belongs; it offers a mapping of the marital alliances that this local descent group has contracted with other groups in the past four or five generations. Narivelo Rajaonarimanana (1996: 38–39) translates *tetiharana* as *parcours-de-rocher*—that is, 'going through the rocks' or 'wandering through the rocks' (*mitety*: 'going through'; *harana*: 'rocky mountain')—and suggests that the word refers to the tombs that are often located in the mountains in southern Betsileo country. Giving a genealogical speech is like 'wandering through the rocks'; it is a metaphorical journey among the tombs and the ancestors. The *tetiharana* can thus be seen as both a genealogy and, borrowing from James Fox (2006), a 'topogeny'.

Since *tetiharana* speeches should be given by both parental sides of the deceased, when a marriage between free and slave descendants has taken place, it is deemed extremely shameful (*hafa-baraka*) to have the marriage spoken about in a *tetiharana*. In such cases, the families agree to skip the *tetihara* speeches, at the demand of the free descent side. This dissimulation, I was told, is not necessary when a 'mixed' marriage with a descendant of a noble has occurred in the family, since even though they are disapproved of for the reasons explained above, there is nothing intrinsically shameful in being allied with a family of noble descent and the *tetiharana* can be given.

The importance of *tetiharana* at funerals is crucial for southern Betsileo local descent groups since it is a way of demonstrating their 'clean' origins and the cleanliness of their marital alliances. In consequence, skipping *tetiharana* because of an inappropriate marriage in the family is not an easy decision; the guests may speculate that the family has something to hide. I was told, however, that it is sometimes better than taking the risk of being publicly seen to be allied with a family considered to be of slave descent, since the status of being unclean (*tsy madio*) could be ascribed to the whole family that has allowed one of its members to marry a slave descendant. Expressions such as 'lowering the ancestry' (*manambany ny raza*) are used to say that the person who marries a slave descendant will lower the status of the dead/ancestors but also that of the group as a whole and, consequently, the status of all its members. We have here an explanation of why the members of southern Betsileo descent groups are so adamant about not letting one of their own marry inappropriately. This is true for the senior members heading the group, but junior members, too, need to worry: if their family is suspected of being of slave descent or of marrying slave descendants, they will increasingly have difficulties finding a spouse with 'clean' origins for themselves or for their children.

The southern Betsileo feel they all know each other—in spite of their mobility, incessant migrations and population growth—because of the *tetiharana* speeches given at funerals. Through this means they keep alive the memories of origins, alliances and migrations—memories that are distributed across all people who live and regularly attend funerals in a particular region. I was often told that *tetiharana* speeches provide the best opportunities to learn about someone's slave descent or at least to become suspicious about the possible slave origins of some families. It is noteworthy that southern Betsileo's memories of alliances and ancestry are, like the *tetiharana*, essentially topogenic. The names of villages, particularly those of incoming spouses, are what may provoke suspicions that some of the descendants recounted in the *tetiharana* have slave origins.

Customary marriage

Vigilance about places of origins reaches its highest level among free descendants when parents are informed by their children that they are seeing someone and would like to perform the marriage customs. Since customary Betsileo marriage often consists of a long process involving exchanges of increasing formality and 'seriousness', free descendants have much time to check their potential marriage partner's origins (*fiavina*) and clean status. In what follows, I describe the process of customary marriage, to give a sense of the context in which the marital investigations take place.

The first steps in the process start as soon as teenagers become sexually active. Young men and women enjoy relative sexual freedom. When girls reach puberty, their parents often give them the option of moving to a separate room in the house, where they will sleep away from their brothers, because of the incest taboo, and where they will be able to host their lovers (*sipa*) for the night. Other sexually active female relatives, often sisters, can share the room. If the family house is two-storey, the room for the girls is always on the ground floor, whereas the parents occupy the first floor.

The room's location on the ground floor makes it easily accessible to lovers, who come after dusk and leave before dawn so that the girl's father, brothers or other male relatives do not see them. The furtive nature of these nocturnal visits does not mean that parents are unaware that their daughters see lovers at night. On the contrary, the girls are given the option of a separate room precisely to allow them to see their lovers without having to leave the house at night, which is considered a dangerous thing to do. It also prevents them from being forced to engage in more serious relationships, which would be the case if they were to introduce their lovers to their parents. For these affairs, it is always the boy who comes to the girl's place, and never the reverse. Yet sexual encounters are not limited to nocturnal visits or the confined space of the girl's room. They also happen during the day, often in the late afternoon, on a discreet riverbank or in some nearby undergrowth. Market days offer particularly good opportunities to meet up with lovers, as do all sorts of large gatherings or ceremonies, including funerals (Dubois 1938; Kottak 1980).

If a boy is accidentally seen by a male relative of the girl, or if he wants to be able to come to see his girlfriend without hiding himself, he has to give the 'closing of the eyes' (*tapi-maso*), which is the first formal relationship of exchange between a potential husband and his potential in-laws. The boy pays a small sum of money, which will be divided between the males of the girl's family, including her brothers. The boy, however, does not give the money directly to the father—which is taboo (*fady*)—but to his mother, who will then pass it on to the girl's mother, who in turn will talk to the father and give him the money. The father will then explain to the male family members who reside locally that the girl is 'seeing' someone, and he will give each of them a share of the money. At this stage, formal relationships between the two families do not take place and parents rarely take such unions too seriously, since they are very unstable and frequently break up.

Yet from this moment the boy can come at any time of the day to see his girlfriend in her village, since they are already accepted as a couple by the girl's family. Half-jokingly, people start using the term *vady* (spouse) alongside *sipa* (lover). The boy may further show respect to his girlfriend's parents in various ways—for example, by bringing small gifts of firewood or food and by taking part in the household's activities, especially in agricultural work. He does not reside permanently in his girlfriend's village, however, because he has to fulfil various duties in his own village. The young couple enjoy a relationship that is, to a certain extent, already marriage-like, and indeed people refer to the situation of a young girl living by herself and receiving a lover by saying that the girl *manao kitokantrano*—an expression that comes from *mitokantrano* ('having a hearth in the house') and can be translated as 'she pretends to have a hearth'.

If the relationship lasts and develops, the boy will soon inform his girlfriend's parents that members of his family will come to do the 'removal of the taboo' (*ala-fady*). On an agreed date—often chosen with the help of a *mpanandro* (diviner) so that it brings good luck—a small party called the *mpanala-fady* (literally, 'givers of the *ala-fady*'), consisting of a few men from the boy's local descent group, arrives at the girl's parents' house. They explain to the head of the family that the boy and the girl like each other and that they would like the girl to come to live for some time with the boy in their village. If the head accepts, the *mpanala-fady* gives him a sum of money that is often enough to buy a few chickens and he gives his blessing. As for the *tapi-maso*, this sum will be divided and distributed among the girl's male relatives. A meal is served—usually chicken and rice—and local rum is offered. If night is about to fall or the journey back will take a long time, the guests are invited to stay for the night. When they return to the boy's village, they take the girl with them. She brings only a small amount of luggage: people in her village and family say, euphemistically, that she is going for a walk (*mitsangatsangana*). At the boy's village, if possible, the young couple will occupy a room in the parents' house—usually a room on the ground floor. If there is no room available at the parents', the couple will temporarily dwell in a relative's house. The girl lives with her partner's kin and works with the women for several months, and sometimes for much longer. This time is clearly thought of by everyone as a kind of probation, to see whether she can get along well and work with people. During this period, however, the couple is now constantly referred to as *vady* (spouses) and the word *sipa* (lovers) is not used any more.

After some time, the boy's father calls his son and tells him that the girl has been among them for long enough. If there have been serious issues during her stay and the parents are concerned that the girl will not make a good wife, they may tell him that she should be taken back to her village. If, on the contrary, the parents and family members in the village are satisfied with her, the boy's father says that the *tandra vady* ('gift for the spouse', often simply called *tandra*) should now be given to her family. Father and son discuss the possibility of paying for the *tandra*. Ideally, it should be the father who offers it, but in poor families it is common for the sons to work and save enough to pay for it, although it will always be presented as coming from the father.

The girl is then sent off to her family to announce that the boy's parents will come to give the *tandra* on a date they have chosen with the help of a *mpanandro* that will bring good luck to the couple. The girl's relatives prepare for the event. Parents buy chickens and rum. Women start weaving mats and collecting items for the girl's trousseau. Members of the girl's local descent group are invited to attend the meeting.

The representatives of the boy's family attending the *tandra vady* meeting consist once again of a few men. This time, the party is called the *mpanandra-vady* ('givers of the *tandra vady*'). As in the case of the *ala-fady*, the boy's parents are not among the *mpanandra-vady*, nor is the boy, who will wait for his wife in his village. When the *mpanandra-vady* arrives at the girl's village, they do not enter the house straight away but instead stay on the threshold. The girl's relatives insist that they should go further into the house to find a better place, but they refuse. One of the male *mpanandra-vady* gives a speech explaining that they come in the name of the head of the boy's local descent group. Then he puts a small amount of money (usually a note of 100 or 200 Ariary [A4–8 cents]) into his hat and puts it on the floor, asking for permission to open the door (*mivoha varavarana*) and enter the house, which is a metaphorical way of asking for the opening of the discussion on the *tandra*. The girl's relatives respond: 'But you already entered. Please come in, sit in the room.' The *mpanandra-vady* comes in a bit further but still stays close to the door, as if they were ready to leave. They then explain that the boy and the girl like each other and would like to set up their own hearth in the boy's father's village. The speaker (*mpikabary*) for the girl's family replies that the girl has already given her consent and so there is nothing they can do to prevent her from leaving, even if no *tandra* is given. The *mpanandra-vady* insists that they want to follow the customs and offer something to the parents. They propose a *tandra*, in the form of either a sum of money or, more rarely, an ox that they may have brought with them. A discussion then starts that takes the form of a ritualised bargaining on the value of this *tandra* (for an example, see Dubois 1938: 400–4). During this discussion, the *mpanandra-vady* is exhorted to come further into the room and 'go upstairs' (*miakatra*) in the house, which is a metaphorical way of asking for a higher *tandra*.

After an agreement on the *tandra* is reached, the *mpanandra-vady* is invited to enter the room to sit in a better place. Up to this point, they have stayed on the western side, where the door is located in all southern Betsileo houses. This time they accept and sit on the eastern side, which is the side where elders and honoured guests should sit. Rum is passed around. The women of the girl's family who were busy cooking the meal are now told to prepare the girl because she will leave the house. During the talks, the girl has been waiting in another room of the house, getting dressed and doing her hair with the help of other women. A meal of chicken and rice is served to the guests and the men of the family, while the women and the girl eat with the children in the kitchen. The rump of the chicken (*vodi-akoho*), which is normally given to the oldest male present, is given instead to the man who talked in the name of the boy's family, even if he is young and there are elders in the room. This is a sign of respect towards the boy's 'fathers-and-mothers' (*ray amandreny*—that is, the parents in the classificatory sense and by extension all the senior members of the group), who have now to be honoured as relatives (*havana*). When the meal is over, the head of the family calls the girl. She appears in her nicest clothes with her hair newly plaited. People bring her luggage, which consists of her personal belongings and also various household items bought for the occasion or given by relatives: suitcases, mats, baskets, clothes, cooking pots, buckets, spoons, a mattress, a bed and so on. The girl's family makes an inventory, calling out each item and writing a list on a small notebook or sheet of paper. This list is for the boy and is given to his representatives. The couple must keep it, because these items belong to the girl and if the couple separates, she will come back to her village and bring these items with her.

The head of the girl's local descent group proceeds to the 'blessing' (*tsiodrano*). Everyone remains seated but turns their body and face towards the eastern wall of the room. The head of the family explains that the family is losing a girl but acquiring a boy since they are exchanging a daughter for a son (see Dubois 1938: 404). Holding a large cup with water, he asks for God's and the ancestors' blessings, and then blesses the girl, sprinkling her and the audience with water from the cup. Everyone shouts '*Soa tsarà e!*' ('Be nicely well!'). After the *tsiodrano*, the head of the family enunciates the ancestral *fady* (taboos) of the girl, which will have to be respected in the new hearth. They are written down in the notebook or the paper used for the inventory to be given to the boy.

The *mpanandra vady* now sets off with the girl and her luggage. It is taboo for the girl to greet people on her way to her new village. When they arrive at the village, the *mpanandra-vady* and the girl are welcomed by a large number of the boy's relatives, who have been waiting in the parents' room—usually upstairs in the house. The family meeting that takes place on the boy's side is called *mampody vady vao* (literally, 'bringing a new spouse home again') or simply *vady vao* ('new spouse'). The girl is invited to sit beside the boy on the eastern side of the room. The luggage (*entana*) she brings is placed in the middle of the room, so everyone can see it. The leader of the *mpanandra-vady* reports on the meeting at the girl's village, detailing the negotiations on the amount of the *tandra*, and he reads out the list of the girl's luggage and taboos. Then a meal—again consisting of chicken and rice—is served to all, but the girl is given an unusually large share of chicken. She receives a tureen full of rice and her own bowl of *loaka* (side dish) on a special placemat, whereas young people receive only a plate of rice topped with a tiny piece of chicken and elders share bowls of *loaka*. A senior female member of the group who has never separated from her husband is asked to bring the first spoon of rice to the girl's and the boy's mouths. During the whole meeting, the couple stays quiet, since they are not expected to talk. After the meal, all the girl's items are placed on the eastern side of the house and she sits in front of them, looking at the eastern wall. All the people present look in this direction, too. The head of the family makes a speech asking God and the ancestors to bless the girl and the couple, and he stresses that the boy's parents have received not a spouse but a daughter. He sprinkles the girl with water, and then her luggage and the audience. When the blessing is over, everybody says '*Soa tsarà e!*' ('Be nicely well!').

The couple should now live for some time in the boy's parents' house, even if a separate house is already available; ideally, the boy should have built a new house in the period between the *ala-fady* and the *tandra vady*. After a month or two, the couple asks the permission of the boy's father to set up their own 'hearth-in-the-house' (*tokantrano*). If the father agrees, this is announced to the boy's family and friends, who are invited to share the morning meal (*sakafo maraina*) the day after the couple have moved to their house or to a separate room. This morning meal must be very simple and usually consists of rice broth (*vary sosoa*), cassava or sweet potatoes, sometimes sweetened with honey. People are invited to eat a small portion of the meal, after which they congratulate the couple, wishing them: 'Let your house be hot!' ('*Mafanà trano!*'). They then depart to leave room for other visitors. With the morning meal completed, the couple can now enjoy having their own hearth in the village.

Marital investigations

When the potential marriage partner is from a family or a village about which little is known, it is expected that the free descent parents will check the family's ancestry by undertaking an extensive investigation (*enquête* in French; *famotorana* in Malagasy). These investigations are not usually conducted during the first stage of the marriage process (the *tapi-maso*) since relationships easily break up. But if children notify their parents that they would like to go further with the customs (*fomba*) then parents and senior members of the family set off, often on foot and sometimes for more than 100 kilometres, to visit their relatives in the region where their child's lover has his or her 'origins' (*fiaviana*). I was told that this inquiry may last for weeks, as parents and relatives gather information about the potential partner's family and 'the kind of ancestry' these people have. My Betsileo friends stressed that, when performing such an inquiry, it is important to take the time to travel around the 'places of origin' (usually the villages of the parents and grandparents) of the potential marriage partners. It is also essential to ask only one's relatives, even remote ones, because other people could be friends or, worse, relatives of the family in question, in which case there is a risk of being told lies. One's own relatives are said to be the only trustworthy informants for this kind of inquiry. It is assumed that they will not lie and will take the gathering of information very seriously, because they all have an interest in not having a slave descendant marrying into the family.

Relatives living close to the village of the family under investigation will often have an idea about whether or not these people have slave ancestry. If they do not, they will know how to get more information. Members of their own kinship networks may have relationships with this family and may go to their funerals. At these funerals, they may have listened to the *tetiharana* and noticed marriages with people from suspicious villages. The final outcome of the parents' inquiry will be that the family is judged 'clean' (*madio*), 'unclean' (*tsy madio*) or 'not clear' (*tsy mazava*). The family's status is considered 'not clear' when, for some reason, the inquiry did not allow the parents to ascertain 'clean' origins. In that case, parents would usually not run the risk of discovering in the future that their counterparts are of slave descent and would therefore refuse the marriage, just as they would had they found out the family was 'unclean'.

Conclusion

Tetiharana (genealogical speeches) and *famotorana* (marital investigations) are practices that are still central to southern Betsileo culture and society. It seems, however, that these two 'journeys', undertaken to check people's origins, had a slightly different role in the precolonial past. Before abolition, Betsileo *olompotsy* (commoners) were mainly concerned with marrying equals—that is, members of descent groups who were of equal rank—so their vigilance about origins was directed mainly at contracting isogamous marriages. In the present day, I would argue that these practices have been entirely hijacked by free descendants, who use them to identify slave descendants and ascribe to them unclean or 'unclear' status. In other words, whereas in the past these two practices were an intrinsic part of the elaborate hierarchical systems found in the Malagasy highlands and were used to make distinctions for the purpose of marriage between descent groups according to prestige and rank, today these practices serve one main goal: to avoid marrying slave descendants.

References

Astuti, Rita. 1995. '"The Vezo are not a kind of people": Identity, difference, and "ethnicity" among a fishing people of western Madagascar.' *American Ethnologist* 22(3): 464–82. doi.org/10.1525/ae.1995.22.3.02a00010.

Bloch, Maurice. 1993. 'Zafimaniry birth and kinship theory.' *Social Anthropology* 1(1b): 119–32. doi.org/10.1111/j.1469-8676.1993.tb00245.x.

Dubois, H. 1938. *Monographie des Betsileo* [*Monograph of Betsileo*]. Paris: Institut d'Ethnologie.

Evers, Sandra. 2002. *Constructing History, Culture and Inequality: The Betsileo in the extreme southern highlands of Madagascar*. Leiden: Brill.

Fox, James. 2006. 'Genealogy and topogeny: Towards an ethnography of Rotinese ritual placenames.' In James Fox, ed., *The Poetic Power of Place: Comparative perspectives on Austronesian ideas of locality*, pp. 89–100. Canberra: ANU E Press. doi.org/10.22459/PPP.09.2006.05.

Freeman, Luke. 2013. 'Speech, silence and slave descent in highland Madagascar.' *Journal of the Royal Anthropological Institute* 19: 600–17. doi.org/10.1111/1467-9655.12052.

Gelman, Susan A. 2003. *The Essential Child: Origins of essentialism in everyday thought.* Oxford: Oxford University Press. doi.org/10.1093/acprof:oso/978019 5154061.003.0009.

Huntington, Richard. 1988. *Gender and Social Structure in Madagascar.* Bloomington: Indiana University Press.

Kottak, Conrad. 1980. *The Past in the Present: History, ecology, and variation in highland Madagascar.* Ann Arbor: University of Michigan Press.

Parker Pearson, Mike and Denis Regnier. 2018. 'Collective and single burial in Madagascar.' In Aurore Schmitt, Sylviane Déderix and Isabelle Crevecoeur, eds, *Gathered in Death: Archaeological and ethnological perspectives on collective burial and social organisation*, pp. 41–62. Louvain-La-Neuve, Belgium: Presses Universitaires de Louvain.

Rajaonarimanana, Narivelo. 1996. 'Les sept pilons de fer: Traditions orales du Manandriana (Madagascar) [The seven iron pestles: Oral traditions of the Manandriana (Madagascar)].' *Études océan Indien* [*Indian Ocean Studies*] 20: 1–160.

Regnier, Denis. 2012. 'Why not marry them? History, essentialism and the condition of slave descendants among the southern Betsileo (Madagascar).' PhD thesis, London School of Economics and Political Science, London.

Regnier, Denis. 2015. 'Clean people, unclean people: The essentialisation of "slaves" among the southern Betsileo of Madagascar.' *Social Anthropology* 23(2): 152–68. doi.org/10.1111/1469-8676.12107.

Regnier, Denis. 2019. 'Forever slaves? Inequality, uncleanliness and vigilance about origins in the southern highlands of Madagascar.' *Anthropological Forum* 29(3): 249–66. doi.org/10.1080/00664677.2019.1624501.

Regnier, Denis. 2020. *Slavery and Essentialism in Highland Madagascar: Ethnography, history, cognition.* London: Routledge. doi.org/10.4324/9781003086697.

Southall, A. 1986. 'Common themes in Malagasy culture.' In Conrad Phillip Kottak, Jean-Aimé Rakotoarisoa and Aidan Southall, eds, *Madagascar: Society and history*, pp. 411–26. Durham, NC: Carolina Academic Press.

Wilson, Peter. 1992. *Freedom by a Hair's Breadth: Tsimihety in Madagascar.* Ann Arbor: University of Michigan Press. doi.org/10.3998/mpub.13491.

5

Journeys in quest of cosmic power: Highland heroes in Borneo

Monica Janowski

To travel is to take a journey into yourself. — Danny Kaye

In this chapter, I will explore the nature and purpose of the journeys in which Kelabit heroes,[1] talked of in legend,[2] engage. I will focus in particular on the legend about a hero called Tuked Rini (Plate 5.1), a version of which I recorded in 1986, recited by Balang Pelaba ('Very Much a Tiger'), in the community of Pa' Dalih on the Kelapang River in the Kelabit Highlands of Malaysian Borneo.[3] The legend of Tuked Rini is a *sekono*, a type of Kelabit oral literature. It tells of the adventures of a group of men, led by Tuked Rini, who explore the inner and outer reaches of the cosmos to do battle with powerful beings and bring back heads. It was told to encourage young men to carry out headhunting expeditions themselves and young women to support them in this. Tuked Rini's wife, Aruring Menepo Boong (Plate 5.2), is also an important cultural hero—her female nature balancing his male nature.

---

1   I define hero, as does the Oxford dictionary, as: 'A person who is admired for their courage, outstanding achievements, or noble qualities' (en.oxforddictionaries.com/definition/hero).

2   I define legend here, as does Timothy Tangherlini (1990: 385), as a 'traditional, highly ecotypified historicized narrative performed in a conversational mode, reflecting on a psychological level a symbolic representation of folk belief and collective experiences and serving as a reaffirmation of commonly held values of the group to whose tradition it belongs'.

3   I have published a book with a full version of the legend as recited by Balang Pelaba, using the legend as a means of exploring the way of life and the cosmology of the Kelabit (Janowski 2014/16).

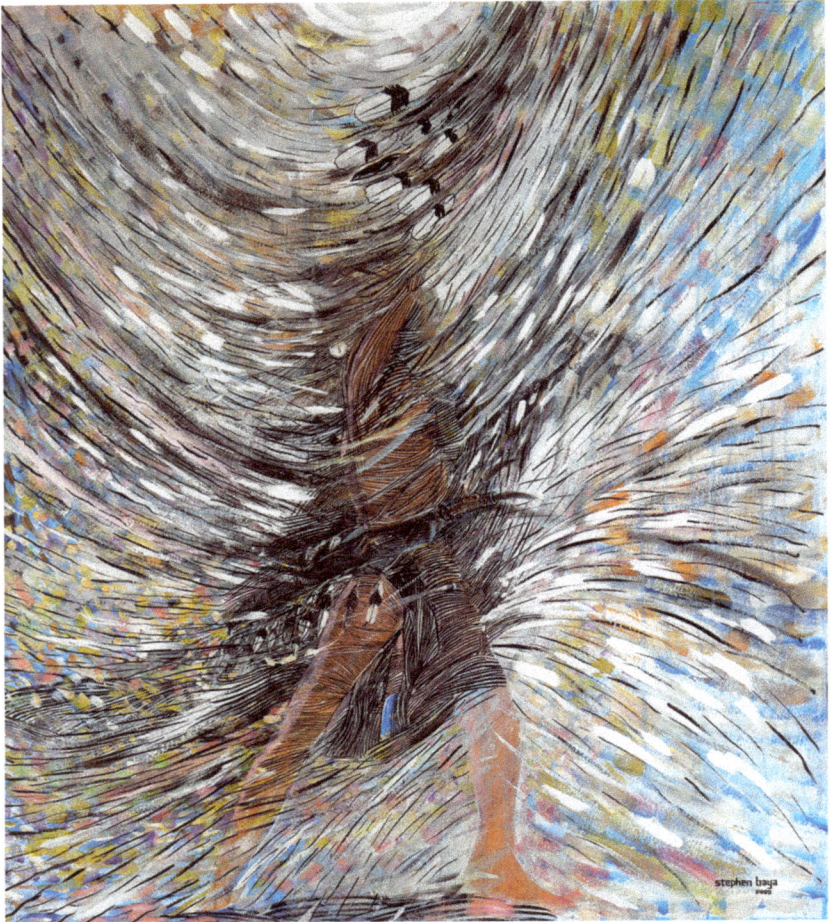

Plate 5.1 Tuked Rini Luun Atar shimmering with lalud (cosmic power) and only semi-visible

Source: Painting by Stephen Baya, 2009.

I will explore the role of *lalud* ('life force' or 'cosmic power') in the legend of Tuked Rini. I will suggest that the concept of *lalud* is key to understanding the role of these legends and their central heroes. I will focus in particular on the role of male heroes and the significance of the headhunting that lies at the core of Tuked Rini's journey through the cosmos. Finally, I will make some remarks regarding present-day journeying to gather *lalud*.

First, I provide an outline of the legend of Tuked Rini as related to me by Balang Pelaba on 25 November 1986.

Plate 5.2 Aruring Menepo Boong, Tuked Rini's wife, carried inside his earring on the way to a feast Above the Sky (Palaii Langit)
Source: Painting by Stephen Baya, 2009.

Outline of the legend of Tuked Rini

The story begins in the early morning in the longhouse at Luun Atar ('On the Flat Land') led by Tuked Rini ('Rini Who is Support for All') and his wife, Aruring Menepo Boong ('She Who Gathers Huge [Beads]'). Aruring prepares a rice meal and invites her husband and others to eat. She recites a chant about her preparation of the rice and her carving of the door through which Tuked Rini will come.

After breakfast Tuked Rini recites a chant about his hunting ability and his desire to go hunting for a tiger. He begins to talk to his close kin about going headhunting. They decide to go to fight another powerful leader, Tuked Rini Lobang Uli' Bario Langiyung ('Rini of the Hole of the

Moaning Wind'), and other heroes living with him inside Batu Balang Tekinang Lungung ('the Vastly Tall and Powerful Spirit Tiger Rock'). These heroes are extremely powerful, and therefore worthy enemies.

Tuked Rini and the other heroes, his close kin, get ready. Tuked Rini recites a chant describing the headhunting clothes he will put on: a tiger-skin jacket and a huge and beautiful knife exchanged for beads, which is so powerful that it causes thunder to roll and blood rain to fall.

They jump off into the sky from the great stone in the river below their longhouse, with the lesser people hanging off the sword sheath of one of the heroes. His close kin accompanying Tuked Rini include Agan Bulan Makub Lungung ('Agan Who Jumps up to Knock against the Moon and the Clouds'), Agan Pun Tolang Na'an Mitun ('Agan Whose Bones Go Straight for His Target'), Lian Balang Olong ('Lian the Spirit Tiger Who Raises Many Poles at Feasts'), Tama Baru' Lanawa Balang Tolang Kayuh Ngelungung ('Father Creator Shadow-Making Spirit Tiger with Bones of Wood Who Makes a Huge Powerful Shadow'), Tagio' Balang Pekeling Kuman ('Havoc-Causing Spirit Tiger Who Exchanges Food with Others at Feasts') and Balang Katu Anak Belawan ('Descendant of Spirit Tigers, Son of Iron').

They fly for a day and a night and land at Ra'an Ayun Langit Temubong ('Pass of the Shadow of the Highest Sky'), near Ru'ib Boong ('the Huge Waterfall'). Here they make camp. Two of the heroes go to collect bamboo in which to cook their food; they are able, because of their great power (*lalud*), to walk on the surface of the water to reach the bamboo. They see that someone has already cut some bamboo and realise that this must have been the people living inside the Spirit Tiger Rock. When the lesser people hear about this, they are terrified and want to return home, but the heroes convince them to continue.

The people of Luun Atar now need to fight the Spirit Tiger Rock itself to get inside it to fight the people living there. The heroes battle with it for a long time and eventually one of the heroes, Agan Whose Bones Go Straight for His Target, leaps up into the sky and comes down right on top of the Spirit Tiger Rock, driving him into the ground. Tuked Rini puts his whetstone into the Spirit Tiger Rock's mouth and they go inside.

They travel for 10 days and nights before reaching a lookout point on top of a hill, from which they can see a longhouse. It is beautiful: the roof shines like silver and there are gongs hanging at each end of the house. Obviously, there are powerful people living in the house.

That evening, Tuked Rini and Agan Whose Bones Go Straight for His Target go into the house—invisible because of their *lalud*. They see that everyone is drinking rice beer; the people of the longhouse have clearly just come back from a successful headhunting expedition. They see two of the heroes of the longhouse, Sewan the Spirit Tiger with Breath of Walking Fire and Siok the Spirit Tiger Who Distributes Smoke with His Fingers. Both of them are wrapped in power (*lalud*), which flows and flickers around them.

The next morning, Agan Whose Bones Go Straight for His Target lets out a war cry (*kit*), which fells many of the lesser people of the longhouse inside the Spirit Tiger Rock, and the lesser people from Luun Atar attack the longhouse and kill more of the lesser people there. Then the heroes of Luun Atar and the heroes of the longhouse inside the Spirit Tiger Rock introduce themselves formally to each other and agree to fight. They begin fighting on the ground outside the longhouse. Tuked Rini Luun Atar recites a chant about the power of his war cry, declaring that he will bring back heads for the beautiful red lady—his wife, Aruring. Thousands more of the lesser people of the Spirit Tiger Rock fall dead because of his war cry. He then joins in the fighting with the heroes of the Spirit Tiger Rock.

The heroes fight and fight. One of the heroes of the longhouse inside the Spirit Tiger Rock uses his power (*lalud*) to send fire sweeping across the land and kills the lesser people from Luun Atar. Only the heroes from Luun Atar are left.

At this point, the old couple up in the Highest Sky notice what is happening in the battle. One, Sinah ('Mother') Sepudau, is the ancestor of the people of Luun Atar and the other, Agan the Upright Bird, is the ancestor of the people of the longhouse inside the Spirit Tiger Rock. Sinah Sepudau, concerned for her descendants from Luun Atar, who are losing the battle, calls out to other descendants of hers, heroes living in the Kerayan River Basin who are related to the people of Luun Atar, and tells them to go to help. They drop down from the sky and set to in the battle.

Tuked Rini of Luun Atar recites a chant about the heroes coming to help, declaring that he will take his enemy's head, to take back to his longhouse at Luun Atar. The battle continues. One of the heroes from the Spirit Tiger Rock, Siok the Spirit Tiger, catches many of the lesser Luun Atar people and drops them, killing them. Only the strongest heroes are left.

One of the Luun Atar heroes, Father Creator Spirit Tiger with Bones of Wood Who Makes a Huge Powerful Shadow, turns into a tree and falls on many of the people of the Spirit Tiger Rock.

One of the heroes from the Spirit Tiger Rock, Sewan the Spirit Tiger with Breath of Walking Fire, fights for aeons with one of the heroes from Luun Atar, Agan Whose Bones Go Straight for His Target, until Agan gets the better of Sewan and ties him up. Then they hear a woman's voice—that of The Great Spirit Mother. She declares that Sewan the Spirit Tiger and Siok the Spirit Tiger, two of the strongest heroes from the Spirit Tiger Rock, are actually from Luun Atar; they had been discarded as babies (because they were born at an inconvenient time). So Agan releases Sewan. There is a happy reunion.

Then the people of Luun Atar realise that all of the people of the Spirit Tiger Rock are dead. They have won the battle. Their own lesser people are also dead; however, one of the heroes of Luun Atar, Descendant of Tigers, uses his powerful *lalud* water to bring them back to life.

So, all of the people of Luun Atar return home, together with their newfound relatives, Sewan the Spirit Tiger and Siok the Spirit Tiger, and two of the heroes from the Kerayan River who had dropped down from the sky to help them. The high-born women of Luun Atar, wives of the heroes, prepare rice beer as soon as they see their husbands coming. Everyone drinks and visits with each other.

The next morning one of the heroes, Descendant of Tigers, tries to persuade Tuked Rini's wife, Aruring, to drink (and sleep) with him. She, however, refuses, reciting a chant about her high status, her desirability, her beauty and her ability to grow lots and lots of rice and to pound and husk it magically with her huge mortar—and declaring that she wants only Tuked Rini.

The people of Luun Atar now harvest their rice fields. The people of the Luun Plain, who live across the river, are also harvesting, and the two groups of people engage in banter and play in the river, including exchanging partners for one night.

Then the people of Luun Atar hold a feast to celebrate the harvest, the new rice and the headhunting success of their heroic men. The men hunt lots of wild pigs for the feast.

Highland heroes

Tuked Rini (known as Tuked Reminii among the Lundayeh) is one of a number of heroes featuring as central figures in Kelabit and Lundayeh legends. These were regularly told or chanted around the fire or during communal work in the rice fields—some until relatively recently. The legend of Tuked Rini was no longer told regularly after World War II and was probably rarely told even in the first half of the twentieth century. This is probably because it was particularly closely linked to headhunting expeditions and these ceased around the turn of the nineteenth and twentieth centuries. Other legends survived until the late 1980s; the story of Agan Tadun was still being chanted in the rice fields while we were living in Pa' Dalih at that time.[4]

---

4   The first time any of the highland legends about heroes were recorded appears to have been when Tom Harrisson (1947–48) noted a small chanted fragment (*sedarir*; see below) of the legend of Tuked Rini as recited by Penghulu Miri. Guy Arnold (1956) noted a fragment of the legend of Tuked Rini during his visit to the Kelabit Highlands in 1956. In 1972, Carol Rubenstein, an American poet, recorded, transcribed and, with the assistance of Kelabit informants Masna Ulun and Lian Labang, translated versions of the legends of Tuked Rini (recited by Ngemong Raja) and those telling of two other heroes, Agan Ngadtang (recited by Niar Ayu) and Balang Lipang (recited by Inan Diu'). The legends as recorded by Rubenstein (1973: 807–1125) were included in a special issue of the *Sarawak Museum Journal* in 1973. My husband, Kaz Janowski, and I recorded the legend of Tuked Rini in 1986 (recited by Balang Pelaba) and I have transcribed and translated these with the help of Kelabit informants (Janowski 2014–16). A version of the legend of Tuked Rini as told by Rian John Pasan was also recorded by his daughter Cindy when she was at school (shortened version in Rethinasamy et al. 2013). Ricky Ganang recorded a version of the legend of Tuked Reminii, a Lundayeh hero equivalent to Tuked Rini, and an outline of the legend of Ufai Semaring (also known as Upai Semaring) in the 1970s, which he has transcribed (Ganang and Yansen 2018: 480–507 [Tuked Reminii]; and Ganang 2002: 26–27 [Ufai Semaring]). Kaz and I recorded versions of the legend of Agan Tadun (who is the same hero whom Rubenstein calls simply Agan) and that of Agan Tchan in 1987, both recited by Balang Pelaba. These have not yet been transcribed or translated. Rubin Jalla (who is Kelabit) has recently given me the outline of another Kelabit legend, that of Balang Lemudan, as told to him by his father, Penghulu Henry Jalla, when he was young, and as noted down by his sister Garnette Jalla and her son Ryan. This is not yet published.

Being heroic

The legends about heroes function as projections of ideal humans and ideal human behaviour. They provide models to be emulated—in particular, models of male behaviour, because most of the central heroes are male. Legends about heroes have as their central characters one or several young men. Except for the legend of Tuked Reminii as recorded by Ricky Ganang, a major theme—even the main theme—of all of the legends is the adventures of young male heroes as warriors, telling of their headhunting expeditions and focusing particularly on their long battles with enemies, whom they always ultimately vanquish and kill. The legend of Agan Tadun—called Agan Ngadtang or simply Agan by Rubenstein (1973: 857–967)—has as an important thread the eventually successful meeting and mating of two young men and two young women, after complex adventures involving mistaken identities and lost children. However, this legend, too, includes a long description of a war expedition—the two young male heroes prove their mettle by battling with and beating two powerful enemies.

Male heroes are, then, the main focus of these legends, although female heroes are also key to the narrative. While the central achievement of the male heroes is to bring back heads from their expeditions, that of the female heroes is to grow and cook the rice and to make the rice beer that makes it possible to have the feasts at which the achievement of headhunting can be confirmed. At these feasts the heads are—in the legends and as they were in real life after a headhunting expedition—paraded by the women and then placed on huge bamboo poles erected outside the longhouse. The partnership of men and women means that the exercise of headhunting 'makes sense'; if the men had no women to whom to bring back heads and who could 'process' them through a feast, there would be no point in headhunting. This echoes the complementarity of men and women in constructing what I have described as rice-based kinship (Janowski 2007a, 2007b). The high status associated with heroes as male+female couples and the feast made possible through their complementary activities also echo the way in which the feeding of rice meals generates hierarchy among highland peoples (Janowski 2007a). Hero couples like Tuked Rini and Aruring Menepo Boong are of the highest status—known as 'really good people' (*lun doo to'oh*).

An important characteristic of heroes and of *lun doo to'oh*—both male and female—is effectiveness. They are good at everything they touch. Men speak well, hunt well and carve wood and bone well; women also carve well, weave mats well, grow rice well and make delicious meals. Both male and female heroes are physically strong. Male heroes can jump and run huge distances, covering them in no time, making deep marks on the earth and on stones in the river as they do so. They have the stamina to keep going for aeons while battling with their enemies. The strength of female heroes is also emphasised; in the legend of Agan Tadun as recorded by Rubenstein, for example, a tall pole is erected made of a tree from which the bark has been stripped for female heroes to test themselves by climbing up to reach a jar full of rice beer and drink from it. Not all of the women of the longhouse can get up there; only female heroes (Rubenstein 1973: 906–09).

The effectiveness of heroes means they are natural leaders and models for the leaders of the people who used to tell and listen to the legends— and those who would become leaders. Heroes are able to care for all of their followers and ensure they have all that they need. Leading couples ensure that rice grows well, that there is plenty of hunted meat and that the longhouse is kept prosperous. Their people are described as *anak adi* ('young children'). Heroes are not only the leaders of their followers; they are also their 'parents' and 'grandparents'. Male+female hero couples lead longhouses—just as couples led longhouses in the real world—which are imagined as higher-level hearth groups (Janowski 1995, 2007a).

Heroes and *lalud*

Heroes—male and female—are perfect examples of humans. A hero is always beautiful and well-groomed according to ideas of the time—even when he has just returned from war:

> Although he has just come back from fighting,
> His hair is smooth and straight,
> Cut in a straight line across his forehead,
> Hair held over a *sulungan* gourd and cut with a knife.
> His eyes are bright as *damar* lamps, like stars in the sky.
> His eyebrows are plucked out, plucked with iron tweezers,
> The thin skin above the eyes made clear.
> His teeth are darkened in his mouth as it if were closed,
> His upper gums a fine red color and his lower gums white.

His ears are long and hanging,
And his earlobes swing forward in spirals below his neck.
He wears half of the moon for each of his earrings.
The moon shines bright and full from him all through the night
And during the day his earrings are the rays of the sun,
The brightest rays coming from beneath the sky.
(Rubenstein 1973: 859)

Female heroes are just as lovely. Here is the description Ngemong Raja gave of Aruring Salud Bulan, a woman who lives on the Moon and who, after a battle in which her husband is killed, marries the hero who has killed him, Iya Atul Aling Bulan, one of Tuked Rini's brothers:

> She is a young girl lovelier than anyone can dream of, as if she is partly the daughter of Darayah [the Great Spirit; see below], by pure luck dropped from Within the Inner Moon. Light glows from her as from the sun as it moves among the spaces of the Highest Sky. Her headdress sends out rays as from a lamp set firmly on her head, crowning her with light. Like plaited *sanguluh* bands are the long slim loops of her earlobes; like tongs of bamboo, hammered flat and curved, are the long loops hanging far forward beneath her face. And each ear is hung full with one hundred earrings, all big and round. (Rubenstein 1973: 1043)

As this extract illustrates, heroes are beautiful because they have high levels of something that is described by the Kelabit and the Lundayeh as *lalud*. It is this that makes them effective. They are often described as shimmering with *lalud* (see Plate 5.1). Heroes wear lovely *lalud*-laden clothes. Female heroes wear shimmering magical cloths. As Aruring Menepo Boong, Tuked Rini's wife, says in Balang Pelaba's version of the legend: 'I wear a shimmering black bark cloth, like a developing, shimmering shadow [*Klebong itm ko tonang angud lunging*]' (Janowski 2014/16: 77).

Spirit tigers (*balang*), which have high levels of *lalud* because they are spirits (see below), are closely associated with male culture heroes, who wear cloaks made of their skins, sometimes said to be possessed by the tiger spirit itself—which follows the hero—and have headdresses incorporating the faces of tigers (Janowski 2014/16: 39–40, 42–43; Rubenstein 1973: 814, 867–68, 886). As Tuked Rini declares while preparing to depart for war, in Balang Pelaba's version of the legend (Janowski 2014/16: 42):

Before I set off I put on my loose jacket as bright as the baking hot sun	*Ngan nalan sinayong ko sinayong lengu ko tso menotong*
I have put it over my chest	*Senaro' pengaripen luun beropong*
I will cover it with my tiger skin jacket with its wavy stripes	*Pengaratah kulit barur lalikong*
The skin covered with stripes, just like the highest sky, the Langit Temubong.	*Kulit barur iring Langit Temubong.*

And here is Carol Rubenstein's translation of the description Niar Ayu, one of her informants, gave of Agan's preparations for his departure for war:

> He puts on his tiger-skin cloak
> With beautiful feathers attached to it
> He places on his head his headdress
> The cap of which is the face of a tiger,
> Its face stretched so that its nostrils are big,
> Its great fangs overhanging above and below,
> Its eyes gleaming …
> The sound of Agan's footsteps can be heard
> As he strides along the verandah,
> And also heard is the calling sound
> Of Ada' Akang, the spirit that rules the tiger-skin cloak,
> Following along with Agan Ngadtang.
> (Rubenstein 1973: 867–68)

Both men and women wear beautiful, valuable beads; beads are associated with status and themselves carry *lalud* (Janowski 1998). Here is the description Niar Ayu gave of Agan's beads:

> His necklace is a bundle of strands,
> Full of small white beads that look like bone,
> His necklace that gleams also with rust-coloured *alai* beads,
> Is rich with green *alat bayung* beads, beautiful to see,
> With rare *labang pagang* beads,
> And with *lukut bala'* beads bought from the Malay of Brunei.
> (Rubenstein 1973: 859–60)

Things that possess high levels of *lalud* are described as *malih* (Ribuh Balang, Personal communication, 2009). Besides tiger-skin cloaks and headdresses and magical cloths, male heroes have weapons that are *malih*. Tuked Rini, in one of the chants (see below) that form part of the legend, tells of his knife that is so *malih* it is able to cause thunder to roll and blood rain to fall (Janowski 2014/16: 43):

My sharp shiny knife	*Nawi retib tadim ken doo' sira*
Which is so powerful that it causes thunder to roll and blood rain to fall	*Nawi nok merurut leku' udan dara'*
Which causes huge thunderclaps and rain to fall	*Merurut udan leku' kora-kora*

Male culture heroes are associated with many naturally occurring or worked stones in the highlands. It is said that it is only because they possessed such high levels of *lalud* that it was possible for these stones to have been deliberately moved and/or worked or inadvertently marked by them (through, for example, jumping from stream to stream). The size of such stones indicates to the people living now that heroes were giants. Near the current longhouse of Pa' Mada there is a huge block of stone that is said to have been Tuked Rini's whetstone, its size demonstrating that he was a giant (see Plate 5.3). There is another similar stone at Ba' Kelalan said to have been the whetstone of the culture hero Upai Semaring. Tuked Rini is said to have made marks on stones in the river when he was jumping across bends to reach places more quickly (see Plate 5.4) and to have made tracings on stone with his fingers, such as those made around the body of a spirit tiger that he is said to have hunted, laid on a stone and butchered (for full details of this story, see Janowski 2014/16: 51). The Lundayeh culture hero Upai Semaring is associated with a number of sets of stones that are said to have been his hearth stones, in Ba Kelalan and Long Pa Sia'. There is a bank of stones near Pa' Tik left by Balang Lipang (Ribuh Balang, Personal communication, 2009).

The heroes of the legends are often said to be able to transform into another form—something that is possible because of their high levels of *lalud*. In the version of Tuked Rini recited by Balang Pelaba, one of the heroes transforms into a tree trunk and falls on his enemies (Janowski 2014/16: 67); and in the version told by Ngemong Raja to Rubenstein, another hero, Iya' Utul Aling Bulan, transforms himself into rain to break through the roof of his enemies (Rubenstein 1973: 1026). Tagio Balang Pakaling Kuman, one of Tuked Rini's relatives who comes to help in the battle when called by Sinah Sepudau, is able to turn his hair into fire, which he throws at the enemy (Rubenstein 1973: 1051). The ability to transform from one form to another is a characteristic of powerful beings in Borneo; this is particularly evident in beliefs about powerful water snakes and dragons (Janowski In press).

Plate 5.3 Baye Ribuh ('One Thousand Crocodiles') with Tuked Rini's sharpening stone (*batuh iran Tuked Rini*)

Photo: Monica Janowski, 2009.

Plate 5.4 Kaya with giant *batu angan* (stones used to support a cooking pot over a fire) near Ba' Kelalan, which is said to have been used by the culture hero Upai Semaring

Photo: Monica Janowski, 8 August 2017.

Lalud is cosmic power; it is also life force. As our neighbour Balang Pelaba, who recited the legend of Tuked Rini to me, once said to me: *Kalau um eko lalud, um eko mulun* ('If you didn't have *lalud*, you would not be alive'). *Lalud* is believed to be present throughout the cosmos to some degree; the cosmos, in other words, is essentially 'alive', as a whole. However, *lalud* concentrates in certain places. This includes not only beings that are biologically alive, but also certain stones, dragon jars and beads. It is concentrated in human leaders (Janowski 2012, 2016) and most particularly, heroes.

Lalud is closely associated with *ada'*, a term that can broadly be glossed as 'spirits' in English (Janowski 2012, 2016). *Ada'* are believed to be present everywhere, populating the cosmos. They are associated with concrete beings including plants, animals (including humans) and stones, but there are also free-floating *ada'* not associated with any concrete manifestation. The less closely associated with a concrete being an *ada'* is, the more *lalud* it appears to be believed to have. Thus, the Ada' Raya or Deraya, the Great Spirit (Janowski 2014b, 2016), may appear in a semi-concrete form but is essentially pure spirit and may appear in any form he/she/it wishes—male or female, human-like or any other form. Transformation from one form to another and lack of attachment to a particular material form are, in other words, characteristics of *ada'* with particularly high levels of *lalud*.

The heroes of legends like that of Tuked Rini are close to being *ada'*. They are semi-visible (see Plate 5.1) (invisibility is a characteristic of *ada'*) and they are able to transform into other forms, like *ada'*. We saw that Aruring Salud Bulan was described by Ngemong Raja as partly a daughter of Daraya; in the version of Tuked Rini recited by Balang Pelaba, Tuked Rini's wife, Aruring Menepo Boong, is described as 'partly human and partly a child of the Great Spirit, Derayeh, who inhabits the middle of the sky and the depths of the earth' (Janowski 2014/16: 34). Both males and females are described as being red (*sia'*)—a colour associated with spirits among the Kelabit (Janowski 2014/16: 61; also see Rubenstein 1973: 809). Red is said to be the only colour that the spirits, including those of the dead, can see, and when the dead were taken to the megalithic cemetery in pre-Christian times a bracelet of *ba'o sia'* ('red beads') was placed on their wrists because this would enable the spirits to see them (Balang Pelaba, Personal communication, 1992).

Not only the heroes of the legends but also those with whom they battle have high levels of *lalud* and are close to being *ada'*. They are described as beautiful in the same way as the main heroes are described. The heroes on both sides are well mannered and treat the battle as something between gentlemen, as it were; whenever battle is joined between them they first politely introduce themselves to one another. Thus, these battles are not between good and evil; they are between well-matched heroes with equal levels of *lalud*. Indeed, those on the other side are sometimes actually presented as possibly having higher levels of *lalud*; some of them have the word *ada'* as part of their names. While all informants were always clear to me that heroes are not actually *ada'*, as you would not be able to see them if they were, the use of the word *ada'* in a name implies high levels of *lalud*. This means that the achievement of our heroes in eventually beating them is the more remarkable.

Lalud (Janowski 2012, 2014a, 2014/16, 2016) belongs to a group of concepts in different languages and cultures in Southeast Asia referring to cosmic power or life force. I have addressed the implications of belief in such a power or force among the Kelabit and elsewhere (Janowski 1984, 1995, 2003a, 2003b, 2007a, 2007b, 2012, 2014a, 2016; Janowski and Kerlogue 2007; Janowski and Langub 2011).[5] In Javanese, Anderson glosses *kasektèn* as 'power' or 'primordial essence' (1972). In Balinese, the equivalent term is *sekti*, which Geertz describes as 'charisma' (1980). In Malay, the term *semangat* can be glossed as 'a vital or effective force' (Winstedt 1956: 19) or 'spirit of life' (Laderman 1991: 41–42). Among the Luwu (Sulawesi), a cognate term is used, *sumangé*, which Errington glosses as 'potency' (1989). Among the Ao Naga, the term *aren* refers to what Mills called 'life force' (1926: 112). Geertz (1980: 106) has argued that the Balinese concept of *sekti* may be equated with the Polynesian concept of *mana*; and Barbier has argued that the Batak notion of *sahala* is also equivalent to *mana* (1999: 86). The belief in an all-pervading vital force is a fundamental one in the region. This group of ideas about something that is both cosmic power and life force connects upland and lowland, mainland and insular Southeast Asia (Århem 2016). The significance of belief in a vital force was recognised in early ethnographies of insular Southeast Asia, such as Skeat's book on Malay magic (1900) and Kruyt's book on animism (1906). There has also been recognition of

---

5   Although Needham (1976) has argued against any belief in such a life force in Southeast Asia, this is on the (in my view, mistaken) basis that such a belief would necessarily be grounded in a 'Western'-style notion of causality.

the importance of belief in this force on the part of researchers working more recently in both mainland and island Southeast Asia (for example, Benjamin 1979; Endicott 1970; Fox 1987; Kirsch 1973).

Bringing back *lalud*: The importance of return

Vital force is believed to flow, and it can be lost and gained. Loss or gain of it is regarded as central to establishing levels of bodily strength, effectiveness in activities and enterprises, social and political success and levels of spiritual strength. Thus, there is a constant struggle to gain more of it and to prevent loss of it.

The journeys made by Kelabit heroes out into the cosmos, to fight with enemies and take their heads, have as their goal not only the expression of *lalud*, through successful battles, but also, as we shall see, the capture of *lalud* and its return to Luun Atar. The journeys made out into the cosmos always end with return. This is underlined in legend as recited by Tuked Rini, who tells of how the lesser people who have died in the battle inside the Spirit Tiger Rock, and who are in a part of the cosmos where the dead go, are persuaded to return to Luun Atar. As two of the lesser people, Lang Kuang and Merigang, tell the others, who are arguing that in the place of the dead where they are everything grows better than in Luun Atar: 'Even if Luun Atar were really such a dreadful place, it's where our ancestors were born, and we should return' (Janowski 2014/16: 72).

The structure of the legend of Tuked Rini: A narrative anchored in *lalud*-laden chants

The main body of the legend of Tuked Rini is related by the storyteller in a normal voice, using his own words. It includes humorous anecdotes, including ones relating to those who are listening. When Balang Pelaba recited the legend in 1986, in my presence and that of many residents of Pa' Dalih where I was living at the time, he incorporated a number of humorous anecdotes (not included in the outline above, for brevity), including one involving me.

However, the body of the narrative of the legend is anchored to a string of chants, which are central to the legend. The chants are recited at key points along Tuked Rini's journey with his close kin and followers. By contrast with the main body of the story, they are recited in a sing-song voice. Also by contrast to the main body of the story, they are learnt by heart, passed from teller to teller (which means they are often very difficult to understand and translate as they are not only in archaic language but also have been somewhat transformed through the process of 'Chinese whispers').

In the legend of Tuked Rini as recited by Balang Pelaba, there are six chants: four recited by Tuked Rini and two by his wife, Aruring. In the version recited by Ngemong Raja there are 10: five recited by Tuked Rini, three by his brother Agan Bulan Makub Lungung, one by his brother Iya' Utul Uling Bulan and one by Aruring Salud Bulan, a lady living originally on the Moon who eventually marries Iya' Utul Uling Bulan.[6] These chants are only present in the legend of Tuked Rini; they are not part of any of the other legends of which we have a record.

The chants—which can be seen as parallel to beads, which the Kelabit traditionally regarded as both precious and powerful (Janowski 1998)— are not necessarily strung in the same order through the legend. It seems that there was originally a considerable repertoire of chants relating to Tuked Rini, his fellow heroes and their wives. They have sometimes been recited on their own.[7] Different tellers chose different chants and strung them in different orders, presenting the sequence of the journey of Tuked Rini and his fellows differently in consequence.

Chants are described as being *dalim* ('deep'), as are many of the words used in them. This means that the words themselves, as well as the combinations of words within the chants, carry *lalud*. The words and phrases themselves make things happen. They make the person reciting them able to achieve what he/she is about to do (Ribuh Balang, Personal communication, 2009). They declare the possession of *lalud* on the part of the heroes chanting them, and they draw on that *lalud* to utilise it, particularly before battle on the part of the male heroes:

> I will make a powerful and effective man's *kit* call
>
> My call will fill the whole world, under the Highest Sky, the Langit Temubong,
>
> It will chase the children [a metaphor for enemies] playing under the *olong* pole. (Janowski 2014/16: 60)

---

6   I was told that these are called *sedarir*; Rubenstein describes them as *nadadir* (1973: 967).

7   Penghulu Miri recited one chant to Tom Harrisson (1947–48) and Ribuh Balang recited several to me.

The meaning of the words and the combinations of words are not fully comprehensible to the audience or even the teller. Balang Pelaba was only partly able to explain the meaning of the chants he had recited to me. Younger people found it very hard to understand the bulk of the chants. This means that my translation of the chanted parts of the story (Janowski 2014/16) is much more tentative than that of the rest of the legend.

The cosmos-scape of Tuked Rini's journey

The cosmos-scape within which the journey and battles of the legend take place seems to be in some respects laid over the real world in which the people of the highlands live. According to Balang Pelaba and others from the Kelapang River who discussed the legend of Tuked Rini with me, the site of the longhouse led by Tuked Rini, Luun Atar, is at the mouth of the Mada' River, where it flows into the main Kelapang River. This is the current site of a longhouse called Pa' Mada. The site is one of a string of sites along the Kelapang River where there is physical and/or orally related evidence of settlement. Through the recent interdisciplinary Cultured Rainforest project, for which I led the anthropological component, we now have physical evidence from earth cores and/or archaeological excavation for some of these sites that they have been the focus of settlement for centuries—and some at least for millennia (Barker et al. 2008, 2009; Lloyd-Smith et al. 2010, 2013). Many of them, including Pa' Mada (Luun Atar), are places where there are palaeochannels of the river that have been used for rice cultivation for the past 400 years or so and which may well have been used for wet taro cultivation long before that (Barker et al. 2008, 2009). Thus, there is a deep cultural link between the cosmos-scape in which Tuked Rini lived and travelled and that in which the people of the highlands themselves live. The two are overlaid one on the other. I should note here that in other parts of the area inhabited by the Kelabit it is said that Tuked Rini did not live in the Kelapang area but elsewhere; in the community of Long Lellang, it is said that he lived in a longhouse near the Pa' Adang, in the shadow of the great stony mountain of Batu Lawi (Rubin Jalla, Personal communication, 2019).

However, although they are rooted in a landscape that is shared with and accessible to people living in the world now, Tuked Rini and his fellows travel to places that are outside the known and accessible parts of the cosmos. In both Balang Pelaba's and Ngemong Raja's versions of the legend, Tuked Rini and his fellows travel into the interior of a huge rock and do battle with people living there. Ngemong Raja calls this the Huge Rock (Batuh Agong), while Balang Pelaba describes it as the Vastly Tall and Powerful Spirit Tiger Rock (Batuh Balang Tekinang Lungung).[8] In Balang Pelaba's version, the heroes do battle with the Spirit Tiger Rock before forcing it below the ground and entering it to find the people living inside and do battle with them (Janowski 2014/16: 48–61). In Ngemong Raja's version of the legend, they also travel to a number of places in the sky, to the Moon and deep under the earth.[9] The legend of Tuked Rini is the only legend in which the heroes travel to such places; in the other Kelabit legends mentioned above, they remain within the known and easily accessible parts of the cosmos.

In travelling, heroes in all of the legends travel, drawing on their *lalud*, much faster than normal people—leaping, for example, over bends of rivers. In the process, the heat and power of their *lalud* leave marks such as that on a stone in the bed of the Kelapang River near Pa' Dalih, which I was told had been made by Tuked Rini (see Plate 5.4). In the legend of Tuked Rini, he and the other heroes do not just leap; they also often fly to their destinations. Other heroes drop down from the sky to join Tuked Rini in the battle inside the Spirit Tiger Rock (Janowski 2014/16: 64). The lesser people of Luun Atar, however, cannot fly. They hang on to Tuked Rini's brother's sword sheath when he leaps into the air to fly to the Huge Waterfall (Janowski 2014/16: 45). In flying, the heroes display high levels of *lalud*.

The places to which heroes journey in the legend of Tuked Rini are places that are *lalud*-laden—loci of *lalud* within the cosmos-scape. Here, they do battle with heroes who are semi-spirit, and with beings that are not human at all, such as the Spirit Tiger Rock. Travel to such places and doing battle with beings there not only demonstrate the possession of *lalud*, but also allow heroes to gather large amounts of *lalud* through vanquishing their opponents. They take this *lalud* back home to Luun Atar in the form of the heads of their enemies.

---

8   I was told by another elderly informant who recited some of the chants in the legend of Tuked Rini to me that Ngemong Raja had forgotten the full name of the Rock, which should indeed be Batuh Balang Tekinang Lungung (Ribuh Balang, Personal communication, 2009).

9   Rubenstein calls this place—to which the captured hero Aruring Salud Bulan is taken and from which she is rescued by Tuked Rini, Iya Atul Aling Bulan and other heroes from Luun Atar—Puruk Panah Liang, which she translates as 'Within the Inner Moon' (Rubenstein 1973: 968). However, other informants have told me this should be Puruk Tanah Liang and that it is not inside the Moon but should be translated as 'Deep Under the Earth' (David Labang and Ribuh Balang, Personal communication, 2009).

Headhunting and *lalud*

The purpose of the journeys made by Tuked Rini and his fellows is to do battle and to take heads, carrying *lalud*, back to Luun Atar. Headhunting was central to the culture and cosmology of the Kelabit until they became Christian from the 1950s. While the Kelabit did not engage in headhunting as often as did some other peoples—particularly the Iban, who were rapidly expanding across Sarawak in the eighteenth and nineteenth centuries and taking heads as they went—headhunting occurred sporadically as part of the feuding that was endemic in the highlands for centuries until Rajah Charles Brooke, the second 'white Rajah' of Sarawak, brought an end to this at the beginning of the twentieth century. Kelabit settlements in the Kelapang Valley, where I have done most of my fieldwork, were often not sited along the main river, despite the fact that this was where the small wet fields in which most of the highly prized rice was almost certainly grown until 300 or 400 years ago, but on ridges above the river. This was for defence against headhunting attacks (Barker et al. 2008: 143).

The reasons for headhunting have been discussed in anthropological literature since Hutton and Kruyt first tackled the topic in the early twentieth century (Hutton 1928; Kruyt 1906). While other reasons for taking heads have been put forward and there has been a tendency in recent years to conclude that there may be multiple reasons for headhunting (see chapters in Hoskins 1996a), many scholars have argued that heads bring fertility or life force into communities (Davison and Sutlive 1991; Freeman 1979; Hoskins 1996b, 1996c; Hutton 1928; Izikowitz 1979; Kruyt 1906; Needham 1976). For the Kelabit, as for many other peoples in Borneo (for example, Metcalf 1982; Uchibori 1978), heads were necessary to bring to an end the period of mourning after a death, particularly where the death was that of a leading individual. Such an individual was not taken to the cemetery for a long period after death.[10] It is likely that the reason for headhunting associated with death, particularly that of an important person, is that heads were believed to bring *lalud* into the community—a fresh source of vitality to replace that lost through the death.

---

10 According to Balang Pelaba of Pa' Dalih, who was previously a shaman (*dayong*) and was centrally involved in dealing with the dead when he was young, the Kelabit practised secondary disposal of the dead for all those who died as respected adult members of the community, keeping them in the longhouse until the flesh had rotted off their bones. A series of *irau* feasts was held to commemorate them and to send them off for good (Balang Pelaba, Personal communication, 1992).

Heads taken in headhunting were treated as kin, feted when they arrived, fed and cared for. The importance of recruiting enemy heads as friends is something pointed to by researchers working in other parts of Southeast Asia (McKinley 1976; Mills 1935). Proper care of the heads meant that their spirits (*ada '* in Kelabit) were kept friendly and helpful, protecting the longhouse and adding to the sum total of *lalud* present in the community. It was considered very important to continue to feed them, as their spirits could become angry and vengeful against the community if they were not cared for properly. This is a widespread belief in Borneo, and remains strong.[11] While the Kelabit no longer keep any heads, as they have become keen evangelical Christians and have discarded them all, some people within other tribal groups, including the Iban and the Bidayuh, continue to keep heads and to use them for ritual purposes. I even know of individuals who have brought old heads to keep in their houses in town, believing that this will make their lives more successful.

After a headhunting expedition, heads were taken back to be handed over to the wives of headhunters; the relationship between Kelabit husband and wife was central to the processing of the *lalud* brought back in heads. The wife of a warrior, receiving heads he has taken, is as *lalud*-laden, as spirit-like, as her husband. She is semi-visible, like a spirit; she is red, the colour of the spirits. As Tuked Rini says:

> I will string the fish [a metaphor for enemy heads] on *kusah* rottan
>
> I will give them to the sparkling red lady to carry
>
> The well-known lady who shimmers like a rainbow
>
> The well-known lady like a shining rainbow, sometimes visible, sometimes not. (Janowski 2014/16: 60–61)

The relationship between headhunting husband and head-receiving wife may, I would suggest, be seen as parallel to that which I have argued exists between them in their roles as providers of the rice meal to their dependants; as a wife processes the *lalud* brought in through the hunting of meat by bringing it together with rice at the rice meal (Janowski 2007a), so she may be seen as processing the *lalud* brought in through the hunting of heads.

---

11   When the heads present in the old building of the Sarawak Museum, hanging in reconstructions of parts of longhouses belonging to different ethnic groups, were moved out of the building in October 2016, a *miring* ceremony was held (at which I was present) to appease the spirits of the heads. There was serious concern among museum staff about the possibility that there would be problems otherwise. I was told of this concern by Dora Jok, the head of the Ethnography Section and in charge of the ethnographic collections (Dora Jok, Personal communication, October 2016).

Bringing back discarded children: Repatriating *lalud*

There is another way in which *lalud* may be regarded as being brought home as part of the legends. This is through the repatriation of what are known as *anak na'ol* ('discarded children'). These are children who have been exposed to die at birth because they were born at a time that was inconvenient—for example, because they were born during the rice harvest, during a visit to another place or because they were considered unlucky or dangerous, such as if they were twins. In the legends of Tuked Rini and of Balang Lipang, the heroes from Luun Atar encounter other heroes who turn out to be *anak na'ol* from Luun Atar. Sometimes, as in the legend of Tuked Rini as recited by Ngemong Raja, other heroes brought in to fight with the main heroes by Sinah Sepudah (= Sinah Sepudau in Balang Pelaba's version—see above) immediately declare themselves to be *anak na'ol* and Tuked Rini's first cousins, join straight away in battle alongside Tuked Rini and go on to prove themselves good fighters (Rubenstein 1973: 990–91). In the legend as recited by Balang Pelaba, the heroes brought to fight with Tuked Rini by Sinah Sepudau are not *anak na'ol*, though they are kin to Tuked Rini, but the theme of *anak na'ol* is present here, too: Tuked Rini and his fellow heroes first battle at length with other heroes, finding them worthy opponents, before the Great Spirit Mother, Sinah Purid Derayeh, informs them that they are kin because those they are fighting are *anak na'ol* from Luun Atar (Janowski 2014/16: 69). In the story of Agan Ngadtang as recited by Niar Ayu, *anak na'ol* also appear: Agan encounters, fights alongside and eventually brings home his brother, Lian Aran Ngadtang Balang, another *anak na'ol* (Rubenstein 1973: 901). Lian, like his brother Agan, is a great fighter. *Anak na'ol* also appear in the legend of Balang Lipang as recited by Inan Diu': Balang Lipang encounters his father's brother, Pun Anan, who turns out to be an *anak na'ol* (Rubenstein 1973: 822). Pun Anan is a smith who transforms Balang Lipang into an invincible iron man who goes on to vanquish his foe. Balang Lipang eventually takes Pun Anan back home to be re-united with his brother, Balang Lipang's father.

All of these *anak na'ol* have a great deal of *lalud*. They return home in the end—along with their *lalud*. Thus, these stories of repatriating *anak na'ol* are also stories of repatriating *lalud*.

Getoman ngan lalud: 'Joining with power'

The high levels of *lalud* displayed, drawn on and gathered by heroes relate to the fact that they are said to be in a state of *getoman ngan lalud* or 'joining with power'. This is a mysterious and fascinating concept. It is not clear whether this term refers to a time in which the heroes live or to the condition of their lives; perhaps it refers to both. In the sense that it refers to a time, this does not appear to be situated in an entirely chronological relationship with the present. There is a sense in which it is situated in a time long ago, ancestral to the present—but a time not connected in any direct way with the present. Balang Pelaba saw *getoman lalud* as a context at the beginning of time in which humans were closer to God: 'Our ancestors at the beginning were linked to *lalud* ... they were very close to God and to Jesus. Jesus gave them *lalud* [*Lun merar let puun puun getoman ngan lalud malem ... moneng moneng ngan Tuhan Allah, ngan Tuhan Jesus. Tuhan Jesus mre lalud ngan idah*]' (Personal communication, 1988). *Getoman ngan lalud* is in a sense, then, a time in the mythical past. It is an idealised version of the real world—what it once was.

Getoman ngan lalud is also what could be if people behaved as they should. In some sense, *getoman ngan lalud* also exists now. Some Kelabit men living in town have shown a good deal of interest in the legend of Tuked Rini, seeing it as exemplifying the way in which humans, and particularly men, should live. In other words, *getoman lalud* remains as a possibility. Some men say that they aim to live it out in their own lives, in the sense that they are living to their full potential as the heroes did, using all their powers (Lian Labang, Personal communication, 1989; Rubin Jalla, Personal communication, 2019). Perhaps we can see *getoman lalud* as somewhat similar to the semi-spirit world of Panggau Libau in which Iban heroes are said to live, which is said to coexist with the world in which normal Iban live (Kedit 2009).

In a state of *getoman ngan lalud*, *lalud* is very evident and is expressed through the heroes of the legends who exist in this state. The heroes—beautiful, *lalud*-laden giants—possess much more *lalud* than humans do now, making them able to do things humans cannot do and travel to places to which normal humans cannot travel. When heroes drop down on to the earth from their flights across the cosmos, thunder roars, lightning flashes and blood rain falls (Rubenstein 1973: 980–81, 990, 993, 1011, 1012). They have, as we have seen, powerful possessions, including knives (which also cause thunder, lightning and blood rain) and clothing derived from the *balang* or spirit tiger. In Balang Pelaba's version of the legend, Tuked Rini is said to have done battle—both in the legend and in a tale told to me separately (Janowski 2014/16: 51)—with a spirit tiger. Tigers are considered to be possessed of great cosmic power throughout Southeast Asia (see, for example, Hutton 1920; Sellato 1983; Wessing 1986). In Borneo, where there are no material tigers, they are by definition spirits (in Kelabit and Lun Bawang, *ada'*). Spirits are considered to be particularly powerful—more so than beings that exist in material form. In the legend, the spirit tiger is a being called the Batuh Balang Tekinang Lungung ('Hugely Tall and Powerful Spirit Tiger Rock'). This being is both rock and spirit tiger. Stone is believed throughout Southeast Asia to be a repository of cosmic power/life force (Janowski 2020).

Seeking *getoman ngan lalud* in the modern world

Lian Labang, who left the highlands in 1948 to go to work at the Sarawak Museum, declared to me: 'Tuked Rini is in my life [*Tuked Rini lam dueh ulun*]' (Personal communication, 16 November 1992). In other words, he, in his own life, was living out a modern version of the heroic journey of the legend. He, like Tuked Rini, had ventured out of the highlands into the cosmos beyond, seeking adventure and success. For Lian, in making airplanes, in making journeys to the Moon, we are doing the same thing as Kelabit heroes like Tuked Rini and Agan Tchan. The essence of being a hero is exploration, finding out new things, going where no-one has been before.

Lian was followed in his journey out of the highlands to town by a number of Kelabit, who left the highlands in the 1960s and 1970s to enter secondary education. A significant number of them went on to higher education and became very successful. They, like Lian Labang, are in some sense equivalent to the heroes of legends like that of Tuked Rini. They have journeyed out into the cosmos, expressed their own *lalud* through their success and accumulated *lalud*—not through head-taking but through their achievements. They are regarded by other Kelabit as potentially powerful centres of *lalud*. When Idris Jalla from the community of Batu Patong became a federal minister, prayers were offered within the Sidang Injil Borneo Church for his wisdom and that he might become a 'Joseph' (an Israelite who, according to Genesis, was sold into slavery in Egypt but nevertheless became vizier of that country) representing the Kelabit and other Orang Ulu (Dora Jok, Personal communication, 28 February 2019).

It is the Kelabit belief that they have gained privileged access to *lalud* through their adherence to Christianity. It is very common to hear urban Kelabit attribute success in education and in getting good jobs to Christianity. In headhunting times, *lalud* was sought through shamanic relationships with spirits (Janowski 2016), through friendships with the Great Spirit in its male form as the Ada' Raya or Puntumid (Janowski 2014b) and through headhunting. Now, the Kelabit regard Christ as their source of *lalud*. The Kelabit have been keen to make a 'break with the past' (Lian-Saging 1976–77: 211) and this relates in particular to their adoption of Christianity after World War II. Particularly since the 'Revival' of 1973 (Bulan and Bulan-Dorai 2004), the Kelabit have abandoned relationships with spirits and previous beliefs and practices. At the Revival, they discarded all of the heads taken in headhunting raids in the past. They rely entirely on Christianity, practising a fundamentalist variety as part of the Sidang Injil Borneo Church. Amster (2009) has argued that Christianity allows them to have more 'portable' potency; this makes sense in the context of the fact that most of the Kelabit now live on the coast.

The Kelabit concern with seeking and accumulating *lalud* is part of wider concern in the region with gathering vital force—one that was important not only in the past but also continues to be important in the present. The successful concentration of vital force is associated with and leads to concentrations of people and the growth of political centres, eventually leading to the development of small states. As Walker has pointed out, 'leadership and power derived from the fact that *semangat*, as potency, could be infused to differing degrees, with individuals ranking themselves according to the amount of potency they possessed' (2002: 18). Headhunting—intended to concentrate vital force—was practised not only by small-scale societies, but also by states (McWilliam 1996; Maxwell 1996). In other words, the transition from 'tribal' to 'state' does not mean that it ceases to be important to concentrate vital force. Attempts to concentrate vital force, as well as the belief that important, charismatic leaders are indeed a concentration of vital force, continue into the present day. As Walker puts it: '*Semangat* is charisma, localised' (2002: 18). Anyone who has lived anywhere in the region will have heard stories about concentrations of powerful objects and *bomoh* around political leaders in the region.

Thus, it should be no surprise that incorporation into the 'modern' urban world does not mean that tribal people like the Kelabit abandon an interest in accumulating and gathering *lalud*. They continue to seek *getoman ngan lalud*. However, the dynamics of accumulation and the personal significance and social contextualisation change radically. Individual Kelabit spend a good deal of psychological and emotional effort trying to deal with the complexity of these dynamics.

The hero in the present day: No return

Tuked Rini's journey was circular; it ended with his return to Luun Atar, bringing back *lalud* to feed into his home community. Nowadays, however, successful Kelabit do not return to the highlands after they have completed their education; they look for work outside the highlands. To stay in the highlands as a young person is, in fact, to be a failure. Some Kelabit do eventually retire to the highlands to live permanently. A larger number build a house in the highlands and spend part of their time there. Increasing numbers look likely, however, to spend the rest of their lives outside the highlands, near their children, who would not countenance any more than short holidays in the highlands—somewhere they have never lived.

Thus, present-day heroes do not return. The journeys of modern-day Kelabit heroes are not circular. The *lalud* they accumulate is not taken back home. The powerful centres that heroes create are physically located in town, and even in foreign countries, as many have moved abroad.

This lack of return is problematic at various levels. Town-based Kelabit themselves feel that they have lost something vital because they no longer live in the highlands. They are nostalgic about their lives there as children. An important part of this nostalgia is for the loss of the feeling, living in a longhouse, that they were part of a bigger community in a way that is impossible in town. Another significant loss is of contact with nature. This has been expressed in recent years in a series of conversations on a Kelabit Facebook group in which young men have toyed with the idea of trying to make contact with the Great Spirit, Ada' Raya, also known as Puntumid ('Grandfather Heel') (Janowski 2014b).

The lack of return also has implications for the relationships between leaders and others. In the past, leading couples like Tuked Rini and Aruring Menepo Boong were at the very core of their longhouse. Longhouses were rebuilt every few years and the leading couple, the *lun doo to'oh* ('very good people'), would lead the rebuilding, building their hearth at the centre with close kin on each side and more distant kin further along the longhouse at each end. They were responsible for all of the enterprises in which the people of the longhouse engaged. The lady of the couple led the rice growing, making the biggest fields with the help of others and taking responsibility for ensuring everyone, including visitors, was fed. Her husband led the men in hunting, ensuring that there was adequate meat to feed everyone. The *lalud* of a leading couple in the past was at the service of others. The *lalud* brought back from headhunting, led by the leading man of the longhouse, fed into the pool of *lalud* held by the whole community and benefited all.

In town, things are very different. Nowadays, a successful couple does not lead a longhouse or take responsibility for the daily lives of others. Life in town makes this impossible; success in the urban world is individual success and tends to benefit the immediate family rather than a wider group. This means that the relationship between successful people and other Kelabit has changed. In the past, being of high status among tribal people in Borneo meant profound respect—even what has been described to me as 'adoration', among the Kayan (Dora Jok, Personal communication, 28 February 2019). Nowadays, this is no longer true. Arguably, this is because those who gather *lalud* are not seen to be taking it back to benefit the wider group from which they come. The Kelabit are, I was told by a town-based Kelabit, losing their *lalud* as a community (Robert Lian-Saging, Personal communication, 27 February 2019). I think this remark reflects a sense that the Kelabit community has been dispersed and the Kelabit identity is being lost; those in the highlands are fewer and fewer and those in town are being absorbed into a multi-ethnic town community.

Conclusion

I have argued that the Kelabit quest for *lalud* is central to understanding the significance of Kelabit legends about heroes. *Lalud* as a concept is central to all Kelabit legends, but particularly to that of Tuked Rini, strung as it is in the form of a series of *lalud*-laden chants, like precious beads.

Lalud belongs to a family of concepts important throughout the region relating to ideas about vital or cosmic force. Heroes like Tuked Rini and his wife, Aruring Menepo Boong, have high levels of *lalud*. This means they have the highest status—they are *lun doo to'oh* ('really good people'). They are ideal humans, more beautiful and effective than their fellows, able and willing to lead and care for their kin and dependants. Not only do they possess *lalud*; male heroes like Tuked Rini also seek *lalud*. They go out journeying across the cosmos to seek *lalud*, visiting *lalud*-laden places and doing battle with worthy enemies, who are themselves heroes representing other communities. In bringing back the heads of these enemies, they bring back *lalud* to their communities. Heroes feed this into their communities through their relationships with their wives, via the same mechanism I have explored elsewhere in relation to the rice meal (Janowski 2007a).

The journeys of heroes like Tuked Rini are expressions of exploration and curiosity, displaying willingness to try new things and go to new places. In the same spirit, the Kelabit took up the opportunity to enter into the wider world through education, when this became available from the 1950s. However, I have suggested that the journey on which these young people embarked led them to a place they had not quite bargained for. It led them away from their origins and essentially barred the way to any return to the life they had left. They had entered another world with a different structure and radically different values from the one they had left. The new world of the town does not allow for leadership and heroism of the old kind. It does not allow for a clear mechanism for them to feed the *lalud* they built up in their journey towards success back into their home communities. Their journeys are not, then, circular as were those of Tuked Rini and the other male heroes of the legends. They are linear, onwards and upwards—but with no clear destination.

I want to return here to the quote with which I began this chapter. The heroes of the legends, like those Kelabit who have taken up opportunities in town, take a journey into the wider world. Such a journey into the unknown carries with it a journey into oneself. The heroes of the legends find themselves in the collective, in the group of kin to which they belong. In accumulating and bringing back *lalud* through their journeys, they were building up their home longhouse as a *lalud*-laden centre. While they, as high-status *lun doo to'oh*, were at the core of that centre, it did not stop with them. It included all of the people who lived with them, their enspirited heirlooms (*pusaka*) and also, most probably, the rice spirits that coexisted with humans. Kelabit who have made the journey to success in the world outside the highlands also try to find themselves in the collective, in the community, placing importance on themselves as embedded at the centre of a wider Kelabit grouping seen as kin. But without a return to the highlands, without living at the centre of a longhouse, the location of that collective, of that belonging, is proving hard to find.

References

Amster, Matthew H. 2009. 'Portable potency: Christianity, mobility and spiritual landscapes among the Kelabit.' *Anthropological Forum* 19(3): 307–22. doi.org/10.1080/00664670903278429.

Anderson, Benedict R.O'G. 1972. 'The idea of power in Javanese culture.' In Claire Holt with Benedict R.O'G. Anderson and James Siegel, eds, *Culture and Politics in Indonesia*, pp. 1–69. Ithaca, NY: Cornell University Press.

Århem, Kaj. 2016. 'Southeast Asian animism in context.' In Kaj Århem and Guido Sprenger, eds, *Animism in Southeast Asia*, pp. 3–30. London: Routledge. doi.org/10.4324/9781315660288-1.

Arnold, G. 1956. Unpublished field diary from visit to Kelabit Highlands in 1956.

Barbier, Jean Paul. 1999. 'Batak monuments: In the shade of the petrified ancestors.' In Jean Paul Barbier, ed., *Messages in Stone: Statues and sculptures from tribal Indonesia in the collections of the Barbier-Mueller Museum*, pp. 79–155. Milan: Barbier-Mueller Museum and Skira.

Barker, G., H. Barton, D. Britton, I. Datan, M. Janowski, J. Langub, L. Lloyd-Smith, B. Nyiri and B. Upex. 2008. 'The Cultured Rainforest project: The first (2007) field season.' *Sarawak Museum Journal* LXV(86)(NS): 121–90.

Barker, G., H. Barton, E. Boutsikas, D. Britton, B. Davenport, E. Ewart, L. Farr, R. Ferraby, C. Gosden, C. Hunt, M. Janowski, S. Jones, J. Langub, L. Lloyd-Smith, B. Nyiri, K. Pearce and B. Upex. 2009. 'The Cultured Rainforest project: The second (2008) field season.' *Sarawak Museum Journal* LXVI(87)(NS): 119–84.

Benjamin, Geoffrey. 1979. 'Indigenous religious systems of the Malayan Peninsula.' In A.L. Becker and Aram Yengoyan, eds, *The Imagination of Reality: Essays in Southeast Asian coherence systems*, pp. 9–27. Norwood, NJ: Ablex.

Bulan, S. and L. Bulan-Dorai. 2004. *The Bario Revival*. Kuala Lumpur: HomeMatters.

Davison, J. and V.H. Sutlive. 1991. 'The children of *Nising*: Images of headhunting and male sexuality in Iban ritual and oral literature.' In V.H. Sutlive, ed., *Female and Male in Borneo: Contributions and challenges to gender studies*, pp. 153–530. Williamsburg, VA: Borneo Research Council.

Endicott, Kirk. 1970. *An Analysis of Malay Magic*. Singapore: Oxford University Press.

Errington, Shelly. 1989. *Meaning and Power in a Southeast Asian Realm*. Princeton, NJ: Princeton University Press. doi.org/10.1515/9781400860081.

Fox, James J. 1987. 'Southeast Asian religions: Insular cultures.' In M. Eliade, ed., *The Encyclopedia of Religion. Volume 13*, pp. 520–30. New York: Macmillan.

Freeman, J.D. (Derek). 1979. 'Severed heads that germinate.' In R.H. Hook, ed., *Fantasy and Symbol: Studies in anthropological interpretation*, pp. 233–46. London: Academic Press.

Ganang, Ricky. 2002. *Laba' em idi serita' luk mekemu'* [*Myths, Legends and Short Stories*]. Self-published.

Ganang, Ricky and T.P. Yansen. 2018. *Dayak Lundayeh idi Lun Bawang. Budaya serumpun di dataran tinggi Borneo* [*The Lundayeh and Lun Bawang Dayak Peoples: The culture of the indigenous peoples of the highlands of Borneo*]. Palangka Raya, Kalimantan Selatan, Indonesia: Lembaga Literasi Dayak.

Geertz, Clifford. 1980. *Negara: The theatre state in nineteenth century Bali*. Princeton, NJ: Princeton University Press.

Harrisson, T. 1947–48. Kelabit Songs and Sekono and Heads. Malaysian National Archives, Accession no. 2006/0035307.

Hoskins, Janet, ed. 1996a. *Headhunting and the Social Imagination in South East Asia*. Stanford, CA: Stanford University Press.

Hoskins, Janet. 1996b. 'Headhunting as practice and as trope.' In Janet Hoskins, ed., *Headhunting and the Social Imagination in Southeast Asia*, pp. 1–49. Stanford, CA: Stanford University Press.

Hoskins, Janet. 1996c. 'The heritage of headhunting: History, ideology, and violence on Sumba, 1890–1990.' In Janet Hoskins, ed., *Headhunting and the Social Imagination in Southeast Asia*, pp. 216–48. Stanford, CA: Stanford University Press.

Hutton, J.H. 1920. 'Leopard-men in the Naga Hills.' *Journal of the Royal Anthropological Institute* 50: 41–51. doi.org/10.2307/2843373.

Hutton, J.H. 1928. 'The significance of head-hunting in Assam.' *Journal of the Royal Anthropological Institute* 58: 329–413. doi.org/10.2307/2843630.

Izikowitz, Karl Gustav. 1979. *Lamet: Hill peasants in French Indochina.* New York: AMS Press.

Janowski, Monica. 1984. 'Chieftainship among the Naga of north east India.' MPhil dissertation, University of Cambridge, Cambridge.

Janowski, Monica. 1995. 'The hearth-group, the conjugal couple and the symbolism of the rice meal among the Kelabit of Sarawak.' In Janet Carsten and S. Hugh-Jones, eds, *About the House: Levi-Strauss and beyond*, pp. 84–104. Cambridge: Cambridge University Press. doi.org/10.1017/CBO9780511607653.004.

Janowski, Monica. 1998. 'Kelabit beads.' In Lidia D. Sciama and Joanne B. Eicher, eds, *Beads and Bead Makers: Gender, material culture and meaning*, pp. 213–46. Oxford: Berg.

Janowski, Monica. 2003a. *The Forest: Source of life. The Kelabit of Sarawak.* London and Kuching: British Museum and Sarawak Museum.

Janowski, Monica. 2003b. 'Masculinity, potency and pig fat: The Kelabit of Sarawak.' In Harlan Walker, ed., *The Fat of the Land*, pp. 130–42. London: Footwork.

Janowski, Monica. 2007a. 'Being "big", being "good": Feeding, kinship, potency and status among the Kelabit of Sarawak.' In Monica Janowski and Fiona Kerlogue, eds, *Kinship and Food in Southeast Asia*, pp. 93–120. Copenhagen: NIAS Press.

Janowski, Monica. 2007b. 'Feeding the right food: The flow of life and the construction of kinship in Southeast Asia.' In Monica Janowski and Fiona Kerlogue, eds, *Kinship and Food in Southeast Asia*, pp. 1–23. Copenhagen: NIAS Press.

Janowski, Monica. 2012. 'Imagining the forces of life and the cosmos in the Kelabit highlands, Sarawak.' In Tim Ingold and Monica Janowski, eds, *Imagining Landscapes: Past, present and future*, pp. 143–64. London: Ashgate. doi.org/10.4324/9781315587899-8.

Janowski, Monica. 2014a. 'Pigs and people in the Kelabit Highlands, Sarawak.' *Indonesia and the Malay World* 42(122): 88–112. doi.org/10.1080/13639811.2013.869383.

Janowski, Monica. 2014b. 'Puntumid: Great spirit of the heart of Borneo.' *Indonesia and the Malay World* 42(122): 120–22. doi.org/10.1080/136398 11.2014.869381.

Janowski, Monica. 2014/16. *Tuked Rini, Cosmic Traveller: Life and legend in the heart of Borneo*. Copenhagen and Kuching: NIAS Press and Sarawak Museum. [Published in paperback in 2014 and in hardback in 2016.]

Janowski, Monica. 2016. 'The dynamics of the cosmic conversation: Beliefs about spirits among the Kelabit and Penan of the upper Baram River, Sarawak.' In Kaj Århem and Guido Sprenger, eds, *Animism in South East Asia*, pp. 181–204. London: Routledge. doi.org/10.4324/9781315660288-9.

Janowski, Monica. 2020. 'Stones alive! An exploration of the relationship between humans and stone in SE Asia.' *Bijdragen tot de Taal-, Land- en Volkenkunde* 176(1): 105–46. doi.org/10.1163/22134379-bja10001.

Janowski, Monica. 2019. 'Protective power: The *nabau* or water dragon among the Iban of Sarawak.' *Sarawak Museum Journal* LXXXI(81)(NS).

Janowski, Monica and Fiona Kerlogue, eds. 2007. *Food and Kinship in Southeast Asia*. Copenhagen: NIAS Press.

Janowski, Monica and Jayl Langub. 2011. 'Footprints and marks in the forest: The Penan and the Kelabit of Borneo.' In Graeme Barker and Monica Janowski, eds, *Why Cultivate? Anthropological and archaeological approaches to foraging–farming transitions in Southeast Asia*, pp. 121–32. Cambridge: McDonald Institute, University of Cambridge.

Kedit, V. 2009. 'Restoring Panggau Libau: A reassessment of engkeramba' in Saribas ritual textiles.' *Borneo Research Bulletin* 40: 221–48.

Kirsch, Thomas A. 1973. *Feasting and social oscillation: A working paper on religion and society in upland Southeast Asia*. Southeast Asia Program Data Paper No. 52. Ithaca, NY: Cornell University.

Kruyt, A.C. 1906. *Het animisme van den Indische archipel* [*Animism in the Indonesian Archipelago*]. 's-Gravenhage: Nijhoff.

Laderman, Carol. 1991. *Taming the Wind of Desire: Psychology, medicine and aesthetics in Malay shamanistic performance*. Berkeley, CA: University of California Press. doi.org/10.1525/california/9780520069169.001.0001.

Lian-Saging, R. 1976–77. 'An ethno-history of the Kelabit tribe of Sarawak: A brief look at the Kelabit tribe before World War II and after.' Graduation exercise, BA Hons, Jabatan Sejarah, University of Malaya, Kuala Lumpur.

Lloyd-Smith, L., G. Barker, H. Barton, E. Boutsikas, D. Britton, I. Datan and B. Upex. 2013. 'The Cultured Rainforest project: Preliminary archaeological results from the first two field seasons (2007, 2008).' In Marijke J. Klokke and Veronique Degroot, eds, *Unearthing Southeast Asia's Past: Selected papers from the International Conference of European Association of Southeast Asian Archaeologists. Volume 1*, pp. 34–51. Singapore: National University of Singapore Press. doi.org/10.2307/j.ctv1qv3nd.9.

Lloyd-Smith, L., G. Barker, H. Barton, I. Datan, C. Gosden, B. Nyiri and E. Preston. 2010. 'The Cultured Rainforest project: Archaeological investigations in the third (2009) season of fieldwork in the Kelabit highlands of Sarawak.' *Sarawak Museum Journal* LXVII(88)(NS): 57–104.

McKinley, Robert. 1976. 'Human and proud of it! A structural treatment of headhunting rites and the social definition of enemies.' In George N. Appell, ed., *Borneo Societies: Social process and anthropological explanation*. Center for Southeast Asian Studies Special Report No.9. DeKalb, IL: Northern Illinois University.

McWilliam, Andrew. 1996. 'Severed heads that germinate the state: History, politics, and headhunting in southwest Timor.' In Janet Hoskins, ed., *Headhunting and the Social Imagination in Southeast Asia*, pp. 127–66. Stanford, CA: Stanford University Press.

Maxwell, A.R. 1996. 'Headhunting and the consolidation of political power in the early Brunei state.' In Janet Hoskins, ed., *Headhunting and the Social Imagination in Southeast Asia*. Stanford, CA: Stanford University Press.

Metcalf, Peter. 1982. *A Borneo Journey into Death: Berawan eschatology from its rituals*. Philadelphia, PA: University of Pennsylvania Press. doi.org/10.9783/9781512818079.

Mills, J.P. 1926. *The Ao Nagas*. London: Macmillan & Co.

Mills, J.P. 1935. 'The Naga headhunters of Assam.' *Journal of the Royal Central Asian Society* 22(3): 418–28. doi.org/10.1080/03068373508725375.

Needham, Rodney. 1976. 'Skulls and causality.' *Man* 11: 71–88. doi.org/10.2307/2800389.

Rethinasamy, Souba, Norazila Abd. Aziz, Fitri Suraya Mohamad, Mohd Hafizan Hashim and Dayang Sariah Abang Suhai. 2013. 'Developing literacy and knowledge preservation skills among remote rural children.' In Ambigapathy Pandian, Christine Liew Ching Ling, Debbita Tan Ai Lin, Jayagowri Muniandy, Lee Bee Choo and Toh Chwee Hiang, eds, *New Literacies: Reconstructing education and language*, pp. 94–107. Cambridge: Cambridge Scholars Publishing.

Rubenstein, Carol. 1973. 'Poems of indigenous peoples of Sarawak: Some of the songs and chants. Part II.' *Sarawak Museum Journal* XXI(12): 723–1127.

Sellato, B. 1983. 'Le Mythe du Tigre au Centre de Borneo [The myth of the tiger in central Borneo].' *ASEMI* 14(1–2): 25–49.

Skeat, Walter William and Charles Otto Blagden. 1900. *Malay Magic: Being an introduction to the folklore and popular religion of the Malay Peninsula.* London: Macmillan.

Tangherlini, Timothy R. 1990. '"It happened not too far from here": A survey of legend, theory and characterization.' *Western Folklore* 49(4): 371–90. doi.org/10.2307/1499751.

Uchibori, Motomitsu. 1978. 'The leaving of this transient world: A study of Iban eschatology and mortuary practices.' PhD thesis, The Australian National University, Canberra. Available from: hdl.handle.net/1885/111352.

Walker, John H. 2002. *Power and Prowess: The origins of Brooke kingship in Sarawak.* Sydney and Honolulu: Allen & Unwin and University of Hawai'i Press.

Wessing, R. 1986. *The Soul of Ambiguity: The tiger in Southeast Asia.* Center for Southeast Asian Studies Monograph Series on Southeast Asia Special Report No.24. DeKalb, IL: Northern Illinois University.

Winstedt, Richard. 1956. *The Malays: A cultural history.* London: Macmillan.

6

Life, death and journeys of regeneration in Saribas Iban funerary rituals

Clifford Sather

Introduction

My concern in this chapter is with what Penelope Graham (1991: 217), in her study of 'paths of life' in eastern Flores, has called 'regeneration'— that is, the sociological process by which a younger generation in society accedes to the social and ritual roles previously performed by members of the preceding generation. Here, I focus, in particular, on Saribas Iban funerary rituals and the way in which these rituals represent societal regeneration through imagery of paths and journeys and by an analogic association of societal regeneration with the seasonal renewal of botanic life, particularly the life of cultivated crops.

The Iban are the single most populous 'Dayak' group in western Borneo. Although they trace their origins to the Kapuas River Basin of present-day Indonesian Borneo, the majority of Iban today inhabit the Malaysian state of Sarawak, where, in 2010, they numbered just over 700,000 (Department of Statistics Malaysia 2012; Sather 2004). Iban death rituals differ notably from one region of Sarawak to another and are everywhere now rapidly changing. The material presented in this chapter derives primarily from fieldwork carried out intermittently from 1977 to the present in Iban communities along the Paku and Rimbas tributaries of the main Saribas River, which, together with the smaller Krian and Awik rivers, form the main arteries of Iban settlement in what is now the Betong Division of western Sarawak.[1]

Life and death as journeys of renewal

Both life and death are described by the Iban as 'ways' or 'journeys' (*jalai*), each of which is thought to unfold in a different cosmic realm: the 'way' or 'journey of life' (*jalai idup*) in what the Iban describe, literally, as 'this world' (*dunya tu'*); the everyday visible world inhabited by living human beings; and the 'way' or 'journey of death' (*jalai mati*) in Sebayan, the invisible afterworld of the dead. In Iban, the word *jalai* (PMP **zalan* [Blust 2013]) means not only 'path', 'way', 'road' or 'journey', but also, more abstractly, for any kind of activity, the prescribed manner in which it should be done.[2] Thus, for example, *jalai bumai* refers not only to the act of rice farming (*bumai*), but also to the methods by which rice farming should be carried out. *Jalai* thus often has a normative connotation and inscribes a linear and/or temporal dimension to whatever activity it refers. *Jalai* may also refer to the 'path' one traverses in the course of a journey. Understood in this way, an Iban saying has it that 'the path of life is as narrow as the pith of a palm tree that grows on the site of a former longhouse' (*sekut jalai idup mesai lumut aping tembawai*), while 'the path of death is as broad as two rice storage bins placed side by side' (*senang jalai midang mesai tibang dua berimbai*)—namely, life is perilous; death is inevitable. The journeys of life and death not only follow a circumscribed path of varying width, but each is also of limited duration. Under ordinary

---

1   I wish to thank the Sarawak Government for permission to carry out this work and the Universiti Sains Malaysia and the National University of Singapore for their early support. For 12 months in 1993–94, my research in Sarawak was funded by a Fulbright translation grant and, since 1991, has been carried out under the auspices of the Tun Jugah Foundation. I am especially grateful to the foundation and its founding director, Tan Sri Datuk Amar Leonard Linggi Jugah, for their unstinting support. In addition, I thank Jantan Umbat, Jim Fox and Moto Uchibori for their insightful comments on earlier drafts of this chapter.

2   *Jalai* is a fundamentally important concept that resonates in many areas of Iban life. Thus, for example, before a new longhouse is constructed, its site must first be measured out and ritually constituted as a *jalai*. This is done through a rite called *ngerembang jalai* (literally, 'to clear' or 'trod down a path') (Sather 1993: 108n.5). The purpose of the rite is to remove obstructions, particularly those that may be presented by the spirits displaced from the site. After its performance and the completion of the longhouse, those who come to occupy the house resume their life journeys as longhouse members with a reduced likelihood of spiritual interference.

circumstances, sooner or later, both journeys come to an end. On the other hand, the two are connected and interdependent. Thus, the second, the journey of death, represents a continuation of the first, the journey of life, and concludes with a return of life-renewing power to this world, the place from which the first of these two journeys begins.

In this world, each person's life journey begins at birth, and ideally, before it ends, passes through three successive stages, each defined by the traveller's generational level (*serak*) vis-a-vis others of adjacent generations. These stages are 'child' (*anak*), 'parent' (*api/indai*) and 'grandparent' (*aki'/ini'*).[3] In everyday social interactions, persons are constantly reminded of their generational positioning relative to others by the universal use of generational teknonyms. To live a complete lifespan, passing through all three of these stages, is, the Iban say, to be *gayu* ('long-lived')—a condition frequently wished for in Iban prayers and blessing formulas.

On the other hand, those who live beyond what normally constitutes a complete lifespan are treated differently at death from others. Persons who live to extreme old age are thought to begin their transition into death even while they are still alive. Thus, their 'soul' (*semengat*)—the vital component of each person's living self—is said to depart from their body for long periods to spend time in Sebayan in the company of the spirits of their deceased friends and relatives, returning to this world only occasionally to re-inhabit their body. Such persons are described as being *setengah antu*—literally, 'half-spirits' (Sather 2003b: 180).[4] The families of the rare few who live beyond a normal three-generation lifespan, and so attain the status of 'great-grandparents' (*umbuh*), need not observe a period of formal mourning (*ulit*) for them when they die. This is because they are said to have already transitioned into Sebayan, so that, when they cease to breathe, they 'do not die' (*enda' mati*) but, rather, are said to simply 'return home' (*pulai*). With the passage of a full three-generation cycle, the birth of a fourth generation of descendants is marked by the re-bestowal (*ngangkatka*) of the personal names (*nama*) that, in life, belonged to ancestors of the *umbuh* generation. By this time, these ancestors are assumed to have died. This practice of name inheritance

---

3   *Serak*, the term used to refer to 'generation' (for example, *serak ke dulu*, 'previous generation'; *serak ke baru*, 'younger generation'), more generally means a 'layer' or 'level' (Ensiring et al. 2016: 1504).
4   As we shall see, once a person dies, he or she is said 'to become a spirit' (*nyadi antu*).

not only marks the passage of a full three-generation cycle of life, but also helps to perpetuate a memory of deceased ancestors and their this-worldly achievements.[5]

At the other extreme, those who die prematurely, are stillborn, aborted or die in infancy are described as *anak mati lulus* ('stillborn'). At death, their bodies are simply buried without ceremony. Although it is said that infants are born with a soul, until their first tooth has erupted, their soul lacks a firm point of anchorage inside the body. Hence, a newborn's connection to life is precarious. Like the elderly at the opposite end of life's journey, they have only a weak attachment to this world.[6] Following death, the souls of the *anak mati lulus* are said to journey to a special place within Sebayan called Kendi Aji, where the road entering the afterworld branches into multiple paths (Sather 1978: 329–30). Here, the *anak mati lulus* are thought to continually interrogate newly arriving souls to find the parents from whom they were separated at birth. Similarly, the souls of those who die untimely or violent deaths—such as by falling from a height (*mati labuh*), drowning (*mati lemas*), taking their own lives (*mati makai tubai*) or, in the case of a woman, dying in childbirth (*mati beranak*)—also journey to separate regions within Sebayan. Here, like the *anak mati lulus*, they live lives removed from the ordinary dead and, in this state, are believed to be beyond ritual recall. Consequently, they are no longer able to involve themselves in the lives of the living and so make no further contribution to the process of this-worldly regeneration.

Every person's 'soul' (*semengat*) at the time of death is said to take permanent leave of the body (*tubuh*). Escorted by the soul of a female 'soul guide' (*tukang sabak*), this now disembodied soul is taken on a ritual journey to Sebayan. Here, it eventually takes up its proper place as determined by the circumstances of its death. In Sebayan, the constant arrival of souls is said

---

5   *Nama* ('name') in Iban also means 'reputation'. Those whose names are re-bestowed are typically men and women of renown, former leaders and persons of exemplary character. Conversely, the names of those who were known in life as troublemakers or adulterers or who died prematurely or as a result of a sudden or violent death should not be passed on to the young lest they inherent these traits or suffer a similar fate. Names, I was told, cannot be bestowed earlier, while the name-bearer and the recipient of the name are both alive, because of the rules of name avoidance that apply among living kin. This practice of re-bestowing names is clearly apparent in Iban genealogies and, in the Paku region where I did most of my fieldwork, can be traced back in local genealogies over at least 12 generations.

6   For this reason, when treating small infants, shamans re-insert their recovered souls not into the infant's body, but usually into that of the mother. On the other hand, if a family provides a substitute for the absent tooth—either a shell armlet (*rangki'*) or an object made of iron (*besi*)—they may, in burying this object with the infant's body, perform the usual death rites observed for a young child.

to continually replenish the numbers residing there. With the departure of the soul from the body, the Iban say that the deceased 'becomes a spirit' (*nyadi antu*). The term 'spirit' (*antu*) has two meanings in this context. In the first, it refers to the deceased's now inanimate corpse (*bangkai*). Thus, at the time of burial, transporting the corpse to the cemetery is described as *nganjung antu* (literally, 'to send the spirit [to the cemetery]'), while burying it is called *numbak antu* (literally, 'to bury the spirit'). Upon burial, the corpse rapidly decomposes. In the process, it returns to the material from which it was created—namely, 'earth' (*tanah*). In its second meaning, *antu* refers to what is now thought to be a newly emergent spirit identified with the deceased. For most persons, this spirit, after lingering for a time in this world, is also said to journey to Sebayan, where it remains in a transitional state until the conclusion of the final rite of the funerary cycle, the Gawai Antu.[7]

For the souls of the ordinary dead, life in Sebayan is thought to be generally similar to life in this world. In arriving there, the great majority of souls take up residence along the Mandai River of the Dead (Batang Mandai Mati).[8] Here, they live in longhouses, cultivate rice and other food crops and rear families much as the living do in this world. Like life in this world, life in Sebayan is also finite. Unlike mortal life, however, it unfolds in a series of further lives, deaths and rebirths—generally seven in all. After a seventh death, the final material residue of the soul dissolves into a watery mist. This condenses, especially in the early hours of the morning, and falls to earth as 'dew' (*ambun*). This occurs especially at the end of the dry season, just after families have finished planting their annual rice fields. The dew is then taken up and nourishes the newly germinating rice plants. Thus, in this way, the soul stuff of the ancestors is incorporated directly into rice, which, as the staple food of the Iban, serves to sustain each new generation of human life in this world (Sather 2012: 122).

The total journey of each person's soul through life and death is thus ontologically connected. Life in this world ends in death, whereupon the soul transitions to Sebayan, where it resumes its journey, this time through a series of rebirths and deaths, ending with its final transubstantiation

---

7   As Reed Wadley (1999: 599) notes, in practical terms, when addressing prayers or making offerings, the Iban generally refer to their deceased ancestors not as 'ancestors' (*aki'ini'*), but either as *antu* (spirits) or, as I will explain later, following the Gawai Antu, as *petara* (gods).

8   The Mandai River has a visible counterpart in this world, an actual river: a southern tributary of the Kapuas in Kalimantan Barat, known to the Iban as the Batang Mandai Idup ('Mandai River of the Living') (Sather 2012: 123).

and return to this world as dew, which, through the medium of rice, is re-embodied in a new generation of humans. The connection of both these journeys with the parallel cycling of life through cultivated crops is predicated on the coexistence both in this world and in Sebayan of what Penelope Graham, in reference to Flores, has called 'separate productive systems' (1991: 259). Thus, subsistence in both this world and the next similarly depends upon the cultivation and consumption of plant crops. Successful cultivation requires husbanding the generative power inherent in the seeds of these crops or their cuttings. The work of tending this material makes possible the continuous cycling of plant life from one farming season to the next. As living humans subsist on these crops, the parallel cycling of human life is therefore dependent on this same work of husbandry. For the people of Léwotala described by Graham, the living, at the time of death, ritually take back from the dead the seeds of all the vegetable food crops they consumed during their lifetime so that the total seed stock available to the living is never depleted, but remains available for each new season's planting. In this way, the living receive from their ancestors the generative potential inherent in their cultivated crops. During Iban funerary rituals, a similar transfer occurs, but in the opposite direction. Here, the surviving family shares its stock of seeds and cuttings with the dead, so that the latter are able to use this material to establish themselves as self-sufficient cultivators in Sebayan. Hence, the ancestors are the ones who, for the Iban, are dependent upon the living. While expressed differently, the outcome is the same: the living and the dead, between them, by cultivating crops, each in their own realm, promote a mutually dependent cycling of life through both plants and humans.

Funerary rituals and societal regeneration

Funerary rituals have been a subject of special interest to anthropologists in Borneo ever since the publication in 1907 of Robert Hertz's classic essay *'Contribution à une étude sur la représentation collective de la mort'* ('A contribution to the study of the collective representation of death') (Hertz 1960). In Hertz's essay, as in this chapter, the central question concerns how the ritual treatment of the dead relates to the temporal renewal of society. In this connection, Hertz argued that death, especially in societies of the Malayo–Indonesian archipelago, is seen as a transformative process, rather than a single momentary event. In consequence, funerary rites typically extend over a protracted period and are divided into stages marking distinct points of transition within this process. Hertz was particularly struck by the parallels he found in Borneo between the treatment of the corpse of the dead and beliefs relating to the fate of the deceased's soul and to the ritual condition of the mourners. In explaining these parallels, he drew attention to the fact that the deceased is not only a biological individual but also a social being. Hence, death not only extinguishes 'the visible bodily life of an individual; it also destroys the social being grafted upon the physical individual' (Hertz 1960: 77).

Hence, Hertz argued, funerary rites are always double, for there are two tasks that must be achieved. On the one hand, the individual must be 'disaggregated' from the collectivity, both socially and in regard to his or her bodily remains, and, on the other hand, society itself must be 'reinstalled', by which Hertz meant that the roles once played by the deceased must be allocated to others. In the course of this reallocation, the dead are believed to attain a permanent place in the afterworld, as the social void left by their death in this world is filled by others, while the mourners, in a parallel way and following a period of seclusion, rejoin the collectivity and resume their everyday social lives. These two phases of the mortuary process—disaggregation and reinstallation—are thus linked both with beliefs about the fate of the soul and with ideas concerning the ritual condition of the mourners.

It takes time, Hertz argued, for the collectivity to readjust to the death of one of its members. This fact is expressed in notions that the period immediately after death is one of special danger during which the departed soul is believed to be potentially malevolent. Paralleling this idea, the mourners, too, are in a perilous state and must be isolated for a time from society. Following a transitional interval of readjustment, the final stage of the funerary process asserts the ultimate triumph of society over physical death. This is represented by a termination of mourning restrictions and, in a parallel way, a belief that the deceased's soul is now fully incorporated in the society of the dead (Hertz 1960: 86).

Hertz's essay was a groundbreaking contribution, particularly to an understanding of how the structure of funerary rituals relates to the temporal processes by which a society regenerates itself over time. But for all his insight, Hertz never fully escaped a narrow conception of 'bodily life', and so failed to see that interposed between society and the physical body are often complex conceptions of the self that may equally well shape social constructions of death. He also failed to see the way in which the particular circumstances of an individual's death may bear upon his or her role in societal regeneration. Unlike the Ngaju, whose double funerals and protracted secondary treatment of the dead strongly influenced Hertz's analysis, the Iban, like a number of other Borneo peoples, while also performing complex and protracted funerary rituals, do not, under ordinary circumstances, practice secondary treatment or reburial of the dead.[9] Instead, the body, upon death, is buried almost at once and plays no further part in the rituals that comprise the Saribas funerary cycle. Instead, the complexity of this cycle is related to a view of the self as an internally differentiated entity, comprising components that participate in the ontological conditions of 'life' and 'death' in different ways. Consequently, death, when it occurs, is perceived, not as a single event, but as a complex process involving the disaggregation and independent transformation of these components. The primary components involved in this process are the 'soul' or *semengat*, the 'plant-image' or *bungai* and the 'spirit' or *antu*. Each of these components is the focus of a separate ritual and, together, these rituals make up, in sequential order, the main rites of the Saribas Iban funerary cycle.

Life, death and the differentiated self

For the Iban, death is characterised not by a total annihilation of the self, but by a gradual disassociation and transformation of its constituent elements. The beginning of this process is signalled by the cessation of breathing (*abis seput*). Some say that the 'breath' (*seput* or *nyawa*), as a source of this-worldly life, inhabits the veins, together with the blood (Sather 2001: 50–55). At death, these and other elements making up the body (*tubuh*), including the bones and flesh, are said to begin to decompose and so return to 'earth' (*tanah*), the medium from which they were created. As earth, these elements are said to be repeatedly remoulded and reforged by the Iban creator god, Selempandai, who, as a blacksmith, fashions each human body at his forge at the time of conception (Sather 2001: 105–8). In this way, new bodies are continually refashioned from the elements that formerly made up the bodies of the dead, as the earth from which they were made is constantly recycled by Selempandi.

---

9 There is, however, a significant exception—*ngelumbung* or 'entombment'—described later in this chapter.

The 'soul' (*semengat*), on the other hand, as a second component of the self, is 'not extinguished' (*enda' abis*) when breathing ceases, but, rather, in contrast to the body, 'remains alive' (*bedau idup*). At death, however, it takes permanent leave of the body that, until then, served as its 'container' (*karung*).[10] Indeed, shamans say that a person's *semengat* leaves the body and begins its journey three days before breathing stops. On the fourth day, as the soul crosses over Lanjan Ridge, well inside Sebayan, at the point where shamans can no longer recover it and bring it back to this world, breathing ceases, the blood stops circulating and the body begins to decompose (Sather 2001: 55–58).[11]

In addition to the body and soul, each living person is also composed of a 'plant-image' (*bungai* or *bunga*).[12] This image is said to exist separately from the body in an unseen region of the cosmos closely associated with the shamanic god Menjaya. Here, some say, it is tended by the spirit-companions of living shamans.[13] Some identify these companions with the spirits of deceased shamans who once lived as humans. The *bungai* appears in the form of a plant—most often likened to a bamboo or banana plant. Like the latter, it typically 'grows in a clump' (*bepumpun*) from a common rootstock called the *pun* or *pugu' bungai*. Each clump is said to represent a single *bilik*-family and each *bungai*, an individual family member. These clumps grow in gardens, each of which, some say, represents a longhouse community. Thus, these gardens are sometimes described as *rumah semengat* ('longhouses of the souls'). The condition of the plants growing in them reflects the collective vitality of all who live in the same longhouse. Menjaya, by inspecting these gardens, is therefore able to monitor the wellbeing of the various human communities present in this world. The *bungai* is thus, at once, both an individual and a socially encompassing image. Unlike the *semengat*, a person's *bungai* 'dies' when

---

10 Some Iban claim that humans have multiple souls and describe this primary soul as the 'body soul' (*semengat tubuh*) (for a detailed discussion, see Sather 2001: 51 ff.).

11 Iban shamans use crystals (*batu karas*) as a diagnostic tool to spy out their patients' *semengat*, which may be revealed in this way as having strayed prematurely into Sebayan (Sather 2001: 130–32, 274–77).

12 The term *bunga* or *bungai* literally means 'flower'. *Ayu* is sometimes used as an alternative term to refer to essentially the same plant image, but in a context where it often has a somewhat different meaning (see Sather 2001: 58–65). In general, the term *bungai* tends to be used—as in the *beserara' bungai*—in connection with mortality, while *ayu* is more frequently associated with longevity (*gayu*), healthful vigour and reproduction. Thus, the plants tended in the upper world by the spirits of ancestral shamans are, some say, more fittingly described as *ayu*.

13 As Uchibori (1978: 20) notes, conceptions of the *bungai* are less well articulated than most other aspects of the self. Among the Layar Iban, he writes, the *bungai* is believed to grow not in another cosmic realm, but inside the family apartment, at the foot of one of the posts supporting the drying rack above the family's cooking hearth.

breathing ceases and the soul departs from the body. In this sense, the *bungai* mirrors each person's this-worldly state of health and mortality. When a child is born into a family, a new *bungai* is said to sprout from the family's *pugu' bungai*. In good health, this *bungai* grows and flourishes like a healthy young plant, while in ill health or old age, it yellows and withers (*nyadi layu'*), and in death, it dies (*mati*) and falls to the earth (*gugur*). As an encompassing life image, the *bungai* reflects the condition of both the body and the soul. If, for example, the soul is absent from the body, a person 'feels withered' (*berasai nyadi layu'*). Similarly, if the *bungai* is ill, scorched by heat or overgrown with weeds, the body and soul are said to suffer. At death, however, unless this death results in the extinction (*punas*) of the entire family, the family's rootstock lives on, capable of generating new *bungai* to replace those who have died (Sather 2001: 61; 2003b: 207). In this way, the *bungai* symbolises not only an individual's vitality and mortal life, but also family continuity and the capacity of society for renewal.

Finally, with the cessation of breathing, the departure of the soul and the death of the *bungai*, the deceased is said 'to become a spirit' (*nyadi antu*). This spirit, as we have noted, is identified at first with both the deceased's corpse and what is described as a newly emergent spirit. At first, as a spirit, the deceased is reluctant to leave the society of the living. Almost at once, however, it begins to lose its human attributes, appearing as an increasingly frightening spectre. Thus, its lingering presence is perceived in largely negative terms as a threat to the living. For the first three nights after burial, during a period called *pana*, a bonfire (*tungkun api*) is built not far from the longhouse and kept burning throughout the night. Here, a simple shelter is erected, where, during each of the three nights of *pana*, the deceased's *antu* gathers to warm itself. In addition, by the light of the fire, it sees itself as it now appears, no longer a mortal human being, but a spectre, and so realises that it no longer has a place among the living. Thus, the deceased's spirit, at the end of *pana*, quits this world and, like the soul, journeys to Sebayan. Once established there, it is gradually transformed into a benevolent *antu Sebayan* (literally, a 'spirit of the afterworld'). Here, in Sebayan, an individual's *antu*, rather than the now disembodied *semengat*, becomes the principal component of the self that represents the deceased in his or her interactions with the living. While in this world the embodied soul functioned as an individual's primary source of agency—what Raymond Firth (1967: 342) calls, in reference to Tikopia, an individual's 'vital personality'—in death, this personality is replaced with the deceased's spirit, or *antu Sebayan*, representing what Firth calls the 'survival personality', or what I would term his or her 'post-mortal self', which functions, in the Iban case, as its 'afterworld counterpart'.[14] At the culmination of the funerary cycle, the spirits of the most recent cohort of longhouse dead are recalled to this world, where, as we shall see, they undergo a final transformation, shedding the last traces of their corpse-like materiality, and so become deified ancestral spirits. From what is now a realm of their own, separate from the living world, they join the preceding generations of ancestral dead to play a role in the lives of their living descendants analogous to, and ultimately merging with, that of the gods.[15]

The journey of each person through life and death is not only protracted, but also involves multiple transformations. Some of these transformations occur in the course of a person's journey through this world, while others are a result of death or occur in the final return of life-renewing potency back to this world. In addition, shaping these journeys are what James J. Fox (1987: 523) has described as elements of a common Austronesian conceptual heritage—specifically, 'a belief in the immanence of life and in the interdependence of life and death'. As life depends on death, 'the ancestral dead or specific deceased persons, whose lives were marked by notable attainments, [are thereby] regarded as capable of bestowing life-giving potency' (Fox 1987: 525). Hence, the ancestral dead—most notably, those who enjoyed long and successful lives in this world—play an important part in the regeneration of life, and the achievements they attained while journeying through this world help define the conditions they and others will experience during their own subsequent journey through Sebayan.

---

14   In Tikopia, the two are terminologically distinct (see Firth 1967: 337). The 'soul'—that is, the 'life force' or 'vital personality' that animates a living person—is called the *mauri* or *ora*. At death, a person's *mauri* ceases to exist and is replaced with the *atua*, the deceased's 'spirit', representing what I would call his or her postmortal self.

15   Although the Iban terms *antu* and *petara* are often defined, respectively, as 'spirit' and 'god', the Iban in fact do not make a clear distinction between the two, often using both terms interchangeably. Generally, however, once the spirits of the dead have been recalled during the Gawai Antu, they are thereafter addressed in prayers as *petara* or, more specifically, in couplet form as *petara aki'/petara ini'* (literally, 'grandfather god/grandmother god').

The immanence of life and the interpenetration of life and death

While I have stressed here the Iban notion that life and death unfold in different cosmic realms, it is important to add that this notion coexists with another that asserts that the living and the dead live in close proximity and that, if our eyes were not covered by a thin, translucent membrane, we would be able to see the dead and share directly in their experiences (Sather 2001: 111–15). Moreover, the conditions that define life and death are thought to interpenetrate. Thus, while still alive, an individual may experience aspects of death, such as soul loss (*semengat lelung*) or a withering of his or her plant-image (*bungai layu*) (Sather 2003b: 179–82). Thus, at some level, the separation of the living from the dead is a matter more of visual perception than of spatial distance. Although the living may no longer be able to see those who have died, they and the dead can still communicate with one another. A person wishing to make contact with a deceased parent may, for example, wrap himself in a ritual *ikat* cloth before going to sleep at night. In so doing, he 'makes himself visible' (*ulih peda'*) to the dead, so that they may, in response, appear and converse with him in his dreams (*mimpi*).

In fact, some persons say that the dead do not really depart from this world at all, but that Sebayan is, in actuality, an inverted realm that exists beneath the floor of the longhouse (see Sather 1993: 111, n.42). Thus, at night, people say, the spirits of the dead may sometimes be heard as they go about their daily affairs—night in this world being day in Sebayan. For this reason, too, the living, before eating meals, often drop small bits of food through the floor of the longhouse as a share for the dead. Similarly, just before the corpse is placed inside a coffin prior to being carried to the cemetery, a final meal is served to the deceased, after which the plate and cup that were used are broken—broken objects being whole in Sebayan—and these, too, are dropped beneath the longhouse floor. Similarly, on ceremonial occasions, when asked by a host to drink rice wine, it is customary for the drinker to first pronounce a formula, 'Give the ancestors drink' (*meri' petara ngirup*), and then to pour a small amount of wine through the floor slats, before drinking himself (Wadley 1999: 599).

The Saribas Iban funerary cycle

For the Saribas Iban, death rituals, at least through the 1970s, comprised a tripartite series in which each major ritual was performed by a different ritual specialist. The first of these rituals, called *nyenggai' antu* or *rabat*, focuses on the deceased's 'soul' and is conducted by a female soul guide (*tukang sabak*). The second, the *beserara' bungai*, focuses on the deceased's 'plant-image' and is performed by a shaman (*manang*), while the third, the Gawai Antu, focuses on the deceased's 'spirit' and is conducted by a company of priest bards (*lemambang*).

The soul's journey to Sebayan: *Rabat*

The moment a dying person stops breathing, a rice-pounding pestle (*alu*) and mortar (*lesung*) are placed across the entrances at each end of the longhouse to prevent the spirits of the dead from entering. Inside the family apartment, the body is bathed and dressed, while on the gallery, a rectangular enclosure called the *sapat* is constructed of ritual cloth. After being bathed, the corpse is placed on a finely woven mat, carried from the apartment and placed inside the *sapat*.

Inside the apartment, over the next few days, the family makes a collection of personal belongings, including necessities for the deceased's use in the afterworld. Together, these things are called *baya'* and, at burial, they are either interred with the body or placed on top of the grave. In addition, there is a special category of objects called the *baya' pandang* ('display baya"') that are not taken to the cemetery, but instead are retained by the family and are first 'opened' (*diketas*) during *ngetas ulit*, a small rite that marks the end of mourning, and then put away again until they are brought out for display during the Gawai Antu.

After the body has been placed inside the *sapat*, a date is set and preparations begin for *rabat*, a night-long vigil that immediately precedes burial. Four major things take place during *rabat*: first, an announcement is made of the cause of death; second, the deceased's life history is recounted, and, related to this, third, the longhouse elders specify the duration of mourning (*ulit*) and announce the amount of the deceased's *adat pemati*. *Adat pemati*, narrowly defined, refers to the size of fines (described as *adat*) to be levied should the rules of mourning be violated. More significantly, however, it stipulates the type of *garung* basket that will be woven for the deceased during Gawai Antu. The amount of *adat pemati* is set beforehand by the deceased's immediate kindred and, after its announcement, it must be discussed and affirmed by the vigil guests. For the Saribas Iban, the amount is a matter of utmost importance because, in this highly competitive society, it is taken to be a measure of each individual's lifetime accomplishments. Fourth, to conclude *rabat*, a soul guide sings the *sabak*,[16] a travel narrative in which her soul escorts the soul of the deceased on its journey to Sebayan.

The *tukang sabak* typically begins to sing the *sabak* well after dark and continues until an hour or so before daybreak the following morning.[17] In the *sabak*, the soul's journey is related chiefly from the point of view of the *tukang sabak's* soul, with dialogue, conversational exchanges and descriptions of boundary crossings (Sather 2003b: 187–91; Sutlive 2012).[18] In the opening stanzas, the deceased is addressed directly and informed that his or her presence in the living world is now at an end. This opening is set inside the longhouse interior. It begins on the gallery, inside the *sapat*, where the soul guide sits beside the deceased's body as she sings, and from there the narrative moves across the *tempuan* passageway and into the family apartment. Here, each important feature of the apartment is now introduced and taken leave of, beginning usually with the family's cooking hearth (*dapur*). These parts of the house now appear as they do to the deceased's soul. Hence, they are personified and speak. The imagery is thus, at once, both familiar and alien. While the deceased is now able to see beneath visible appearances and so converses directly with the *semengat* of the objects of which he is taking leave, he himself, being now disembodied, can no longer touch or feel them.

---

16   *Sabak* is the root form of the active verb *nyabak*, meaning, literally, 'to weep', 'cry' or 'lament'.

17   Since my initial fieldwork in the 1970s, many Christian families have replaced the singing of the *sabak* with a simple Christian service. Some have also dispensed with the *sapat*.

18   It is important to bear in mind that what is described here relates specifically to the Saribas (Saratok and Skrang) Iban. In the Rejang, the Iban funerary cycle is quite different. The Rejang Iban typically perform not one, but two, *sabak*. The first, called the *sabak kenang*, is much like the Saribas *sabak* and is performed, like the latter, during the night preceding burial. The Rejang counterpart of the *beserara' bungai*, generally called the *beserara' bungai layus*, is performed much earlier than in Saribas, on the third night after death, and is the occasion, like the Saribas *rabat*, on which the length of mourning is fixed (Sather 2003b: 205n.21). In the Rejang, the second *sabak* is called the *sabak lumbung* or, particularly in the upper Rejang, the Gawai Lumbung. As the final rite of the funerary cycle, the *sabak lumbung* is performed some time after the conclusion of *ulit*, usually within a year or so of death. Although it is performed by a *tukang sabak*, and so is not a major bardic ritual like the Saribas Gawai Antu, the ancestral dead are similarly recalled to the longhouse of the living, where they are honoured and exchange goods with their human hosts, including cultivated crops (see Sutlive 2012: 4). In contrast with the Saribas and despite the ritual's name, there is no association of *lumbung* with the construction of a tomb to enshrine the physical remains of the dead.

The ancestral dead, barred from entering the longhouse, gather at the bottom of the entry ladder. Leaving the family apartment, the deceased now passes along the *tempuan* passage and from there descends to the ground. From there, in the company of the *antu Sebayan*, the party journeys along the same path that the deceased's corpse will take on its way to the cemetery. Beyond this point, the surroundings they pass through become increasingly unfamiliar, until, at last, they reach the dark, gloomy frontier where Bunsu Bubut, the coucal bird goddess, makes her home.[19] The party has now arrived at Titi' Rawan (the 'Bridge of Fear'), across which the deceased's soul must pass to reach Sebayan. The brave pass over easily, but for others the Titi' Rawan shrinks to the size of a small quivering pole. On reaching the other side, the party finds the grave goods (*baya'*) left at the cemetery. The party now comes to a second barrier, the Pintu Tanah ('Earthen Door'), which only Bunsu Belut, the worm goddess, can open for them. On the other side, they pass, one after another, the areas inhabited by the souls of those who died ill-fated deaths. Close by, at a river landing, they find boats awaiting them. Using these, they journey downriver, then up the Mandai River to the landing place of the dead, where the deceased is welcomed by the spirits of his ancestors.

As soon as the *sabak* is finished, the deceased's body is removed from the *sapat*, placed in a coffin and carried to the cemetery. There, burial takes place just before dawn, while it is still daylight in Sebayan. Returning to the longhouse, the burial party and other mourners are invited into the deceased's *bilik*. Here an elderly woman, ideally the oldest in the community, is called upon to feed the newly widowed spouse, if the deceased was married, or, if not, the eldest surviving member of the family, the first of three balls of black rice called the *asi' pana*. Each ball stands for one day of *pana*, during which time no-one may leave the house to work or travel outside. In the past, during these three days, the deceased's family remained in total seclusion. To mark its disjunctive status, during daylight hours, windows and skylights were closed, so that the apartment was kept in darkness. The family was not permitted to light a fire on its hearth and, instead, other families had to prepare special meals for them. After the last ball of *asi' pana* was eaten, at dawn, a chicken was sacrificed and its blood smeared on the window frames, after which the windows and skylights were reopened to introduce daylight back into

---

19 The plaintive call of the greater coucal or crow pheasant (*Centropus sinensis*), when heard in this world, is believed to signal the passage of a human soul into the afterworld.

the apartment. Much as in the manner described by Hertz, *pana* reflected the family's temporary disengagement from the life of the community, while, similarly, the deceased, now neither able to return to the longhouse of the living nor yet fully installed in Sebayan, is thought to gather each night to warm itself at the *tungkun api*.

Pana is followed by a longer period of mourning called *ulit*. *Ulit*, literally, refers to a small container in which a few of the personal effects of the deceased were placed at the time of death, including the items of *baya' pandang* mentioned earlier. The lifting of *ulit* restrictions is marked by a small ritual called *ngetas ulit* (literally, 'to cut open the *ulit*'). In the past, a man of prowess, a warrior or seasoned traveller was often invited to open the *ulit*, and, even today, the ritual is often preceded by a mock headhunting raid—now frequently performed as a predawn or early morning game hunt. At its conclusion, the man invited to open the *ulit* shouts a war cry (*mangka'ka selaing*) as he approaches the longhouse or fires a shotgun into the air. Those inside respond by beating gongs, thereby breaking the silence enjoined by mourning.[20] Entering the house, the performer cuts the fastenings binding the *ulit* and removes the personal effects from inside. After this, he cuts a small bit of hair from each member of the deceased's family and waves a cockerel over them, thereby releasing them from mourning restrictions.[21]

Severing the plant-image: *Beserara' bungai*

The second major ritual of the Saribas funerary cycle, the *beserara' bungai* (or *bunga*), is usually performed during the night immediately following *ngetas ulit*. Like *rabat*, it takes place on the bereaved family's section of the longhouse gallery. *Beserara'* means, literally, 'to sever', 'separate' or 'cut away'. What is cut away during the ritual is the branch of a plant stalk representing the deceased's 'plant-image'.

As with other rituals performed by Saribas shamans, the *manang* begins by first inviting his hosts to assist him in constructing a shrine called the *pagar api* ('fence of fire'), which serves as the focal point of his

---

20   In the past, the *ulit* period was much longer than it is today, particularly for prominent individuals, and mourning restrictions could be automatically lifted by carrying out a successful headhunting raid (see Sather 2003b: 201–2; Uchibori 1978: 114–21). During the colonial era, the length of *ulit* was reduced to a maximum of one month.

21   With the exception of widowed spouses, who are released from mourning by a separate ritual called *muai tebalu*, which is generally held well after *ngetas ulit* (see Sather 2003b: 204–5; Uchibori 1978: 121–26).

performance. In the case of *beserara' bungai*, the distinctive feature of this shrine is a freshly cut plant stalk—most often bamboo or, alternatively, *kayu kemali* (*Leea aculeata Bl.*). This is fastened to an upright spear, the top of which is securely attached to a horizontal pole, just above head height, which is extended between house pillars perpendicular to the long axis of the house. The base of the spear is inserted into an earthenware jar, representing the rootstock of the *bungai*. The *manang* chooses one of the stalk's branches to represent the deceased's *bungai* and, to signify this, he attaches to it a bead or shell armlet. Over the end of the pole nearest to the family apartment he drapes a ritual cloth and either a bundle of undyed cotton thread or a white cotton cloth. This latter is called the *kembai bungai* and is said to draw to itself the straying souls of members of the bereaved family. At the conclusion of *beserara bungai*, the *manang* gathers together these souls and reinserts them in each owner's body. While the *manang* completes his preparations, women inside the *bilik* prepare offerings, consisting of various kinds of cultivated food plants, including fruit, plus popped rice, bamboo tubes of steamed rice and packets of glutinous rice. When the *pagar api* is completed, the women bring these offerings from the *bilik* and place them beside the earthenware jar representing the *pugu' bungai*.

Like *rabat*, the main feature of *beserara' bungai* is an extended narrative, which, in this case, concludes, like the *sabak*, with a journey to Sebayan. The opening stanzas are—again, like those of the *sabak*—set in the longhouse interior. Similarly, spirits of the ancestral dead have gathered outside at the base of the longhouse entry ladder. In this case, the leaders of the dead ask permission to sever the *bungai* and to take it, together with a share of the family's property, back with them to Sebayan. The *manang*, in replying, identifies himself with Selempandai, the god of creation. Not only does Selempandai fashion human bodies, but he also determines the length of each individual's lifespan. In performing the *beserara' bungai*, the *manang* assumes the role of Selempandai, as both a life-giver and an undoer of life—one who determines both the time of a person's birth and the time of his death (see Sather 2003a). Speaking as Selempandai, the *manang* informs the spirits that they must allow him not only to sever the *bungai*, but also to divide the family's property, including its stock of seeds and plant cuttings. The first half of the shaman's narrative describes this division. After announcing his intentions, the shaman briefly adopts the voice of the deceased. Here, and later in his chant, by giving voice to the deceased, the shaman in effect creates a dialogue between the living and the dead in which each acknowledges their grief in parting and describes their newfound responsibilities towards one another (Sather 2001: 336–37):[22]

Bedua' leman utai ditanam, anang kurang	Divide everything we cultivate, let neither receive less
Telesak tambak ubi enggi' aku dibai' aku mati	My cuttings of cassava, I take with me to die
Pulai ngagai menua kami di Bukit Lebur Api	Returning to our country at Lebur Api Hill [in Sebayan]
Ke menjadi, malam padam	Lit by day, extinguished by night
Tang pagi menjadi mau' rerendang	Comes morning, it [again] blazes brightly
Enggi' sida' ditanam ba' emperan tanah lelanji	Theirs, they [the living] plant on a fertile plain
Nyadi ubi madang jabang	Growing well in the cassava garden
Sapa babi berani ngenchuri ubi	No wild boar dares to steal them
Laban sida' takut mati kena' tunang sendiri' leka senapang	*For fear of being killed by a torrent of shotgun pellets*

Depending on the ingenuity of the shaman, the list of cultivated crops (*utai ditanam*: 'planted things') is often extensive. On the occasion recorded here,[23] in addition to cassava (*ubi/jabang*), it consisted of sugar cane (*tebu*), Job's tears (*nyeli'*), mustard (*chabi'*), longbeans (*retak*), gourds (*labu'*), pumpkins (*entekai*), maize (*jagung*), hill rice (*padi bukit*), swamp rice (*padi paya*) and glutinous rice (*padi pulut*). It also included rubber gardens. Having received their equal share of these crops, the deceased, still speaking, now reciprocates with gifts of charms and medicines for the use of the living (Sather 2001: 352–53):

Uji sambut nuan enggau kukut jari kanan	Receive with the nails of your right hand
Taring uting babi dupan enggau batu tanduk rusa' ngulam	The rooting tusk of a pig and the petrified antler of a grazing sambar deer

---

22 Fox (2003) describes these dialogues as a distinctive feature of Austronesian funerary rituals.
23 On 28 October 1977 at Tanjong longhouse, Ulu Paku, Betong Division (see Sather 2001: 326).

Enggau batu ai' ulih ngambi' di kaki kerangan	Together with a water-stone charm found at the foot of a gravel bed
Ditambah enggau batu gumbang ke besegang ngalun kerangan	Add to it a petrified wave that dashed against the shingle
Tu' batu buah pauh laba berendam dikemeranka ikan bam	This is a petrified pauh laba fruit taken from beneath the sea where it was guarded by a whale
Kena' nuan nyeridika simpuli padi rutan	Use it to tend your rutan rice
Ngambika belayan ia kedil jampat mansang	And your crops will be abundant and grow quickly

Beserara' bungai is essentially a rite of separation. The bereaved family, by dividing its property, particularly its stock of seeds and plant cuttings, erases its future material obligations towards the dead. Each is now provided with the necessary resources for a self-sufficient existence—the living in this world, the dead in Sebayan. This does not mean, of course, that the living will cease to make offerings to the dead or cease to expect benefits in return. With the exchange completed, the time has come to sever the *bungai*. Now transformed, the deceased again appears as a menacing spectre (Sather 2001: 360–61):

Ke begamal rigam-rigam ke tinggi jam-jam …	Now appearing huge and tall like a leafy tree …
Bemata mesai buah terung kanggan	With eyeballs as big as eggplants
Sintak seput iya munyi ai' surut matak langan …	His breathing sounds like the ebbing rush of waves …
Nyawa iya seruran dengam-dengam	His open mouth is forever eager to eat
Ngeli' ka sigi' mesai tempan	His teeth are as large as anvils

As the shaman severs the branch representing the deceased's *bungai*, he reminds the deceased that, although they are now separated, he must not forget his descendants, particularly those who continue the *bilik*-family to which he belonged (Sather 2001: 368–69):

Diatu' kitai nyau besarara'	Now we are severed, separated
baka ira' tabu' tali	like strands of a once
	braided cord
Bekejang meh kitai baka	We are parted like logs once
batang tampung titi	joined to form a footbridge
Tang nuan amang enda'	But you must not neglect to
nganjungka kami ubat	send us charms that cause us
ngasuh kaya	to be rich
Ngasuh raja, ngasuh gerai,	That bring us wealth, health
ngasuh nyamai	and happiness
Kena' kami nampung nerujung	So that we who continue this
bilik penaik nuan ke di	bilik-family may prosper in
menua tu'	this land

With the *bungai* now severed, the *manang* leads a party of mourners to the river where they cast the severed branch and offerings into the flowing water. Returning to the longhouse, the *manang* recovers the souls from the *kembai bungai* and restores them to the members of the bereaved family. He then returns to the *pagar api* to sing the final stanzas of his narrative. In them, his soul accompanies the spirits of the dead as they return to Sebayan. This time, the path they take is quite different from the one taken by the *tukang sabak*. It is more direct and has none of the barriers that the deceased's soul had to overcome on its initial journey to Sebayan.

Recalling the spirits of the dead to the living world: The Gawai Antu

The Gawai Antu focuses on the deceased as *antu*, hence its name. Its purpose, bards say, is *diperantu* ('to confirm the status [of the dead] as *antu*'), thus making them fitting recipients of future prayers and offerings (see Umbat and Ensiring 2004: 5). In contrast to *rabat* and *beserara' bungai*, the Gawai Antu is a major community undertaking jointly sponsored by most, if not all, of the families making up the longhouse. It is also the most complex and costly. Performing it is an enormous economic investment, requiring years of planning and saving. Consequently, it is held at most once in a generation and is frequently deferred even longer. It is typically held only after a majority of families living in the longhouse have at least one deceased ancestor to be memorialised. By sponsoring it, a longhouse not only celebrates the achievements of its most recent generation of dead, but also demonstrates its own material success, thus advancing the status of its living members while, at the same time, validating that of their immediate ancestors.

The Gawai Antu is often described by Saribas elders as a work of 'house-building' (*berumah*). This is signified at the beginning of the Gawai by the collection and fashioning of building materials and, at its conclusion, by the use of these materials to erect a wooden tomb hut (*sungkup*) over the grave of each of the newly memorialised dead. These tomb huts are described as *rumah Sebayan*—that is, as forming an 'afterworld longhouse'. Together, their construction symbolises the reconstitution of the longhouse dead as an independent longhouse community in which the newly deceased are now fully integrated members as a result of having been provided with a *sungkup* and the various other grave goods supplied to them during the Gawai. During the first stage of the Gawai, men thus prepare the materials for constructing the *sungkup*, while women cut bamboo, which they split and peel into weaving materials.[24] During the next stage, the women, working inside the longhouse, weave these materials into special cylindrical baskets called *garung*, while men erect altars (*rugan*), which they attach to the main passageway pillars outside each family's apartment. From these pillars, family members hang items of remembrance that formerly belonged to the dead. Here, each evening and night during the Gawai, they set out food offerings in the *rugan* for the spirits of their family's dead.

After these preliminaries, the main Gawai opens at dawn with a ceremonial reception of guests, beginning with the specially invited men of prowess, who, taking the role of warriors, will drink one or the other of the two sacred rice wines served to them at the climax of the Gawai. Invited guests are called *pengabang*. The same term is also used to refer to the visiting spirits of the dead and gods of Sebayan who are invoked during the Gawai. In marked contrast to the informality that otherwise characterises longhouse life, the reception of visitors and the major ceremonial events that follow are carefully structured according to status, age and gender. As in all traditional Gawais, human hosts and guests assume the ceremonial roles of the spirit-heroes and gods, thus recreating in their seating and outward behaviour a numinous world of idealised precedence that characterises not only the realms of the gods and spirit-heroes, but also those of the dead (Sather 1996: 98–99). Accordingly, a major task of each family head is to *bedijir*, 'to line up' or 'array in order', the visitors he seats at his family's section of the gallery. At major ritual

---

24 This work is done in a special area outside and separate from the longhouse called the *taba'* (Sather 2003b: 228).

junctures before feasting, oratory or ritual processions, the *tuai gawai*, the elder chosen to be the principal festival leader, walks the length of the longhouse, notifying each family head to begin arranging his or her visitors in order of precedence. At other times, guests are free to move about and mingle informally with their kin and neighbours.

The welcoming of guests ends at sundown. After serving rice wine and an evening meal, the *tuai gawai* announces the beginning of the main ritual events. These open with processions by the guests around the longhouse gallery accompanied by welcoming music (*ngalu petara*) played for the gods and spirits of Sebayan whose presence the visiting guests enact. Next, the men of prowess, in ceremonial dress with drawn swords, dance along the gallery to 'clear' (*ngerandang*) and 'fence' (*ngelalau*) a pathway for the priest bards, who, once this is done, begin their invocation to recall the dead to the longhouse. From this point, the bards sing throughout the remainder of the night. As they sing, they move slowly forward in a continuously rotating motion, circumambulating, as they do, the entire longhouse gallery. Their movements are said to mimic those of the gods and spirits.[25] Starting first in the *tuai gawai*'s apartment, the priest bards begin to sing of the coming of the gods and spirits, led by the principal gods and goddesses of Sebayan, who travel as married pairs—first, Raja Niram and his wife, Ini' Inan, and then their daughter Dara Rambai Geruda and her husband, Bujang Langgah Lenggan.[26] They are followed by others and then by the spirits of the ancestors down through the most recent longhouse dead. The song relates that before the spirits of the dead take leave of Sebayan, they first pick charms to take for their Gawai hosts. These are described as fruits that hang from the branches of a miraculous palm tree called the *ranyai*.[27] Described by some (Heppell et al. 2005: 26) as the Iban 'Tree of Life', the *ranyai* in fact grows not in this world, but in Sebayan, where its fruits can only be collected by the dead. Left behind by the spirits of the dead at the conclusion of the Gawai, they again take the form of charms meant for the use of the living.

---

25 Note that during the Gawai Antu, the spirits of the dead actually begin their nightly visits to the longhouse before this formal invocation takes place.
26 The latter is said to have taught the ancestors how to perform the Gawai Antu.
27 There is, in fact, considerable ambiguity about the *ranyai* (see Sather 2003b: 189), as it is also represented by a variety of shrines constructed on different ritual occasions. In one of its forms, also represented as a palm tree growing in Sebayan, its 'fruits' are trophy heads that only the bravest of the dead are able to collect.

With the departure of the dead from Sebayan, the bards—still singing—now leave the *tuai gawai*'s apartment and enter the gallery. Here, as they move from one family's section to the next, they narrate the journey of the spirits as they travel through the cosmos to this world. As they sing, each bard carries a drinking bowl (*jalung*) in the palm of his right hand filled with rice wine. During this singing, the wine is said to change colour and acquire a magical potency so strong and lethal that only the brave may drink it. Shortly before dawn, as the invocation draws to a close, the dead arrive in the living world. In the words of the invocation, they are received with offerings, rice wine, cockfights and songs of praise. At this point, each bard, as he finishes singing, hands his bowl of *ai' jalung* to an elderly woman,[28] who sits facing one of the warriors assembled at the centre of the longhouse gallery. Here, she presents her cup, which the warrior receives and, after first clearing it with the tip of his sword, drinks down with a loud war cry.[29]

The next set of drinkers then destroys the *rugan* altars and throws them beneath the longhouse floor. For many, this is a poignant moment as it signals the impending departure of the dead. It is also a time of heightened danger. By inviting the dead directly into the public areas of the longhouse, the Gawai Antu temporarily dissolves the separation between the living and the dead that the singing of the *sabak* and the rite of *beserara' bungai* helped to create.[30] As a consequence, the potential for calamity is enormous. Thus, while the Gawai enjoins a massive amount of feasting and drinking, the greater part of this occurs within a highly regulated setting, with publicly announced rules and carefully scheduled events, each signalled beforehand by the *tuai gawai*. Danger is thus managed through an explicit display of order.

---

28 This woman, in presenting the bowl to the warrior, is said to be acting on behalf or playing the role of the principal goddesses of Sebayan, Ini' Inan and Dara Rambia Geruda.

29 The role of these drinkers clearly highlights the continuing significance of male prowess in Saribas society. During the 1970s and 1980s, most of those who were asked to perform the part of warriors were policemen or soldiers in the Malaysian Army. When I first began fieldwork in Sarawak, there was still an active communist insurgency in which a number of younger Iban men were then fighting. Others had seen military action in the 1960s during Konfrontasi or, earlier yet, as trackers with the British Army during the Malayan Emergency. To be eligible to drink these ritual wines, a man should have either received a dream command or taken a human life in combat (*bedengah*) (Sather 1993: 101).

30 Note that, during these earlier rituals, the spirits of the dead must remain at the foot of the longhouse entry ladder.

This display reaches its climax as contact with the dead intensifies, culminating with their arrival in the longhouse and the drinking of the sacred wines. After the first group of warriors has finished drinking the *ai' jalung*, and while the guests, both living and dead, are still present in the house, a final morning meal is served. For the living, this is characteristically a joyous feast, with heavy drinking. Typically, many who have had little sleep since the Gawai began now become intoxicated. The dramatic climax of the Gawai then follows: the drinking of the *ai' garung*. The hosts, each representing one of the families with dead to be memorialised, now form a series of processions to 'present the *garung*' (*nganjung garung*) to the most honoured group of warriors. The first is led by the *tuai gawai*, who carries his family's *garung* baskets, each containing a bamboo tube filled with rice wine. After a series of mock combats, the drinkers receive the wine and drink it down with a war cry. The *ai' garung* is believed to be even more poisonous (*bisa'*) than the *ai' jalung*. Some bards compare it to the *ai' limban* (or *beru'*), the fluids that flow from a decomposing corpse (Sather 2003b: 236). After drinking repeatedly, the warriors typically vomit.

As I have argued elsewhere (Sather 2012: 129–30), by drinking the sacred wines, these warriors 'consume' and so obliterate the last remaining traces of corpse-like materiality that still adhere to the dead. They thereby confirm their status, not only as *antu*, but also as potential *petara*, propelling them beyond the cycling of life and death to a future of immortality, as gods.

Life as a journey of achievement

As Fox asserts, in the indigenous religions of the Austronesian-speaking world, 'Creation' is characteristically seen as having 'produced myriad forms of being'—in short, 'a celebration of spiritual differentiation'—that typically express themselves in social terms in institutions of precedence and achievement (1987: 526). Thus, a common Austronesian image of this-worldly life is that of a metaphorical 'journey of achievement', in which '[l]iterally and spiritually, individuals are distinguished by their journeys. Rank, prowess, and the attainment of wealth can be taken as evident signs of individual enhancement in a life's odyssey' (Fox 1987: 526).

This enhancement is typically validated at death, when each person's life journey comes to an end, so that mortuary rituals and feasting not only give recognition to the position each individual attains in life, but also translate 'this position into a similarly enhanced position in the afterlife' (Fox 1987: 526).

The Gawai Antu is very much a celebration of social and spiritual differentiation. A basic ideological premise of Saribas Iban society is that all individuals are essentially alike at birth (see Sather 1996). At the same time, however, Saribas society is also intensely competitive. Personal accomplishment is highly valued and is judged to be a sign of both individual merit and spiritual favour. The outcome of competition is differentiation—a process likened by the Iban to the art of weaving (Sather 1996: 74). Just as each cotton thread begins this process alike, in the end, after dyeing and weaving, it assumes a distinctive colour and place in a finished fabric. While some persons die at birth, or prematurely, before they have had a chance to gain social recognition, or suffer ill-fated deaths and so achieve no enduring place as ancestors, for the great majority, the Gawai Antu constitutes the principal occasion on which differences of achievement are publicly displayed and celebrated. Earlier, during *rabat*, the deceased's life history was recounted, his journey of achievement assessed and, on this basis, the amount of his *adat pemati* was fixed (Sather 1996: 100; Umbat and Ensiring 2004: 11). This amount is remembered and, during the Gawai Antu, determines the type of *garung* basket that is woven for him.

One basket is woven for each person who was old enough at the time of death to have been given a personal name (*orang ke benama*). Infants who die before being named receive only woven 'playthings' (*ayam*). In the Paku and Rimbas areas, seven different *garung* designs were recognised in the 1970s and 1980s, including one (called *gelayan*) to which everyone who bore a name—male, female, married or unmarried—was entitled. The other six denoted ascending levels of attainment. In the past, the highest-status designs were reserved for male war leaders, warriors and regional chiefs and, in the case of women, especially accomplished weavers. The special importance of each *garung* basket is that its design directly expresses the deceased's achieved status. Thus, the Iban say, it is a 'sign' (*tanda*) of the deceased in regard to his or her social and spiritual standing.

As signs, the *garung* baskets, together with grave furnishings and the display of personal objects formerly belonging to the dead (today often including photographs), make it possible for those who participate in the Gawai to remember the now absent dead and so, briefly, to 'relive' their presence in this world. The provision of *garung* baskets and tomb huts is described as a means of 'remembering' (*ngingat*). In the course of being provisioned, the ancestral dead are feasted and invited into the public areas of the longhouse to mingle with the living. In this way, experiential distance is obviated and the living are made to feel that the dead are present among them, not anonymously, but intimately, as individual visitors. Among the dead, it is the most recent cohort, whose former presence is still freshest in the memories of their hosts, who are especially honoured and whose presence is the main object of the ritual. By the time the sponsoring community holds another Gawai Antu, its present hosts will have traded places with those who were children before, becoming the next generation of ancestral dead, dependent now upon a succeeding generation 'to remember' and so to assure them a place among the ancestral dead appropriate to their accomplishments in this life. By being remembered, the dead are at the same time empowered, emerging in the process as benevolent beings—*antu* and future *petara*—capable for as long as they are remembered 'of returning benefits to the living' (Fox 1987: 526).

After the conclusion of the Gawai Antu, the *garung* baskets are carried to the cemetery where they are hung inside the tomb huts together with offerings and other objects meant for the use of the dead, including miniature farm baskets. The spirits of the dead are said to take these *garung* back with them to Sebayan, where they serve as signs of status. The ancestors, in departing, thus take the status they achieved in this world with them to the afterworld. In so doing, they leave their living descendants still journeying in this world free to embark upon status-enhancing journeys of their own devising (Sather 1996: 100–01). Death thus returns each new generation of descendants to a state of relative equality, while at the same time, it installs precedent and hierarchy as the organising principles of life in Sebayan. Finally, the construction of tomb huts reconstitutes the ancestral dead as a newly refurbished longhouse community, spatially differentiated and sufficiently independent of the living for its members to be safely invited to future Gawais as ritual visitors from beyond the human world.

Death as a source of differentiation

While each person's life journey is seen as a potential source of social and spiritual differentiation, so, too, is death. The transition from life to death is thus perceived as having a variety of possible outcomes. For the majority, it results in the transit of their souls to Sebayan. But there are many exceptions. At death, shamans, for example, are buried with their heads oriented upriver (*ke ulu*), rather than downriver (*ke ili'*)—the orientation of ordinary laypersons. This is because their souls, at death, are believed to travel not downriver to the Mandai River of the Dead, but upriver to a separate afterworld of their own located at the summit of Mount Rabung.[31] From this abode, the spirits of deceased shamans continue to play an active role in this world, but one specifically associated with shamanism. During curing performances, living *manang* invite them to join them as spirit companions on their journeys into the unseen world. Some shamans also engage them as their individual spirit-helpers (*yang*).[32] Although Iban shamanism is not, strictly speaking, an inherited calling, it tends to pass down along family lines, as does the transmission of healing charms, medicine boxes and the other ritual paraphernalia. Thus, most shamans maintain close ties to the spirits of their shamanic ancestors. In addition, the summit of Mount Rabung, where these spirits reside after death, is directly accessible to the upper-world home of the shamanic gods, Menjaya and his sister, Ini' Inda. Consequently, they are regularly called upon to accompany Menjaya and his sister whenever they are summoned to this world as ritual visitors. In addition, they are also responsible for tending the gardens where the *bungai* grow, which some shamans say are located on the slope of Mount Rabung (Sather 2001: 29–32; 2012: 123–24).

---

31   Like the Mandai River of the Dead, Mount Rabung is believed to have a visible counterpart in this world. Its identity, however, is less certain. Bukit Rabung is not visible from the Rimbas and Ulu Paku where I did my fieldwork but can be readily seen from higher elevations along the Sarawak–West Kalimantan border. It is easily identifiable by its distinctive profile, which resembles that of a gong, with a high rounded protuberance forming its summit (Sather 2001: 117). From its profile and the direction in which it appears, Mount Rabong would seem to be the same mountain that people in the upper Kapuas call Gunung Tilung, Tevilung or Tebilung, and which a number of other Dayak groups, like the Taman, regard as the abode of the dead (Bernard Sellato, Personal communication). According to Sellato, this mountain is identified on maps of West Kalimantan as Gunung Liang Sunan and is on the left bank of the Mandai River. In Iban, *rabung* means, literally, 'apex', 'summation', 'zenith' or 'highest point' (Sather 2001: 116). In Saribas chants, Bukit Rabung is described as being immediately beneath the 'zenith of the sky' (*perabung langit*).

32   *Yang* refers specifically to the spirit-helpers of ritual specialists—notably, shamans and priest bards. By contrast, *tua'* are personal guardian-spirits who assist those they take under their care by safeguarding their lives and aiding them in their quest for material wealth and renown.

At death, the spirits of women who die in childbirth often become malevolent spirits known as *antu kuklir* and so remain for a brief time in this world to take revenge upon the living (Sather 1978). Others metamorphose at death directly into spirits, often malevolent ones such as *antu gerasi* (demon huntsmen), mythic beings such as *nabau* water serpents or animal spirits, usually dangerous ones like crocodiles or tigers. In the past, those who metamorphosed in this way were usually men of prowess, often war leaders or ritual specialists who engaged animal and demonic spirits as their spirit-helpers (Sather 2012: 39–40; Uchibori 2019: 229–30).

By contrast, the spirits of those who were especially successful in life often pay periodic visits to this world to protect their descendants or offer them assistance. In so doing, they sometimes assume the role of a personal guardian-spirit or *tua'* (Béguet 2012; Sather 2012: 137–40). In entering the visible world, *tua'* are typically 'concealed' (*ngarung*) in the visible form of animals. For this reason, guardian-spirits, in addition to *tua'*, are also known as *antu ngarung* (literally, 'concealed spirits'). In Saribas, the spirits of dead ancestors who return to this world as *tua'* most often 'conceal' themselves as snakes, typically pythons (*sawa*) or, less often, cobras (*tedung*). Charles Hose, writing more than a century ago, referred to the animals in whose form the *antu ngarung* appear as 'totems', in that the animal spirit's protection frequently extended to a whole family or, over time, to a line of family descendants whose members, in return for the spirit's protection, refrained from killing, eating or injuring it (Hose and McDougall 1966: Vol. II, pp. 90–96). As Hose noted, however, not all *antu ngarung* are ancestors or even deceased humans.

Finally, there existed in the past an alternative form of ritual practice that was reserved for individuals of exceptional renown. Called *ngelumbung* ('entombment'), the corpse of the deceased was not buried in the earth, but instead was placed in a coffin (*rarung*), which was then set on a raised platform above ground and covered with a roof resembling a *sungkup* (Sather 2003b: 238–39; Uchibori 1978: 263–89, 1984). This whole structure was called a *lumbung* (or 'tomb'). Fluids were drained from the coffin and, after the fleshy parts of the corpse had decomposed, the bones were removed, cleaned, bundled together and placed inside a permanent container, either a jar or a hardwood coffin. In Saribas, almost all entombments occurred during the first generations of pioneer settlement, some 14–16 generations ago.[33] Unlike the spirits of the ordinary dead, those who are entombed are believed to remain in this world. In this regard, their fate was modelled on that of the spirit-heroes and heroines (*Orang Panggau*). Thus, the purpose of entombment, for the most potent of the dead, was to bring about their immediate apotheosis. Rather than dispatching them, like the ordinary dead, on a journey to Sebayan, it instead served to retain their presence in the living world as powerful immortals—invisible, yet accessible to their descendants (Uchibori 1984: 30).

Conclusion

For the Iban, life and death are seen as interconnected journeys that unfold in different cosmic realms. Bridging these realms and connecting the living and the dead are additional journeys, including the ritually enacted journeys of the soul-guides, shamans and priest bards that make up, as we have seen, the principal events of the Saribas Iban funerary cycle.

The journey of life, or *jalai idup*, begins at birth and concludes at death. The self that undertakes this journey is an embodied self, which thereby differs from the disembodied postmortal self that undertakes the journey of death. Within the visible this-worldly realm in which this first journey occurs, it is the body, animated by the *semengat*, that is the conscious agent that initiates and executes a living person's actions (Sather 2018: 57–63). At death, the soul disengages from the body and journeys to Sebayan, where it is said to live on, merging in the minds of many with the *antu Sebayan*, which, after death, takes its place as the source of the deceased's continuing agency.

While still embodied, each person's life journey is seen as an arena of achievement. At death, an accounting is made of each individual's accomplishments and on this basis the amount is set of his or her *adat pemati*. This amount in turn determines the type of *garung* basket that is woven for the deceased during the Gawai Antu. At the conclusion of the Gawai, this basket is taken by the deceased's spirit, as it returns from this world to Sebayan, where, now fully incorporated into the society of the dead, it determines the deceased's status in the afterworld.

---

33   Uchibori, writing of the Skrang and Layar Iban in the mid-1970s, describes a number of more recent entombments (1984: 23–28). See also Sather (2012: 141).

Death, coming between these two main journeys, represents both a transition and a source of potential transformation. With the departure of the soul, a new component of the self emerges, the *antu Sebayan*. Appearing initially as a spectre, the deceased's spirit, like his or her soul, journeys to Sebayan, where it gradually sheds its menacing form and becomes a generally benevolent spirit—that is, an *antu Sebayan*. There are exceptions, however. Death, like life, gives rise to a variety of new forms of being. Among them are the spirits of deceased shamans, who journey at death to a raised afterworld on the summit of Mount Rabung, where, as the spirit-companions of the living shamans, they assist the latter in their healing work. Others may metamorphose directly into nonhuman demonic or animal spirits or become beneficent guardian-spirits or *tua'*, while the most potent of the dead may be entombed and so, by avoiding burial, remain, like the Iban spirit heroes and heroines, active spirit agents in the living world. For the majority of the dead, usually within a generation of having settled in Sebayan, they are recalled by their living descendants to this world to complete their transformation. Here, reconstituted as a separate community, their status is confirmed not only as spirits, but also as potential future gods, capable of assisting the living as ritual visitors from beyond the human world.

Finally, the representation of these two journeys as journeys of regeneration rests upon an association of the temporal cycling of human life with that of plants.[34] The most explicit expression of this association is with the 'plant-image' or *bungai*. As a component of the embodied self, the *bungai* directly mirrors, in the form of a living plant, the health and mortality of the embodied self of which it is an image. The conditions of its birth, growth and even its reproduction and death precisely replicate those of its human counterpart. At the same time, the *bungai* is also an image of regeneration and social renewal. By severing and removing the dead *bungai* during *beserara' bungai*, the shaman makes room on the parent rootstock for the appearance of new *bungai*. Thus, his action promotes continuity and reflects the capacity of the *bungai* to renew itself. At the same time, the *bungai* also symbolises the social dimensions of embodied selfhood. Individual *bungai* grow in family clumps in gardens representing

---

34   For a more general discussion of the use of 'botanic icons' in the Austronesian-speaking world as metaphors for human lifecycle processes, see Fox (1996).

'longhouses of the souls'. Here, the rootstock (*pugu' bungai*) symbolises the capacity of these groups to replenish themselves and so persist beyond the lifetimes of their individual members.

A second way in which this analogy is represented is through an exchange of seeds and plant cuttings between the living and the dead, as each, through the husbandry of these planting materials, maintains a parallel, but separate productive system. Thus, during *beserara' bungai*, members of the bereaved family share with the spirits of the deceased their productive assets, including their food crops and stock of seeds and plant cuttings. In this way, the living provide the dead with the necessary resources to join them in promoting a parallel cycling of life through both the food crops they each cultivate and the successive generations of human cultivators, both living and dead, who subsist upon these crops.

Finally, at the end of the second and final of these journeys, the souls of the dead or, more accurately, the final material residue of these souls, are transformed into a watery mist that returns to this world, where it condenses and falls to earth. Here, in this form, it nourishes and is absorbed into each family's rice crop. Rice, in turn, as the staple food of the Iban, nourishes the families who cultivate it. And so, in this way, the final transformation of the souls becomes the ultimate metaphor of regeneration. Through rice, life-engendering potency is returned from one generation to the next and from Sebayan back to this world, thereby completing the ontological cycle of human life and death.

References

Béguet, Véronique. 2012. 'Iban *petara* as transformed ancestors.' In Pascal Couderc and Kenneth Sillander, eds, *Ancestors in Borneo Societies: Death, transformation, and social immortality*, pp. 243–77. Copenhagen: NIAS Press.

Blust, Robert. 2013. *The Austronesian Languages*. Rev. edn. Canberra: ANU Asia-Pacific Linguistics.

Department of Statistics Malaysia. 2012. *Population Distribution and Basic Demographic Characteristics Report 2010*. Kuala Lumpur: Department of Statistics Malaysia.

Ensiring, Janang, Joanne Veydt Sutlive, Robert Menua Saleh and Vinson H. Sutlive, eds. 2016. *A Comprehensive Iban–English Dictionary*. Kuching: The Dayak Cultural Foundation in cooperation with The Tun Jugah Foundation.

Firth, Raymond. 1967. 'The fate of the soul.' In Raymond Firth, *Tikopia Ritual and Belief*, pp. 330–53. Boston: Beacon Press.

Fox, James J. 1987. 'Southeast Asian religions: Insular cultures.' In Mircea Eliade, ed., *The Encyclopedia of Religion. Volume 13*, pp. 520–30. New York: Macmillan.

Fox, James J. 1996. 'The Austronesian botanic idiom.' In Tony Whitten and Jane Whitten, eds, *Plants: Indonesian Heritage. Volume 4*, pp. 66–67. Singapore: Archipelago Press.

Fox, James J. 2003. 'Admonitions of the ancestors: Giving voice to the deceased in Rotinese mortuary rituals.' In Peter J.M. Nas, Gerard A. Persoon and Rivke Jaffe, eds, *Framing Indonesian Realities: Essays in symbolic anthropology in honour of Reimar Schefold*, pp. 15–25. Leiden: KITLV Press.

Graham, Penelope. 1991. 'To follow the blood: The path of life in a domain of eastern Flores, Indonesia.' PhD dissertation, The Australian National University, Canberra.

Heppell, Michael, Limbang anak Melaka and Enyan anak Usen. 2005. *Iban Art: Sexual selection and severed heads*. Leiden: KIT Publishers.

Hertz, Robert. 1960. 'A contribution to the study of the collective representation of death.' In Robert Hertz, *Death and the Right Hand*, Rodney and Claudia Needham, trans, pp. 27–86. London: Cohen & West.

Hose, Charles and William McDougall. 1966 [1912]. *The Pagan Tribes of Borneo*. 2 vols. London: Frank Cass & Company.

Sather, Clifford. 1978. 'The malevolent *koklir*: Iban concepts of sexual peril and the dangers of childbirth.' *Bijdragen tot de Taal-, Land, -en Volkenkunde* 134: 310–55. doi.org/10.1163/22134379-90002590.

Sather, Clifford. 1993. 'Posts, hearths and thresholds: The Iban longhouse as a ritual structure.' In James J. Fox, ed., *Inside Austronesian Houses: Perspectives on domestic designs for living*, pp. 65–115. Canberra: Department of Anthropology, Research School of Pacific Studies, The Australian National University.

Sather, Clifford. 1996. '"All threads are white": Iban egalitarianism reconsidered.' In James J. Fox and Clifford Sather, eds, *Origins, Ancestry and Alliance*, pp. 70–110. Canberra: Department of Anthropology, Research School of Pacific and Asian Studies, The Australian National University.

Sather, Clifford. 2001. *Seeds of Play, Words of Power: An ethnographic study of Iban shamanic chants*. Kuching: Tun Jugah Foundation and the Borneo Research Council.

Sather, Clifford. 2003a. 'The shaman as preserver and undoer of life: The role of the shaman in Saribas Iban death rituals.' In Mihály Hoppál and Gábor Kósa, eds, *Rediscovery of Shamanic Heritage*, pp. 153–77. Budapest: Akadémiai Kiadó.

Sather, Clifford. 2003b. 'Transformations of self and community in Saribas Iban death rituals.' In William D. Wilder, ed., *Journeys of the Soul: Anthropological studies of death, burial and reburial practices in Borneo*, pp. 175–247. Phillips, ME: Borneo Research Council Monograph Series 7.

Sather, Clifford. 2004. 'The Iban.' In Ooi Keat Gin, ed., *Southeast Asia: A historical encyclopedia. Volume 2*, pp. 623–25. Santa Barbara, CA: ABC Clio Press.

Sather, Clifford. 2012. 'Recalling the dead, revering the ancestors: Multiple forms of ancestorship in Saribas Iban society.' In Pascal Couderc and Kenneth Sillander, eds, *Ancestors in Borneo Societies: Death, transformation, and social immortality*, pp. 114–52. Copenhagen: NIAS Press.

Sather, Clifford. 2018. 'A work of love: Awareness and expressions of emotion in a Borneo healing ritual.' In James J. Fox, ed., *Expressions of Austronesian Thought and Emotions*, pp. 47–79. Canberra: ANU Press. doi.org/10.22459/EATE.04.2018.03.

Sutlive, Vinson H. 2012. *Tears of Sorrow, Words of Hope: An ethnographic study of Iban death chants*. 2 vols. Kuching: Tun Jugah Foundation and the Borneo Research Council.

Uchibori, Motomitsu. 1978. 'The leaving of this transient world: A study in Iban eschatology and mortuary practices.' PhD dissertation, Research School of Pacific Studies, The Australian National University, Canberra.

Uchibori, Motomitsu. 1984. 'The enshrinement of the dead among the Iban.' *Sarawak Museum Journal* 33: 15–32.

Uchibori, Motomitsu. 2019. 'Spirits as the others: From the Iban ethnography.' In Kawai Kaori, ed., *Others: The evolution of human sociality*, pp. 325–45. Kyoto and Melbourne: Kyoto University Press and Trans Pacific Press.

Umbat, Jantan and Janang anak Ensiring. 2004. *Ripih Pengawa' Gawai Antu* [*Stages of the Gawai Antu*]. [In Iban]. Kuching: The Tun Jugah Foundation.

Wadley, Reed L. 1999. 'Disrespecting the dead and the living: Iban Ancestor Worship and the violation of mourning taboos.' *Journal of the Royal Anthropological Institute* 5(4): 595–610. doi.org/10.2307/2661150.

7

The long journey of the rice maiden from Li'o to Tanjung Bunga: A Lamaholot sung narrative (Flores, eastern Indonesia)

Dana Rappoport

Introduction

The 'long songs'[1] I have been working on in Indonesia, in both the Toraja and the Lamaholot regions, have a basic similarity: they tell the story of journeys. In the Toraja region (Sulawesi), they were called *ossoran*, from the verb *mangosso'* ('to tell in an ordered way, according to a succession'). They described the origin of something—an object (iron, a cordyline leaf), a human, a spirit (the *bugi'*)—and recounted its progress from a distant place (the sky or elsewhere) to the site of narration in the human world. These were not genealogies, because there was no question of a succession of filiation. They were about journeys or peregrinations in space. These stories, in octosyllabic lines, performed through songs and dances during many days, bringing the whole community together, were banned by the

---

1   I use the expression 'long songs' to refer to sung narratives from 500 to 1,000 lines long at least. Some may extend to more than 10,000 lines and require six days and six nights of singing (cf. Toraja: *Gelong maro*).

Christian authorities in the middle of the twentieth century. They have now fallen into oblivion except for the few that have been transcribed (van der Veen 1965, 1966; Rappoport 2009).

In the Lamaholot-speaking region (eastern Flores), the long songs also tell the stories of beings (humans or spirits) moving from one place to another. Several men can still sing and explain them. Unlike the situation in the Toraja region, among some of the Lamaholot, these long songs have not been eradicated, although they are now threatened due to literacy and lifestyle changes.

It would be interesting to extend the comparison to other populations of Insulindia (island Southeast Asia). From the route of the Bunaq ancestors (Berthe 1972) to the initiatory journeys of the heroes of Palawan epics (Revel 2000), it is likely that most of the long songs in Insulindia are based on the storytelling of paths and journeys. And more broadly, we may underline that even the famous long stories of Indo-European literature also have as their narrative springboard the quests taking place in space. Think of *The Odyssey*, *Don Quixote* and the story of the Holy Grail, to name a few, even though these stories were not sung. All of them raise the same basic interpretative questions. We want to understand the reason for the journeys and the geographical extent of the travel, with points of origin and points of arrival. What brings the journey to an end? Is it the final goal that is important or the journey itself? What do these trips teach those who tell them? Why is the content of these narratives so important for the societies that maintain them? What are the performance rules of their telling?

To address some of these questions, I look at a Lamaholot long song that I recorded in 2006 on the Tanjung Bunga peninsula, at the eastern tip of Flores, in the *desa* of Ratulodong (or Waiklibang).[2] The conditions for recording this narrative were surprising. I was called in November 2006 to attend the Dokan Gurun ritual, which means literally 'to wrap, to protect'. The ritual began in the village's 'big house' (*lango bélen*). On the altar, stained with goat's blood, sat three main clan leaders next to a young woman around 20 years old. I would understand much later

2   My thanks go to the singers of the villages of Waiklibang and Waibao who have shared with me, since 2006, part of their ritual life, part of their knowledge and part of their time. I also want to warmly thank my faithful friend Philip Yampolsky, who edited the English version of this article, and James Fox for his long-inspiring reflections and his invitation to write in this volume. This research is part of various fieldwork done since 2006 with the permission of the Indonesian Government.

that she embodied the figure of the rice seed to be wrapped in the granary (inside the 'big house' in this village). Everyone went to the yard in front of the house around 11.30 pm and began to sing and dance the 'long song', which lasted until early morning. I was able to record the whole session, without any battery failure. The singers danced around the ceremonial *nuba nara* stones (considered the seat of the rice maiden) in a counterclockwise direction. Some songs were performed by men, others by women, but from song to song, piece by piece, the entire narrative was told. At daybreak, during the last song, all the women who were singing, including the young woman I had seen the previous day, were wrapped in single file by the ritual leader (a single wrapping enveloped all of the women) in a very old Indian cloth (*ketipa réda*), and were then led into the house where the rice granary was located. The young woman was therefore the embodiment of the rice seed that was to be wrapped and placed in the storehouse before sowing.

In this chapter, I analyse the content of the song that was performed that night—the story of the origin of rice—together with its oral performance. This Lamaholot narrative has already been the subject of a few studies (Tukan 1996; Kohl 1998). As it can be told in different forms, in its entire ritual sung version or in summary narrative versions without song, the story can vary in length and the steps and the end of the journey vary widely from village to village even though the place of departure is the same (Li'o).[3]

Variation is one of the common features of the oral tradition. In the eastern Insulindian region, aesthetic variability seems to be at its height, in terms of both style and content. On the Tanjung Bunga peninsula alone, more than six musical styles are counted. Add to this the intense dialectal variability. It is therefore not surprising that versions of the same story are different in realisation yet similar in outline. This inexhaustible variability—already noted a long time ago—is one of the great attractions of this region (Adams 1971). The version collected in its summarised form (and not sung) by Karl-Heinz Kohl (1998) in the neighbouring village of Waiklibang (20 kilometres away) is very different from the full sung version I recorded (I will not detail the similarities and differences here).

---

3   Li'o (also written Lio) is in central Flores, west of Sikka, around Paga and Dondo. It is both the name of a region and the name of a linguistic group of around 100,000 speakers, according to the census of 2009 (Eberhard et al. 2020), and is considered a dialect chain with Ende (Grimes et al. 1997: 85).

Similarly, if singers of the village where I work are asked to summarise the story, they will not give all the elements of the myth, and their versions will vary even from one singer to another. Often, they add elements that are not sung in the versified story, which is why I must constantly go back and forth between the lines sung that night and the summaries made by the people, together with the observation of rituals and people's feelings towards rice.

First, I will look at the topic of the journey inside the song of the origin of rice itself. Then I will describe the performative aspects of this song. Finally, I will consider the time of this long journey and the way it is expressed in the song.

Paths and journeys in the song of the origin of rice

Road songs in Lamaholot culture

Road songs are a useful ethnomusicological category, for at least two reasons: on the one hand, because in the Lamaholot area, songs performed while walking are common, and on the other, because songs that narrate paths and journeys, performed while dancing, are also prevalent. These two types of road songs differ in their duration (the former can be termed 'short songs', while the second corresponds to 'long songs'), but they are related because they are part of the same ritual: the first, called 'road song' (*berasi pana laran*), is performed before the second, which is sometimes called 'narrative of the road [of someone]' (*opak moran laran*).

At Waiklibang, great rituals (involving more than one clan) begin with road songs, sung literally on the road. On their way to the ritual, men sing two-by-two as they walk along the road towards the place of the ritual (whether to the 'big house' or to the ceremonial rice field).[4] This song is a male vocal duet (a pair of singers), a tight and technically difficult counterpoint, which is on the verge of extinction because of its required virtuosity and the decline of all traditional vocal forms. The rhythm is unmeasured. The men's high and sharp voices overlap at close intervals

---

4   Each sovereign clan is in charge, alternately, of a ceremonial rice field each year in which animal offerings, songs and dances will take place.

(smaller than a tempered major or minor second).[5] The singers make their voices echo from the mountain. Why do they sing while walking? First, to notify those who have already arrived at the dance square. The host clan hears its guests from afar and prepares for their arrival.[6] But this repertoire is not only an announcement, it is also, above all, a request for permission to pass in front of the dwelling places of *nitun*, the spirits who live in the tall trees and in certain features of the landscape. The song tells about the places passed by the singers. The words differ according to the calendar. Here is an example of lines sung while walking:

Duli pi'in osé Munak Ina	This site here is called Mother Monkey
pali Pao Laka Dodo	site Mango Laka Dodo
Duli pi'in déo dase	This site is almost reached
ni pi'in di no'on naran	this site with a name
Lei ka'an lali pana laran	My legs walk on the path of the setting sun
lei lali pana laran	legs walk on the way to the setting sun
Pana kala hiko waén'	Walking, crossing what's in front
gawé' liwa lolon	passing through the summit
Duli be'ena' tana	This site a landslide land
pali balébo-lébo rié	site of water-inundated poles
Luat buno ha'é	If we maybe go down
pana ka'an tiro léwo	walking to the village

Source: *Berasi Pana Laran* song, Waiklibang, 2006.[7]

Once the request for permission to pass has been issued, the singers continue on their way. No manifestation of permission is expected from the singing, except ease of travel on the road, which is a positive sign of protection. The lyrics of this kind of song are made up of toponyms and

---

5   Thirteen examples of this kind of song can be listened to at: archives.crem-cnrs.fr/archives/items/CNRSMH_I_2007_006_001_208/.
6   A singer explained to me: 'In the past, when there were rituals like this, when we went to the place of the ritual, we had to sing the *berasi pana laran*, so people would say, "Hey, they're already there, here they are." From a distance, they prepared the betel. We would sing to the door of the house. In the song itself, we said: "Prepare the areca nut."'
7   '(Flores Waiklibang) Men's Duo "Chant De Route" 1', Sound Archives, available at: archives.crem-cnrs.fr/archives/items/CNRSMH_I_2007_006_001_208/.

places (*duli pali*) with metalinguistic expressions of a performative type describing the singers walking on the path. When the singers arrive at the performing place, they will, at night, begin the second type of 'road song', not by walking anymore but by dancing until dawn.

The second type of road song consists of long sung narratives, called *opak bélun* ('singing narrative') or *opak lian naman* ('singing narrative with songs on the dancing place', as they are most often danced in village dance squares).[8] Their content varies according to each village and each ritual. In Waiklibang, these 'long songs' tell of journeys, linked to the origins of rice, sovereign clans or, less often now, sharp weapons (when villages went on raids). Their importance in the Lamaholot region may be related to the way this area was populated, through waves of migration from the west (Sina Jawa), from the east (Keroko Pukén) or, more rarely in Tanjung Bunga, from the north (Seram Goram).[9] In consequence, in a village, the various clans come from different points of origin, but on the ritual communal house, one origin is indicated through the position of the head of the crocodile on the top of the house. The crocodile points to the place of origin of the main sovereign clan (*tana alat*).

This *opak lian naman* repertoire is distinguished by the length of its narratives, the length of the performances and the intense participation of people during these long night vigils that bring together all the clans of a ceremonial domain (*lewo tana*: 'village land'). A 2,000-line song in hexasyllabic distichs is performed until dawn; there are no narrative stops in the middle of the night and the song must end when the day is up. All these narratives—for rice, clans or war—recall journeys (of the rice maiden, of ancestors, of spirits). The memory of the routes is fixed by the recitation of sequences related to migration, referring to placenames enunciated in a fixed order—places that can be written on a map (Map 7.1).

---

8   They are also called *opak hodé' ana'* ('sung narrative with duets') or *mura lian* ('lively songs'). *Opak* ('storyteller'); *Bélun*, always paired with *opak*, means 'to sing' (Pampus 2001). *Hodé' ana'* ('to receive the child') is the name of the two duets in the form of an interlude within the narrative. *Lian* means 'songs, singing'.

9   These three names are constantly told by the various clans, coming from one or the other places, which designate mythical origins. These are the names of mythical places, always cited by the various clans as their place of origin.

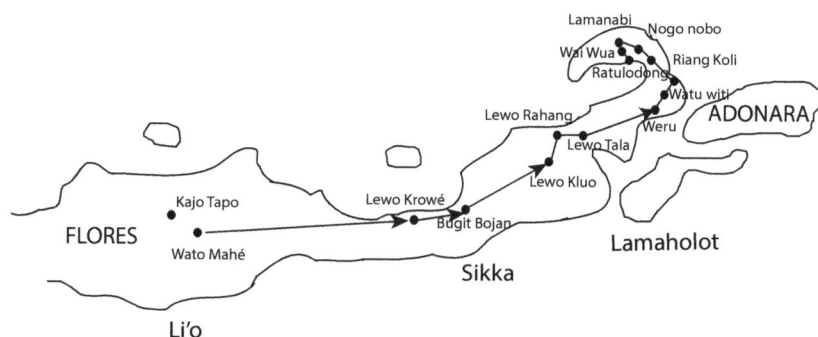

Map 7.1 The journey of Nogo Ema' according to the sung narrative (Waiklibang, 2006)
Source: Dana Rappoport.

The various paths in the song of the origin of rice

Sometimes referred to as 'the narrative of Tonu Wujo's road' (*Opak moran laran Tonu Wujo*), after one of the names of the maiden who will turn into rice, this song of the origin of seeds develops a myth widespread throughout island Southeast Asia in many variations (Mabuchi 1964): the killing of a human (child, woman or man) who will turn into edible plants. While the motif of the personification of the seed is found from Southeast Asia to Oceania, it is in eastern Insulindia that it seems to be most widely developed. Not only is it danced and sung, it is also sometimes enacted by humans, who personify the seed. Among some Lamaholot of eastern Flores, a maiden is chosen each year to perform the role of the victim, who, in the story, will be transformed into rice and maize (the young woman I saw at the altar); her presence is not only real during the ritual but also materialised each year by artefacts that, for the most part, will last only a year (a stake and a stone altar, representing the place where she will be killed in the rice field; fabrics and objects representing her comb and hair oil).[10]

---

10 In its agrarian function, *méran bélédan* refers to the sacrificial altar on which the maiden, who will embody herself in rice, sits before being sacrificed. This altar is made of a stone (*méran*), depicting the young woman's seat, and a stake (*belegat*), depicting the backrest, topped with a coconut with which to wash the young woman's hair and covered by a shelter constructed in the rice field (*mau Tonu Wujo*) (Rappoport 2017).

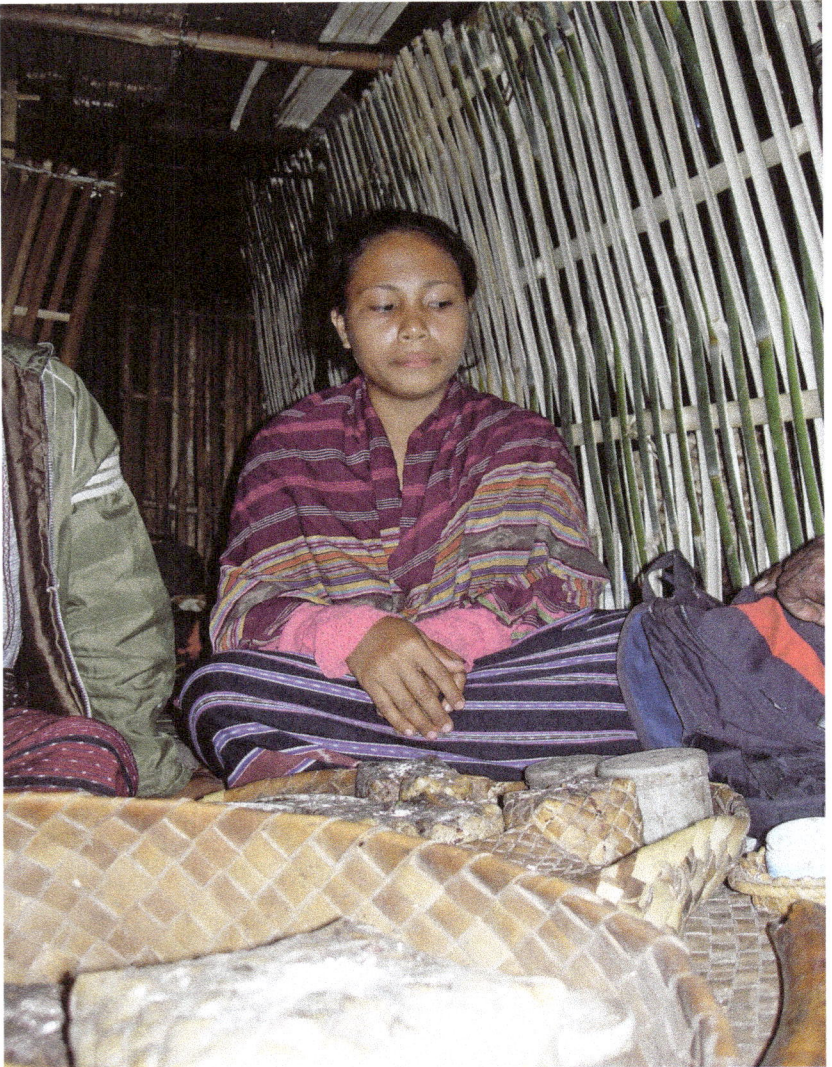

Plate 7.1 A rice maiden, *dokan gurun* ritual, Waiklibang, 2006
Photo: Dana Rappoport.

Plate 7.2 A rice maiden, *helo nikat* ritual, Waiklibang, 2007
Photo: Dana Rappoport.

Plate 7.3 Ema' Klara Kesi Liwun, the *opak* narrator, performing the song of the origin of rice, 2006

Photo: Dana Rappoport.

This song of the rice origin is organised around an essential issue: the survival of a society threatened with famine. In the past, humans—ignorant of agriculture—were hungry; they ate beans, ingested their own excrement and drank their own urine. To ensure the survival of the group, a maiden known as Nogo Ema' (or Tonu Wujo) ordered her seven brothers to find machetes, cut down and burn all the trees in the field and then kill her. Stabbed to death by her youngest brother, her body metamorphosed eight days later into rice and other edible plants. From the harvests of this field, the brothers filled seven granaries; with the sale of this rice, they bought elephant tusks (to get married). So, a woman 'paid' for seven brothers so that they could take wives. But these seven brothers no longer got along and fought, which is why Nogo Ema' left to be shared in all the villages.[11] This is the crux of this sung story.

The sung narrative that I recorded during the night of the Dokan Gurun ritual is called *Opak bélun gurun gawak bé'ola tugu* ('The narrative of the wrapping up of the results of working in the fields'). It comprises

---

11   Although the body of Nogo Ema' is dead, she keeps living in another form.

more than 2,200 lines (hexasyllabic and octosyllabic) arranged in four parts:[12] 1) The life of Nogo Ema's male ancestor, with a quest for a child (Pati Sogén) and the quest for his future wife in the Li'o region (lines 1–500); 2) the family of Nogo Ema' with her seven brothers and the invention of agriculture by Nogo Ema' (lines 501–1,270); 3) the killing of Nogo Ema' and transformation of her body into a plant (lines 1,271–437); and 4) Nogo Ema's journey and her unfortunate adventures (lines 1,438–2,268) and her arrival at the place of enunciation of the story (from 1,982 to the end). While the first half of the story is devoted to the ancestors of Nogo Ema' and unfolds over more than 1,000 verses, the dramatic knot about the killing and transformation of the maiden into a plant appears only halfway through (sung in 100 verses), after which the journey to and arrival at the village of enunciation take place over 800 verses.

It should be noted that, throughout the song, this maiden bears several names. She is most often called Nogo Ema' or Tonu Wujo, and more rarely Bési Paré Nogo Gunun, Nogo Gunun Ema' Hingi or Biné' Bési Ana' Paré[13] (shortened to Bési Paré when she metamorphoses into edible plants, in line 1,404 and after).[14] *Biné' ana'* is also a kinship term used to name her. Until the end of the song, she appears mainly under the two names Nogo Ema' and Tonu Wujo. This striking multitude of names can be explained by the constant metamorphoses of this young woman, whose status varies with her roles as a child (*ana'*), a girl (Nogo or Tonu),[15] a sister (*biné'*), a woman (*ema'*), a plant (Bési Paré) or a spirit (Tonu Wujo, Nogo Ema').

I will consider now two sequences of the narrative that unfold two paths: a downward path and an eastward path.

The downward path to the ancestors

The first part of Nogo Ema's narrative (lines 1–500) concerns the period of cultural foundation, when humans were still only 'earth spirits' (*nitun*). This period, evoked by the naming of places and of Nogo Ema's ancestors

---

12   This narrative has been written down by a team I gathered during one week, comprising a storyteller accompanied by two singers and a script (teacher from elementary school). The text was then translated to Indonesian by a teacher from a secondary school.

13   *Biné'* ('sister on the father's side'), *ana'* ('child'); *biné' ana'* is a kinship term that can designate the father's sister's child.

14   *Bési* ('pumpkin'); *paré* ('growing rice').

15   A name that can be given to girls or women.

over four generations before her, covers, on the one hand, the sterility problem of her paternal grandparents and, on the other, her father's search for a wife. So, two initial conflicts set the characters in motion: the longing for a child in the grandparents' generation and the quest for a woman in the parents' generation. These quests determine the spatial progression in search of a child and a woman.

The narrative therefore goes back a long way in time and space. It begins in a place on the border between the Li'o-speaking country and the Sikka country, 200 kilometres west of Tanjung Bunga. The distant land (*tana léla*, says the poem, circa line 1,140) is evoked as follows:

Tonu ukut lewo doan	The traces of Tonu lie in a distant village
Wujo raran tana léla	the path of Wujo is a remote land[16]

Source: Excerpt from the song *Opak bélun gurun gawak bé'ola tugu*, lines 1,139–1,140.[17]

Throughout the first part of the narrative, the story takes place in Li'o, between the two villages of Nogo Ema's grandparents: that of her paternal grandparents (named 'Village of the Altar Stone, Land of the White Bamboo')[18] and that of her maternal grandparents (named 'Village of the Coconut, Land of the Areca Nut').[19] Whereas the first is on the Earth, the second is located underground and is populated by humans and spirits (*nitun*) in the place of the setting sun. The place of her paternal grandfather is recalled in the name of the ceremonial domain, ancestors, ceremonial stones, spirits, mountains and lands:

---

16 Lamaholot poetry relies on pairs of words that are complementary, synonymous or antonymous. These pairs are disjunctive when they are sung (in the above lines: *Tonu/Wujo, ukut/raran, lewo/tana, doan/lela*). *Ukut raran* literally means 'the trace of the path, the memory of the road'.

17 All the following quotes are taken from the narrative I collected on 8 November 2006. The whole narrative can be heard in eight audio files at: archives.crem-cnrs.fr/archives/items/CNRSMH_I_2007_006_001_232/.

18 Lewo Wato Mahé Tana Belan Burak.

19 Kajo Tapo Wua' Poné. The entire name is Lewo Lali Kajo Tapo Tana Lali Wua' Poné ('To the Setting Sun Village of the Coconut, to the Setting Sun Land of the Areca Nut') (lines 175–76). All place and character names have simple and elaborate forms. The simple form requires only the first words (so the villages are usually called Wato Mahé and Kajo Tapo), as in Rote island (Fox 2006: 91).

Lewo Wato Mahé	Village of the Altar Stone[20]
Tana Belan Burak	Land of the White Bamboo
Raja Pati Mangu	Raja Pati Mangu
Tuan Boli Li'o	Sovereign Boli Li'o
Tonu Osé Longo	Tonu Osé Longo
Wujo Laju Burak	Wujo Laju Burak
Nuba Sogén Sara Boro	[Stone] *Nuba* Sogén Sara Boro
béla Kéwa Kala Midi	[stone] *béla* Kewa Kala Midi
Guna Siga Buga	[Spirit] *Guna* Siga Buga
déwa Tuli Nara	[spirit] *dewa* Tuli Nara
Ilé Wato Téna	Mountain of the Stone Boat
Woka Wai' Wuri	Mount of the Wuri River
Duli Kebo Lolon Buto	Site of the Eight Palms
pali Hulu Hala Lolon	Site of the Warm Leaves

The places inhabited by humans are defined by the association between a toponym (*lewo tana*), a patronym of a sovereign (*raja tuan*), ceremonial and potent stones (*nuba béla*), auxiliary spirits (*guna déwa*), a mountain (*ilé woka*) and a site (*duli pali*).

The story begins with a quest for a child and a quest for a wife. In the paternal village (Wato Mahé), a couple, in despair of sterility, adopts a baby boy, Pati Sogén, who had been abandoned in the forest. Later, when Pati Sogén has become a young adult, sitting in the temple and playing a flute, the flute tells him to go to the Coconut Tree village (Kajo Tapo) to choose his wife, who is Koka Tuli Sanganara's daughter. He goes there, far away. Upon arrival, his bride, Gowin Burak, asks him to go to meet her grandparents, who are underground spirits (*nitun*). The task looks difficult because their place is located on a precipice. So Pati Sogén thinks about it, and a rat (or snake/chicken) appears to help him get underground (*ula rogo nolo, manuk béka doré*: 'the snake moves forward, the chicken follows', line 474). The animal, which is an auxiliary spirit (*guna déwa*),

---

20 *Mahé* means the trace of a landslide. This word is also found in the neighbouring Tana 'Ai region with the *grén mahé* ritual—*mahé* referring to an altar of stone and wood (Lewis 1988a: 32).

helps him to break the stones, and there he discovers two villages[21] whose ruler has the double male–female name Ina Rimo Ama Gaja. To take a wife, he is only asked to eat and drink with them in mind. Thus, Pati Sogén Laga Li'o (Nogo Ema's father) marries Tonu Gowin Burak Bubu Jawa Rérek (Figure 7.1).

The path Pati Sogén has walked goes from the Earth to the world below—that of the underground spirits. The motion is vertical. From the beginning of the narrative, the toponyms are overwhelming and there are no temporal indicators. The names of villages, mountains, rulers and cultivated fields and the mention of attributes of sovereignty—ceremonial stones planted (*nuba nara*) and mobile auxiliary stones (*guna déwa*)—refer to an ancient time, that of Nogo Ema's grandparents.

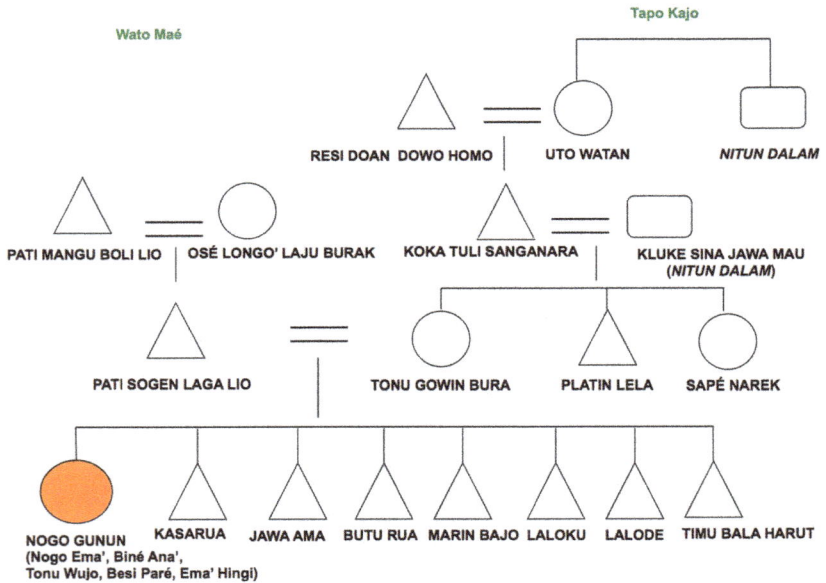

Figure 7.1 The ancestors of Nogo Ema' according to the narrative (Waiklibang, 2006)

Source: Dana Rappoport.

---

21   Sodok Lewo Bélen', Tana Haban Wawe Utan ('Great Mountainous Village, Dangerous Wild Boar Land'), whose sovereign is Ina Rimo Ama Gajak.

The eastward path to Tanjung Bunga

In the last part of the narrative (from line 1,438 to the end), Nogo Ema', after her death, leaves Li'o, the region of her ancestors, to share herself from village to village. The song does not say in what form she leaves. Some say she goes in her invisible spirit form, but as soon as she arrives in a village, she transforms herself into a young woman. A remarkable feature of the story is Nogo Ema's constantly changing state and her continuous progress eastward.

What is the first reason for her departure? Why does this young woman's spirit leave her brothers? In Kohl's (1998, 2009) study, first published in German and then in Indonesian, the author uses the term 'wandering' (Ind.: *pengembaraan*) to describe the journey. Is it a wandering or a purposeful journey? In the song I recorded, the maiden moves eastward, towards the rising sun, towards the village of the storyteller, without wandering. The reason for her departure is given in the song: thanks to the harvest resulting from her metamorphosis into rice, her seven brothers fill seven rice granaries, allowing them 'to buy elephant tusks' (*hopé bala*) to 'buy a wife' (*hopé wéli*). But they quarrel, both outside and inside the house, which causes Nogo Ema' to flee:

Lodo mala geni wekit	They go down and fight[22]
géré mala guat onet	they come up and tear each other apart
Na'a pali ata pito	The seven brothers
ama pali ata léma	the five brothers
Nogo nala ikit léin	Nogo goes on her feet
Ema' nala hajan lima	Ema' wings her arms

The last distich, 'goes on her feet, wings her arms' (a common refrain in the song), indicates the departure of the rice maiden, without any other words. Human pride results from prosperity, which fosters rivalry and encourages the brothers to compete for goods and women. Shame and disgust at her brothers' actions are what drive Nogo Ema' to separate from her family, as Bapa' Krowé's explanation shows:

---

22   Line 1,438 ff.

The brothers asked their mother: 'Mother, there are seven of us and there is only one daughter, so who is responsible for the bride price?' She said that, with the result of the harvest, they could each buy elephant tusks. The harvest of the field was endless. For a year, the harvest lasted, they harvested and it continued. In the end, with this success beyond all expectation, pride went to their heads. They felt superior. Nogo Gunun, in her form of rice, but also as a human being, was saddened. 'For my sake, they became proud. I will go away, I will go from one village to another.' Then she left in the form of an invisible spirit. From time to time, we either saw her as a human being or we didn't see her. And when she arrived at a village, then she took on her human form. (Bapa' Krowé, Personal communication, Waiklibang, July 2018)

Nogo Ema's departure is the beginning of a long journey, which will be marked by stops in the villages she encounters, from Li'o to Tanjung Bunga. The route she takes runs from west to east, from the Li'o country to the eastern tip of Flores (Map 7.1), passing through different places with long names.[23] For example, Lewo Rahan, a village on the coast opposite Tanjung Bunga, is mentioned as follows:

Lewo raé Tapo Toban	Village upwards of the Fallen Coconut[24]
Tana Lewo Rahan	Land of the Coconut Basket Village
paken wai lau	whose name is River Seaward
Raja Merin Miten	Raja of the Black Stone
Tuan Ina Rua	Sovereign of Two Women
Raja Butu Rua	Raja Butu Rua
Rua Marin Bajo	Rua Marin Bajo[25]

Each village name refers to a ceremonial domain (*lewo tana*) associated with a sovereign (*raja tuan*). Nogo Ema's journey is marked by her meetings with different rulers, almost all of whom want to have intercourse with

---

23   Here are the various village names told in the song: Lewo Krowé Tana Tukan Henga Rua Hama (around Maumere), Lewo Peli Bugit Bojan Tana Peli Tulé Walén, Lewo Keluok Wojon Tobo Tana Napen Hapén, Lewo Raé Tapo Toban Tana Lewo Rahan, Kawaliwu, Lewotala, Oka, Wéru, Watuwiti, Riang Koli, Lamanabi.

24   Line 1,496 ff.

25   The names of two rulers at Lewo Rahan. These two names, Butu Rua and Marin Bajo, are the names of two of Tonu Wujo's brothers (see Figure 7.1).

her. Twice she is almost raped (in Lewo Rahan and Ratulodong) and twice she is raped (in Lewotala and Riang Koli). In Lewotala, she is raped at night by the sovereign Raja Nara Boki, inside the temple. In the poem, the word 'rape' is never sung:

Pati bunu bauk	When it gets dark[26]
beda nodo nokok	in the deep of night
Teka nala pali	Wants to make a friend
buno nala pera	needs a relation
Raé koké tukan	Up in the middle of the temple
teka raé balé' bawan	up in the centre of the ritual house
Tonu mia mata	Tonu is ashamed
Wujo rure eret	Wujo shows an undone face
Lutu nala bai	Pregnant with a baby
nara nala béda	waiting for a child

From this rape in the ritual house, a child is born whom she chooses to abandon; she places him in a shell and sends him to the sea, from the coast of Flores to Adonara. Beached on the opposite coast, the child's crying is confused by the people of Adonara with the sound of a great man. The child is then killed by them (around line 1,558), which explains why rice did not spread to Adonara, the neighbouring island. Once killed, the baby is pushed back to where it came from, stranded at Watuwiti and buried by the local ruler, which is why they attribute good harvests to this village. Nogo Ema', for her part, continues on her way and is raped again, at Riang Koli. This time, rape is represented by the donation of areca nut:

Ikit nala lein téna	Moves fast on her legs[27]
tiro nala lewo	arrives at the village
Koli Tana Wutun	Koli, the End Land
Lajo Ekan Wakon	at the Lajo Land[28]

---

26 Line 1,529 ff.
27 Line 1,570 ff.
28 Complete name of Riang Koli's village.

Raja Bési Burak	Raja Bési Burak
Tuan Talu Wai	Sovereign Talu Wai[29]
Soron wua hiku	Gives an areca nut
nein malu padak	gives hungry touches her hand
Nogo mia mata	Nogo is ashamed
Ema' rure eret	Ema' shows an undone face
Hiko nala tion	Continues on her way
liwat nala gete	going on her way

The rape is never told, only suggested through a litotic expression specific to this type of poetry. From this new rape, she gives birth not to a child but to rice itself. She continues her journey to Lamanabi where different events happen. When she climbs a mountain and observes the surroundings, she goes swimming and takes off her ring (line 1,599). Throughout the journey, Nogo Ema' loses objects: bracelet, ring, comb. The villagers of Muleng, while hunting, find the ring. By this means, they recover some of the harvest.[30]

Never feeling comfortable in the places through which she passes, but vulnerable, Nogo Ema' continues on her way to the narrator's village. There, she meets the narrator's ancestor, more than 14 generations earlier, and a new adventure occurs. The ancestor of the Maran clan (Raja Kélu Béra Tuan Bélawa Burak) meets the young woman while hunting. He tries to abuse her, but she deflects his attention by playing a trick on him, making him believe that a scorpion was there and the village was burning. Then she disappears. The next day, his dream tells him to return to the place where he met her, to the stone where she sat (*Nogo méran*: 'the woman's seat'), and when he returns he finds her golden earrings. In his dream, he is asked by Nogo Ema' to replant them, and the harvest from this planting is exceptional and, above all, endless. However, the ruler of the neighbouring ceremonial domain (Lewotala), who had raped and impregnated Nogo Ema', hears about this extraordinary fact and comes to see the harvest. He sets fire to it and Nogo Ema' disappears again.

---

29   Complete name of Riang Koli's ruler.
30   So, every time they leave to sow, these inhabitants give food to the ring. Nogo Ema's objects are kept in traditional houses and are fed.

Here ends the story of Nogo Ema' in the sung version of the myth, on the evening of the wrapping of the maiden to enter the storehouse. But in fact, a continuation was told to me by Bapa' Krowé in 2018:

> Once she disappeared again, Nogo Ema' ascended to heaven, at a place called Bubu Loti Bui Lomek, without being able to go down again. For 300 years (six generations), the population suffered from hunger. One of their ancestors, Bapa' Béra, sought a solution. And once again, an animal assistant made it possible to go up to the sky to search for her. He flew up to heaven in an attempt to bring her down. He talked to her, cut her hair while Bapa' Bera stayed down below. When she fell from the sky, he caught her. She turned into an egg. He told her not to turn into a chick and to stay inside. He told her that he would feed her eggs. He told his brother to go hunting to meet her. His brother went hunting in Kung Belen' and found a grain of rice in the belly of a deer and replanted it. Since then we have been growing rice and the Maran clan has shared it with all the others for at least 300 years. Bapa' Hawan and Bapa' Bera (ancestors from the Koten and Maran clans from Waiklibang village) found it, cultivated it and shared it. They lived in a single house up there (in the old village). There were seven of them in Béra's family, and seven in Hawan's family. We became the Koten clan and the other Marans. The rice journey is more or less that. (Bapa Krowé, Personal communication, July 2018)

Despite the fantastic and cryptic aspects of the story, several generations of the narrator's ancestors emerge in the song. The following are mentioned: Pati Puru Hawa, Pain Béra Jon Nara, Kélu Béra and Sédu Dowé Dua Ama. Myth is then connected to lived reality; fiction and history intertwine.

Why sing and tell about the rice maiden's journey? Attending the ritual, one realises the importance of the act of wrapping the seed so that she does not leave again. A common fear is that the seed will go away; in the story, Nogo Ema' is constantly disappearing. The farmers' wish is to wrap her up, to keep her, to protect her, to do everything possible to prevent the seed from leaving again, which would risk leading them to starvation.

A singer explains to me that this narrative is a way to welcome the rice maiden:

> We want to welcome Tonu Wujo to her village of origin. So, we go there by flying, not by walking. Once there, we move hither and thither by walking, from Li'o to eastern Flores, so the story which ends in the village begins with recounting her clans, her

temple, her beach; we tell of her mountains, her spirits [*nitun*], her days; we tell everything, we must not make a mistake. That's why only one man knows it. If many of us know it, there will be war because nobody likes to be defeated. (Storyteller Anton Siku Mukin, 68 years old, Personal communication, Karawutun, March 2006)

The sung narrative fixes the memory of routes through the recitation of sequences of placenames linked to migration, referring to a historical knowledge of these places, which are evoked in an unchanging order.

To tell the rice maiden's journey

During an agricultural year, the narrative of the rice maiden's journey is sung four times: before sowing, harvesting, threshing and storage. A large number of people from the different clans of the ceremonial domain gather for a long musical vigil.

One narrative through various dances

The 2,200-line narrative of the origin of rice is conveyed in a number of distinct musical forms, performed alternately by men and women. Several storytellers will sing, following one another, from 11.30 pm to 6 am, according to a succession of narrative sequences sung to six different dances. Each is distinguished by its name, its variety of steps, its melodic-rhythmic configurations and its choreographic structures (disjointed centripetal line, circle, semicircle, separate bodies and so on). The various genres are named *haman opak bélun, nama nigi, lian kenolon* and *nama néron, goken, berasi*.[31] Most can be sung several times during the night. All involve few singers—only six or seven—according to a complex alternation: a storyteller (male or female: *opak*) and his or her 'embroiderer' (*nukun opak*),[32] two pairs of singers (*hodé' ana'*) and sometimes a soloist (*nukun blaha*). Thus, whereas the story is continuous, the songs made to tell it are discontinuous, even though the variety of musical genres never breaks the narrative continuity.

---

31   Compare with the sound files at: archives.crem-cnrs.fr/archives/items/CNRSMH_I_2007_006_001_232. For the succession of the dances, see Rappoport (2016: 184).

32   A duet cannot mix male and female singers. Thus, if the storyteller is a female, the embroiderer must also be a woman. The Maran clan had a female storyteller, but she had recently passed away.

I would like to focus on the most important musical genre and dance common to the whole of eastern Flores. The dance is the same everywhere: it is performed by a chain of dancers adorned with white feathers, moving counterclockwise.[33] It is usually called *haman opak bélun*, which means 'to thresh to sing the narrative'. This is the famous dance of the Tanjung Bunga and Bai Pito areas, recognisable by the clothes of the dancers, who stand in a row with feathers and bells on their backs and feet. The dance has been partly described by Ernst Vatter (1932) and Jaap Kunst (1942: 7). Vatter also recorded a silent movie of the dance in 1929 (Vatter 1963). In this, the ground is threshed (*haman*) in the place of the dance (*naman*) and a narrative is told (*opak*) in a lively song (*mura lian*). The name of the dance itself shows that it is much more than a series of motions; it is a ceremonial narrative. Unlike all the other main round or chain dances of the neighbouring areas, in which the dancers hold hands or arms (like the *dolo-dolo*, *lilin* and *lian naman* on Adonara), the *haman opak bélun* is performed in a chain without holding hands. The dancers stand in a semicircle, while the singers stay inside the circle and move around the ceremonial stones (*nuba nara*). All move in a sequence of six steps, performed all night—left, right, left, right, right, left—in an obsessive circular motion. The pulse is beaten on the ground and marked by bells. On the last beat, there is no threshing; rather, it is almost mute. What is important in the dance is the motion of the pelvis, which is visually and sonically emphasised by bells, chains and shell decorations—all of which reinforce the energy conveyed.

Two things are important to keep in mind: the variety of dances does not interfere with the continuity of the story (the story is paramount), but without dance there is no other possibility of telling the narrative (that is why in regions where storytellers have disappeared, the dance also disappears). Narrative, songs and dance are intrinsically linked.

---

33   This could be related to the way the rice fields are harvested. The harvesters are arranged in a single line that progresses from left to right to surround the divinity of rice, represented by the altar. To the left of the line are the men and to the right, the women, each singing different songs. The movement progresses inwards and to the right.

The musical form of the rice maiden's long journey

What is the link between the musical performance and the content of the song? To answer that question, it is useful to understand how the narrative is performed. The organisation of the song is based on a clear assignment of musical tasks to specific performers.

In the *haman opak bélun* dance, the storyteller (*opak*) is introduced by his embroiderer (*nukun opak*) on an isochronous pulse. He chants the narrative while his embroiderer repeats the narrator's last words, adding a layer of vocal flourishes to the former's voice. After 100 lines of narrative, the storyteller takes a break and there is a lyric interlude sung by two duettists (named *hodé' ana'*): two pairs of singers sing an identical musical phrase in alternation. This musical sequence contrasts with the preceding account of the story; now dancers shout enthusiastically, infusing energy into the dance, whereas the lyrics of the *hodé' ana'* duets do not seem really meaningful. The first duo is called *ana' puken* ('children trunk'); the second duo, *ana' wutun* ('ending children'), repeats the words of the first.[34] The duettists dance close to each other, so that the two pairs of singers form a unit. Within one pair, the first voice is called *hodé'* ('to receive'), while the second is called *nuku* ('second voice'). This sequence marks a rest during the narrative performance. After the *hodé' ana'* duet sequence, there is sometimes a soloist, *nukun blaha* ('long second voice') or *nukun ana'* ('second voice child'), singing for a long period, following the story, as a kind of junior, second storyteller. Then, the main storyteller (*opak*) goes on again.

In the course of the sung performance, the 2,000-line narrative is constantly interspersed with lyrical breaks. One may wonder what the purpose of these breaks is. A singer explains:

> *Opak* [storyteller] stops first, then comes *hodé' ana'* [duets]. They stop because people who listen are bored. In this dance, *opak* [storyteller] is paired with *hodé' ana'* [duets], alternating with *nukun blaha* [storyteller], in order to feel that night can last a little bit longer. (Bapa' Arnoldus Kebojan Maran, *opak* storyteller, Personal communication, January 2007)

---

34 There is a possibility of double meaning, suggested by a local performer, who told me that *ana* means 'songline' and not 'child' (*ana'*), which would make sense 'to receive the line' from the previous duet.

In this quotation, boredom arises from narrativity, which may explain why these lyrical breaks do not advance the narrative; instead, they force a pause in the narrative. Perhaps, like a long walk on a hiking trail, the telling of the journey is inconceivable without breaks. Lyrical breaks in the great narrative repertoires are essential to the telling of the story, as if to highlight it, to relieve the narrator and to stimulate collective energy. What do these lyrical musical breaks actually tell us? During the rice maiden's journey, from line 1,462 to line 2,080, 25 narrative sequences sung by the storyteller are interrupted by 18 lyrical duet sequences (*hodé' ana'*) that occur almost every two minutes. Here is an example of an alternation between narrative sequence and what I call 'lyrical pause':

The soloist narrative and embroiderer (*opak + nukun opak*)

Duli Kaléba Lama diké	The site Kaléba Lama Diké
pali Lolon Lama Hadi	the site Lolon lama Hadi
Matan nala noi	[Pati Sadi] watches
wekin nala lilé	he observes
Tonu wai' bui'	Tonu looks
matan nala noi	she watches
wekin nala lilé	they observe each other
Tutu nala ema'	she [Nogo Ema'] tells to the mother
marin nala bapa'	says to the father
pé'én nala bapa'	to this father

The duetting lyrical pause (*hodé' ana'*)

Hajon é Béra	Hajon e Béra[35]
Raran tala Bama lali	The road to Bama to the setting sun
raran pi Bama ga'é	where is the road to Bama?
Suban sepat to Waidoko	Suban [male name] stops to see Waidoko
Luhi pi malé ga'é	Where is the thread for this needle?
limak ko malé pidan limakko	The yarn wraps in my hands

---

35 Ancestors' names.

The soloist narrative and embroiderer (*opak + nukun opak*)

Tonu néku tutu gokok	Tonu comes back to talk
Wujo néku marin hajat	Wujo then speaks
Nékun géte-géte	Then questions
pai ahak data	keeps questioning
Na'an léké létak	They want to arrow her[36]
pai ama ahak dat tali	lure her with a rope
Na'an léké letak hala	They do not arrow her
taha tali hala	[she] cannot free herself from the rope
Nogo wekan lewo	Nogo is shared in the village
Ema' dawin tana	Ema' is distributed on the land
pe'en dawin tana	distributed on this land

The duetting lyrical pause (*hodé' ana'*)

Hajon Béra	Hajon! Béra!

These examples illustrate the whole process of singing narration. The link between the narrative and the duetting lyrical *hodé' ana'* sequences seems rather loose. The *hodé' ana'* duets tell about a village (Bama, Waidoko, line 1,773), but are also about thread and weaving—perhaps as a comment on the narrative. They disconnect the narrative from the necessity of continuity and offer, through this semantic discontinuity, a poetic moment. These lyrical sequences may also sometimes interact as an echo and make it possible to value and resonate what has just been said. The flow of the song is structured by series of semantic and musical pauses that behave like narrative stopping points. Thus, the musical form itself expresses in a way the journey of the rice maiden, made by successive stops.

The requirements of sung narrative performance

Two criteria govern the singing of the journey: continuity and correct naming. On the one hand, the journey must be sung continuously; on the other, the storyteller must not make any mistakes in the itinerary.

---

36 The men want to shoot Tonu Wujo with an arrow, like a game animal.

Only specialists can satisfy these requirements. Knowing how to set out the path in the right order without omitting any step is a challenge for all storytellers, who risk their lives in the event of performative error. I have shown elsewhere the importance of the persons in this society in charge of speech (whom we may call storytellers, chanters or master poets) (Rappoport 2016). *Opak*—called also *bawa* ('drum') or *todo bawa* ('to beat the drum continuously')—is the name of the storyteller, and is a title awarded to those who are able to sing long narrative sequences. As they have the capacity to memorise the genealogies and the routes of migration, these chanters are the guardians of custom. It is believed that they have an innate ability to recite the history of the ceremonial domains without having inherited it from the mouth of another and indeed without even being born in the place of which they sing.

The memory they demonstrate in singing and storytelling and their mastery of lexical complementarity are shared only by a small number of people. As a poetic element, lexical complementarity is a prerequisite of any kind of ritual speech.

The song itself says:

Tutu pali rala roi	To tell, they have to know
marin rala kéna	to say, they must have knowledge[37]

Despite the fact that the storytellers are excellent singers and poets, these performers are viewed not as artists but rather as key persons in maintaining the harmony of society. Their responsibilities put them in danger should a performative fault occur, because words can influence the fate of the community. Their mission—mastering and performing ritual poetic narrative, thereby facilitating the reproduction of life—can lead to the performer's death. In eastern Flores, as in many places in the Austronesian world, these persons possess religious authority, which is expressed through the performance of ritual poetry considered as offerings to various kinds of spirits.

To sing the narrative is a cognitive skill that has a specific aim: to set out the path. However, should this path be wrong, danger might befall the community:

---

37 Lines 929–30.

> We, as storytellers, tell of long journeys, from Larantuka, Ende
> or Maumere. I remember I was still a child when they rebuilt the
> great temple. They were dancing. One of the storytellers was from
> Belogili [a neighbouring village]. I moved to stand close to him.
> He was reciting. My father laughed: 'Ah, is this the right way or
> not? Is he acquainted with the temple or not?' After he returned
> home, two weeks later, he was dead. He did not know the [right]
> road. He knew a wrong road. We must know the way back. If
> we do not know it, we become lost. For example, [although] this
> way is said to be a good road, but it is a fire road, a wrong road.
> I was still in the second class of primary school, around 1959.
> (Storyteller Paulus Platin Maran, Personal communication,
> Waiklibang, 2010)

The idea of 'knowing the right road' is fundamental if one is to avoid being
lost. To know the right path is to know the path of your ancestors. Not all
the clans can tell the journeys. In this region, this task is exclusive to the
sovereign clans (*raja tuan*)[38] and, in particular, to the Maran clan, who are
responsible for the poetic ritual speech (*tutu marin*: 'to say, to tell') before
animal offerings. In the sociopolitical model of the region, four main
clans (Koten, Kélen, Hurit and Maran) share sacrificial functions, with
each of the names relating to their obligations during the killing of a pig
(*koten*: 'head'; *kélen*: 'tail'; *hurit*: 'slice'; *maran*: 'pray'). The Maran clan's
role as oral performers (singing, telling, praying) dates back to an ancestor
who gave one of his sons the task of singing, speaking and telling the story
by 'standing towards the sea and looking towards the mountain'—an
expression meaning that these persons can speak to all the invisible spirits,
both maritime (*harin*) and terrestrial (*nitun*). This distribution of mastery
of public speaking is also found among their Sikka-speaking neighbours
(Tana' Ai dialect), in whom it implies the attribution of a higher status
to the clan responsible for the custodianship of the historical sequences
relating to the ceremonial domain during the *grén mahé* ritual (Lewis
1988b: 98).

The narrative musical performance shows the need for completeness
and the taste for musical breaks. This way of constantly interrupting
the narrative raises the question of the relationship between space

---

38 At Waiklibang, the social structure comprises two types of clans: the sovereign clans (*suku raja
tuan*) and the support clans (*suku nipa talé*). The former have the right and duty to make offerings
to the land (*huké tana*). Penelope Graham (1991), who has done fieldwork in a neighbouring area
(Lewotala), explains in detail the notion of clan in this part of Flores.

(required by the narrative) and time (which music shapes). One could suggest that the length of the singing performance expresses the length of the journey. But let us turn the question around: what does the length of the journey tell us about time?

The length of the rice maiden's road

In the narrative of the rice maiden's journey, there is no linguistic marker of time and the Lamaholot expression for 'time' (*ékan nuan*) never appears. Instead, to express the idea of time, the song says:

Tutu kala Bési kolé	Tell the Pumpkin stem
marin kala Paré matan	tell the Rice receptacle
Bési kolé lewo doan	The Pumpkin stem lies in a distant village
paré matan tana léla	the receptacle of Rice is a distant land
Nian tasik ketiko to'u	Far beyond a sea
nian wai' begura rua	far away like two rivers[39]

The meaning of these three distichs conveys the long distance from the rice's origin—a distance expressed by three spatial markers (*doan, léla* and *nian*), which signify 'far away' and two nouns, the river and the sea, which are two elements that, like time, are limitless and sourceless. This spatial distance possibly also means a great distance from the present. In addition, the idea of origin itself is suggested through the botanical metaphor (*kolé/matan*: 'peduncle/receptacle'), referring to a stalk from which a flower emerges. Temporal depth through this narrative seems to be marked by space, as though there was no possibility other than to express the past through space.

The complementary pair *kolé/matan* ('peduncle/receptacle') deserves our full attention because, with other pairs, it expresses a framework of thought common all over Tanjung Bunga. It can be compared with another pair,

---

39　Line 112 and ff. In these distichs, various pairs are expressed: 1) *tutu marin* ('to tell, to say'), to talk ritually; 2) *Bési paré* ('Pumpkin rice'), rice; 3) *Kolé matan* ('stem receptacle'), a botanic metaphor referring to the origin; 4) *lewo tana* ('village land'), the ceremonial domain; 4) *Tasik wai'* ('sea river'), 'flooding'.

which organises the vocal duets in this region, *puken/wutun* ('the trunk' and 'the tip'). In this region, vocal duets proceed in pairs. The first duo, the most expert, chooses the lyrics and the second completes them, using the same melodic-rhythmic motif. The first pair is called 'children of the trunk' (*ana' pukén*) and the second 'children of the tip' (*ana' wutun*). The first organises not only the singers, but also the song lyrics. It marks the importance, in their musical language, of the complementarity between anteriority (the one that begins) and posteriority (the one that follows). This ordering can be seen on three levels: at the level of a duet (one singer always starts before the other), at the level of the relationship between duettists (one duo always starts before another) and at the level of the spatialisation of the songs on the agricultural work lines (men sing a repertoire at the beginning and women sing another repertoire at the end of the harvest line).

These two complementary pairs (peduncle/receptacle and trunk/tip), which are prevalent in the field of orality (Fox 1988), indicate the need to respect an order of precedence. Why should this order of precedence be linked to the time of the rice maiden's journey? My hypothesis is that the perception of time in this region depends, in the general framework, on a relationship of authority organised in hierarchical pairs (between people, genders, clans and singers), between those who manage to associate the two ends of a story (the origin and the stem, the receptacle and its peduncle) and the two ends of a song, both literally and figuratively (able to tell the story and able to sing it; to begin and to end) (Rappoport In press).

Let us come back to space. In the narrative, time is imagined in terms of a path, according to the ceremonial domain that separates the place of enunciation from the place of origin, in a progression from the past to the singer's present. The progression is shown by the character's itinerary. The itinerary is told in the account of the journey, which is defined by the variety of places crossed—seas and rivers (*tasik uai*), ceremonial domains (*lewo tana*), fields and valleys (*duli pali*), large or small mountains (*ilé bélen', wokan réren*)—and encounters. The song's narrative consists, then, of telling the 'trace of the path':

Tutu kala Tonu ukut	To tell the trace of Tonu[40]
marin kala Wujo raran	to say the path of Wujo

---

40   Line 1,137 and ff.

Tonu ukut lewo doan	The trace of Tonu lies in a distant village
Wujo raran tana léla	The path of Wujo is a remote land

James Fox (2006: 89) uses the term topogeny to refer to an ordered succession of placenames, showing that some Austronesian societies prefer topogeny to genealogy because successive generations are perceived only in space. One of the functions of these topogenies may be to establish the precedence of a group over a territory through the ability to store knowledge about the relationships and interconnections between past events and the secret names of spirits and places encountered during migration.

The temporal thickness may be perceived in the accumulation of places crossed, which requires time to be told and thus increases the length of the performance—a particularity of this kind of narrative—sung continuously for about five or six hours. A sort of homology can be established between the length of the performance and the length of the journey. We have seen above how the narrative is interspersed with interludes, within a continuous flow. About every hundred verses, the narration gives way to duets whose role is to pause in the story, like a pause on a path. Their function is not narrative but lyrical. While the essence of the song lies in its narrative, this song would not take place without these alternating duets that do not serve the narrative but help to rest, to endure the length of the path.

When music, at the time of agrarian rituals, calls to mind the myth of the origin of rice, singing no longer corresponds to a time lived in the present but calls to mind an ancient 'imagined' time. Everything that is told in the song is about the extraordinary: the communication with spirits, the metamorphosis of a maiden into an edible plant and the nonhuman ancestry of Tonu Wujo, born from the earthly spirits. Yet, during the telling of the myth, and for a whole agrarian year, from sowing to harvesting, one or two young women personify that seed. Through the ritual replaying the dramatic knot, the ancient time suddenly becomes actualised through a form of 'presentification'. It is as if the ritual, through storytelling and personification, makes the ancient times present. Thus, this myth of the origin of rice connects the personal history of clans to the arrival of rice in the region.

Time lived and time represented are combined by myth—what Ricoeur (1983: 330) calls the intertwining of fiction and history. Indeed, the storyteller inscribes the ruling clans of the place of enunciation in the continuity of the imagined time by connecting them to Nogo Ema', the spirit of rice. The master poet connects himself to history by telling only of his own ancestors who met the rice maiden.

Conclusion

This chapter addressed the theme of the journey in the myth of the origin of rice. I have shown how the narrative rehearsed the journey of Nogo Ema', the maiden turned into rice, who travelled from west to east, from Li'o country to Tanjung Bunga. Her trip tells the story of the dispersal of rice in the eastern part of the island, to places that did not grow rice. This journey is distinguished by its length and also by its violence. Her ultimate destination is the village of the storyteller's family, some of whom may have known of the arrival of rice in the region.

This trip teaches something profound: in this society, as in many societies in eastern Insulindia, time is expressed by the recollection of the paths (in Lamaholot, *ukut laran*). The further away are these traces, the longer is the narrative. Only the storytellers know 'the traces of the paths', and this knowledge engages them vitally. For, to make a mistake in the enunciation of paths is to make a mistake about oneself and one's group. In these societies, orality is the only history book. We know how much a mistake in a history book can cost its author in Western societies, but in eastern Indonesia a mistake in stating the itinerary can bring death and illness to the group in question. Because the performance of these stories engages the bodies of the humans who tell them, it can be understood why the knowledge of roads and the ability to sing them are, in Lamaholot society, so important for the consciousness of the group.

References

Adams, Marie-Jeanne. 1971. 'Cultural variations in eastern Indonesia.' *Manusia Indonesia* 5(4–5–6): 425–40.

Berthe, Louis. 1972. *Bei gua. Itinéraire des ancêtres. Mythe des Bunaq de Timor* [*Bei Gua: Route of the ancestors—Timor Bunaq myth*]. Paris: Editions du CNRS.

Eberhard, David M., Gary F. Simons and Charles D. Fennig, eds. 2020. *Ethnologue: Languages of the world.* 23rd edn. Dallas: SIL International. Available from: www.ethnologue.com.

Fox, James J. 1988. *To Speak in Pairs: Essays on the ritual languages of eastern Indonesia.* Cambridge Studies in Oral and Literate Culture. Cambridge: Cambridge University Press. doi.org/10.1017/CBO9780511551369.

Fox, James J. 2006. 'Genealogy and topogeny: Toward an ethnography of Rotinese ritual place names.' In James J. Fox, ed., *The Poetic Power of Place: Comparative perspectives on Austronesian ideas of locality,* pp. 89–100. Canberra: ANU E Press. doi.org/10.22459/PPP.09.2006.05.

Graham, Penelope. 1991. 'To follow the blood: The path of life in a domain of eastern Flores, Indonesia.' PhD dissertation, The Australian National University, Canberra.

Grimes, Charles, Therik Tom, Barbara Grimes and Max Jacob. 1997. *A Guide to the People and Languages of Nusa Tenggara.* Kupang: Artha Wacana Press.

Hatto, Arthur Thomas. 1980. *Traditions of Heroic and Epic Poetry. Volume One: The traditions.* London: The Modern Humanities Research Association.

Kohl, Karl-Heinz. 1998. *Der Tod der Reisjungfrau: Mythen, Kulte und Allianzen in einer ostindonesischen lokal Kultur* [*The Death of the Rice Maiden: Myths, cults and alliances in an east Indonesian local culture*]. Stuttgart: Kolhammer.

Kohl, Karl-Heinz. 2009. *Raran Tonu Wujo: Aspek-aspek inti sebuah budaya lokal di Flores Timur* [*Raran Tonu Wujo: Core aspects of a local culture in eastern Flores*]. Maumere: Penerbit Ledalero.

Kunst, Jaap. 1942. *Music in Flores: A study of the vocal and instrumental music among the tribes living in Flores.* Leiden: E.J. Brill.

Lewis, E. Douglas. 1988a. 'A quest for the source: The ontogenesis of a creation myth of the Ata Tana Ai.' In James J. Fox, ed., *To Speak in Pairs: Essays on the ritual languages of eastern Indonesia,* pp. 246–81. Cambridge: Cambridge University Press. doi.org/10.1017/CBO9780511551369.010.

Lewis, E. Douglas. 1988b. *People of the Source: The social and ceremonial order of Tana Wai Brama on Flores.* Dordrecht, the Netherlands: Foris Publications.

Mabuchi, Toichi. 1964. 'Tales concerning the origin of grains in the insular areas of eastern and Southeastern Asia.' *Asian Folklore Studies* 23(1): 1–92. doi.org/10.2307/1177638.

Pampus, Karl-Heinz. 2001. *Mué moten koda kiwan: Kamus bahasa Lamaholot. Dialek Lewolema, Flores Timur* [*Mué moten koda kiwan: Lamaholot–Indonesian Dictionary, Lewolema Dialect, Eastern Flores*]. Frankfurt am Main: Frobenius-Institut.

Rappoport, Dana. 2009. *Songs from the Thrice-Blooded Land: Ritual music of the Toraja (Sulawesi, Indonesia)*. Paris: Édition de la Maison des sciences de l'homme.

Rappoport, Dana. 2016. 'Why do they (still) sing stories? Singing narratives in Tanjung Bunga (eastern Flores, Lamaholot, Indonesia).' *Wacana, Journal of the Humanities of Indonesia* 17(2): 163–90. doi.org/10.17510/wacana.v17i2.439.

Rappoport, Dana. 2017. 'Singing in dangerous places (Flores, Lamaholot, Indonesia).' *Asia Pacific Journal of Anthropology* 18(5): 462–82. doi.org/10.1080/14442213.2017.1372515.

Rappoport, Dana. In press. 'Le temps de chanter. Pratiques musicales et perception du temps dans l'Est indonésien (Flores, Indonésie) [Time to sing: Musical practices and perception of time in eastern Indonesia (Flores, Indonesia)].' In Grégory Mikaelian, ed., *Temporalités khmères: de près, de loin, entre îles et péninsules* [*Khmer Temporalities: Near, far, between islands and peninsulas*]. Bern: Peter Lang.

Revel, Nicole. 2000. *La quête en épouse. Une épopée palawan chantée par Mäsinu* [*The Quest for a Wife: Mämiminbin—A Palawan epic sung by Mäsinu*]. Paris: Éditions UNESCO, Langues & Mondes, L'Asiathèque.

Ricoeur, Paul. 1983. *Temps et récit* [*Time and Narrative*]. Paris: Seuil.

Tukan, Simon Suban. 1996. 'Masyarakat Lewolema dalam interpretasi mitos Nogo Ema' Besi Pare [The Lewolema society in the interpretation of the myth of the Nogo Ema' Iron Pare].' Masters thesis, Ledalero School of Philosophy, Flores, Indonesia.

van der Veen, Hendrick. 1965. *The Merok Feast of the Sa'dan Toraja*. The Hague: Martinus Nijhoff. doi.org/10.26530/OAPEN_613374.

van der Veen, Hendrick. 1966. *The Sa'dan Toradja Chant for the Deceased*. The Hague: Martinus Nijhoff. doi.org/10.26530/OAPEN_613381.

Vatter, Ernst. 1932. *Ata kiwan: unbekannte Bergvölker im tropischen Holland* [*Ata Kiwan: Unknown hill tribes in tropical Holland*]. Leipzig: Bibliographisches Institut.

Vatter, Ernst. 1963. *Spiel und Tanz* [*Games and Dance*]. (D828/1961). Göttingen, Germany: Institut für den Wissenshaftlichen film.

8

Paths of life and death: Rotenese life-course recitations and the journey to the afterworld

James J. Fox

Introduction

The idea of the path and of the journey that the path implies is a prominent and persistent conception among the Rotenese. There are many paths, but all such paths are referred to in ritual language by the paired terms 'path and road' (*eno ma dalan*). In rituals, paths have a direction, a beginning and an end, and journeying can be from west to east or from east to west: towards sunrise at the 'head' (*langa*) of the island or towards sunset at the 'tail' (*iko*) of the island.

On Rote, this movement is through a specific nominated space. All of the 17 traditional domains (*nusak*) of the island have their dual ritual names and, within each of these domains, particular places and prominent locations—fields, streams, hilltops—have their ritual names as well. Rotenese ritual recitations rely on topogenies—the formal ordered recitation of ritual placenames—to give direction to movement along a particular path and thus trace a recognised progression. This recitation of topogenies forms an essential part of the knowledge of origins.

Journeying can go beyond Rote to places with ritually designated names on neighbouring islands and further to places about which Rotenese can only speculate. Not only is life full of journeying, but also life itself from birth to death is conceived of as a journey. This conception is particularly prominent in the life-course recitations that mark the main rituals of death.

From a comparative perspective, these Rotenese life-course recitations are remarkable and distinctive. While many Austronesian societies in their mortuary rituals focus on a journey—often complex and precarious—that leads to an afterworld, the Rotenese at their funeral ceremonies focus on selecting one chant from a variety of patterned life-course recitations that is intended to fit the life of the deceased. This life-course chant is then recited in celebration of the deceased on the evening or evenings prior to burial.

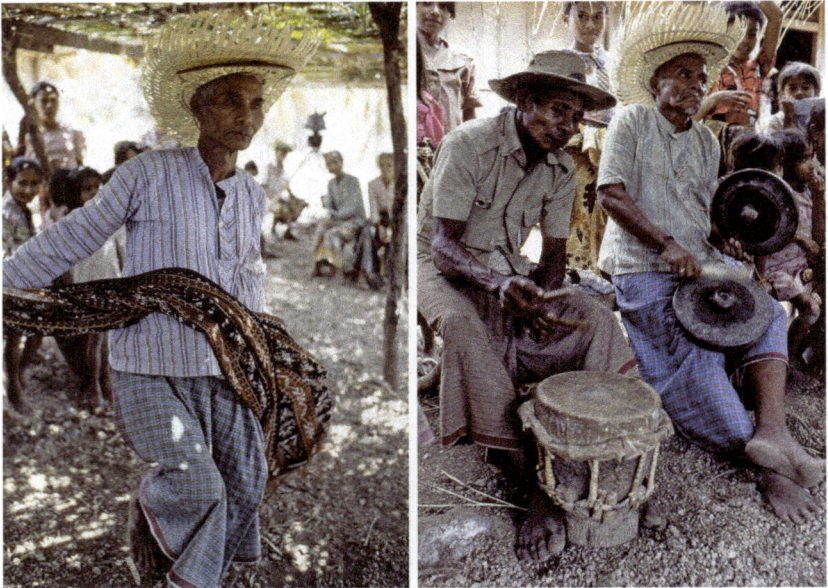

Plates 8.1 and 8.2 Rotenese funerals are generally convivial gatherings spent in meeting, talking and feasting, often interspersed with drumming, gong-playing and dancing

Before the burial, the personal affairs of the deceased are discussed, debts are settled and the close kin of the deceased offer their ritual exchanges to presiding maternal relatives. Burial is in the late afternoon before sunset, with Christian prayers for the deceased. There is—or once was—a ritual framework to all these proceedings although it was rarely made evident (see Fox 1988a). Only on the night or nights before burial were life-course chants recited to the accompaniment of circle-dancing.

Photos: James J. Fox.

All life-course recitations in the Rotenese repertoire are conceived of as particular paths that define a diversity of human possibilities. They identify the deceased by a life pattern and, in some cases, by manner of death. Many of these recitations include or invoke journeys within this life-course, producing an array of alternative avenues, some criss-crossing the island or venturing to destinations on other islands. If life is seen as a grand journey, it often consists of a variety of lesser journeys. All these fanciful imaginary biographies are metaphorical excursions for which there can be multiple interpretations.

Following the burial, there can also occur a final dirge that sends the spirit of the deceased on its way. This lament is a simple, sad and succinct instruction of farewell. It, too, describes a journey—a final journey to the afterworld.

This chapter discusses the repertoire of these life-course recitations gathered in the central domain of Termanu on Rote. From this rich repertoire, the chapter considers a selection of these recitations and some of the paths they set forth. It then presents and provides exegesis on one particular recitation entitled *Kea Lenga ma Lona Bala* and concludes by providing an example of the farewell instructions to the deceased for the final journey to the afterworld.

The genre of life-course recitations: Some illustrative examples

Life-course recitations form part of a much larger body of Rotenese oral literature composed in strict canonical parallelism—the specific, obligatory pairing of words to create formal ordered compositions. These different compositions are named after the particular chant character who is most prominent in them. In the case of life-course recitations, this is the chant-name given to the deceased.

In general, compositions are also identified by their ritual use. Thus, what I refer to here as life-course recitations are all simply classified as 'death chants' (*bini mamates*). A persistent theme in all of these chants is that of the 'orphan and widow' (*ana-mak ma falu-ina*). One enters life as an orphan and widow, journeys through life and departs, as one began, once more as an orphan and widow.

'Orphan and widow' can be used as a category to describe a number of general life-course recitations including some origin chants that can be altered, recomposed and recited as life-course recitations. A good example of these possibilities is the chant *Suti Solo do Bina Bane*—a chant known throughout Rote. As an origin chant, *Suti Solo do Bina Bane* recounts the journeying of two shells, a nautilus and a baler shell, that become either clappers to ward off birds from a rice field or the container for indigo and the base for spooling cotton for weaving. With its emphasis on the journeying of the two shells, *Suti Solo do Bina Bane* can also be composed to be told as a general orphan and widow life-course recitation (for 21 versions of this chant in both formats, see Fox 2016).

In the discussion of life-course recitations, there is what would seem to be a proliferation of dual names of persons and places plus the names of various creatures of the heavens, of the earth and of the sea, as well as of plants, especially trees. All of these names carry a weight of symbolic significance defined by implicit cultural conventions. Some of these names can be translated while others are more elusive, with parts that hint at their significance. In the Rotenese, because these names are doubled, the verbs that can accompany them can be either singular or plural. In a maddening fashion, which is intolerable in English, singular and plural can alternate even in a short sequence of lines, as if the poet intended to pair them to increase his use of parallelism. In translations and exegesis in this chapter, I have tried to use singular for most persons except where two different creatures or objects are invoked and the plural is critical. I consider, in summary fashion, a number of different life-course recitations and then focus on one particular example, which I present as a good illustrative reference text.

Manu Kama ma Tepa Nilu

Soon after my arrival in Rote in April 1965, I began to study ritual language, working with three master poets from Termanu: Meno Tua ('Old Meno'), the 'Head of the Earth' of Termanu; Seu Ba'i, an already accomplished poet who had attached himself as an apprentice to Old Meno; and Peu Malesi, a fellow clansman of Seu Ba'i but someone whom Seu Ba'i saw as a rival. Most of the first compositions I recorded were life-course recitations.

The first of these was a composition by Peu Malesi that, once I had managed to transcribe it, I took to Old Meno for help in understanding it. Gradually, after several months, when I had begun to comprehend various compositions, I realised that included in a volume of Rotenese texts, *Rottineesche teksten met vertaling*, that the Dutch linguist J.C.G. Jonker published in 1911, there was a beautiful life-course recitation entitled *Manu Kama ma Tepa Nilu*, which Jonker described as 'obscure' and had left untranslated, providing instead commentary and notes on its content. When I read the Rotenese text to a couple of elders, their assumption was that it was another of the compositions that I had recorded from Malesi.

I then took the text to Old Meno and offered to read it to him. Instead, he insisted that I read it to an assembled group of elders at the end of a court session. I did this a week or so later, explaining before I began that I was bringing back Rotenese knowledge that the Dutch had recorded from their ancestors. The reading was a success. Old Meno had given me the opportunity of a public performance, which established a degree of credibility and seriousness to my status and opened the way for wider participation for my recording of oral compositions.

More significant for my research was Meno's reaction. After initially telling me how he had stayed awake at night wondering about my arrival and my motivations for coming to Termanu, he accepted me and my tape recorder as means of transmitting his knowledge to subsequent generations. At one point in another life-recitation, *Lilo Tola ma Koli Lusi*, he interpolated his own commentary on *Manu Kama ma Tepa Nilu* and, in just 28 lines, summarised a Rotenese understanding of all life recitations and their significance.

His lines assert that the human condition is one of dependence, which is expressed as being an orphan and widow. Using a traditional paired phrasing, 'those who wear black hats//those who wear yellow slippers'—an expression that originally referred to the Dutch and Portuguese but is now applied to anyone who adopts superior airs—Old Meno, as Head of the Earth, whose position is in polar opposition to the Lord of the Domain, gave insistent emphasis to the idea of mortality as the levelling feature of human life that does not differentiate between the great and the weak:

Hu ndia de neda masa-nenedak	Therefore consider, do consider
Ma ndele mafa-ndendelek	And remember, do remember
Basa lesik-kala lemin	All you great ones

Do basa lenana-ngala lemin	Or all you superior ones
Boso ma-tei telu	Do not have three hearts
Ma boso ma-dale dua.	And do not have two insides.
Se neu langa le	Whoever suffers lack and hindrance
Na basang-ngita teu ndia	We all go there
Ma se neu toa piak	And whoever suffers need and distress
Na basang-ngita teu ndia.	We all go there.
Se ana-mak?	Who is an orphan?
Na basang-ngita ana-mak.	All of us are orphans.
Ma se falu-ina?	And who is a widow?
Na basang-ngita falu-ina.	All of us are widows.
Fo la-fada lae:	They speak of:
Manu Kama dala dain	Manu Kama's road to Dain
Ma Tepa Nilu eno selan.	And Tepa Nilu's path to Selan.
Na basang-ngita ta enon	All of us have not his path
Ma basang-ngita ta dalan.	And all of us have not his road.
Sosoa-na nai dae bafak kia nde bena	This means that on this earth then
Ana-mak mesan-mesan	Each person is an orphan
Ma falu-ina mesa-mesan.	And each person is a widow.
De manasapeo nggeok	Those who wear black hats
Do manakuei modok ko	Or those who wear yellow slippers
Se ana-ma sila boe	They will be orphans, too
Ma falu-ina sila boe.	And they will be widows, too.

Meno's interpolation is both powerful and personal. It acknowledges that people follow different paths. Not everyone has 'Manu Kama's road to Dain and Tepa Nilu's path to Selan', which is distinctive and remarkable.

This life recitation begins with the marriage of Manu Kama//Tepa Nilu's mother, Silu Lilo//Huka Besi, and his father, Kama Lai Ledo//Nilu Neo Bulan, part of whose names, 'Sun//Moon' (*Ledo/Bulan*), signifies a heavenly origin. As Manu Kama//Tepa Nilu (MK//TN) is growing up, first his father and then his mother dies, leaving him an orphan. Another woman, Bula Pe//Mapo Tena (BP//MT), offers to be his true mother and aunt but when he asks her to provide bridewealth so he can marry, she is unable (too poor) to do so. This request is metaphorically phrased as a request to buy him 'a friarbird's voice and a parrot's whistle', but BP//MT replies that she is a 'woman without a ring on her finger and a girl without copper on her legs'. MK//TN therefore leaves BP//MT, sets forth and meets another woman, Lide Mudak//Adi Sole, who offers to take him in and be his true mother and aunt, but again she, too, is unable to provide him the bridewealth he needs. So, MK//TN grabs his 'friarbird-hunting bow and parrot-hunting blowpipe' and sets off once more. Next, he meets the woman Lo Luli//Kalu Palu (LL//KP), who offers to be his true mother and aunt.

One night, he hears the beating of drums and gongs and asks what is happening. LL//KP tells MK//TN that the Sun and Moon are holding a great feast at Rainbow Crossing//Thunder All-Round. So, MK//TN goes to attend the feast that is in progress. He is recognised but then insulted when he is offered millet in a rice basket and lung in a meat bowl. He leaves the feast and meets yet another woman, Leli Deak//Kona Kek (LD//KK), who becomes his mother and aunt. He moves with her to 'Lini Oe's birth group and Kene Mo's descent group', where he taps lontar palms and prepares fields for his mother and aunt, LD//KK. A perahu appears selling 'nine fine things and eight delightful objects' and its captain invites LD//KK to come on board, saying: 'What pleases you, buy it and what displeases you, put it back.' While LD//KK is looking through the offering, the owner sets sail, stealing LD//KK to take her to Selan do Dain. When MK//TN returns from the field, he is told that his mother has been carried away to Selan do Dain. He climbs on to a 'pig's feeding trough and a giant clam shell' and sets off to Selan do Dain in search of LD//KK. When he arrives at his destination—now referred to by its full ritual name, Sela Sule ma Dai Laka—he instructs the owner of the perahu to take a message back for him:

'Mai leo Lini Oe mu	'Go back to Lini Oe
Do leo Kene Mo mu!	Or go back to Kene Mo!
Mu mafada lena Lini-la	Go and tell the lords of Lini
Do mafada lesi Kene-la,	Or tell the headmen of Kene,
Mae: "Sek-o makanilu neo-la	Say: "Come to see me

Tasi-oe pepesi-la	Where the water of the sea strikes the land
Dae lai Dain boe	There is a homeland on Dain, too
Ma oe lai Selan boe.	And there is native water on Selan, too.
De au lo-ai kada Selan	My tomb-house shall be on Selan
Ma au late-dae kada Dain. "'	And my earthen-grave shall be on Dain."'

As a funeral chant, this life-course recitation, which ends with Manu Kama//Tepa Nilu's journey to Selan do Dain, is open to speculation and interpretation. It is not clear precisely what category of person it can be used to celebrate. As an all-purpose widow and orphan chant, it could possibly be used for any variety of persons. For Meno, Manu Kama's road to Dain and Tepa Nilu's path to Selan was a passage to the grave and a general commentary on all human endeavours that led finally to a tomb-house and earthen-grave.[1]

Dela Kolik ma Seko Bunak

Dela Kolik ma Seko Bunak is another fanciful life-course recitation that involves more of a pursuit than a journey. Meno recomposed an origin chant from Termanu to create this recitation, which he claimed was appropriate for the funeral of a child who dies as an infant. Dela Kolik ma Seko Bunak (DK//SB) is this male child, who is snatched from his mother and is only regained after his death. DK//SB's name includes the paired placename Kolik//Bunak, which is a ritual designation for the domain of Termanu. This gives the recitation a specific setting from which to trace the pursuit of the child.

This recitation begins with the birth of DK//SB's mother, Pinga Pasa ma So'e Leli (PP//SL), to Koli Faenama ma Bunak Tunulama (KF//BT). The critical cultural premise that underlies this recitation—and other ritual recitations—is that a mother's cravings in pregnancy reflect and reveal the character of the child to be born. Almost one-third of this recitation is taken up with KF//BT's efforts to satisfy the cravings of his wife. First,

---

1   The complete reference text of *Manu Kama ma Tepa Nilu* can be found in Fox (1988b) and has been reprinted in Fox (2014: 229–64).

PP//SL craves 'goat's liver and buffalo's lung'; then, 'bees' larvae and wasps' larvae'; then, 'chucks of turtle meat and strips of seacow flesh'; and then, fatally, 'a hawk's egg and an eagle's child'. KF//BT has to employ 'a three-toed lizard and a two-toothed mouse' to obtain the egg and child of a particular named hawk and eagle, Tetema Taenama and Balapua Loni (TT//BL), nesting in two high *nitas* and *delas* trees. These two trees, the *nitas* (*Sterculia foetida*; Indonesian: *Kelumpang*) and the *delas* (*Erythrina Spp.*; Indonesian: *Dedap*), are large, prominent flowering trees of ritual importance in this and other ritual compositions.

Soon after the birth of DK//SB, the hawk and eagle, TT//BL, takes her revenge by stealing the child and carrying him eastward to Sepe Ama Li's *nitas* tree and Timu Tongo-Batu's *delas* tree (again, the paired terms Sepe// Timu ['Dawn//East'] indicate the direction of the hawk and eagle's flight). DK//SB's mother, PP//SL, 'strikes her ribs in anger and beats her thighs in distress' and sets out in pursuit of her stolen child. When she reaches the place where the hawk and eagle are perched, she kicks the tree but cannot dislodge her child. It is at this point that the eagle and hawk, TT//BL, speak to her, saying:

'O sue anam leo bek,	'Just as you love your child,
Na au sue anang leo ndiak	So I love my child
Ma o lai tolom leo bek,	And just as you cherish your egg,
Na au lai tolong leo ndiak boe.	So I love my egg also.
De o muä au-anang-nga so	You have eaten my child
De besak-ia au uä o-anam-ma	Now I eat your child
Ma o minu au-tolong-nga so	And you have drunk my egg
De au inu o-tolom-ma bai.'	So I drink your egg also.'

TT//BL then flies back to her original perch in Taoama Dulu's *nitas* and Loniama Langa's *delas* and from there to Loma-Loma Langa's *nitas* and Pele-Pele Dulu's *delas* with PP/SL in pursuit (again, the names of the owners of these trees, both of whom have Dulu//Langa ['East//Head'] as part of their names, indicate that the flight of the hawk and eagle is in the east of Rote). However, as PP//SL approaches, TT/BL takes wing again and this time flies to the far western end of Rote at Dela Muli//Ana Iko. When PP//SL finally arrives, the eagle and hawk fly out to sea but PS//SL 'cannot wade the waves nor cross the swell' and she is forced to return home.

TT//BL then flies into the heavens and perches on the 'Moon's *delas* and the Sun's *nitas*', where she continues to munch and chew DK//SB. Finally, when all that remains are 'chicken bones and buffalo sinew', the eagle and hawk return to earth and drop what remains of DK//SB near two large rock formations off the coast of Termanu, Batu Hun ma Sua Lai, where his mother, PP//SL, can gather them. And so, the recitation ends with the lines:

Besak-ka tetema tapa henin	Now the hawk throws him away
Ma balapua tuu henin.	And the eagle casts him away.
Boe-ma inak-ka Pinga Pasa	The mother, Pinga Pasa
Ma teon-na So'e Leli neu	And his aunt, So'e Leli
De tenga do hele nenin.	Takes or picks him, carrying him.
De la-toi dui manun	They bury the chicken bones
Ma laka-dofu kalu kapan.	And they cover with earth the buffalo sinews.

The path of pursuit in this recitation transverses the island of Rote, shifting heavenward to the Sun and Moon before returning to the coast of Termanu at the centre of the island. As an imaginary biography to celebrate the death of an infant, this recitation presents a moving life-course where there has been little of life to celebrate.[2]

Ndi Lonama ma Laki Elokama

Ndi Lonama ma Laki Elokama is a life-course recitation for the death of a rich man. This recitation was gathered from Old Meno's contemporary, the master poet Stefanus Amalo. It is remarkable for its long personal admonition from the deceased addressed to the members of his family. The genealogical introduction to this recitation begins with the marriage of the woman Lisu Lasu Lonak//Dela Musu Asuk to Ndi Lonama//Laki Elokama (NL//LE), who in this case is the principal chant character and

---

2   The complete reference text for *Dela Koli ma Seko Bunak* can be found in Fox (1971) and has been reprinted in Fox (2014: 91–128). Knowing that Old Meno had composed this version as a funeral chant, Seu Ba'i, years later, provided me a version of this same chant that recounts the origin of the rock formation Sua Lai//Batu Hun, on Termanu's north coast. This version initially follows Meno's version, but then diverges significantly. The eagle and hawk do not drop Dela Koli//Seko Bunak back in Termanu but fly on to Timor and drop the child there. The child survives, marries and gives rise to the rocks Sua Lai//Batu Hun. Eventually, these rocks return to their place of origin and fix themselves on Termanu's coast.

subject of this recitation. The recitation continues with the birth of their children: a son, Solu Ndi//Luli Laki (referred to in ritual language as 'a cock's tail feathers and a rooster's plume'), and a daughter, Henu Ndi//Lilo Laki. NL//LE's wealth in herds of animals is described at length:

Te hu touk Ndi Lonama	But the man Ndi Lonama,
Ma ta'ek Laki Elokama	And the boy Laki Elokama,
Tou ma-bote biik	Is a man with flocks of goats
Ma ta'e ma-tena kapak.	And is a boy with herds of water buffalo.
De basa fai-kala	On all the days
Ma nou ledo-kala	And every sunrise
Ana tada mamao bote	He separates the flock in groups
Ma ana lilo bobongo tena	And forms the herd in circles
Na neni te tada tenan	Bringing his herd-separating spear
Ma neni tafa lilo bote-na …	And bringing his flock-forming sword …
Fo bote-la dai lena	For the flock is great
Ma tena-la to lesi …	And the herd is extensive …

NL//LE is suddenly struck down by illness and, as he is about to die, he gives instructions to his son and daughter on how to use his wealth. These instructions are long and elaborate injunctions to recognise and care for widows and orphans. When they are concluded, NL//LE sets out in poignant detail his journey to the afterworld:

Te au touk Ndi Lonama	For I am the man Ndi Lonama
Ma au taëk Laki Elokama	And I am the boy Laki Elokama
Na au tonang sanga sosokun	My boat is about to lift
Ma au balung sanga sasaën	And my perahu is about to rise
Fo au ala u tunga inang	For I am going to search for my mother
Ma ala u afi teong	And I am going to seek my aunt
Nai muli loloe	In the receding west
Ma iko tatai.	And at the tail's edge.
Fo au leo Dela Muli u	For I go to Dela in the west

Ma leo Ana Iko u.	And I go to Ana at the tail.
De se au tonang ta diku-dua	My boat will not turn back
Ma au balung ta lolo-fali	And my perahu will not return
Te dae saon doko-doe	The earth demands a spouse
Ma batu tun tai-boni	And the rocks require a mate
De se mana-sapuk mesan-mesan	Those who die, this includes everyone
Mana-lalok basa-basan	Those who perish, this includes all men
De neuk-o fai a neu fai	As day follows day
Ma ledo a neu ledo.	And sun follows sun.
Te au dilu Ana Iko len	I turn down to the river of Ana Iko
Ma au loe Dela Muli olin	I descend to the estuary of Dela Muli
Nde be na iu sio lai dalek	There are nine sharks down below
Ma foe falu lai dalek.	And eight crocodiles down below.
De ala silu dope lai dalek	They show their knife teeth down below
Ma ala dali noli lai dalek	And they sharpen their fangs down below
De neuk-o se au balung ta diku-dua	Now my boat will not turn back
Ma au tonang ta lolo-fali.	And my perahu will not return.

At a funeral ceremony, these sad words of departure foreshadowing the personal journey to the afterworld were intended to be sung as a message from the deceased to his descendants.[3]

---

3   The complete reference text for *Ndi Lonama ma Laki Elokama* was first published in Fox (2003) and reprinted in Fox (2014: 283–95).

Pau Balo ma Bola Lungi

Pau Balo ma Bola Lungi is yet another life-course recitation, intended for the funeral of a young man who dies before he has married and had a family. It is an explicitly erotic celebration of the many illicit loves of a Don Juan–like figure, who, in the version from Termanu, comes to a violent end. This chant is popularly known throughout Rote in many diverse versions, some even more explicitly adulterous than Termanu's.

This version was also obtained from the master poet Stefanus Amalo. It is one of the longest chants in my collection of life-course recitations. Pau Balo ma Bola Lungi's exploits take him on lengthy journeys to and through the domains of Rote.

This recitation begins with an extended genealogical introduction starting two generations before the birth of Pau Balo ma Bola Lungi (PB//BL). The woman Henu Elu//Bula Sao marries Lai Lota//Sina Kilo and gives birth to Malungi Lai//Balokama Sina (ML//BS). When ML//BS reaches maturity, he sets off in search of a noble wife, sailing first to the island of Savu, referred to as Seba Iko ma Safu Muli, in the west. When he is unable to find a wife on Savu, he returns to Rote, Kale do Lote, and encounters the woman Si Solu Hate Besi//Kona Boi Kado Lofa, whom he marries. When she becomes pregnant, she craves 'chucks of turtle meat and strips of seacow flesh'. These cravings can be interpreted as a sign of PB//BL's eventual character. In the Rotenese mythological imagination, the turtle and seacow were originally women who were condemned for their adultery to their sea creature condition. While seeking the food to satisfy his wife's cravings, ML//BS also gathers small sharks and stingrays to give to her—again, signalling PB//BL's future nature. PB//BL is born, twisting and lashing like a shark and stingray.

When PB//BL is growing up, he plays with some young girls who mock his claim to nobility. Stung by this taunt, PB//BL asks his mother to provide him with the variety of bamboo he needs to fashion a blowpipe and a bow to hunt parrots and friarbirds—a metaphorical declaration that he is ready to seek a woman to marry.

PB//BL sets off with his parrot-hunting blowpipe and his friarbird-hunting bow. The first woman he encounters is Liu Pota//Menge Solu (LP//MS), whose father has died. She sits upon her father's grave grieving over her situation as an orphan and widow. PB//BL decides not to use his bow and blowpipe but instead returns to his mother to tell her about LP//MS and to lament the condition of the world:

'Seuk-ko teman ta dae bafok	'Integrity is not of the earth
Ma tetun ta batu poi …'	And order is not of the world …'

As a result, he changes his resolve to marry and instead chooses to seek pleasure before he dies, asking his mother to buy lovemaking sorcery medicine to aid him in his efforts:

'Mu asa fe au nai	'Go and buy for me some sorcery stuff
Ma tadi fe au modo	And get for me some herbal medicine
Fo nai masamu siok	Sorcery stuff with nine small roots
Ma modo maoka faluk	And herb medicine with eight large roots
Fo ela Paung neu sosoa	Allowing my Pau to make love
Ma Bolang neu piao,	And my Bola to take pleasure,
Te se Paung pu lemu lon na	For my Pau's thigh will be a dolphin in the ocean
Ma Bolang ao malo sain na.	And my Bola's body will be an eel in the sea.
Neuk-ko dae holu lalutun	Later the earth will embrace it as fine dust
Ma batu luni laselan …'	And the rocks crush it into rude lumps …'

PB//BL then sets off on his lovemaking journey. His exploits are many and varied and carry him across the island. His adventures are explicitly proclaimed:

De ana sosoa basa oe la	He makes love in all the waters
Ma piao ndule dae la.	And has intercourse through all the land.

On his journey, he travels to Soni Manu ma Koko Te, the domain of Lelenuk, on the south coast of Rote. There he has the chance to sing enticingly to the accompaniment of gongs and drums:

Boe ma ta'ek-ka Pau Balo	The boy Pau Balo
Ma touk-ka Bola Lungi	And the man Bola Lungi
Lole halan no meko	Lifts his voice with the gongs
Ma selu dasin no labu.	And raises his words with the drums.
De hala filo fani-oen na	His voice as fragrant as bees' honey
Nafeo fani-lasi	Spreads round like forest bees
Ma dasi loloa tua-nasun na	And his words as sweet as lontar syrup
Naleli bupu timu.	Wander round like hovering wasps.

Women drop their fishing nets and come running to make love with him:

'Hala Pau Balo ia	'That is Pau Balo's voice
Ma dasi Bola Lungi ia.'	And those are Bola Lungi's words.'
Boe te ala nggafu heni nafi tasi nala	So they shake sea cucumbers back into the sea
Ma ala toko heni si meti mala.	And they throw the molluscs back into the tide.
De lalai lelena	They come dashing
Ma tolomu sasali.	And they come running.
De leu te Paung loloi aon	They go for Pau's rayfish twisting body
Ma Bolang fefelo aon.	And Bola's shark lashing body.
Boe ma ala tu lale'ak Paun	They wed by ravishing Pau
Ma ala sao lanolek Bolan.	And they marry by forcing Bola.

PB//BL continues on his way, making love to a married woman whose husband threatens to kill him but instead curses him. PB//BL makes light of this curse and continues his lovemaking:

Boe ma Paung sosoa lali	So Paung makes love once more
Ma Bolang piao seluk.	And Bolang takes pleasure again.
De leo dulu oen neu	To the eastern water, he goes
Ma leo langa daen neu.	And to the headland, he goes.

Finally, he meets a woman planting rice, Nggeo Lao//Pila Selu, who rejects his overtures by refusing to share betel–areca nut with him. She sends him on his way and, as he strides forward into yet another village, the curse takes effect: the rainbow cuts across him and lightning spears him.

De ana sapu no tene-tuk	He perishes quickly
Ma ana lalo no ha'e-laik	And he dies suddenly
Nai Bafi Sole dulu mon	In Bafi Sole's eastern field
Ma nai Diu Ama langa fuan.	And in Diu Ama's headplain.
De late-dae neme ndia	The earthen grave is there
Ma lo-ai name na.	And the wooden tomb is at that spot.

Although his death is sudden and violent, PB//BL remains something of a heroic figure among Rotenese men and references are frequently made to him as a recognised cultural figure.[4]

Life-course recitations as literary compositions

All life-course recitations are literary compositions. Composed according to cultural norms that require the strict pairing of words, these formal recitations are formulaically structured and follow an array of recognised conventions. Journeys are ordered according to a directional template that looks east or west, north or south through a landscape clustered with ritually designated dual names. The dual names of chant characters overlap with placenames, adding to the evocative significance of each recitation. The names of other creatures from the heavens, the earth and the sea as well as the names of plants form part of this same system. By convention, some creatures and some trees are specifically male or female. Their associations are the literary vehicle for cultural understandings.

For the Rotenese today, these recitations are literary compositions in another sense. They continue to be preserved by the poets and elders of the island, but they are rarely performed at rituals. Virtually all funerals

---

4   I have already gathered several versions of *Pau Balo ma Bola Lungi* recited in different dialects that provide varying accounts of Pau Balo//Bola Lungi's exploits. I am still hoping to gather at least another two versions to be able to compare them with one another with a particular focus on their erotic language.

are now conducted with Christian rituals, which allow, at best, fragments of the past—snatches and segments of a recitation—to emerge. That these recitations are still maintained as an oral tradition is a tribute to the perseverance of the past and the recognition of a rich ancestral tradition that continues to evoke cultural respect.

Attempting to interpret any single life-course recitation requires careful attention to the conventions on which it draws. It is therefore instructive to consider one life recitation in detail—one that, like many similar recitations, involves journeying back and forth across the island with messengers and messages sent to convey sentiments of symbolic significance about the nature of life, death and memory.

Kea Lenga ma Lona Bala: A life-course reference text

Kea Lenga ma Lona Bala is perhaps an inappropriate name for this life-course recitation. Kea Lenga//Lona Bala is the chant character who figures most prominently in the recitation but, as a funeral chant, this composition concerns the chant character Delo Iuk//Soma Lopa, a woman who dies in childbirth. This composition offers an excellent example of many of the chief features of a life-course recitation, including the journeying and messaging that link its protagonists.

Unlike most life-course recitations, this composition, gathered from the master poet Seu Ba'i in 1965–66, does not begin with a genealogical introduction. Its opening lines posit a time when Kea Lenga//Lona Bala is old enough to begin the search for a spouse.

Kea Lenga//Lona Bala hears that there are beautiful women to be wed on the tiny island of Ndao, referred to as Ndao Dale//Folo Manu, and he sets off in a perahu to find a wife:

1.	*Touk-ka Kea Lenga*	The man Kea Lenga
2.	*Ma ta'ek-ka Lona Bala.*	And the boy Lona Bala.
3.	*Faik esa manunin*	On one certain day
4.	*Ma ledo esa mateben*	And at one particular time [sun]
5.	*Ndii na namanene*	Ears hear
6.	*Nggata na namania*	Hearing listens

7.	*Benga lafafada*	Words are spoken
8.	*Dasi lakatutuda*	Voices let fall
9.	*Ina lena Ndao Dale la*	There are extra women on Ndao Dale
10.	*Feto lesi Folo Manu la*	Additional girls on Folo Manu
11.	*Dani la lahe lolek*	Unmarried girls of rivalling loveliness
12.	*Leo lutu lahe lolek*	Like smooth stones of rivalling loveliness
13.	*Sopa laka'i kalek*	Unwed girls of imposing beauty
14.	*Leo dongi laka'i kalek.*	Like barbed spears of imposing beauty.
15.	*Boe ma touk-ka Kea Lenga*	The man Kea Lenga
16.	*Ma ta'ek-ka Lona Bala*	And the boy Lona Bala
17.	*Nakandolu tona ofan*	Builds a perahu ship
18.	*Ma nalela balu paun.*	And designs a sailing craft.
19.	*Faik esa matetuk*	On one right day
20.	*Ledok esa matemak*	On one perfect time
21.	*Boe ma laba nala tona ofan*	He mounts the perahu ship
22.	*Ma tinga nala balu paun.*	And steps aboard the sailing craft.
23.	*De ana pale uli titidi de neu*	He guides the splashing rudder
24.	*Ma leko la kukulu de neu*	And manoeuvres the flapping sails
25.	*Neu tasi Ndao balu buin*	Toward Ndao's sea anchorage
26.	*Ma neu meti Folo beu te'en.*	And toward Folo's tidal harbour.

When Kea Lenga//Lona Bala (KL//LB) arrives in the harbour of Ndao, he meets the man Ndao Eli-Sama//Folo No-Do'o (NE//FN), who is fishing. NE//FN interrogates KL//LB and KL//LB asks him about marriageable women on Ndao. NE/FN tells him that all the women of Ndao have married except for one woman in the house of Iu Ai//Lopo Maka. This turns out to be the woman Delo Iuk//Soma Lopo:

27.	*Boe ma neu tongo lololo*	There he meets with his arms
28.	*Tou Ndao Eli-Sama*	The man Ndao Eli-Sama
29.	*Ma neu nda lilima*	And he encounters with his hands
30.	*Ta'e Folo No-Do'o*	The boy Folo No-Do'o
31.	*Pili lide tetele*	Bending over to pick out *lide*-fish
32.	*Nai tasi Ndao balu buin*	In Ndao's sea anchorage
33.	*Maku moka luluku*	And stooping to spy minnows
34.	*Nai meti Folo beu te'en.*	In Folo's tidal harbour.
35.	*Boe te ana lole halan neu*	He raises his voice
36.	*Ma a'e dasi neu, nae:*	And lifts his words, saying:
37.	*'Baluk se balun o*	'This boat, is it your boat
38.	*Tonak se tonan o?'*	This ship, is it your ship?'
39.	*Boe te touk-ka Kea Lenga*	So the man Kea Lenga
40.	*Ma taëk-ka Lona Bala nae:*	And the boy Lona Bala says:
41.	*'Baluk au balung ia*	'This boat is my boat
42.	*Tonak au tonang ia.*	This ship is my ship.
43.	*Ndii nga namanene*	My ears hear
44.	*Ma nggata nga namania*	My hearing listens
45.	*Ina lena Ndao Dale la*	There are extra women on Ndao Dale
46.	*Feto lesi Folo Manu la*	Additional girls on Folo Manu
47.	*Sopa la kai kalek*	Unwed girls of imposing beauty
48.	*Ma dani lahe lolek.*	Unmarried girls of unrivalled loveliness.
49.	*De au pale uli titidi*	I guide the splashing rudder
50.	*Ma au leko la kukulu*	And I manoeuvre the flapping sails
51.	*Fo sanga leo Ndao Nusa u*	To seek Ndao Nusa
52.	*Ma sanga leo Folo Manu u.'*	And to seek Folo Manu.'
53.	*Boe te taë Folo No-Do'o*	The boy Folo No-Do'o

54.	*Tou Ndao Eli-Sama*	And the man Ndao Eli-Sama
55.	*Ana selu dasi neu*	He raises his words
56.	*Ma ana aë halan neu, nae:*	And he lifts his voice, saying:
57.	*'Ina lena Ndao Dale la*	'The extra women on Ndao Dale
58.	*Tu lama-noü so*	Have all wed
59.	*Feto lesi Folo Manu la*	The additional girls on Folo Manu
60.	*Sao lama-dai so.*	Have already married.
61.	*Ala dani lai to'on lon*	There is a girl unwed in her mother's brother's house
62.	*Sopa lai aman uman*	And a girl unmarried in her father's home
63.	*Lai Iu Ai Ndaok uman*	In the house of Iu Ai of Ndao
64.	*Lai Lopo Maka Folo lon.'*	And in the home of Lopo Maka of Folo.'

Kea Lenga//Lona Balo marries Delo Iuk//Soma Lopo and she becomes pregnant. Unexpectedly, KL//LB hears that Pele-Pele Dulu//Loma-Loma Langa has died and he has to board his perahu to return home. The paired terms *Dulu//Langa* ('East//Head') in the name Pele-Pele Dulu//Loma-Loma Langa indicate that KL//LB must traverse the island from Ndao at the western tip of Rote to somewhere at the eastern end of the island. He returns to the 'Dawning East//Reddening Head' (*Timu Dulu//Sepe Langa*):

65.	*Nadeka tu nala Delo Iuk*	Now he weds Delo Iuk
66.	*Sao nala Soma Lopo*	And marries Soma Lopo
67.	*Boe ma tu nala Delo Iuk*	He weds Delo Iuk
68.	*Ma sao nala Soma Lopo.*	And he marries Soma Lopo.
69.	*Faik esa mateben*	One particular day
70.	*Ma ledok esa manunin*	And one certain time [sun]
71.	*Boe te inak-ka Delo Iuk*	The woman Delo Iuk
72.	*Ma fetok-ka Soma Lopo*	And the girl Soma Lopo
73.	*Tei-na daä -fai*	Her womb enlarges
74.	*Ma su'u-na nggeo-lena*	And her breasts darken
75.	*Nggeo-lena bobongin*	Darken to give birth

76.	*Ma daa-fai lalaen.*	Enlarge to bring forth [a child].
77.	*Boe te halak-kala mai*	But voices come
78.	*Ma dasik-kala mai*	And words come
79.	*Touk Pele-Pele Dulu*	The man Pele-Pele Dulu
80.	*Ma taek Loma-Loma Langa*	And the boy Loma-Loma Langa
81.	*Ana lalo ma ana sapu.*	He has died and he has perished.
82.	*Boe ma taëk-ka Kea Lenga*	So the boy Kea Lenga
83.	*Tinga-nala balu paun*	Steps aboard his sailing craft
84.	*Ma touk-ka Lona Bala*	And the man Lona Bala
85.	*Sae-nala tona ofan.*	Climbs on top his perahu ship.
86.	*Ana leo Timu Dulu neu*	He goes toward Dawning East
87.	*Ma leo Sepe Langa neu.*	And toward Reddening Head.

Time passes and the father of KL//LB's wife, Lopo Maka//Iu Ai, on Ndao asks the Tiny Bat of the Dawning East and the Flying Fox of the Reddening Head to fly to the east to find out about KL//LB. There, where two roads form a circle and three paths come together, they meet Lani Pea//Siti Si'u:

88.	*Teuk lakalaladik*	Time passes
89.	*Bulak lakaseseluk*	Moons change
90.	*Te balun ta lolo-fali*	But the boat does not return
91.	*Ma tonan ta diku-dua.*	And the ship does not come back.
92.	*Boe ma ta'ek Lopo Maka Folo*	So the boy Lopo Maka of Folo
93.	*Ma touk Iu Ai Ndaok*	And the man Iu Ai of Ndao
94.	*Ana tetenin Bau Ana Timu Dulu*	He questions the Tiny Bat of the Dawning East
95.	*Ma ana tata Soi Ana Sepe Langa*	And asks the Flying Fox of Reddening Head
96.	*Nai dala batu sepe langa*	On the stone road to Reddening Head

97.	*Ma eno dae timu dulu, lae:*	And on the earthen path to Dawning East, saying:
98.	*'O eno daen sila boe*	'You on the earthen path
99.	*Ma o dala batu sila boe*	And you on the stone road
100.	*De o leo timu dulu mu*	Go to Dawning East
101.	*Ma o leo sepe langa mu.'*	And go to Reddening Head.'
102.	*Boe ma Bau Ana Timu Dulu la leu boe*	So the Tiny Bat of Dawning East goes
103.	*Ma Soi Ana Sepe Langa la leu*	And the Flying Fox of Reddening Head goes
104.	*Te leu dala dua bobongon*	He goes to where two roads form a circle
105.	*Ma leu eno telu tai-lolon.*	And goes to where three paths come together.
106.	*Boe te leu tongo lololo*	There he meets with arms
107.	*Ma leu nda lilima*	And encounters with hands
108.	*Lani Pea ma Siti Si'u.*	Lani Pea and Siti Si'u.

Lani Pea//Siti Si'u tells the Tiny Bat and the Flying Fox that she is mourning the death of her father, Pea Pale-Sama//Si'u Lele-Lai. They sit at the gravesite, which is marked by two hardwood trees, a *tanga-tea* and *ka-koli*. These trees are, by convention, the signs of a poorly tended grave disturbed by roving animals. In her grief, LP//SS tells the Tiny Bat and Flying Fox to travel further and pose their questions again:

109.	*De natane neme ndia*	He asks there
110.	*Ma teteni neme na.*	And questions at that spot.
111.	*Boe te ala selu dasi neu*	They raise words
112.	*Ma a'e halan neu:*	And they lift voices:
113.	*'Mu manosi seluk bai*	'Go inquire once again
114.	*Ma mu matane seluk bai*	And go, ask once again
115.	*Te Si'u Lele-Lai sapu*	For Si'u Lele-Lai has died
116.	*Ma Pea Pale-Sama lalo.*	And Pea Pale-Sama has perished.
117.	*De lalo ela Lani Pea*	He has perished leaving Lani Pea

118.	*Ma sapu ela Siti Si'u.*	And he has died leaving Siti Si'u.
119.	*De ami mangatu late dae*	We sit on the earthen grave
120.	*Ma ami masalai lo ai*	And we lean on the wooden tomb
121.	*De lo ai tanga-tea la*	A tomb of wood-hard *tanga-tea* tree
122.	*Ma late batu ka-koli la.*	And a grave of rock-hard *ka-koli* tree.
123.	*Ala pila bala dededen*	It is now a deep-burnt red
124.	*Ma ala nggeo lasa kekenin.*	And is now a dark, glossy black.
125.	*Ami mangatu tunga seli*	We sit on one side
126.	*Na manu kali tunga seli*	While chickens scratch on one side
127.	*Ma ami masalai tunga seli*	And we lean on one side
128.	*Bafi tofi tunga seli.*	While pigs uproot the ground on one side.
129.	*De mu teteni seluk bai*	Go, question once again
130.	*Ma mu tata seluk bai.'*	And go, demand once again.'

The Tiny Bat and the Flying Fox fly on to another site where two roads form a circle and three paths come together and there they meet Dano-La Lalata//Beu-La O'oko, part of whose names (*dano*: 'lake') and actions evoke an aquatic scene. This spot attracts the Tiny Bat and Flying Fox to stay and they do not return to Ndao:

131.	*Boe ma neu natane seluk*	So he goes to ask again
132.	*Ma neu tata seluk.*	And he goes to demand again.
133.	*De neu dala dua bobongon*	He goes to where two roads form a circle
134.	*Ma eno telu tai-lolon.*	And where three paths come together.
135.	*Boe te neu nda lilima*	There he encounters with hands
136.	*Ma neu tongo lololo*	And he meets with arms
137.	*Dano-La Lalata*	Dano-La Lalata

138. *Ma Beu-La O'oko.*	And Beu-La O'oko.
139. *De oko lo dene buna*	They wade there with kapok flowers
140. *Ma lata lo mea lilo.*	And they float there with golden red buds.
141. *De Soi Ana Sepe Langa*	The Flying Fox of Reddening Head
142. *Ma Bau Ana Timu Dulu*	And Tiny Bat of Dawning East
143. *Ala lili dene leme ndia*	They love the kapok plants there
144. *Ma neka dano leme na.*	And crave the lake plants at that place.
145. *De ala ta tulek Ndao*	They do not go back to Ndao
146. *Ma ala ta falik Folo.*	And they do not return to Folo.

When the Tiny Bat and the Flying Fox do not return to Ndao, Iu Ai//Lopo Maka (IA//LM) demands that the Friarbird and Green Parrot fly off to the Dawning East and Reddening Head to find Kea Lenga//Lona Bala and tell him to come back to Ndao because his wife has died giving birth. This initiates a dialogue: the Friarbird and Green Parrot explain that they need two specific trees—a *nitas* tree and a *delas* tree—on which to alight. IA// ML then instructs them to alight on Timu Tongo-Batu's *nitas* tree and Sepe Ama-Li's *delas* tree. Again, the terms Timu//Sepe ('East'//'Dawn') in these names indicate a location in the east of Rote. By convention, the Friarbird and Green Parrot are considered to be female. Their gentle, sweet song is an important aspect of the message they are intended to convey:

147. *Boe ma ta'ek Iu Ai Ndaok*	So the boy Iu Ai of Ndao
148. *Ma touk Lopo Maka Folo*	And the man Lopo Maka of Folo
149. *Ana tata Koa Ndao*	He demands of the Friarbird of Ndao
150. *Ma teteni Nggia Folo*	And requests the Green Parrot of Folo
151. *Fo leo Timu Dulu neu*	To go to Dawning East
152. *Ma leo Sepe Langa neu*	And to go to Reddening Head

153. *Do na-lo Kea Lenga*	To call Kea Lenga
154. *Ma na-nggou Lona Bala*	And to shout for Lona Bala
155. *Fo falik Folo Manu mai*	To return to Folo Manu
156. *Ma tulek Ndao Nusa mai*	And to come back to Ndao Nusa
157. *Te Delo Iuk bongi*	For Delo Iuk was giving birth
158. *Te ana lalo*	But she died
159. *Ma Soma Lopo lae*	And Soma Lopo was bringing forth
160. *(Te) ana sapu.*	But she perished.
161. *Boe te Koa lole halan*	But the Friarbird raises her voice
162. *Ma Nggia aë dasin, nae:*	And the Green Parrot lifts her words, saying:
163. *'Au koa mana taidok*	'I am a leaf-clinging Friarbird
164. *Ma au nggia manasae baëk.*	And I am a branch-perching Green Parrot.
165. *De au u Timu Dulu*	If I go to Dawning East
166. *Fo au sae baëk u be*	On what branch will I perch
167. *Ma au(u) Sepe Langa*	And if I go to Reddening Head
168. *Fo au tai dok u be?'*	To what leaf will I cling?'
169. *Boe ma taëk Iu Ai Ndaok*	The boy Iu Ai of Ndao
170. *Ma touk Maka Lopo Folo*	And the man Lopo Maka of Folo
171. *Ana lole halan neu*	He raises his voice
172. *Ma a'e dasin neu, nae:*	And lifts his words, saying:
173. *'Mu Timu Tongo-Batu nitan ba'en*	'Go to a branch of Timu Tongo-Batu's *nitas* tree
174. *Ma Sepe Ama-li delan poin*	And go to the top of Sepe Ama-Li's *delas* tree
175. *Fo sa'e baek mu ndia*	Go, perch on the branch there
176. *Fo bebenu mu ndia*	Go, balance there
177. *Ma tai dok mu ndia*	And go, cling to the leaf there
178. *Fo dodoko mu ndia.'*	Go hang there.'

The Friarbird and Green Parrot fly off to the east to perch on *nitas// delas* trees. There they meet the woman Buna Sepe//Boa Timu (BS//BT: 'Reddening Flower//Eastern Fruit'), who asks them who they are. They explain that they are the Friarbird and Green Parrot of Ndao and have come to look for Kea Lenga//Lona Bala to tell him that his wife has died giving birth. BS//BT tells them that the mourning is continuing for the death of Loma-Loma Langa//Pele-Pele Dulu (LL//PD), who has left his child, Ka Loma//Pua Pele, an orphan. (It was the news of LL//PD's death that prompted Kea Lenga//Lona Bala to leave Ndao and come back to the east.) BS//BT instructs the Friarbird and Green Parrot to be aware of this situation when they go on to speak to KL//LB:

179.	*Boe te ana leo Sepe Langa neu*	So she goes to Reddening Head
180.	*Ma leo Timu Dulu neu.*	And goes to Dawning East.
181.	*De ana sae ba'ek neu Nitas*	She perches on the branch of the *nitas*
182.	*Ma tai dok neu Delas.*	And clings to the leaf of the *delas*.
183.	*De siluk bei ta dulu*	Dawn is not yet in the east
184.	*Ma huak bei te langa*	And light is not yet at the head
185.	*Te ana kako doko-doe halan*	But she sings pleadingly with her voice
186.	*Ma hele tai-boni dasin.*	And whistles requestfully with her words.
187.	*Boe ma inak-ka Buna Sepe*	The woman Buna Sepe (Reddening Flower)
188.	*Ma fetok-ka Boa Timu*	And the girl Boa Timu (Eastern Fruit)
189.	*Ana kona boke dae mai*	She climbs down to the ground
190.	*Ma tuda nggodi dae mai.*	And slips down to the ground.
191.	*De ana lelu nalamula dulu*	She looks intently toward the east
192.	*Ma lipe nakanae langa.*	And stares carefully toward the head.

193. *De ana selu halan neu*	She lifts her voice
194. *Ma lole dasin neu, nae:*	And raises her words, saying:
195. *'Koa be nde o*	'What sort of friarbird are you
196. *Ma nggia hata nde o?*	And what kind of green parrot are you?
197. *De siluk bei ta dulu*	Dawn is not yet in the east
198. *Ma hu'ak bei ta langa,*	And light is not yet at the head,
199. *Te o mu amang nitan-na lain*	But you go to the top of my father's *nitas*
200. *Ma to'ong delan-na lain.*	And to the top of my mother's brother's *delas*.
201. *De o kako doko-doe halam*	You sing pleadingly with your voice
202. *De mahala hataholi*	You have a human voice
203. *Ma o hele tai-boni dasim*	And you whistle requestfully with your words
204. *De madasi daehena.'*	You have a person's words.'
205. *Boe ma Koa a'e dasin neu*	The Friarbird lifts her words
206. *Ma nggia lole halan neu, nae:*	And the Green Parrot raises her voice, saying:
207. *'Koa Ndao nde au*	'I am the Friarbird of Ndao
208. *Ma Nggia Folo nde au.*	And I am the Green Parrot of Folo
209. *Au eme Folo Manu mai*	I come from Folo Manu
210. *Ma au eme Ndao Nusa mai*	And I come from Ndao Nusa
211. *Fo mai a-lo Kea Lenga*	I come to call out for Kea Lenga
212. *Ma a-nggou Lona Bala.*	And I shout for Lona Bala.
213. *Tun Delo Iuk bongi*	His spouse, Delo Iuk, was giving birth
214. *Te ana lalo*	But she died
215. *Ma saon Soma Lopo lae*	And his wife, Soma Lopo, was bringing forth
216. *Te ana sapu.'*	But she perished.'
217. *Boe ma inak-ka Boa Timu*	The woman Boa Timu

218.	*Ma fetok-ka Buna Sepe*	And the girl Buna Sepe
219.	*A'e halan neu*	Lifts her voice
220.	*Ma lole dasin neu:*	And raises her words:
221.	*'Bei huas-sa ia*	'Just yesterday
222.	*Ma bei nakas-sa ia*	And just a little while ago
223.	*Loma-Loma Langa lalo*	Loma-Loma Langa died
224.	*Ma Pele-Pele Dulu sapu.*	And Pele-Pele Dulu perished.
225.	*De sapu ela Pua Pele*	He perished, leaving Pua Pele
226.	*Ma lalo ela Ka Loma.*	And he died, leaving Ka Loma.
227.	*De leo Kea Lenga uman mu*	When you go to Kea Lenga's house
228.	*Ma leo Lona Bala lon mu*	And to Lona Bala's home
229.	*Fo mafada nai ndia*	Speak there
230.	*Ma manosi nai na.'*	And talk at that place.'

The Friarbird and Green Parrot fly on to speak to Kea Lenga//Lona Bala to tell him of the death of his wife in childbirth. He explains that he is in mourning for LL//PD and then gives them an areca nut and coconut, instructing them to plant the coconut at the head of his wife's grave and the areca nut at the foot of her grave so that he will recognise the grave when he returns to Ndao:

231.	*Boe ma ana la lida neu*	So she flies wings
232.	*Ma ana meli ei neu.*	And she hastens legs.
233.	*De nafada Kea Lenga*	She speaks to Kea Lenga
234.	*Ma nanosi Lona Bala, nae:*	And talks to Lona Bala, saying:
235.	*'Saom-ma Delo Iuk bongi*	'Your wife, Delo Iuk, was giving birth
236.	*Te ana lalo*	But she died
237.	*Ma tum-ma Soma Lopo lae*	And your spouse, Soma Lopo, was bringing forth
238.	*Te ana sapu.'*	But she perished.'
239.	*Boe ma touk-ka Kea Lenga*	The man Kea Lenga
240.	*Ma ta'ek-ka Lona Bala*	And the boy Lona Bala

241. *Lole halan neu*	Raises his voice
242. *Ma aë dasin neu:*	And lifts his words:
243. *'Bei heni huas-sa ia*	'Only just yesterday
244. *Ma bei liti nakas-sa ia*	And barely a little while ago
245. *Loma-Loma Langa lalo*	Loma-Loma Langa died
246. *Ma Pele-Pele Dulu sapu.*	And Pele-Pele Dulu perished.
247. *De sapu ela Pua Pele*	He perished, leaving Pua Pele
248. *Ma lalo ela Ka Loma*	And died, leaving Ka Loma
249. *Bei doe-doe nita osi*	Still succulent as a *nitas* garden
250. *Ma bei nula-nula nupu no.*	And still unripe as a coconut shoot.
251. *De o tulek diku [-dua] Ndao*	You go turning back to Ndao
252. *Ma falik lolo-fali Folo*	And return back to Folo
253. *Fo muni pua nde ia*	Carrying this areca nut
254. *Ma muni no nde ia*	And carrying this coconut
255. *Fo Delo Iuk sapu so*	For Delo Iuk has died
256. *Na sele pua neu ein*	So plant this areca nut at her feet
257. *Ma Soma Lopo lalo so*	And Soma Lopo has perished
258. *Na tane no neu langan*	So sow this coconut at her head
259. *Fo ela no laboa langan*	And let the coconut grow fruit at her head
260. *Ma ela pua langgi ein*	And let the areca grow flower stalks at her feet
261. *Fo ela au falik leo Ndao u*	So that when I return to Ndao
262. *Na au lelu u late dae*	I may go to look upon her earthen grave
263. *Ma au tulek leo Folo u*	And I go back to Folo
264. *Na au lipe u lo ai.'*	I may stare at her wooden tomb.'

The final journey to the afterworld

Just as life is conceived of as a journey, so, too, is death. Rotenese life-course recitations celebrate the possibilities of many different paths for life's journeying. These celebrations were given voice by a chanter (or sometimes a succession of chanters), who would lead a long night's round-dancing before the burial. The dirge that accompanied or immediately followed the burial recounted a different journey—a perilous journey on a single path to an unknown land westward, where the sun sets and from which there is no return.

The dirge has long since ceased to be performed in Termanu. In eastern Rote, particularly in Ringgou, such dirges (*boreu*) are still carried out to instruct the dead on this final journey. This long dirge was recorded from the master poet Ande Ruy. To perform it, he had to imagine for himself a setting and chose to remember the death of an elderly woman to whom he refers as 'grandmother' (*besa*). It constitutes an extended dialogue between the chanter and the deceased, remembering her life but at the same time firmly instructing her on her journey to the afterworld.

This long lament heaps image upon image, mixing the remembrance of moments of joy with the stark realities of departure, describing the coffin as the ship of the dead about to set sail. To emphasise the nature of the journey to the afterworld, the chanter states that when one goes to Kupang (referred to, in grandiose terms, as Kota Batu//Di'i Lilo: 'the Stone-Wall Town//the Golden Pillars'), one can return, but from the journey to the afterworld, there is no return.

In pre-Christian beliefs, it was thought that some aspect of the person did return briefly to partake of the food offerings left for the dead. In this chant, that belief is evoked and the deceased is referred to as a remnant creature with the eyes of a bumble bee. However, even this visitation is fleeting. At its conclusion, the deceased is described as 'a fallen coconut//a withered areca nut' and instructed: 'Just fix your eyes on your path and direct your nose to your way.'

He'e a'u we o besa o	Ah, wee … O Grandmother
Mana-sue o nei	Who was so loving …
Ma mana-lai o nei	And so affectionate …
Masa mao o nei	So caring …

Boi o nei.	So supporting …
He'e a'u we	Ah wee …
Ua ia tao le'e boe	What fortune is this
Ma nale ia tao le'e, besa?	What fate is this, Grandmother?
De rina basa nusa ara boe	There through all the domains
Ma basa iku ra boe, besa	And all the lands, Grandmother
Bei ro dudi no-nara	Still with relatives
Ma ro tora tuke-nara	And with kin,
Fo au afarene lolo, besa ei	For I remember, Grandmother
Do ameda rara.	Or I ponder.
Au ia isa apa	Here I am like a single buffalo
Boe ma au ia mesa manu.	Here I am like a lonely chicken.
Te nae:	It is said:
Dale leo pila lolo	An inside like stretched red threads
Ma tei leo keo tenu,	And a heart like black woven threads,
Tei mamadai dulu	Your heart reaches to the east
Soa neu buna	Taking care of (your) flowers [children]
Ma dale mamano'u laka	Your inside extends to the head
Bati neu boa leo.	Fending for (your) fruit [descendants].
Te nae:	It is said:
He'e a'u we, mana-sue o nei	Ah wee … one so loving
Ma mana-lai o nei,	And one so affectionate,
Mata malua ia	The eye of the day is dawning now
Ma idu maka ledo ia	The hint ('nose') of the sun is shining now
Te neuko su'i besi neu ko	But the coffin nails are for you
Ma koe riti neu ko.	And the coffin lock closes for you.
O besa, londa asa neu dulu	O Grandmother, drape cloth at the east

Ma ba pou neu laka.	And wrap the cloth at the head.
He'e au we o neu ko	Ah wee ... for you
Tika mala balum lain,	Climb aboard your perahu,
Balu pao-ma lain	Aboard your sailing perahu
Ma hene mala tondam lain	Mount aboard your boat
Tonda ufa-ma lain,	Aboard your sailing boat,
Ma neuko hapa nunu balu paom	Your banyan-wood sailing perahu
Ma ba e'a tonda umam.	Your waringin wood sailing boat.
De au afarene lololo	I do continue to remember
Ma asa neda rara, besa.	And I do continue to ponder, Grandmother.
Na neuko au dale boe rasala	Here my heart feels wrong
Ma teik boe rasiko.	And my stomach feels off target.
He'e au we mana-sue o nei	Ah wee ... one so loving
Ma mana-lai o nei	And one so affectionate
Fo hida bei leo hatan	At a time long ago
Ma data bei leo don	At a time since past
Honda rolam papa	Your walking stick creaking
Ma te aim boboto	And your wooden spear sounding
Ifa mala buna leo	You cradled the flowers of your clan
Ma o'o mala soro mala leo.	And you carried the descendants of your clan.
Faina ledo neu peu tua	During that day, going to tap the lontar
Fo [ami] mala meu peu tua	We went to tap the lontar
Te hu dadi mu nama hena.	This became our hope.
Ma fai neu lele hade,	And on that day, going to tend the rice
Na ami mala meu lele hade	We went to tend the rice
Tehu dadi mu nabani, besa a.	This became our prospect, grandmother.
Nai lo a dale	Within the home

Ma nai uma a dale	And within the house
Ifa mara upu mara	Cradling your grandchildren
Ma o'o mara soro mara.	And carrying your descendants.
Au dalek boe dola edu	My heart is full of sorrow
Ma au teika boe koko redo	And my insides are filled with regret
Besa a, maka ledo ia leo	Grandmother, the sunlight has past
Ma malua ia leo.	And the daylight has gone.
Neuko mori mu hapa nunu	Now is time to lay the *waringan* [coffin]
Ma dadi mu ba e'a.	And the moment to set your banyan [coffin].
De fain nea peu tuan	The day to watch the lontar tapping
Na bea neu mete upuma	Then to see your grandchildren
Ma ledo neu lele haden	The time to tend the rice
Na bea neu relu soro mara.	Then to look after your descendants.
Fain a beka ra-fafada	On that day, voices might say
Ma dasi rama-tuda, rae:	And words might fall, saying:
'Seo dai Kota Batu	'Go to the Stone-Walled Town [Kupang]'
Seo dai te fali	If you go, you can come back
Ma deru dai Di'i Lilo	'And journey to Golden Pillars [Kupang]'
Na deru dai te tule.	If you journey, you can return.
Tehu balakai ia leo.	But now stiff like this …
Ki kalutu Folo	Green Parrots caw on Folo
Ki' rae malua	Green Parrots speak to the dawn
Ma dolo kateu Ndao	Friarbirds twitter on Ndao
Dolo rae makaledo.	Friarbirds speak to the sunlight.
Neuko hene mala tondam lain	Now climb on board your boat
Tonda ufama lain.	On board your boat and perahu.
Idu maka ledo ia	The nose of dawn is here

Dolo kateu Ndao	Friarbirds twitter on Ndao
Neuko dolo rae maka kedu	Now the Friarbirds speak sobbingly
Na hene mala balum lain	Now step on board your vessel
Balu pao ma lain.	On board your vessel and canoe.
He'e au we mana-sue o nei	Ah wee, one so loving
Ma mana-lai o nei	And one so affectionate
Neuko leko la fo mu	Now set sail to go
Ma pale uli fo mu	And turn your rudder to go
De neuko leko la Safu Muri	Set sail for Savu in the West
Ma pale uli Seba I'o.	And turn your rudder to Seba at the tail.
De tule ta di'u dua so	Do not return, having turned your back
Ma fali ta soro lele so.	And do not come back, having turned round.
De nae:	It is said:
Ela dea-dea, besa o	Let's speak and speak, O Grandmother
Ma ela ola-ola dei, besa o.	And let's talk and talk, O Grandmother.
Sadi rene mafa-rene	Only remember, do remember
Te nai oe ma so	Where your water once was
Ma sadi neda masa neda	And only recall, do recall
Te nai dae ma so.	Where your land once was.
Tehu au dalen boe dola edu	But my heart is also full of sorrow
Ma teik boe koko redo	And my insides are filled with regret
Afa rene lololo	I continually remember
Ma ameda rara	And I constantly recall
Mata esa ko matan	Eye to eye
Ma rolu esa ko rolu	Knowing each other
Ma idu esa ko idu	Nose to nose
De lela esa ko lela.	Understanding each other.

De mana-sue o nei	One so affectionate
Ma mana-lai o nei.	One so loving.
Te neuko fati ara tao lada	But in the middle of the night
Ma boro ara tao do	And late in the night
O tule di'u dua mai	You can return, turning back
Ma fali soro lele mai	And come back, turning round
Te ma-mata bupu timu	But with the eyes of a bumble bee
Fo mahara bupu timu	The voice of a bumble bee
Ma ma-idu fani lasi	And the nose of a honeybee
Fo madasi fani lasi.	The sound of a honeybee.
He'e au we mana-sue o nei	Ah wee … one so affectionate
Ma mana-lai o nei	And one so loving
Au ameda neu upu mara	I recall your grandchildren
Ma au afarene neu soro mara	And I remember your descendants
Buna bei nai bui	Flowers not yet at the tip
Modo bei nai odan.	Green not yet at the head.
De dila bei ta nasa-e'e	Wings not yet able to fly
Ma ei bei ta na-pa'i.	Legs not yet able to crawl.
Ledo esa nai ria	One time like this
Ma fai esa nai na	One day like that
Besa, te doko doe reu dua	Grandmother, begging twice
Ma tai-boni reu telu	And requesting thrice
Ratane reu dua	Questioning twice
Ma teteni reu telu.	Asking thrice.
He'e au we mana-sue o nei	Ah wee … one so affectionate
Ma mana-lai o nei	And one so loving
Te idu bara te tasi	As close as the spines of a sea urchin
Ma idu esa ko idun	Nose to nose
Ma mata soro siu meti	And as close as the *gewang*-leaf ocean net
Mata esa ko matan.	Eye to eye.

Na neuko tei boe o dola edu	Now [our] insides are filled with regret
Ma dale boe koko redo	And hearts are full of sorrow
Te hu sale dale taa na	But regret does nothing
Ma tue tei taa ria.	And sorrow does nothing.
He'e au we mana-sue o nei	Ah wee … one so loving
Mana-lai o nei	And one so affectionate
Mori mu batu tue	You go to the stone of regret
De ami tue tei meu dua	Our inner regret is doubled
Ma mori mu ai sale	And you go to the tree of sorrow
De ami sale dale meu telu.	Our hearts' sorrow is tripled.
Te se manu oa lasi	The noisy chicken of the wood
Se o sala so	What has gone wrong
Ma dilu bafi noli nura	The tusked pig of the forest
Dilu o siko so?	What is mistaken?
He'e au we mana-sue o nei	Ah wee … one so loving
Ma mana-lai o nei	And one so affectionate
Sama leo nura Lole	Like the forest of Loleh
De tati heni nura Lole	Cut down the forest of Loleh
De ami ode Lole be kako?	Then where will our Loleh monkey hoot?
Ma sama leo nura Dela	And like the forest of Dela
De dede heni nura dela	Burn down the forest of Dela
De ami bafi Dela be tofa?	Then where will our Dela pig root?
Tehu sale dale ta'a na, besa	Regret of the heart is not here, Grandmother
Ma tue tei ta'a ria.	And inner sorrow is not there.
Te hekene basa so	Promises are past
Ma bara-tà basa so	Restrictions are past
Ua esa ko ua	Fortune with fortune
Nale esa ko nale	Fate with fate
Ami mafarene lolo	We continually remember
Ma masaneda rara	And bear in mind

Ua leo besak ua	Fortune like the present fortune
Ma nale besak nale.	Fate like the present fate.
Mama lasi leo no	Mother, old as a coconut
Fo ono aom leo no	Your body falls like a coconut
Ma mama latu leo pua	And mother, withered as an areca nut
Fo refa aom leo pua.	Your body drops like an areca nut.
Mita mai leo be a	We will see what happens
Fo balaha leo be a	What tomorrow will be
Ma ami bulu mai leo be a	And we will learn what will be
Fo binesa leo be a.	What the day after next will be.
Ria neme ria leo	Let this be as this
Ma na neme na leo.	And let it be as it is.
Tule di'u dua mu	Go, turning, turning back
Mu oe ma leo	Go to the waters and onward
Ma fali soro lele mu	Go, go back, turning round
Mu dae ma leo	Go to [your] lands and onwards
Sadi pasa mata neu eno	Just fix your eyes on your path
Ma sunda idu neu dala	And direct your nose to your way
Besa ei.	Grandmother.

Conclusion

Rotenese life-course recitations convey a vital imagined world. Although there are references to ordinary everyday activities in these recitations, much of what they portray is far from ordinary. In this chapter, I have focused on the world of movement these life-course recitations recount: messaging and journeying across the island and to destinations beyond Rote. This is a world of many possible paths. The possibility of many paths is the epitome of life, in contrast to the one-way journey into death.

References

Fox, James J. 1971. 'Semantic parallelism in Rotinese ritual language.' *Bijdragen tot de Taal-, Land- en Volkenkunde* 127: 215–55. doi.org/10.1163/22134379-90002782.

Fox, James J. 1988a. '"Chicken bones and buffalo sinews": Verbal frames and the organization of Rotinese mortuary performances.' In D.S. Moyer and H.J.M. Claessen, eds, *Time Past, Time Present, Time Future: Essays in honour of P.E. de Josselin de Jong*, pp. 178–194. Verhandelingen van het Koninklijk Instituut voor Taal-, Land- en Volkenkunde 131. Dordrecht, Netherlands: Foris Publications.

Fox, James J. 1988b. '"Manu Kama's road, Tepa Nilu's path": Theme, narrative and formula in Rotinese ritual language.' In James J. Fox, ed., *To Speak in Pairs: Essays on the ritual languages of eastern Indonesia*, pp. 161–201. Cambridge: Cambridge University Press. doi.org/10.1017/CBO9780511551369.007.

Fox, James J. 2003. 'Admonitions of the ancestors: Giving voice to the deceased in Rotinese mortuary rituals.' In Peter J.M. Nas, Gerard Persoon and Rivke Jaffe, eds, *Framing Indonesian Realities: Essays in symbolic anthropology in honour of Reimar Schefold*, pp. 15–26. Leiden: KITLV Press.

Fox, James J. 2014. *Explorations in Semantic Parallelism*. Canberra: ANU Press. doi.org/10.22459/ESP.07.2014.

Fox, James J. 2016. *Master Poets, Ritual Masters: The art of oral composition among the Rotenese of eastern Indonesia*. Canberra: ANU Press. doi.org/10.22459/MPRM.04.2016.

Jonker, Johann C.G. 1911. *Rottineesche teksten met Vertaling [Rotinese Lyrics with Translation]*. Leiden: E.J. Brill.

9

Winds and seas: Exploring the pulses of place in *kula* exchange and yam gardening

Susanne Kuehling

To Professor Erhard Schlesier, 1926–2018[1]

Introduction: Movements in the Massim

Austronesians have a common history of seafaring and exchanging, and this chapter explores the movements of people and objects within the *kula* system of gift exchange in southeastern Papua New Guinea as an example of an Austronesian 'matrix of movement' (Ingold 2000: 219). I will demonstrate that their journeys and other movements occur in a social space that is experienced as a multilayered web of clan-based communities and a patchwork of defined, often named, spaces (called *mwatui* in the Dobu language) that are entered and crossed, exited, circumvented or visited depending on the social relation of persons to

---

1 Professor Emeritus Erhard Schlesier passed away in 2018. Without him, I would never have embarked on this long journey and I am forever grateful for his mentorship and teachings. This chapter is dedicated to him, although words will never suffice to express my feelings in February 2018 when I looked at the mountains of Me'udana, where he did his field research, and realised I could never meet him again.

the space. Socially significant movements often occur in regular bursts, or pulses, as the gardening cycle as well as the *kula* activities are responding to the annual seasons and social events that encourage or prohibit them. People cannot walk around freely; they are obliged to respect the wishes of the landowners when they leave their own *mwatui*, hence the choice of routes is limited to certain paths, blocks of land, villages, beaches, reefs and islands. Strangers or trespassers were not treated kindly in the past (see Fortune 1932), and I have more than once witnessed physical harm done to supposed trespassers during my fieldwork on Dobu Island.[2]

The concept of movement on a 'path', as it refers to the journey from A to B, is widespread among Austronesians. I will demonstrate that, rather than being seen as linear and absolute, the term, for the islanders of the *kula* region, describes a motion concerning various *mwatui* that will be involved in an individual's journey, causing moral and practical considerations and challenges at times. Depending on their social role, people may have different *mwatui* at their disposition, using principles of clan, lineage and adoption to negotiate them. Some spaces are considered mostly neutral and public, like the wet line on beaches where the waves lap on the shore, while others, such as cemeteries, are prohibited for anyone who is not part of the lineage. Some *mwatui* are regarded as dangerous and spirit-inhabited while others, like a church, are seen as safe. Time also matters when considering which route to take, as day and night provide different restrictions and opportunities, the seasons and the weather determine which options are feasible and the cycle of feasting changes the usual rules during events. Since warfare ended in the 1890s, overseas exchanges have become the main *'eda* (routes) for men to achieve renown. The *mwatui* of *kula* journeying appear as sea spaces that are different from land only in that they are free for all to enter, cross and exit. Linguistically, they are not different from land spaces, but in reality, the challenge of ocean travel and its opportunities make sea *mwatui* more exciting to travel than paths on land. Sea travel requires complex knowledge of the seasonal

---

2   I conducted fieldwork on Dobu and surrounding islands from 1992 to 1994 and for shorter visits in 1995, 2009, 2012, 2015, 2016 and 2018. My gratitude to the many islanders who worked with me has no limits. This chapter is a collaborative project with those many men and women over the years. Neddy Daniel from Dobu Island never tired of reflecting on semantic questions, but the bulk of information on winds and seas was shared by Synod Timothy, a *kula* master and former captain of a cargo boat who knows the waters and seasons. I am fluent in the Dobu language that serves as lingua franca among the older generation of *kula* masters.

winds and how to navigate them, but in comparison with Micronesia and Polynesia, here island destinations are close enough to travel by waymarks if the weather is favourable.[3]

Kula exchange: The hard work of giving

Kula exchange is famous in the social sciences as the archetypical example of gift exchange with delayed reciprocity. Two kinds of objects are passed between a chain of partners in a large maritime region (the 'Massim'), providing strong networks of support, a competitive element between the participants and the thrill of adventure. The fame of *kula* is based on a classic monograph by Bronislaw Małinowski, titled *Argonauts of the Western Pacific* (1922)—the best-known volume of his ethnographies about the Trobriand Islanders. *Kula* has also been known in sociology since Marcel Mauss elaborated on the notion of reciprocity by using it as one example in his classic monograph *The Gift* (1990). More recent debates on the relevance of *kula* in sociocultural anthropology were published in a *kula* conference volume edited by Leach and Leach (1983) and in the works of Fred Damon (1983a, 1983b, 1990, 2000, 2002, 2017) and Nancy Munn (1986, 1990). Complicated concepts, from reciprocity to value and gender, have benefited from *kula*-related material (see Graeber 2001).

The valuables used for *kula* exchange are cut from shell: one is a wide ring cut from the Conus shell (called *mwali*) and the other consists of tiny red shell disks chipped from the thin red layer inside Chama oysters (called *bagi*, *veigun* or *soulava*). With decorative shells and beads, the valuables are fashioned in specific styles that indicate part of their value. Patina and the knowledge that a valuable has circulated many times add to the beauty of cut and decoration, but the assessment of value remains contested in many cases. There are four categories of rank, from newly made and small to ancient and very fine. Two valuables of the highest rank, called *dagula* (Dobu: 'head decoration'), appear in Plates 9.1 and 9.2.

---

3   For Central Carolinians, comparable named sea spaces are documented (for example, Alkire 1974: 45; D'Arcy 2006: 98) and, although on a much larger scale than the *kula* travellers, many similarities point to common relationships between Austronesian peoples and their seas of islands. Mimi George has recently argued that ancestral *mana* can be directed to manipulate the winds and gods in Taumako Atoll, Polynesia (2012, 2018).

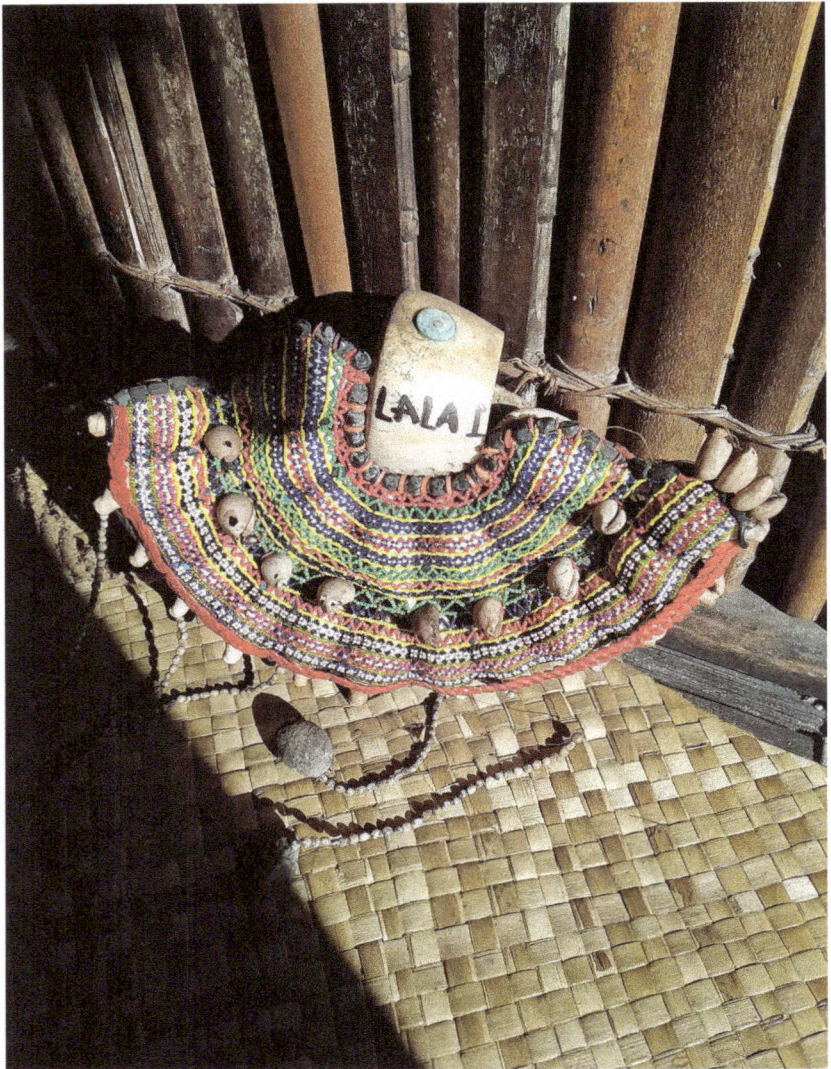

Plate 9.1 *Mwali* named Lala, picture taken in Wabununa (Woodlark Island) at the house of Chief Dibolele in February 2016

Photo: Susanne Kuehling.

Plate 9.2 *Bagi* named Komakala'kedakeda, held by Toulitala in Bihawa (Duau, Normanby Island) in February 2016

Photo: Susanne Kuehling.

As more than 1,000 shell ornaments of each type of *kula* valuable travel on their *'eda* (routes) in opposite directions between the islands, they accumulate individual fame on their journey—on their past *'eda*—that rubs off on to the persons who hold them temporarily. They are mostly given on credit by the host to the guest and returned when the former host visits his former guest. Ideally, these partnerships are not only lifelong but are also passed on as an important part of one's heritage from the maternal uncle, thereby remaining within the matrilineage. The social networks that are maintained for *kula*, the magic, moral principles and stories that are required for successful exchanges and the specific resources on the islands of the *kula* region are at the root of the sociopolitical systems and egalitarian structures. These valuables—*bagi* and *mwali*—can be used to purchase pigs and canoes. They are indispensable in local exchanges between families, regulating social relations—for example, in marriage exchanges, compensation payments and especially in mortuary rituals (see Damon and Wagner 1989). *Kula* travel and subsistence gardening are tied together by the seasons and the varied environments of the region.

For the Austronesians of the *kula* region, as in many other rural areas, movements are mostly restricted to subsistence activities and family events, leaving individuals little room for choosing their paths. After pacification and conversion to Christianity around the 1890s, new opportunities opened up, as markets and church events provided new, good reasons to move about in a morally acceptable manner (Kuehling 2014), but today's islanders continue to encourage each other to *miabaula* (literally, 'to stay at home and mind one's business') (Kuehling 2005: 82). To wander around the island without legitimate purpose (*adadana besobeso*) is regarded as a wasteful, impolite, disrespectful and potentially dangerous activity and travel is legitimate only when it is classified as 'work' (*paisewa*; see Kuehling 2005: 91). *Paisewa* refers to laudable activities that require persons to do things that are for the community (or lineage), such as gardening, childbearing, mourning, building houses, canoes and other structures, household work, weaving, exchanges of food between affinal relatives, mortuary rituals and, in particular, exchanges of the most valuable things: large yams, pigs and *kula* valuables.

Longer journeys across the ocean are normally related to the movement of these most valuable objects. A *kula* expedition provides a perfect reason to travel in a morally acceptable manner; it is a laudable affair, comparable with visiting family, attending feasts and helping with transport for organising pigs and other resources (sago leaf for house-building, betel nuts, pandanus rolls for weaving mats, clay pots and dried sago bundles). To handle *kula* valuables on behalf of one's matrilineage counts as equally important as providing pigs and yams for distribution. These three items are clustered as *'une*, the most important things in an adult's life (see Kuehling 2005). As the late Ruth Lakatani, a *kula* master from Mwemweyala hamlet on Dobu, would tell me, '*'une* are very important [*yage sinabwana*]; other things are worthless [*yage besobeso*]' (Fieldnotes, September 2015).[4]

4   I received funding for this study from the Canadian Social Science Humanities Research Council as well as internal funds from the University of Regina (VP Research Fund and Travel Fund). I am very grateful for the support from my colleagues at the University of Regina—in particular, Nilgun Önder (Associate Dean, Research), Sally Gray and the office of Research Services; Murray Daku and the office of Financial Services; and Tobias Sperlich, who, as head of my department, shifted my classes around the research and showed general support when needed most. The members of both research teams and their leaders, Philip Baloiloi and Synod Timothy, deserve my sincere gratitude, as they volunteered for this project and neither expected nor received any payment for their hard work. The visual anthropologist on our team, Regina Knapp, was cheerful and productive even when the circumstances were impossible (as on the second expedition, when the boat's generator was defective and batteries could only be charged when the engine was running).

In the Dobu-speaking southern region, there are two main reasons to go on a *kula* expedition. First, it is required to cleanse a mourner or reintroduce an heir after the death of a *kula* man or woman (this kind of expedition is called *kwausa*). Second, a strong leader can call out for a competitive journey, in which all participants try to reach a specific goal, called *yawala*. The goal could be to bring back a named shell valuable or a set amount of valuables. In the northern *kula* region—from the Amphlett Islands in the west to Muyuwa (Woodlark, also Muyuw), Nasikwabu, Yanabwa and Egom in the east—*kula* events are also centred on competition and mortuary rituals, but the details and terms differ. Individuals who are involved in *kula*—usually not more than one or two men per matrilineage—negotiate with their wives, sisters and mothers when they can go on a *kula* trip to plan, discuss and eventually formalise the exchanges of *kula* valuables. Those men, often accompanied by a young relative as an apprentice, travel in two directions to visit their partners. Their 'work' (*paisewa*) of *kula* is the sum of their experiences during the journeys, the physical discomfort caused by being at a strange place, drinking 'strange water' and depending on the hosts' generosity, the emotional hardships of passing on a beloved valuable and the hard work of providing for a *kula* visitor, reciprocating the hospitality that the host has previously experienced (Kuehling 2017).

Map 9.1 The *kula* region
Source: Malinowski (1922: Map III).

Going for a spin

Obviously, not all movements can be classified as 'work'. While *kula* expeditions are the only way to experience the larger island world, many men admit they sometimes go for 'a little spin', as they say in English. Due to the predominantly matrilocal residence pattern, men routinely move more frequently between villages as they live with their wives but carry responsibilities for their own matrilineage. Their obligations in both places provide excuses that allow them to stop and chat on their way or take a detour for personal enjoyment. For unmarried men, the restrictions are even more relaxed. At night-time, these spins lead either to the house of a girlfriend (*gwali*) or to a gathering in the 'bush' with peers (*ediu*), where drinking and barbecuing of a (perhaps stolen) chicken are typical activities (as I was told). Girls are strongly advised to stay at home during the night, as pack-rapes by drunken men (called 'line-ups': *lain*) are not unheard of. Women are rarely seen walking to their gardens alone, to avoid encounters with men 'on a spin'.[5] Most women prefer not to travel on the sea, although they enjoy an hour of afternoon fishing just off the village, in the company of a child or two, to provide a little protein for the evening meal. Night fishing, or fishing with nets or kites, is restricted to men, in line with the general concept that women should stay in the house at night.

Daytime spins may include a canoe trip. On a beautiful calm day, the commonly shared desire to spontaneously paddle across the sparkling surface of the ocean, enjoying the beauty and looking out for nothing in particular makes it acceptable for unmarried men to travel by sea without explicit purpose. In a well-known story, the hero paddles around just for pleasure, as he explains to everyone whom he encounters in a slightly apologetic manner after being asked what he is up to (Kuehling 1998: 329–36):

'Ei, niba, mwao tautauya?'	'Hi, cross-cousin, where are you going?'
Enega i gwae: 'Ya, tuga ya eneyaneya.	So he responded: 'Nah, I am just paddling around without purpose.

---

5   Reo Fortune's statement that 'they rarely have to be raped' when encountered alone (1932: 77) does not reflect my experiences and conversations with many girls and women.

Siwalowa nuagu i ewena ga ya eneyaneya.'	The calm sea has attracted my thinking/feeling and so I just paddle around.'
I ona: 'O, bobo'ana.	He said: 'Oh, that's good.
Nate u neyaneya u naonao ebwe'una wate yage iabe u loba.	Paddle to over there and you will find one special something.
Ebwe'una salu ena.'	On one of the islands.'

This exchange represents the appropriate style of an encounter in the region, as persons who move always have to explain themselves to the people they encounter in a deferential manner. The short dialogue also documents the usual way to meet strangers while moving. First, the term for cross-cousin (*niba*) is used to indicate relatedness in a more general manner, implying that they are from a different clan (which in the past indicated a more severe level of strangeness than today). Second, our hero literally justified his purpose-free arrival: he stated that 'my thinking/feeling had been so attracted by the calm sea that I just took off and paddled around'. In response, the local shows his approval to the humble admission of just spinning and regales him with information about 'finding something' when paddling further and then 'crossing' (*naonao*).

Kula journeys

My focus in this chapter is on *kula*-related ocean travel, not on individual adventures ('spins') or land-based journeys. Unlike previous accounts of *kula* exchange that have foregrounded the individual desires and musings of *kula* masters (Damon 1983a, 1983b, 1990, 2000, 2002; Małinowski 1920, 1922; Munn 1986, 1990), I will here dwell more on the communal aspects, the shared environment and belief system and the shared understanding of journeys among *kula* travellers. For generations now, young men have been tested and observed by their fathers and uncles, so that the smartest child of a man's sister would become the principal heir of his *kula* partnerships. These partnerships are ideally self-renewing and most trustworthy. A man 'travels and speaks for himself in public, but he will always have his sisters' children in mind' when transacting and plotting, as I was told many times. *Kula* travellers should therefore be understood as the representatives of their respective matrilineages. They share not only the valuables, but also the stories of their experiences with those left behind, contributing strongly to general conceptions of places in the region.

Plate 9.3 Chief Dibolele of Wabununa (Woodlark Island) displays some of his *bagi* valuables for inspection

Photo: Susanne Kuehling.

In addition to the matrilineage of a man, his household plays a significant role in his success in *kula*. Most men live at the place of their wife and children, who are from a different clan and matrilineage, yet they contribute to the success of the journey in various ways—for example, by exercising *miabaula* during the *kula* journey, as their 'useless walkabout' (*adadana besobeso*) can hurt the traveller or damage the exchanges. While a man crosses the ocean, his entire extended family back home remains linked to his fate, in spite of the distance. A wife and a son will receive some *kula* valuables to thank them for their efforts in supporting the husband's or father's *kula*, but most of the inheritance of *kula* stays within his matrilineage, with a man's sister's children. Through their individual actions—and this includes magic, dream travel and witchcraft—the islanders never feel unobserved or singular (see Kuehling 2005), so neither persons nor places should be seen as disconnected from each other when imagining Austronesian paths. The social syndrome called *gwasa* (or *nadiwala*) speaks to this connectedness, as people in a hamlet suffer from hangover-like symptoms when a visitor has left after staying overnight. *Gwasa* lasts for three days and effectively slows every activity in the hamlet and gardens as people believe that they are more likely to hurt themselves when working hard during *gwasa*.

The *kula* region, from a villager's point of view, forms a web of linked matrilineages that intersect and overlap. Former headmistress Millicent Laibobo recalled the time when she had to travel to strange places as part of her job. She explained:

> *Kula* is very important: when I travel and people hear the names of my mother or her brother, their partners go and prepare my bed, my food, my betel nuts. All for free. (Interview, March 2016, Asagamwana, Bwaiowa)

Over and over, people emphasised this aspect of *kula* as the most desirable 'profit'—the exchanges are roughly balanced over time and there is no material gain involved other than the freedom of travel and the wider horizon that it provides.

Routes and paths: The concept of *'eda*

The English terms 'path' or 'lane' do not translate easily into the Dobu language. Its equivalent, *'eda* (or *keda* or *ked* in other languages of the *kula* region), is less topographically and rather socially defined. A 'path' is not only a lane, footpath or road, but also can be the solution to a problem, a potential route to another person, such as an exchange partner (both in physical and social space) or the journey of a *kula* shell valuable from hand to hand, beach to beach, circulating through the *kula* network.

Only valuables circulate (*sakowasi*) through the *kula* network; persons only visit the next stops in two directions. Dobu-speaking people, in their perspective, do not 'walk on a path' but cross a matrix of named spaces. To the islanders, the world is divided into geographical spaces (*mwatui*) that are subdivided into even smaller *mwatui* in multiple ways. Persons cross these *mwatui* as they go about their lives—for example, when they visit the small outhouse on the beach: they first leave the interior of the house (*toolo*), cross the verandah (*apwesa*), climb down (*mwauta*), cross the village space on the way to the beach (*dolo*), cross the beach (*dolo*) and enter (*lugu*) the small hut over the sea after climbing (*mwela*) and crossing (*abala*) a shaky 'bridge'. After finishing their business, persons reverse these actions as they come out (*apwesa*), walk in parallel to the beach (*nao*), go back to the house (*laga*) across the beach and enter (*lugu*) the village space. While this is a simple route, choosing the right path in other contexts sometimes creates difficulties and conundrums and wise men are praised for picking the right *'eda*.

Due to the moral dimensions and wisdom required to move appropriately and successfully, the concept of *'eda* offers itself to metaphorical use, and indeed, I have heard it in many different contexts, ranging from highly formal to casual. In speeches, when discussing the movements of valuable objects as their *'eda* or commenting on incorrect movement as *'edagesi* ('wrong *'eda*'), the term has a legal undertone, but when young people scheme to meet a mate, the term becomes more playful and acquires a sexual undertone. When women talk about their *'eda* to the garden, they often refer to their hard work in even reaching their yam garden. Challenges may be pondered by searching for a suitable *'eda* out of calamity. Taking a 'heavy' (*mwau-*) route may take its toll or lead to glory, depending on the individual's capability. In some contexts, following the appropriate *'eda* is regarded as laudable 'hard work' (*paisewa*). There are *mwatui* of the supernatural—spaces where witches and sorcerers are believed to move, where the spirits of the dead are living, and journeys to such spaces are dangerous. 'There is a hidden world under the cooking stones', as my friend stated in a confidential conversation, referring to the *mwatui* of *welabana* (witches) and *balau* (sorcerers) that the islanders believe exist in parallel to their physical world.

Islanders acknowledge that women and men tend to follow different *'eda* as adults, each gender group using their specific routes to fame. Women spend most of their time in their hamlet and both last year's and this year's gardens, usually working in small groups with their children. They may paddle out to catch some small fish, within sight of the shore, but are not supposed to roam around alone at night or further out on the ocean. Men are more regularly moving around, from their wife's place to their sister's village and to the bush looking for prey or building material. They are the fishermen and canoe builders; their universe is larger for they are mobile on the ocean.

Mwatui: Named spaces

On land, *mwatui* are owned spaces, usually belonging to a number of people at the same time. Dobu Island, for example, is the large *mwatui* with which I am most familiar. On Dobu, the 60-some hamlets—each a few huts on stilts—are spread around the coastline, forming six separate *kula mwatui* that are quite independent and now elect their own councillor. These *mwatui* are Edugaula, Mwanomwanona, Enaia, Balabala, Wabuna and Egadoi. The island itself takes precedence over these subdivisions. When all the *kula* people from Dobu travel together, they call it *Gulebubu yawalina*: the *kula* expedition (*yawala*) of the dormant volcano that forms the island (named Gulebubu: literally, 'the Rock of the Grandparents'). Within each of these *mwatui*, there are bush lands, gardens, swamps and grass areas as well as several hamlets, each belonging to one or two matrilineages, preferably of the same moiety of bird clans, either those residing in nests or those residing in tree holes (see Kuehling 2005: 67). The island is surrounded by *mwatui*: travellers first reach the *mwatui* of the shore (*loniuniuna*: 'seeing stones and movement') and then the shallow part on the beach (*lodababa'ina*: 'where the waves are moving'). If nobody welcomes the travellers, they will sit on the dry sand close to the waves, gazing towards the ocean, waiting to be approached and allowed on to the island by the landowning matrilineage (*susu*).

All *mwatui* are managed by the matrilineages whose male and female elders assign an individual to use it (for gardening or settlement). In all cases, permission is required to enter the *mwatui* of another lineage. Each matrilineage holds a number of exclusive plots of land near the village; one is a little bit further inland, where the storage huts for yams are located, and another one, also in the vicinity of the hamlet and overgrown with shrubs and often marked by croton plants, is their cemetery. Those two *mwatui* are for the exclusive use of the owners; people from different lineages can only enter together with landowners (this includes husbands in this matrilocal setup). Before 1900, primary burials were done in the centre of the hamlet, and these *tabu* spaces still exist, unused but still charged with power, invisible to the stranger but always present to the family who lives around it. In the past, only members of the matrilineage would enter their lineage's central burial space (*ali'ali*); others could not cross the hamlet but walked around its periphery, staying in the less restricted space of a footpath or a beach.

There are six bird clans (*manua*) on Dobu, spread across the island. Being in the *mwatui* of one's bird clan is seen as being with family ('we are one'), as all the food of that land can be consumed without hesitation or repercussions.[6] I learned repeatedly that, in the past, clan was indeed the connection that ensured the partner was safe at a foreign place. One reason was, as I was informed many times over, that fellow clan members could not be eaten in cannibalism times, as eating someone of one's own clan is believed to cause a debilitating fatal disease called *lala*, which causes the abdomen to swell and the blood to turn 'bad'. I witnessed a situation where a man who had passed away during a *kula* expedition in 1993 was left behind on Normanby Island because 'his partner was of the same clan so he could be buried there' (Fieldnotes 1993; also Kuehling 2005: 202). Due to frequent conflicts over land during my fieldwork, I could not map the clan lands outside the hamlets, but Map 9.2 shows the six *kula mwatui* and roughly indicates the dispersed clans and their *mwatui* of residence on Dobu Island.

Often, footpaths (*'eda*) follow the boundary of two clan *mwatui* or are located between the sandy beach and the soil of someone's land. Ownership, clearly, is a complicated matter in this system: while a person may be assigned as the owner of a specific taro plant, the *mwatui* of that plant is situated inside the *mwatui* of the *susu*, which is also part of the clan land of that *susu*. After harvesting that taro plant, seniors of either *susu* or clan level may advise a person to plant the next one somewhere else and so a person's house garden *mwatui* may keep changing, as does one's yam garden (*bagula*) and last year's garden (*yakwala*) in the rhythm of swidden agriculture that is practised in the *kula* region.

---

6   Some clans stored the bones of their deceased in secret and exclusive limestone caves on the Sailele peninsula. This practice is now discontinued and one of the caves has been inaccessible since 2016.

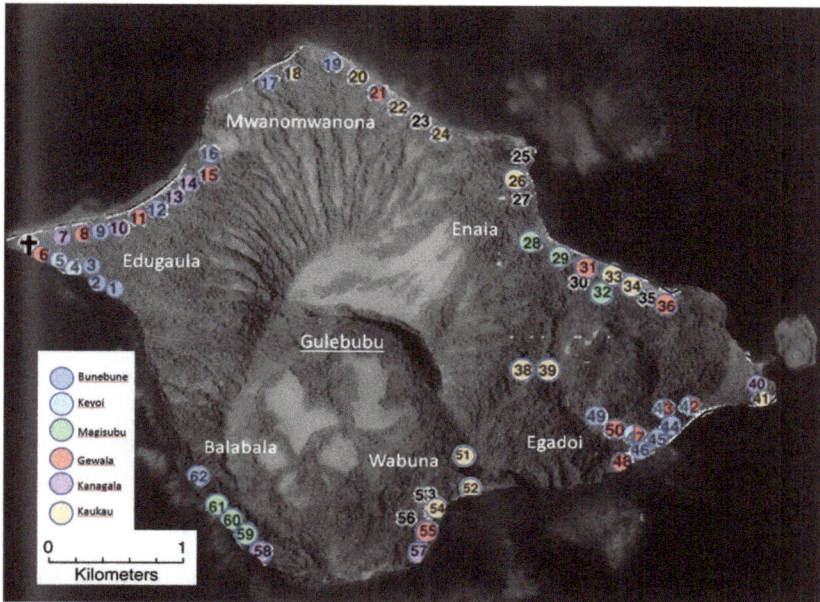

Map 9.2 Map of Dobu Island, with clans from census taken in 1993
Source: Author's creation.

Some key attributes of *mwatui* were created in the past. When a person dies, the house of the deceased will be abandoned and seen as a 'dirty' (*baibaila*) space. No new house will be built on this *mwatui* once it has fallen apart. As long as memory lasts, the space remains connected to the deceased person and the life that once happened there. The children and grandchildren of a man will not eat any food that has been grown near his house or eat pork raised nearby, not just because it is regarded as disrespectful but also because it is believed to cause a dangerous disease. These spaces remain connected to their deceased paternal relative for two generations, no matter how a village changes its appearance over the decades.

In theory, *mwatui* on the islands of *kula* exchange could be mapped according to interlinking bird clans, likely indicating that individuals are intimately related to *mwatui* all across the region. It used to be advisable to marry the daughter of a *kula* partner to ensure stability in the multilinked networks of overseas partners. Such links have left traces, resulting in people on different islands stating that they are 'the same' regarding lineage and clan.[7] The ocean is part of this patchwork of subdivided spaces. Although not linked to clans (as far as I am aware), the routes that can be sailed or paddled are named *mwatui*. These *mwatui* eclipse smaller *mwatui* like reefs, islets, rocks, a vortex 'that pulls the canoe under' named Mwanou (Mwasiuna Taikeu, February 2016) and other features. Mythological tracks of culture heroes abound and connect the region (for example, Fortune 1932: 216–31; Young 1991).

Travel is experienced as the result of moving between *mwatui*, whether on land or by sea. For example, if a man goes to the beach, intending to travel by canoe, he crosses the *mwatui* on land and, pushing (*pela*) the vessel from further up the beach, enters the *mwatui* where the waves lap up to the sand and wades (*gayo*) into the shallow sea (*lodabadaba*). He climbs into the canoe and paddles past the region where he can still see the stones on the ground (*loniuniuna*) while setting up his sail. All these motions fall under the larger category of going seawards (*dolo*) as he reaches the zone of deep ocean (*ola simasimata*). There are reefs (*nuwa*) and spots where certain fish can be caught sometimes—smaller *mwatui* related to subsistence, usually named and owned by a matrilineage or clan. In the Dobu region, one can almost always see some land, so the traveller is unlikely to reach a zone of deep and endless ocean (*bwagabwaga daita*) but will usually reverse the motions to go on land (*laga*) on a neighbouring island to visit a relative or exchange partner. Epeli Hau`ofa has famously argued that, for Pacific islanders, the ocean is not a restricting boundary but a place of opportunity and movement, a 'sea of islands' (1994, 1998). There is no linguistic difference between *mwatui* on land and *mwatui* on the ocean for the *kula* region.

Kula as a regional system

Overseas travel in southeastern Papua New Guinea, as in many other island regions, was dangerous in the past, when raiding and occasional cannibalism caused severe fear of foreign coasts. Many islands had no name as they did not constitute a unit, so the clustering by the early European explorers does not correspond with local notions of island

---

7   In the century since pacification, the relevance of clans as places of the same intrinsic substance has decreased, but Reo Fortune's remark that 'totemism is not important in establishing international exchange partnerships', based on his fieldwork on Tewara Island in the late 1920s (1932: 209), is inconsistent with my data.

space. The sea of *kula* islands excludes many islands, like Goodenough, and only spots on the other large islands of the D'Entrecasteaux archipelago belong to it. It consists of more than 30 islands: the Duau region of Normanby, the Bwaoiwa coast of Fergusson and Dobu in the D'Entrecasteaux archipelago form the southern boundary; the Trobriand Islands and Muyuwa (or Muyuw, Woodlark Island) are the northern extension (see Map 9.3). In between are smaller groups of low islands, reefs and sandbanks, making it a treacherous region to navigate. The *kula* exchange connects at least 10,000 islanders across the region, providing news, assistance and kinship. In the past, essential items like clay pots and canoes, pigs and other resources were included in the network and still today large canoes can be bought with four or so *kula* valuables and a few pigs. Large clay pots are a typical (and welcome) gift to *kula* partners, who pass them on to a wife or other female relative when returning home. The valuables themselves are an important resource for places that do not produce them, like Duau, Dobu and Bwaiowa, as they, like the other *kula* communities, need them for affinal exchanges within their islands, mostly as bride-price and mortuary gifts, but also for the use of land and as compensation 'payment'. I believe that many more communities indirectly benefit from the network, as gossip and objects are always in motion and people are related to places outside the *kula* region, too.

The experience of space is ever changing in time, so in this section I will explore how the winds and seas, seasons and individual knowledge of their patterns contribute to the experience of *kula* travel in the Massim region of Papua New Guinea. Since Małinowski's classic study of *kula* in the *Argonauts of the Western Pacific* (1922), research on the ground has mostly focused on intensive studies in various island communities.

The named sea spaces of the *kula* region and beyond invoke memories—for example, of myths and songs that narrate the mythical wandering of culture heroes in the island world. For *kula* traders, traces of the mythical fights between giant snakes and powerful cockatoos are still visible in the landscape of the Duau coast and the movements of a mythical snake from Goodenough Island to Duau and further northeast are not only visible in the formation of reefs but also present in the minds of the islanders, who are always willing to share the public version of these stories. Mermaids and sprites populate the mind when travelling these *mwatui*, but also stories of wrecked ships, drowned valuables and passengers and brave (or not so brave) captains and crews.

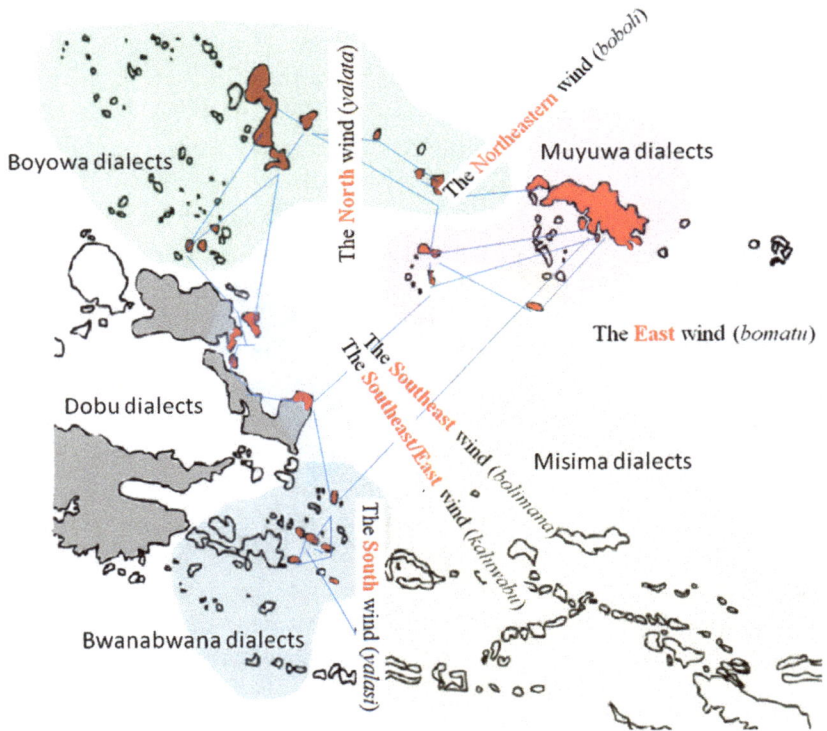

Map 9.3 Languages and winds of the *kula* region (red spots are *kula* communities)
Source: Author's creation.

Since most of the islands in the *kula* region can be reached in steps of two-day canoe trips, it comes as no surprise that the islanders are interrelated and share a sense of community. Yet it could be argued that, without the moral dimension legitimising travel, such connections would not exist in spite of the short distances, and in fact, many islands in the east of the region are less connected since they lost their link to the *kula* network around 1900. The barren, uninhabited Conflict Islands were once a critical stopover point for canoe fleets connecting Misima and Sudest to the *kula* region, bringing red shell strings as part of their exchanges. These strings were fashioned into *bagi* by specialists within the *kula* region (Bwanabwana). While named sea spaces still connect the island regions, they do not constitute *kula* 'paths' of the present but are evidence of a broken link. Strings of shell disks are now peddled (about 20 centimetres for about A$100) through the provincial capital, Alotau, or purchased when visiting Sudest or another island of that region (for about half that price).

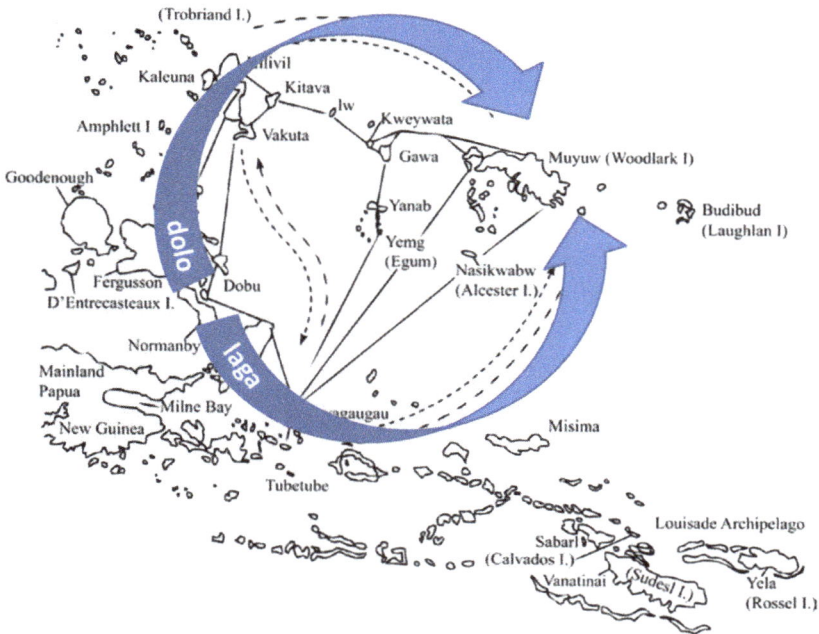

Figure 9.1 Going up and down for *kula*

Source: Author's creation, based on map by Martha Macintyre (1983: xxi).

The notion of 'up' and 'down', as in many Austronesian languages, is connected to the rising and setting of the sun, which crosses its own *mwatui* in the sky on its daily journey. Except for the Trobriand Islands, located at the far northwest of the *kula* region, with no islands to go 'down' to, the principle of this polarity is applied in the various languages of the *kula* region. To complicate matters, the *kula* regions are recognised as separate, *kula*-related *mwatui*, so a canoe crosses over (*abala*) from Dobu Island to Esa'ala on Normanby, the government station, but it goes 'upwards' or 'downwards' when following the *kula mwatui* that connect the islands.

From a Dobu perspective, one travels 'up' (*laga*) to Duau, Koyagaugau and all the way to Muyuwa—a place that most islanders never visit in their lifetimes. They usually know the name and village of their *kula* partners but do not meet them in person. Going west, one travels 'down' (*dolo*) to Fergusson Island, the Amphletts and other islands on the way up to the Trobriands (a place that is now more frequently visited because of the betel nut trade to Kiriwina).

The verbs that qualify direction within and between *mwatui* are based on either physical terrain or the movements of the sun. This is confusing for an outsider, as one can at the same time go 'up' and 'down' when moving in the *kula* network, depending on the context. When a person paddles from Dobu Island to the *kula* region of Fergusson Island (Oyao or Bwaiowa), the *kula*-related motion is 'to go down' (*dolo*). When reaching the physical point where the water becomes shallower before reaching the island of destination, a traveller is going 'up' to the island, even if the general direction in the larger, *kula*-related mental map is 'down'. Only the Trobriand Islanders do not go 'up' and 'down' for *kula*, but 'across' to Kitava and Kaileuna or Sinaketa. I was told by my team members that this is likely related to the relative position of the archipelago in regard to the sun and the *kula* travels.

Passages of the *kula*

The named spaces in the ocean that can be travelled connect *kula* communities and are used to link up further to the southeast as well as to the mainland of New Guinea. Expert knowledge of these spaces is complex; a rich and deep understanding of the relationships between persons, the environment and spiritual forces informs decisions on travel. Some of the high-ranking *kula* valuables are named after these spaces, such as the *mwali* Dalmuyuw, the *mwali* Kepou, the *bagi* Dauya and the *bagi* Kabwaku Tamagwali (literally, 'Sea Swallow of Tamagwali').

The names of these sea spaces thereby turn into the names of valuables that move and leave a trail of loved namesakes behind, just as new babies are often named after the valuables in the possession of a matrilineage at the time of their birth. Before World War II, *kula* valuables of high rank were passed on in chiefly circles only, so that commoners had very little chance to lay their hands on them, but since the war, increasingly it seems, high-ranking *mwali* and *bagi* have been pulled on to different tracks for a variety of reasons (such as bribery, lack of heirs or insufficient *kula* knowledge). There are still circles of partners who handle most of the valuables of high rank, but since they overlap and are switched in places like Koyagaugau Island, confusion about proper routings has become a grievance to these men and women.

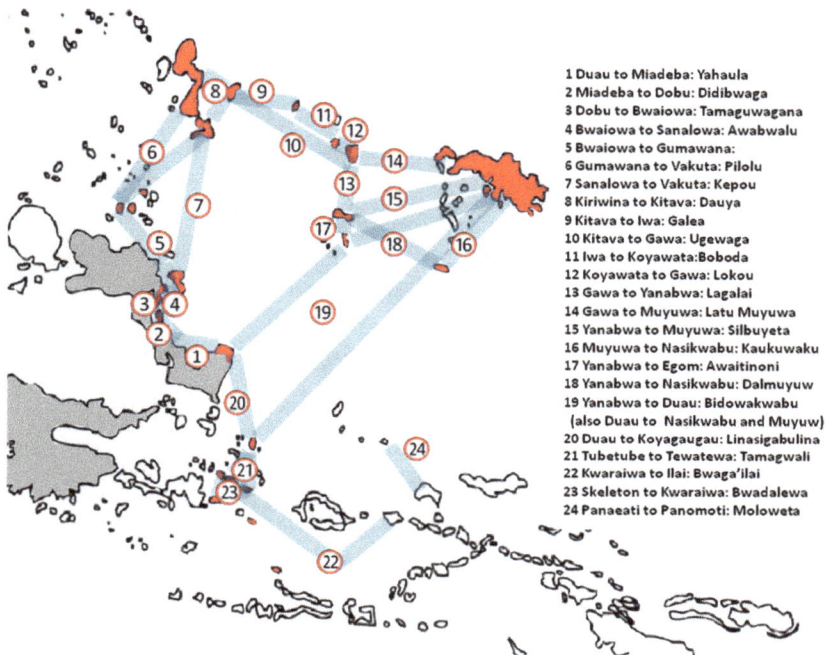

1 Duau to Miadeba: Yahaula
2 Miadeba to Dobu: Didibwaga
3 Dobu to Bwaiowa: Tamaguwagana
4 Bwaiowa to Sanalowa: Awabwalu
5 Bwaiowa to Gumawana:
6 Gumawana to Vakuta: Pilolu
7 Sanalowa to Vakuta: Kepou
8 Kiriwina to Kitava: Dauya
9 Kitava to Iwa: Galea
10 Kitava to Gawa: Ugewaga
11 Iwa to Koyawata:Boboda
12 Koyawata to Gawa: Lokou
13 Gawa to Yanabwa: Lagalai
14 Gawa to Muyuwa: Latu Muyuwa
15 Yanabwa to Muyuwa: Silbuyeta
16 Muyuwa to Nasikwabu: Kaukuwaku
17 Yanabwa to Egom: Awaitinoni
18 Yanabwa to Nasikwabu: Dalmuyuw
19 Yanabwa to Duau: Bidowakwabu
  (also Duau to Nasikwabu and Muyuw)
20 Duau to Koyagaugau: Linasigabulina
21 Tubetube to Tewatewa: Tamagwali
22 Kwaraiwa to Ilai: Bwaga'ilai
23 Skeleton to Kwaraiwa: Bwadalewa
24 Panaeati to Panomoti: Moloweta

Figure 9.2 The *mwatui* of *kula*

Source: By the author.

Most famously, the *mwali* Kibu Tokunuwesi is an example of a valuable with a namesake that has high value (although it has barely moved in almost 40 years, only from Kiriwina to Bwaiowa). The *mwali* shell was found on a reef of this name in northern Kiriwina in the late 1960s by a man named Tokunuwesi (see Kuehling 2017: 186–87). Out of gratitude, the shell was passed to a medical orderly working in the Losuia aid post, who commissioned the cutting and decorating of the enormous *mwali* shell and named his newborn son after the *mwali*. This man is now in his mid-30s and uses this name as one of his Facebook handles. I heard him saying a number of times that 'Kibu is me. I am Kibu'—an expression that reflects the same sense of similarity as that of the mothers or grandmothers who call and cradle a child while showing them a picture of a *kula* valuable, excitedly saying: 'Look, this is your namesake, it is you! Your uncle held it when you were born!'

When I brought back the photographs of more than 1,000 *kula* valuables in 2018, I witnessed such scenes multiple times in all parts of the *kula* region. Valuables build emotional links between people and places as they travel, just as humans leave their traces in the form of narratives when they visit their partners. Namesakes around the network speak to the long duration of circulation and it is an indication of high rank when it is said that 'a valuable is so old, its namesakes have passed already and their *bubus* [grandchildren] are now adults' (as is the case for those valuables that were created after World War II, when *kula* was re-initiated). As personal names are the property of matrilineages, the name is passed on through generations of women, connecting the lineage deeply with the valuable, as names are more than just signifiers but also serve as indicators of close connection.

The winds[8]

The seasonal winds determine whether sea travel is possible, advisable or not recommended, so *kula* expeditions are facilitated and timed by the weather and by *kula* masters who organise their journeys accordingly, thereby creating the desired movement of valuables in what I would like to call a 'pulse' that pushes the objects around the region of islands in large quantities of up to 300 or 500 pieces at a time, out of an approximate total of more than 1,000 valuables of each kind. Planning and leading a *kula* expedition requires much personal investment of time, resources and consensus-building and can involve a lot of logistical organisation and rescheduling. It can be nerve-racking as plans are readjusted all the time, while the pressure is high since much is at stake; to make a name as a successful leader (*toniwaga*), the participants of a *kula* journey need to bring home many baskets filled with *kula* valuables. The term for the desired and expected movement of many valuables together, *ulai*, was sometimes translated by men in all *kula* regions as 'year' when they spoke English, although they were well aware that one *ulai* can take three to five years and refers to the circulation around the chain of partners; it is not a purely temporal but a spatiotemporal measurement. If a 'year' is

---

8   The diagram I published in my monograph (Kuehling 2005: 187) has 'the winds all wrong', as I was told by the late Labenia Ephraim. In this chapter, I wish to correct my errors in that work, but my mistake also indicates the current situation in which knowledge of winds is less important, as *kula* travel can happen at almost all times provided there is a boat. Only in the peak gardening season for men is it unusual to shy from the hard work and travel.

understood as referring to a cyclical temporal unit based on the sun and the winds (rather than the modern calendar year), the error in translation can be explained by a *kula*-centric notion of a spaciotemporality (*ulai*) rather than a yam-centric one in which the word year (*yakwala*, also referring to last year's garden) is used when discussing the movements of *kula* valuables.

The pulse of *kula* and the rhythm of the winds combine to create windows of opportunity and adventure, giving men a chance to prove themselves and to escape the daily grind of subsistence work. In the southern region, November is the season for harvesting taro, but once the yam seed tubers are in the ground, the women close their yam house and manage the remaining tubers. As food at home is limited, *kula* partners like to travel during this period in hopes of receiving their valuables without much delay as the women in their hosts' family are also keen to save their food for the months to come until the next harvest. As all belts are tightened, a *kula* journey is attractive for its culinary delights. The prospect of bringing some yams of the highest quality back to the home village adds to the lust for shell valuables. I was told that, after finishing their own gardens in January during the north wind (*yalata*) season, Duau people can go to Muyuwa, saving their own food while being a burden on their partner's household until he passes on a valuable. This is a strategy of *kula*, although direct exchange between Duau and Muyuwa is technically incorrect. As a form of leapfrogging that leaves out a partner, this is a widely lamented but very common practice.

Malinowski has informed us that northeast winds mark the high season for *kula* sailing in Kiriwina (1920: 103; 1935: Fig. 3, pp. 50–51), probably referring to the time when the *yalata* blows and when the yams are planted. During this period, however, timing is everything as, from November to February, various winds may occur and the islanders need to know how to read the signs of each of them to make safe choices. According to Synod Timothy, these winds come in some kind of order and last for varying periods:

- The north wind (*yalata*): Winds that blow from November to February. This wind is not very strong (other than *bolimana* and *kaluwabu*, see below) and lasts only a few hours at a time. When this wind shifts to the northwest and takes on strength, it is called *otola*. It is the time when *saido* nuts (Pacific almonds) are ripening and falling to the ground. During this time, new gardens should be ready for regular weeding and maintenance work, which is mostly done by women, freeing men up for a journey. During *yalata*, canoe travel from Kiriwina to Muyuwa is possible as the wind hits the sails from the side. Sailing south, however, is impossible, so Trobriand Islanders can travel to Fergusson to visit their partners in Bwaiowa but they cannot return until *yalata* recedes. From Duau to Dobu and back, and from Duau to Muyuwa, is possible, and from Duau to Koyagaugau is difficult but can be done by 'following the wind', as Synod Timothy put it (March 2018). This wind is desired; it gets 'called' (*lo'ulo'uloyei*) by shouting *ku mai* ('come!') and waving one hand down, in hopes that it will appear some days later. Women are often experts in calling this wind (see also Fortune 1932: 211–14).

- The east wind (*bomatu*): This wind is expected to blow from November to January. It calms down and brings a lot of rain, but at infrequent intervals the clouds are moved away when the wind strengthens again. This is the season for kite fishing and for burning newly cut gardens to prepare for planting. It is possible to travel by canoe from east to west (for example, from Duau to Dobu) as well as to sail both north and south. Sometimes *bomatu* can blow strongly (*habolimana*) and these are the times when notoriously slow-moving, high-ranking valuables are passed on to the next partner because only tough people, and only those on inherited high-ranking tracks for these valuables, will brave the wind and visit their partners to receive valuables of high rank. Mwasiuna Taikeu, a *kula* master from Bwaiowa, told me that this was his strategy—to paddle to Vakuta (crossing the *mwatui* named Kepou) or Gumawana (crossing Niupulupulu, literally, 'the round coconut') at times when the others did not dare, and to bring home high-ranking *mwali*.

- The southeast/east wind (*kaluwabu*): Occurring between November and July, this wind is very strong and makes canoe travel too dangerous. When it blows, high waves and occasional rain occur. It joins forces with *bolimana* and brings clouds and rain. In June, when *kaluwabu* is in peak season, southeasterly winds blow (sometimes also as *bolimana* or *yawana bolimana*) and then stop and shift into *yalasi* until December.

- The west wind (*ebwaga*): This also occurs from November to February. This wind moves around and when it comes from the west it is very strong so that waves hit from east to west—for example, the Bwaiowa coast has high waves. When it comes from the east, the surf is wild and the sea is murky but calm on the surface with strong undercurrents. There is a vast amount of plant debris in the water. When it blows from the south, it brings heavy rainfall, with dark clouds forming on the Duau mountains (*bwaula koya*) and low temperatures. When the west wind becomes strong, it can cause cyclones as it covers a large area, allowing it to form into a spiral.

- The northeast wind (*boboli*): This blows from November to February, too. It hits the Duau coast straight from Muyuwa. Both northerly and easterly winds (*yalata* and *bomatu*) can turn into *boboli*.

- A southeasterly wind (*yawana*) may also occur at this time. If it blows from the south or southeast, it joins forces with *bolimana* and becomes very strong, bringing clouds and rain (*yawana bolimana*). If, however, it blows from easterly and southerly directions, it neutralises the *bolimana* and turns steady and quiet (*yawana*).

These winds are interspersed with calm periods when the winds change (around October/November and March/April). Malinowski (1935: 50) has noted that calm periods are used to paddle back to the Trobriands after visiting partners in the south (on the Amphletts, Sanalowa or even as far as the Bwaiowa coast). I have witnessed how the winds can change within an hour, turning a placid sea into a wild and dangerous space. Winds from the south can be especially strong and make canoe travel difficult or even impossible.

- From April to June, the southeast wind (*bolimana*) causes high surf and swells that make it nearly impossible to launch or land a boat. This wind brings no rain. It is the season of new yams, a time of plenty.

- From July until December, the south wind (*yalasi*) brings cold nights and heavy seas.

- From June to August, when the south wind (*yalasi*) and also a southeasterly wind (*yawana*) blow, low tides may block shallow passages through reefs. I witnessed canoes being stranded on corals in the passage between Dobu and Bwaiowa. With long stakes, the canoes were slowly pushed forward until we reached deeper waters again. Most certainly, these situations occur elsewhere as well, limiting the availability of certain *mwatui* at those times.

Plate 9.4 A *kula* canoe from Egom Island
Photo: Susanne Kuehling.

Gardening, *kula* and the winds

Yam gardening and *kula* exchange are interlinked, as men work in the gardens unless they participate in *kula*. Women do most of the weeding work while men are strongly engaged in the heavy lifting involved in preparing new gardens and tending to the yam sticks. While gardening practices differ between the south and the north, the basic idea that there are special yams for *kula* partners is generally shared and the preparation of clay pots with quality food is similar in all *kula* communities I visited between 1993 and 2018. The gardening may differ between the islands, but the same, most delicious yams were prepared for us when we visited in 2016 and 2018. For Dobu Island, I learned that among the cultivars (Dobu: *'uma*) deemed appropriate for serving distinguished visitors are large tubers of purple and white-purple yams as well as white, creamy varieties. Of 39 different cultivars used on Dobu (in 1993), there were 21 different kinds of *Dioscorea alata*, of which seven were deemed appropriate for serving *kula* partners (named Bodalau, Damoni, Dayakulo, Didi or Dubwala, Samulolo, Suwasuwa and Yamosa). Eighteen cultivars of *Dioscorea esculenta* were planted, but only seven were seen as prestige food (Madiyasa, Momouwa, Mwamwa'uwa, Mwanalawa or Gadagada, Tetuboiya, Tetuwale and Uyagasu). On Fergusson Island, in the Bwaiowa region of the *kula*, where this is the only subspecies, the cultivars used are named Awabwaduwe, Gulia, Ututuwau and Uyagasu. Uyagasu, which is a whitish purple colour with a soft, creamy texture and sweetish taste, is valued as the best of all types of yam and used to be cooked only for chiefs and distinguished *kula* partners. The complex knowledge required to oversee the production of sufficient yams for a year's purposes of hosting, gifting, sharing and eating the smallest and least valuable yams marks a good wife and sister, and those women whose yam house is always full and whose cooking fire never cools are highly respected. In the past, men could specialise their efforts in gardening, *kula* or warfare, while women gained a name with gardening and *kula* if they aspired and qualified.[9] Only a few women travel themselves. Since they are often held back by children and the garden and see these journeys as an additional burden to an already busy daily schedule, most women pick a nephew or brother, husband or uncle to visit *kula* partners on their behalf.

The same yams are used for gifts of cooked food (in Dobu: *buyo*) that are required as part of affinal exchanges locally. Large raw yam tubers of these preferred varieties are gifted in large baskets as part of most local exchanges (mortuary feasting, compensation payments, marriage exchanges and so on). Women's contribution to *kula*, the role as perfect host, requires them to grow, manage and provide the yams needed for visiting partners, to prepare delicious meals for them and make them feel as comfortable as possible. Only when the supplies of yam run out will the women interfere and quietly inform their husbands that it is time to send the visitor away with a *kula* valuable, as I was told by various women in all *kula* communities.

The support team behind a *kula* master

Women need clay pots from the Amphletts or Bwanabwana (or mainland New Guinea's East Cape) to prepare this special food. They also need specific kinds of pandanus-leaf bundles to weave the new mats that

---

9   The key position of women in *kula* is in Kiriwina acknowledged and symbolised by a principle called *kailagila*: '[T]he Three stones on which the cooking pot rests' (Malic and Kasaipwalova 1998: 103 ff.).

a visitor will be offered to sit on as soon as he or she arrives. Men are often involved in providing these resources. A man may kill a pig for a visitor, but the entire work behind the scenes is in the hands of his wife, from fetching water to minding the small children while speed-sweeping the hamlet and collecting the laundry, blowing the fire and organising a little sugar for the guest by sending a capable small child to the neighbours. Since the husband needs to sit and talk with the visitor, the wife shows her virtue and respect by never showing exhaustion or discontent and even by keeping babies from crying. I was told by many *kula* masters, male and female, that the services provided by the wife and the rest of the household under her direction are an essential element of *kula* and that a partner would excuse himself and wander off for good if he did not feel welcome due to the attitudes of a wife and children. So, in each location, while men are busy with their *kula* scheming, their wives and other female relatives are equally involved in *kula* 'work' (*paisewa*) by providing the various resources and services that make the exchange system possible. In the southern region, the women control the stored yams, so if there is a need for the support of a *kula* partner, a man needs to cooperate with his wife and sisters as men must not enter their wives' yam houses. Therefore, the movements of *kula* travellers are deeply entwined with those of the gardeners and food providers.

Yet *kula* and gardening are connected on even more levels. It appears that the region has developed a mutually advantageous setup, as the gardening cycles shift between the archipelagos. The Trobriand Islands and Northern Muyuwa complete their new gardens first (in October and November). Bwaiowa and Dobu are next (in November and December); Duau completes new gardens in January and the small islands of the Bwanabwana region have planted their seed tubers by February. When the seed tubers are in the ground, a lean period begins in which yams are only seldom consumed and are stored for feasts or to feed distinguished visitors. In Dobu, this time is named *botana* (literally, 'hunger'). Once the yam plants are well established, two to three months into the gardening cycle, the old tubers are removed. In Dobu, this is called *mweia* and not only is it believed to strengthen the plant and increase the harvest, but also it is used as a way to gauge the upcoming harvest by feeling the size of the new tubers.[10]

---

10   Yam gardening in the northern Massim differs from the south, but space does not permit a more detailed comparison (see Malinowski 1935; Digim'Rina 1995 for Basima).

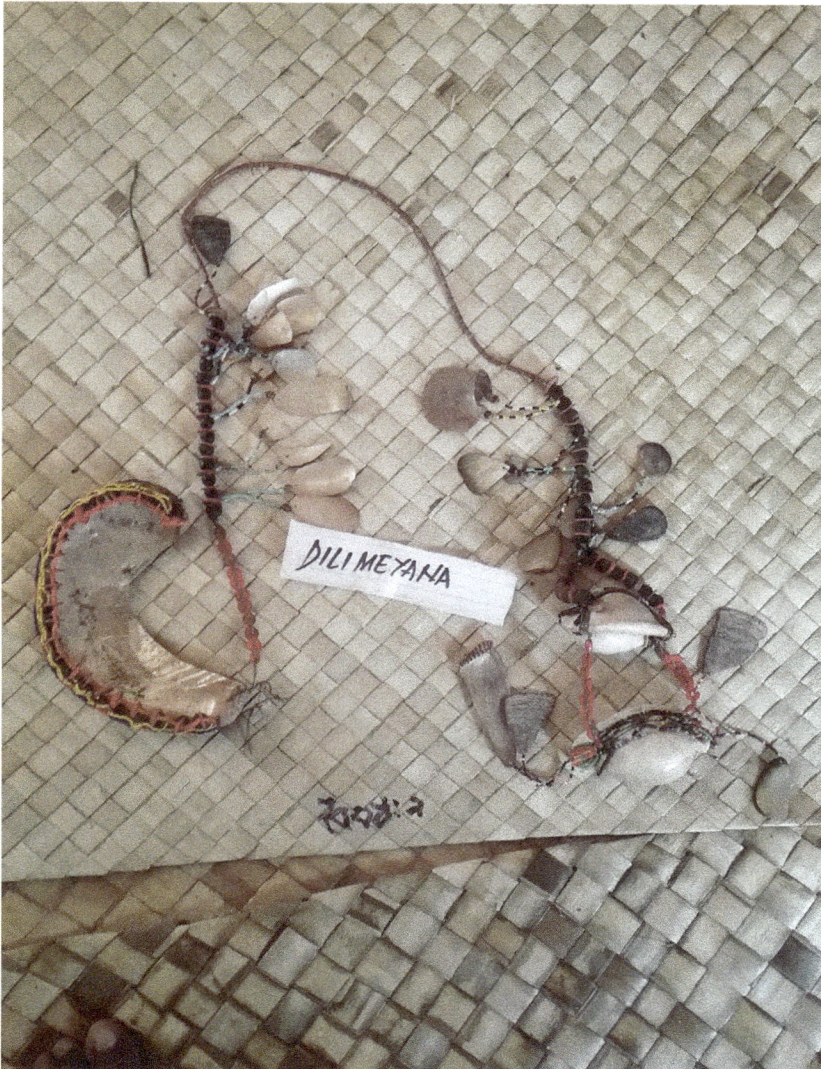

Plate 9.5 *Bagi* Dilimeyana
Photo: Susanne Kuehling.

The different gardening practices and yam cycles in the *kula* region combine to form a safety network for the islands with fragile ecologies, like the Amphletts and the Bwanabwana region, which see many harvests destroyed by floods or droughts, as occurred in 2015–16, when it did not rain from July until February in the Bwanabwana region and the yam seed tubers dried up in the ground. So, in February/March, when the

Bwanabwana islands have planted their yam seed tubers, the northern islands of the Muyuwa region have already started their harvest and can assist their southern partners. In April/May, Amphlett islanders may need to rely on the food security of the Bwaiowa/Dobu region when their seed tubers are planted. In September/October, they can also ask their partners in Vakuta and Sinaketa for assistance if their yam harvest fails. During the time of plenty, short voyages are possible in intervals of calm weather, so knowledge of the seasonal winds directly links with yams and *kula* exchange. Years without any harvest used to happen in the past as well; some are recounted in the stories of high-ranked *kula* valuables. The *bagi* Dilimeyana, for example, was brought by a man from a drought-stricken island in the Bwanabwana region shortly after World War II, when *kula* was taken up after the ban during the war. He asked his *kula* partner in Duau for help as his sister's daughter, named Dilimeyana, was starving. After receiving a generous supply of yams and pork from the abundant gardens of Duau, the man returned to his home island with the shell valuable, finished its decorations, named it Dilimeyana and sent it to his Duau partner, who used it in his *kula* network (see Kuehling 2017: 199).

Subsistence and the winds

Successful gardening depends also on the right timing of the winds, bringing the rain or dry air that yams need. The garden cycle is connected to other subsistence activities that are also markers of time and help people remember incidents from the past.

When the east wind (*bomatu*) blows from November to January, it opens the gardening season in Dobu and Bwaiowa by assisting the burning of dried leaves and branches of the newly cut gardens and preparing them for planting. This wind makes everybody feel tired. This is also the time for kite fishing (as in the song *Tai goma Losina*; see Barton and Dietrich 2009: 120).[11] From December to January, in Duau, the yam seed tubers are prepared for planting. Once the chosen seed tubers are piled up in the yam house, they are sprinkled with magic liquids and treated with incantations as well as other techniques to encourage their growth. One of these

11   It appears as though one specific kite-fishing method in the Massim region only occurred in *kula* communities, suggesting the skill was passed between *kula* partners (Barton and Dietrich 2009: 70).

techniques used to be cat cradles (*'abi'abi*: literally, 'building something'), played during the planting season (*e'sa'e*), which was believed to 'open the eyes of the seed yams' so they would grow once in the ground.[12]

Between November and July, when the strong southeast/east winds (*kaluwabu*) join forces with the southeast wind (*bolimana*), bringing clouds and rain, people are resigned to weeding their gardens while silently complaining about the unpleasantly cool weather, consoling themselves by feeling happy for their growing yam plants.

From June to August, *yalasi* and also *yawana* are marked by low tides, enabling the collection of shellfish. This season is called *kebulabula*. The old yams have been removed from the planting holes and gardeners can estimate their harvest and use up the last stored yams accordingly. From July until December, however, when the south wind (*yalasi*) blows, south-facing coastlines, like Duau's, are sometimes affected by strong gusts and waves, and the yams may be damaged by the wind.

From April to June, the southeast wind (*bolimana*) brings no rain. It is the season of new yams—a time of plenty for the islanders of the northern Massim, Bwaiowa and Dobu. On the Duau coast, the early yam cultivars (such as *Sabewa* in Dobu) are stealthily harvested so as to taste their sweet softness, with people excusing their lust by saying that they need to feed the new babies ('their first yams'), but in spite of the slight stigma attached to those 'greedy' people who harvest too early, there are stories and restrictions linked to the practice. During this time, islanders observe the Pleiades in the night sky, because if they see its 'tail' dropping, this indicates that heavy storms will occur in the evening, 'spoiling dinner time', as I was told.

From July until December, the south wind (*yalasi*) dries up the garden areas after they have been cut in preparation for the *bomatu* season, meaning the leaves and plant materials will burn well when *bomatu* comes up. Bringing very cold nights, this wind effects people's health, and many suffer from respiratory tract infections.

12 According to Damon, 'movement is the point' to string figures. He describes beautifully how string figures are a way to perform stories in motion (Damon 2017: 283–91)—a 'kind of magical geometry' (p. 292).

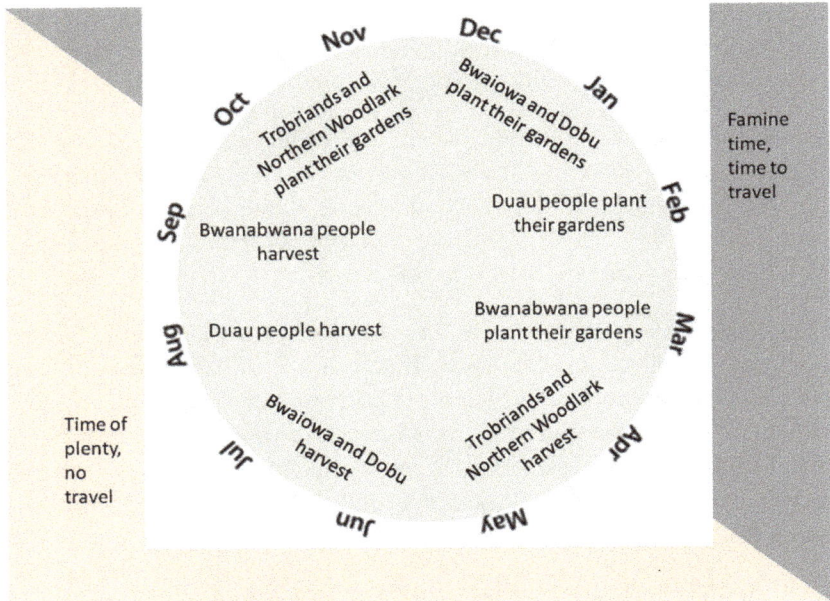

Figure 9.3 Overlapping gardening cycles in the *kula* region
Source: By the author.

Changes

While in the past the privilege to travel to distant exchange partners seems to have been limited to leaders and chiefs (Swadling and Bence 2016), the postwar shifts of power have resulted in a large number of participants in the exchange of *kula* valuables, with certainly more than 2,000 individuals now involved in *kula* travel (see also Young 1983). Generous gifts of yams were a token of appreciation for a partner in the past—a gift called *masula liga* in the southern *kula* region that is now rare as only chiefs can assemble large amounts of yams.

This increase in numbers after World War II led to the splitting of valuables (called *gasi* in Dobu), making two *mwali* out of a former pair; the two *mwali*, Bwaluada and Koka (both meaning 'sea eel'), used to be a pair; similarly, *bagi* strings such as in Dilimeyana 1 and 2 have been halved. Most precontact valuables are out of circulation; only a few greenstone axe blades, beaded belts and pig-tusk pendants are kept as family heirlooms. Quality yams of the appropriate cultivar are still served to *kula* visitors, but rice and canned food are highly desired and are routinely part of meals. Only the two objects *mwali* and *bagi* are now in regular circulation; some are being newly created and decorated by specialists. The decorations have changed in style over the past century, as islanders increasingly gained access to decorative glass beads. Due to pearl diving, empty shells became readily available as headpieces on *bagi* strings and the size of red shell disks has changed significantly. Before, there were two sizes: larger disks (*sapisapi*) were used to decorate the *bagi* string or were sewn on to a piece of cloth to make a belt (*gadiwa'uma* in Dobu), while smaller disks were very fine and thin and were used for the string. Nowadays, *sapisapi* shells are largely replaced with plastic and *bagi* shells are less carefully crafted— not as thin and smooth as they were in the past.

Plate 9.6 *Mwali* Lagim (centre), held by Edward Digwaleu from Tewatewa
Photo: Susanne Kuehling.

Some *mwali* have been bleached to look 'cleaner', while others have retained their patina but have undergone mending and redecorating; some valuables of old have changed their appearance and name. I heard rumours that some high-ranking shell valuables are hidden in Port Moresby, while copies bearing their names are circulating in the *kula*. Often, I heard that the Queen of England has removed the *bagi* Goma'alakedakeda and is hiding it in the British Museum, a story that was credited to John Kasaipwalova by various men on the islands. It seems that the shells themselves are getting smaller while the decorations are getting larger, to the point that a *mwali* can hardly be taken on a canoe journey. These include the 'witchcraft' *mwali* Kabisawali and a new *mwali* Lagim, introduced to the *kula* in 2016—both commissioned by John Kasaipwalova and adorned with large, heavy carvings.

While creating new good reasons to move about in a morally acceptable manner, the market economy also limits people's movements today, as without money, transport is increasingly difficult to find for people who cannot brave the seas on a canoe. Pacific lifestyles have always been subject to change (see D'Arcy 2006). The islanders of the *kula* network were always mobile and inventive. The growing intensity of change in modern education, the global cash economy and various forms of Christianity is blurring the boundaries between 'us' and 'the others', and in the light of fading local belief systems and a loss of subsistence-related skills, location remains a critical element of identification with a group. The named spaces on land and sea are constructs of collective history, memory, personal and shared emotions, based on experiences of movement in the environment, creating social interaction and relationships. On the islands, the rhythm of *kula* is still determined by gardening and travel, and both activities are of equal importance.

With the introduction of rice and other desirable store-bought food items, however, the significance of yam gardening appears to be decreasing. The late chief Digim'Rina from Okeboma, N-Kiriwina, was quoted as saying that 'when the men *kula*, they care for their gardens'—implying that non-*kula* men are more prone to neglecting their subsistence and prestige activities, finding cash more attractive than shell valuables. These days, however, a visitor will expect store-bought food to be served, increasing the burden on the host. Leaving a trail of borrowed money, tobacco, rice and kerosene in Dobu, these debts are called 'bookings' (*bukis*) and should ideally be repaid, to be extinguished (*kwe'u*).[13] *Kula* practice is increasingly shifting from subsistence to a fringe existence in the global cash economy, becoming a burden rather than a blessing for families with access to cash and an impossibility for subsistence gardeners without an income. With low wages and high costs for transportation, store-bought food and fuel for small boats are very expensive. *Kula* indeed makes no sense in

---

13 I have elsewhere discussed the effect of this increasing trend of the cash economy on the islands, where stores are notoriously short-lived and debts rarely repaid in full (Kuehling 2005).

the profit-oriented setting of the global cash economy, when access to goods and *kula* opportunities depends not on personal merit but on cash infusions from helpful relatives in town.

Nowadays, travel by modern boats interrupts the rhythm of *kula* (*ulai*) as these boats can go against the wind and currents, take shortcuts and brave heavy rain that would have soaked the pandanus sails of the past. Modern vessels allow more flexibility for those individuals who can afford a passage, own a dinghy or have relatives with a cargo boat who can provide free travel for *kula* purposes. Those people are not always leaders, as in the past, but display a more entrepreneurial interest in *kula*. John Kasaipwalova falls into this category. He is an Australian-educated playwright from the Trobriand Islands who once called the *kula* a 'development corporation' (1974) and spent time and money travelling the entire 'ring of power' to collect valuables and assist in the creation of a coffee-table book on *kula* (Malnic and Kasaipwalova 1998) and a film featuring a number of these *kula*-for-profit traders (Mitchell et al. 2000).

The *kula* exchange of the Amphlett islanders is critically affected by modern transport and selfish partners. They used to be the western bottleneck of the exchange system, connecting the different languages of the Dobu and the Boyowa dialect chains. The elders on Gumawana explained that they should go first to Vakuta to pick up *mwali* and bring them home so that Bwaiowa people (from East Fergusson Island) can come and pick them up from their partners on the Amphletts. After this main exchange (*ulai*), Bwaiowa people who have established exchange partnerships directly with Vakuta are allowed to leapfrog and travel directly to their partners in the southern Trobriand Islands to collect the leftover *mwali* valuables to create an even larger *ulai* to attract Dobu islanders and excite the *kula* partners on faraway islands who plot and ponder how to get a hold of many, or specific, valuables. Therefore, the frustration is enormous for the *kula* communities of the Amphlett Islands when they are left out, as happened in 2018. I was told that the last *ulai* went past the Amphletts altogether as Bwaiowa people went by modern vessel to Vakuta and so the Amphletts 'did not touch one *mwali* in that *ulai*'.

Similar complaints come from the eastern bottleneck, the small islands of the Bwanabwana region, as well as Yanabwa and Egum further north. In the past, these islands were important stopovers for all vessels, as the long stretches of ocean in the eastern part are demanding and exhausting to cross. There, as well, modern types of transport have reduced the importance of these islands (see Macintyre 1983) and formerly central Tubetube Island has now lost this role, with a young generation exclaiming that '*kula* is a waste of time and money' (Peter Wesley, February 2016). As many of the young men are high school graduates, they have not learned to sail a canoe as expertly as the village men and it is too late (or too embarrassing and insignificant) for them to learn it well enough to be safe. They cannot read the winds and sky and rely on their skills. On the other hand, those islanders who can sail lack the cash to be generous hosts in the new terms of rice and canned meat. As those who have the means to sponsor feasts and *kula* events feel that it is not worth the expense, so islands with a low population that are closer to the mainland are having difficulty recruiting talented heirs. Another issue arising is that the winds are 'changing', weather patterns are losing their relative reliability and, therefore, the valuable knowledge of the past is losing some of its credibility and value. The lack of mutual trust between elders and their successors, many men told me, is the main worry of *kula* nowadays, as clever and diligent young men and women are lost to the towns.

Moving in *kula* space, crossing various *mwatui* in the process, used to be reserved for the smartest sons and nephews of a *kula* man. This privilege is now gone, but the prospect of a free meal and a welcoming family at the end of the journey is still a reality. The advantages of *kula* appeal to the current generation of adult men aged in their fifties and beyond, who argued in all meetings that we held in the major communities that they are trying their best to plan to bring back the vanishing pulse of *kula* (*ulai*), to discourage the exchange of small groups but support the festive, competitive, adventurous, celebratory travel as a larger group. This is seen as a means to attract younger people and gives the older men a chance to watch their performance, teach them strategies and educate them about all the things a *kula* master needs to consider.

Local leaders are currently attempting to revitalise interest in *kula* through sports and United Church events. These are now sometimes connected with *kula* by councillors, teachers and elders who have noticed that *kula*-playing teenagers are better behaved; but every Christmas, when relatives from town come to visit, their role in providing resources and assistance works against the need to cultivate strong *kula* ties. In town, *kula* valuables are shifted around, sometimes used as decoration and as sentimental anchors of identity or sold to tourists, art dealers or museum collectors. *Kula* is currently being converted from a practice of chiefs to merchandise—a 'beloved brand', in Robert Foster's 'coca-globalization' sense (2008).

Since 2008, tourism has reached the *kula* region with force, with the arrival of large cruise ships and the marketing of 'tradition'. For Trobriand Islanders, dancing for tourists, selling simple carvings and even *kula* valuables while neglecting subsistence and education during the tourist visits have become a normal form of income (MacCarthy 2016). On Kirivina, pickpocketing and a general monetarisation of petty exchanges between family and friends are regretfully accepted side effects. Dobu islanders always feared the Trobriand Islanders because of their magic, and recently I witnessed their worry about the use of battery acid as a means of retribution (I was told a number of times: 'When in the Trobs, never hang anything on a line over night. They put it [acid] on your clothes and when you wear them the next day, you die from it'). I find the change from fierce 'Argonauts' to 'Shirt of Nessus' disappointing, as seagoing canoes, and races between them, have disappeared, while clothes on a washing line have gained significance in *kula*-related lore from a Dobu perspective. People on Kiriwina, and increasingly on Kitava, are selling their valuables to tourists and art collectors now, while disinterested partners on Tubetube Island are simply left out by their surrounding partners, as has already happened to other areas such as Boiboi Bay, Muyuwa. The current generation of senior *kula* masters is concerned that their web of relationships will not survive for long as it stretches ever thinner in some places while tattering at the seams elsewhere. Koyagaugau and small Ode (or Ole) Island are now the most important stops in the bottleneck of the Bwanabwana region—a fact that causes frustration, as the heritage of complex *kula* partnership chains and obligations has not been carefully enough maintained since the death of its greatest strategic mind, Mwalubeyai ('King Kula'), in 1995.

While the established churches, the Catholics and Wesleyans/United Church, accept *kula* as a positive social force, evangelical churches have more recently settled in some *kula* communities and are currently attempting to convince the islanders to give up the 'satanic' habit of exchanging demonic objects. So far, their call to burn the objects has not been met with enthusiasm, but some individuals have certainly destroyed their *mwali* and *bagi* in an attempt to quit sinning.

Conclusion

Movements on *kula* paths are manifestations of journeying through space as one of the pillars of humankind—a universal anchor for identity: 'images of place' that help to 'objectify a sense of being and belonging' (Jackson 1995: 19). To Austronesians, the 'lived experience' of travel (Rodman 1992: 641; Kahn 1996: 173), the invisible boundaries of sea spaces and the sensations of routine paths and special events become personal and shared memories through the emplaced and embodied practice of moving between them. Austronesian paths and journeys provide, as demonstrated, a useful vantage point for a comparative analysis of power relations, ecology, subjectivity, questions concerning the dynamics of life as they appear in local concepts of the person, patterns of connectedness with the environment and symbolic meanings of place. Ingold has noted that persons and their movements between places and time are intertwined in lived experience: '[P]laces do not have locations but histories. Bound together by the itineraries of their inhabitants, places exist not in space but as nodes in a matrix of movement' (2000: 219). In a similar vein, Hanlon emphasises the dynamic and 'porous' attributes of place (2004: 210).

From an outsider's perspective, the ocean space of *kula* travel is more spectacular than digging the ground and weeding the garden spaces, so the ocean space has inspired comparisons with the heroic Greek Argonauts (Małinowski 1922). I have argued that, in reality, yam gardening and management are the backbone of *kula* hospitality and, like canoe travel, depend on a high degree of skill and knowledge about the environment, involving a lifestyle of permanent observation and speculation about the weather brought by the winds. The mutual support of an entire household is what enables a *kula* partner to sit and talk with his visitor; the women and young relatives of a *kula* man form the mostly invisible yet highly efficient system that enables the exchange to materialise.

Using toponyms and named winds, I have aimed at the description and expression of experiential realities, which are, in Feld's words, 'deeply linked to the embodied sensation of places' (1996: 113). They are anchors of memory, as they tell stories of the past as well as of individual travels— roots and routes, as coined by Clifford (1997)—'mapping place into identity, conjoining temporal motion and spatial projection, re-inscribing past into the present, creating biography as itinerary' (Feld 1996: 113). Basso has argued that:

place names may be used to summon forth an enormous range of mental and emotional associations—associations of time and space, of history and events, of persons and social activities, of oneself and stages in one's life. (1988: 103)

This reflects my own experience of researching this topic.

My microscopic, sociolinguistic ethnography does not fully support the notion that Austronesians are ordering their social and physical world into a grid of dualisms: inside/outside, back/front, low/high, female/male (for the Caroline Islands, see Alkire 1970: 66, 70, 1972; Alkire and Fujimura 1990: 75 ff.; see also Feinberg 1988). Anne Douglass has argued that these dualisms are practised by following the rules of respect, in spatial movement and language as well as in relationships (1998: 138). This grid is indeed realised in motion verbs that relate to the physical grid of named places, as I have demonstrated, but when more detail is taken into account, the pairs of opposition do not hold but in fact reveal a more fluid structure that allows for shades of grey. I am therefore reluctant to read binary opposites into my data as I find more complementarities than polarising dual opposites. The sun goes up (*laga*) so as to go down again (*dolo*), crossing over (*abala*) the sky and forming a basic axis of orientation, crossed by the motion *nao*, not to separate but to define a temporal or locative motion.

The Malinowskian notion of the *Kula* 'Ring', widely used in the literature, does not represent the movement of people—and only sometimes of the valuables, as they may be de-routed through affinal exchange obligations within *kula* communities. I was told a number of times that the *kula* network is more like a zone as contrasted to the non-*kula* participants, who may or may not be attached in a secondary way to *kula*. Gordon Lakatani (Mwemweyala village, Dobu, September 2015) phrased this difference aptly when he said the idea of a 'ring' should be understood 'more like a boxing ring in which everything happens inside'. Unlike a boxing ring, or ice rink, however, the boundaries are in reality fluid, with intermarriages and friendships intersecting with *kula* partnerships. This imagery matches the notion of *mwatui* spaces: the *kula* region itself is a *mwatui*.

The network of exchange partnerships provided, and still provides, a sense of an imagined community, revitalised every time the islanders are recounting the names of their partners, their islands, villages and the valuables that were travelling between them, sharing stories about the places and journeys involved in moving the objects from beach to beach in an (ideally) endless double-helix through time and space. The image of a spiral was brought up by Trobriand playwright and poet John Kasaipwalova, who shared what he refers to as 'the backbone of any Kiriwinan magic' (Malnic and Kasaipwalova 1998: 142–43): 'The centre of the spiral is called *gum* (essence), and stands for "spiral thinking", the "presence of the past".' I was unable to find evidence of this image in the southern part of the *kula* region, where 'spiral' is translated as *wasi*, the word (and suffix) that refers to a vortex and anything that goes in circles (as in *sakowasi*, the common Dobu verb for moving around). The *kula* masters from the Dobu-speaking region of the *kula*, in considering the metaphor of a spiral, suggested it is a very secret concept, one that has been lost over time or, most likely, evidence of a different spatial conception in the Trobriands due to that archipelago's relative position in the northwestern part of the *kula* region. To the other language communities in the *kula* region, not a spiral but a motion of 'up' and 'down' is used for orientation and linguistic expressions of space.

It is the pulse of movements (*ulai*) of men, women, pigs, *kula* valuables and yams on their *'eda*, their crossings and visiting of *mwatui* spaces, that clusters them as the most relevant living creatures, defining yams as persons and attributing many human characteristics to *kula* valuables (see Kuehling 2005, 2012). This pulse is connected to the seasons and is locally framed as 'work' (*paisewa*) that is both required and laudable, creating opportunities for humans to shine and to gain control over resources and the minds of others. The societies of the region have developed *kula* as a system of extraordinary mechanisms of solidarity and mutual assistance based on trust and respect. For five generations, *kula* has persisted, despite the dire prospects and frequent disruptions caused by the cash economy and an education system that privileges an Australian perspective and often discredits institutions such as *kula* as 'primitive' or 'backwards'. In the capital of Alotau and for descendants of people from *kula* islands living in urban centres, *kula* is embraced as a marketing strategy, and wearing a *bagi* necklace has become a prime identity marker. As a lifestyle, however, *kula* does not sit well in a market economy.

References

Alkire, William H. 1970. 'Systems of measurement on Woleai Atoll, Caroline Islands.' *Anthropos* 65: 1–73.

Alkire, William H. 1972. 'Concepts of order in Southeast Asia and Micronesia.' *Comparative Studies in Society and History* 14(4): 484–93. doi.org/10.1017/S0010417500006812.

Alkire, William H. 1974. 'Land tenure in the Woleai.' In Henry P. Lundsgaarde, ed., *Land Tenure in Oceania*, pp. 39–69. Honolulu: University of Hawai'i Press. doi.org/10.2307/j.ctvp2n5c9.6.

Alkire, William H. and Keiko Fujimura. 1990. 'Principles of organization in the outer islands of Yap State and their implication for archaeology.' *Micronesica Supplement No. 2*: 75–88.

Barton, Gerry and Stephan Dietrich. 2009. *This Ingenious and Singular Apparatus: Fishing kites of the Indo-Pacific*. Heidelberg, Germany: Museum für Völkerkunde.

Basso, Keith H. 1988. '"Speaking with names": Language and landscape among the western Apache.' *Cultural Anthropology* 3(2): 99–130. doi.org/10.1525/can.1988.3.2.02a00010.

Clifford, James. 1997. *Routes: Travel and translation in the late twentieth century*. Cambridge, MA: Harvard University Press.

Damon, Frederick H. 1983a. 'On the transformation of Muyuw into Woodlark Island: Two minutes in December, 1974.' *The Journal of Pacific History* 18(1): 35–56. doi.org/10.1080/00223348308572457.

Damon, Frederick H. 1983b. 'What moves the kula: Opening and closing gifts on Woodlark Island.' In Jerry W. Leach and Edmund Leach, eds, *The Kula: New perspectives on Massim exchange*, pp. 309–42. Cambridge: Cambridge University Press.

Damon, Frederick H. 1990. *From Muyuw to the Trobriands: Transformations along the northern side of the Kula Ring*. Tuscon, AZ: University of Arizona Press.

Damon, Frederick H. 2000. 'From regional relations to ethnic groups? The transformation of value relations to property claims in the kula ring of Papua New Guinea.' *Asia Pacific Journal of Anthropology* 1(2): 49–72. doi.org/10.1080/14442210010001705920.

Damon, Frederick H. 2002. 'Kula valuables: The problem of value and the production of names.' *L'Homme* 162: 107–36. doi.org/10.4000/lhomme.158.

Damon, Frederick H. 2017. *Trees, Knots, and Outriggers: Environmental knowledge in the northeast Kula Ring*. New York: Berghahn Books. doi.org/10.2307/j.ctvswx6vz.

Damon, Frederick H. and Roy Wagner, eds. 1989. *Death Rituals and Life in the Societies of the Kula Ring*. DeKalb, IL: Northern Illinois University Press.

D'Arcy, Paul. 2006. *The People of the Sea: Environment, identity, and history in Oceania*. Honolulu: University of Hawai'i Press.

Digim'Rina, Linus S. 1995. 'Gardens of Basima: Land tenure and mortuary feasting in a matrilineal society.' PhD thesis, The Australian National University, Canberra.

Douglass, Anne Roberta. 1998. 'Children and adoption on Woleai Atoll: Attachment and young children's response to separation.' PhD thesis, Harvard University, Cambridge, MA.

Feinberg, Rick. 1988. 'Socio-spatial symbolism and the logic of rank on two Polynesian outliers.' *Ethnology* 27: 291–310. doi.org/10.2307/3773522.

Feld, Steven. 1996. 'Waterfalls of song: An acoustemology of place resounding in Bosavi, Papua New Guinea.' In Steven Feld and Keith H. Basso, eds, *Senses of Place*, pp. 91–135. Santa Fe, NM: School of American Research Press.

Fortune, Reo F. 1932. *Sorcerers of Dobu: The social anthropology of the Dobu islanders of the western Pacific.* London: Routledge & Kegan Paul.

Foster, Robert J. 2008. *Coca-Globalization: Following soft drinks from New York to New Guinea.* New York: Palgrave.

George, Marianne 'Mimi'. 2012. 'Polynesian navigation and Te Lapa: "The Flashing".' *Time and Mind* 5(2): 135–74. doi.org/10.2752/175169712X 13294910382900.

George, Marianne 'Mimi'. 2018. 'Experiencing *mana* as ancestral wind-work.' *Time and Mind* 11(4): 385–407. doi.org/10.1080/1751696X.2018.1541126.

Graeber, David. 2001. *Toward an Anthropological Theory of Value: The false coin of our own dreams.* New York: Palgrave. doi.org/10.1057/9780312299064.

Hanlon, David. 2004. 'Wone sohte lohdi: History and place on Pohnpei.' In Brij V. Lal, ed., *Pacific Places, Pacific Histories*, pp. 195–215. Honolulu: University of Hawai`i Press. doi.org/10.1515/9780824844158-013.

Hau`ofa, Epeli. 1994. 'Our sea of islands.' *The Contemporary Pacific* 6(1): 148–61.

Hau`ofa, Epeli. 1998. 'The ocean in us.' *The Contemporary Pacific* 10(2): 392–410.

Ingold, Tim. 2000. *The Perception of the Environment: Essays in livelihood, dwelling and skill.* London: Routledge.

Jackson, Michael. 1995. *At Home in the World.* Durham, NC: Duke University Press.

Kahn, Miriam. 1996. 'Your place and mine: Sharing emotional landscapes in Wamira, Papua New Guinea.' In Steven Feld and Keith H. Basso, eds, *Senses of Place*, pp. 167–96. Santa Fe, NM: School of American Research Press.

Kasaipwalova, John. 1974. '"Modernising" Melanesian society: Why, and for whom?' In Ron May, ed., *Priorities in Melanesian Development*, pp. 451–54. Canberra: ANU Press and UPNG.

Kuehling, Susanne. 1998. 'The name of the gift: Ethics of exchange on Dobu Island.' PhD dissertation, The Australian National University, Canberra.

Kuehling, Susanne. 2005. *Dobu: Ethics of exchange on a Massim island, Papua New Guinea*. Honolulu: University of Hawai'i Press.

Kuehling, Susanne. 2012. 'They spear, hit again, bite, get engaged and sometimes marry: Revisiting the gendering of kula shells.' *Anthropologica* 54(2): 319–32.

Kuehling, Susanne. 2014. 'The converted war canoe: Cannibal raiders, missionaries, and *Pax Britannica* on Dobu Island, Papua New Guinea.' *Anthropologica* 56(2): 269–84.

Kuehling, Susanne. 2017. '"We die for kula": An object-centred view of motivations and strategies in gift exchange.' *Journal of the Polynesian Society* 126(2):181–208. doi.org/10.15286/jps.126.2.181-208.

Leach, Jerry W. and Edmund Leach, eds. 1983. *The Kula: New perspectives on Massim exchange*. Cambridge: Cambridge University Press.

Lewis, David. 1972. *We, the Navigators: The ancient art of landfinding in the Pacific*. Honolulu: University of Hawai'i Press.

MacCarthy, Michelle. 2016. *Making the Modern Primitive: Cultural tourism in the Trobriand Islands*. Honolulu: University of Hawai'i Press. doi.org/10.21313/hawaii/9780824855604.001.0001.

Macintyre, Martha. 1983. 'Changing paths: An historical ethnography of the traders of Tubetube.' PhD thesis, The Australian National University, Canberra.

Malinowski, Bronislaw. 1920. 'Kula: The circulating exchange of valuables in the archipelagos of eastern New Guinea.' *MAN* 20(July): 97–105. doi.org/10.2307/2840430.

Malinowski, Bronislaw. 1922. *Argonauts of the Western Pacific: An account of native enterprise and adventure in the archipelagoes of Melanesian New Guinea*. London: Routledge & Kegan Paul.

Malinowski, Bronislaw. 1935. *Coral Gardens and Their Magic. Volume I: Soil-tilling and agricultural rites in the Trobriand Islands*. London: Routledge.

Malnic, Jutta and John Kasaipwalova. 1998. *Kula: Myth and magic in the Trobriand Islands*. Sydney: Cowry Books.

Mauss, Marcel. 1990 [1923–24]. *The Gift: The form and reason for exchange in archaic societies*. Trans. by W.D. Halls. London: Routledge.

Mitchell, Rob Scott, Jutta Malnic and Richard Dennison. 2000. *Kula: Ring of Power*. [Video]. Directed by Michael Balson. 51 mins. National Geographic Explorer USA, ZDF Germany and Finnish Broadcasting Corporation. Produced by Sky Visuals, distributed by University of Hawai`i Press.

Munn, Nancy D. 1986. *The Fame of Gawa: A symbolic study of value transformation in a Massim (PNG) society*. Cambridge: Cambridge University Press.

Munn, Nancy D. 1990. 'Constructing regional worlds in experience: Kula exchange, witchcraft and Gawan local events.' *MAN* 25: 1–17. doi.org/10.2307/2804106.

Rodman, Margaret C. 1992. 'Empowering place: Multilocality and multivocality.' *American Anthropologist* 94(3): 640–56. doi.org/10.1525/aa.1992.94.3.02a00060.

Swadling, Pamela and Polly Bence. 2016. 'Changes in *kula* valuables and related supply linkages between the Massim and the south Papuan coast between 1855 and 1915.' *Archaeology in Oceania* 51(1): 50–60. doi.org/10.1002/arco.5106.

Young, Michael W. 1983. 'The Massim: An introduction.' *The Journal of Pacific History* 18(1): 4–10. doi.org/10.1080/00223348308572455.

Young, Michael W. 1991. 'The sea eagle and other heroic birds of Nidula mythology.' In Andrew Pawley, ed., *Man and a Half: Essays in Pacific anthropology and ethnobiology in honour or Ralph Bulmer*, pp. 380–89. Memoirs of the Polynesian Society No. 48. Auckland: Polynesian Society.

10

On the word *ked*: The 'way' of being and becoming in Muyuw

Frederick H. Damon[1]

Introduction

This chapter describes the concept and practice of the major term *ked* in the Muyuw language, the principal language spoken on Muyuw, otherwise known as Woodlark Island, in the northeast *Kula* Ring, in Milne Bay Province, Papua New Guinea. The concept may be simply translated as 'path' or 'road', yet it abounds in sociological subtleties and cosmological foundations. It simultaneously formulates Muyuw's cultural specificity and orients people to a larger regional context. In facilitating these twined but opposed tendencies, the word is used in a pattern of social thought and action widely distributed throughout the Indo-Pacific. Although this contribution is confined to the northeast *Kula* Ring,[2] it is lodged in a study of Asian-Pacific social histories and dynamics.

1   As always, the information in this chapter flows from the kindness and intelligence of my many Muyuw teachers over the years. Additional thanks must go to David Gibeault and Luo Yang, who facilitated important comparative understandings about the Chinese concept of *dao/tao*; to Liang Yongjia for participating in that discussion; to Malcolm Ross for insights about the historical linguistics of the Austronesian languages of Milne Bay (he encouraged me to make an argument in this chapter); and to James J. Fox for his incisive comments on an earlier draft of this chapter.
2   I use '*Kula* Ring' to refer to this place in Papua New Guinea and *kula* to refer to the institution and practice of circulating 'armshells' and 'necklaces' counterclockwise and clockwise around the island cultures participating in the institution. *Kula* is the Trobriand pronunciation of the word Malinowski made famous. The Muyuw cognate is *kun*. The word is used as a noun and a verb.

When I commenced research in the 1970s, '*ked's*' significance was apparent. One easily realised that its pedantic translation—'path' or 'road'—did not capture the complex nuances inherent in its usage. I was told precisely that by a Muyuw man pulled into the English-language orbit of the country still shy of its formal independence. One of a set of young men drawn from the island to receive Western training, he was, perhaps like me, struggling with the all-too-ready translation into English.[3] With the spirit of that early encounter and with a world of different research behind it now, this chapter attempts to make apparent an important and allusive idea central to the organisation of Muyuw lifeways. I first examine words and their usage. I then turn to some of the origin mythology behind attempts to grapple with what at first seems like the idea's central content: the organisation of exchange. The operational understanding this affords brings the chapter to a conclusion. There I outline the structures by which the idea of *ked* becomes a manifold of complexity.

On (the) words

Words, things and people are said to go 'on' (*wa-*) paths, tracks, *ked*. The Muyuw word translated as road, or path, is a frequently heard and rich concept. 'Way', 'manner' or 'method' and 'meaning' are among the English words its usage conveys. Two words might sound the same but people will say they have 'different paths' (*kweita ked*). Ideally, paths should be 'straight' (*idumwal*)—characteristics often applied to a person's actions or 'intentions' (*non*, or *nanon*, a word that can also be translated as 'mind'). This is judged good. Being 'crooked' (*kaydodog*) or 'moving aimlessly', 'wandering around' (*tapleileiy*), brings a contrary evaluation and is a vice. Asked how a person runs this or that *kula* relationship, the respondent usually says they just go on it, 'follow the path' (*kikun ked*), implicitly straight—an intention sometimes signalled with the movement of a hand, going out from the speaker, not to his side. This is not, however, a passive construct. It is as metaphysical as it is literal. People often speak as though the *ked* determines their action; they are just doing what the way prescribes. In this framework, the *ked* is the agent; people are just the means by which

---

3   Named Naudekon, he was a son of Molotau, the most important person in the northeast *Kula* Ring, if not the whole ring itself. Elsewhere (Damon 1983b), I have given an account of Molotau's extraordinary life objectives. Naudekon brought the word and its myriad possible translations into English, among them 'way' and 'meaning'. His realisation of the word's significance, like his father's, I have always remembered.

its action is accomplished. The stress here is not unlike that for the Chinese concept *dao*—an idea whose implications entail ethical considerations as well as deliberate, straight intentions.[4] A mortuary practice exemplifies the control *ked* holds over people. A death is likened to a tree falling, blocking paths among the living, who are connected by lines of affinity or *kula* (see Damon 2017: 351n.24). People should ignore one another until they have performed a small clearing ritual. Good friends might walk by one another on a dock only a few feet wide because their 'path' was not yet opened. Another epoch in anthropology would understand this behaviour as rationalisation. Informants' descriptions, and some observations, of transactions of *kula* valuables and pigs would seem to support such an assertion—where the invocation of *ked* rationalises interests left unstated (but hardly unknown). However, I believe the idea comes instead from the acute sense of the social, of hierarchy, which the idea of *ked* carries in this region. By focusing closely on the words—in part, their grammaticality—this section begins to explore this complex concept.

If, as is likely, the idea translatable by 'road', 'path', 'way' and 'manner' is important throughout the Austronesian world, the Muyuw—and very likely the greater Milne Bay region—word form *ked* is relatively specific. Green and Pawley (1998: 61) use **zalan* as the Proto-Malayo-Polynesian term and **jalan* as the Proto-Oceanic word for 'path'. These forms seem to be realised as *dalan* in Timor's Tetun language,[5] *hala* in Tonga, *sala* in Rotuman and *ara* in Māori. In the Motu language along Papua New Guinea's southeastern coast, the form is *dala*; that it might be cognate with an important northern *Kula* Ring term—*dala* in the Trobriands and *dal* in Muyuw, which are terms often translated as 'subclan'—raises possibilities with which I end this section. The Muyuw term *ked*, the Trobriand *keda* and Dobuan *eda* all seem unrelated to the **jalan* construction, according to the linguist of the Papuan Tip languages, Malcolm Ross (Personal communication, 31 December 2018). Ross surmises the word:

---

4   *Dào* (道) is written with two characters. The lefthand character, *chuò*, translates to something like 'go' or 'movement'; the righthand character, *shŏu*, translates to 'head' ('Motion by reasoning?'). The term expands into *tiān dào* (天道) and *dàodé* (道德). The first is like natural law; the second, ethics or morality. 彳, *chì* and 'straight' (直, *zhí*) compose the *dé* from *dàodé*. Some months before this essay became well conceived, I asked Mark Mosko if he had considered the Chinese *dao* for his analysis of Trobriand ethnography. His response was that the title *Way of Baloma* intended just that.
5   Therik does not put *dalan* as such in his glossary. See *bein* ('ancestors') and *bein dalan* ('ancestor's path') (Therik 2004: 286).

comes from *keja 'path', which is of Proto Papuan Tip antiquity, although of fairly restricted distribution … It also has cognates in some Ngero languages—the languages of [the] Vitiaz Strait trade network. This makes sense, as Proto Papuan Tip seems to have come from the area, presumably in Lapita times'. (See also Pawley and Ross 1995: 59)

If Ross's speculations are correct, the word form perhaps reflects a synthesis between the region's original inhabitants and East Asian Austronesian currents over the past 1,500–3,000 years.

Although the word *ked* may participate in non-Austronesian language conventions, it shares common Austronesian/Oceanic possession usages. In simplistic terms, *ked* is a noun; its possession is telling. Three affix systems indicate possession in the Muyuw language and, by widespread understanding, the three classes are 'distant', 'intermediate' and 'intimate'.[6] The first two are prefixes, the third is a suffix. *Ked* is possessed with a prefix, placing it in the 'distant' class. One says *gunaked* ('my road'). By contrast, 'my leg' would be *kakeig*, the suffix 'g' indicating the first-person intimate class; *kakeim* is 'your leg', the final *m* being the possessive marker. Using the intermediate first-person possessive to say 'my leg' (*agukakein*) changes the meaning to the leg of a pig—a prestation received in a ritual, for example. Arguably, the possession classes have semantic significance. And the received interpretation of these matters is that they demonstrate qualities of inseparability/separability or inalienability/alienability. Most body parts use the 'intimate', 'inalienable' possessive form, indicating that they are internally related to a larger whole. By contrast, the 'intermediate' designation given in the example of 'my leg'—a piece of pork received in a ritual—specifies something separable and specifiable, individualised in its usage; this kind of debt to this actor, another kind from the same pig to a different person.

Although revealing, the paradigmatic differences the separable/inseparable contrast indicates ignore a processual organisation evident in practice.[7] This leads us, not coincidentally, to the complexity in the Muyuw category *ked*. The word form *ked* is not just in the most separate, distant class, it is also in a class best characterised as tool-like. Included in this

---

6   Blust (2009: 476–84) uses 'direct' versus 'indirect' for the inalienable/alienable or intimate/intermediate/distant distinctions I deploy here.
7   This is probably a generalisable point for Austronesian cultural forms. See Mosko (2017) for his transformation of a well-understood Austronesian classificatory scheme, 'base'/'tip', into the sequence base-trunk-tip-fruit.

classification are axes and knives, a class of *kula* valuables (-*kitoum*), boats and, among others, individual fingers. Although the generic term for 'finger', *didi-*, takes the intimate suffix possessive, individual finger terms are possessed with the 'distant' prefix. This condition may speak to a no longer practised tradition that involved lopping off a digit for mortuary practices. Far more important, however, are the uses of individual fingers for fundamental tasks such as tying, weaving, handling and holding— that is, producing things by digitally transforming certain potentialities into others. Arguably, the experiential structure of this understanding is built into annual and life cycles—that is, basic features of organised consciousness, as I have suggested for learning processes entailed in string figure usage in Muyuw (see Damon 2017: 286–87). Words in this class stand out because they make things, including people.

Details about the *kula* show the processual, sequential quality to the possession system. *Ked* is the fundamental term used with respect to *kula* relationships and, as noted, it is possessed by the distant possessive structure—so, *gunaked* for 'my path'. *Kula* valuables travel on these relationships and they are possessed with the so-called intermediate possessive: *agumwal*, *aguveigun*, for 'my armshell, my necklace'. The exchange of these forms creates a person's ranked 'name' and the word taking the suffix form of the 'intimate' class; hence, *yagag* for 'my name', with the closing *g* the first-person indicator.[8] Although an individual's name is an aspect of an inseparable identity, its value, its rank, depends on the state of affairs of *kula* valuables, and that follows from the travels of specific 'armshells' (*agumwal*, 'my armshell') and 'necklaces' (*aguveigun*, 'my necklace') on specific paths, -*ked*.

A similar sequence is evident in the terms used to specify kinship relationships. Among all of the terms in the 'distant' class are words translated as 'husband' and 'wife': *mwan* and *kwav*.[9] 'Husband' and 'wife' are understood as part of a sequence—that is, a process that transforms this or that into something else.[10] These two categories generate the affinal

---

8   This sequence is also indicated with the individually owned *kula* valuable called *kitoum*, which is in the 'distant' class. Hence *gunkitoum–agumwal–yagag* for 'my *kitoum*–my armshell–my name'.

9   As I have noted in other publications (Damon 1983a; 1990; 2017: esp. pp. 167–68), these categories have to be achieved on the basis of position-appropriate action. The categories exist as modes of action.

10   I discuss the metaphorical use of kinship terms with respect to yams, how a 'husband' (male yam) and 'wife' (female yam) are transformed into alternate generation relationships (*tabu-*) between a dried up old seed tuber and new yams, for eating or planting (Damon 1990: 167–68). Proximate generation relationships are conveyed by taro.

relationship *sinvalam*. This form uses the intermediate possession classifier; one says *agusinvalam*, *inasinvalam* for 'my affines', 'his affines'. By the operation of this relationship (the word can be made a verb, especially with a causative construction like *kabi-*), people are made and with them emerge relationships specified by other kinship terms, most of which are in the 'intimate' class. First and foremost among these are proximate generation in-laws, *yawa-*, and the brother-in-law category, *nubou-*. As noted elsewhere (Damon 1983a; 1990: Ch.4), almost all ritual activity in Muyuw centres on relationships defined in reference to these terms, the *ked*, the manner or way appropriate to the designations. For example, as soon as a young man is seen to be married, he should go to his in-laws' (*yawa-* or *nubou-*) garden to work (if in a sailing village, to their boat); a young woman should carry firewood to her husband's female *yawa-* and *yava—t*, more or less a new bundle every day until she has gifted everyone. And by their interaction flow all those positions following from the productive activities of married couples, 'father'/'mother' (including mbw)/'child' (*tama-/ina-/natu-*), MB/ZC relationships (*kada-*); 'alternate generation' relationships, which include FZ/BC relations (*tabu-*); and same-generation relationships, the same-sex sibling terms, es/ys, *tuwa-/ bwada-*, and the cross-cousin term *nubie-*.[11] Apparent anomalies to this synthesis are the terms for opposite-sex siblings and the sister-in-law relationship, respectively, *na—t* and *yava—t*. In these, the possessive is infixed. A woman would refer to and sometimes call her brother *nagut* and her sister-in-law *yavagut* (both reciprocals). It may be noted that the same possessive anomalies appear in Trobriand kinship terms. If the infixed possessive *—gu-* in this structure suggests this form contains qualities exemplified in the spousal terms—*gunakwav* and *gunamwan*—then this is consistent with affinities that exist between brothers and sisters and husbands and wives; for example, relations between both should not be visible in public. Mosko (2017) has featured this in his recent accounting of Trobriand kinship. The *yava—t* term arguably participates in this form because of specifications concerning the production of children. Muyuw understand that men make children because they produce the food women convey to them in utero and ex utero. By virtue of this claim it is held that men control their children. And, after a father, his sisters (or a still dominating mother) have the next most important say over a child's

---

11 The Muyuw kinship terminological system is nearly identical to the Trobriand set except with regard to cross-cousin terms. In the Trobriands, FZC is *tabu-* and MBC is *latu-*. Muyuw believe that cross-cousins marry in the Trobriands, unlike in their own system, where they are not supposed to marry.

fate (first and foremost concerning marriage). Although these claims are realised in ritual action running through the life cycle (described in Damon 1989, as well as 1983a and 1990), they are symbolised in a little gift right after a baby is born. This gift is the child's first excrement, which is wrapped up and given to the father's sister as a testimony to her claims on his productivity.[12]

All the patterns implied in the foregoing are connoted by the word *ked*; different relationships have different *ked*. This speaks to the sociological subtleties fixed in the term. It contains complex ideas and subtle action. Here I note one other usage of the word and then conclude this initial section with several domains of action that might be understood in similar terms.

A derivative of *ked*

Although a different word, *kut*, is used for a boat's course, a modification of *ked* specifies narrower passages boats follow when passing through reefs. The term is *aniked*. A more than metaphorical use of this term is sometimes applied to the movement of gardens/fields over time. Muyuw practise a version of slash and burn agriculture, yet forests are not randomly cut for new fields. In addition to different regions having different ideal fallow lengths designed to produce different tree products, garden spaces move around plots of ground called *tasim*,[13] which are plots of uncut forest. These groves are so defined because they have more coral than dirt. This is not, however, just a negative because *tasim* generate important forest resources as well as conceived favourable ecological conditions for adjacent fields (see Damon 2017: 132–39). The courses a garden takes around *tasim* over time may be called *aniked*, as if a garden is a boat passing over the forested coral-strewn land like a real boat pilots through passages in reefs. Gardens have boat terms imposed on them and the language of sailing, or paddling, suffuses garden work. The *aniked* usage is part of a rich set of reciprocating understandings between the land and the sea (and sky)—understandings fixed in cosmological constructs.

---

12 This approach to kinship terminologies adopts a 'production' rather than 'exchange' perspective, outlined in Damon (1983a). Piot (1991) deploys this approach in West African Togo.
13 Muyuw say that the word *tasim* derives from their word for island, *sim*, and the word for chop, *tay*.

'Subclan' as the Proto-Oceanic 'path'?

The Motu cognate of the Proto-Malayo-Polynesian term *zalan* and the Proto-Oceanic word *jalan* for 'path' is *dala*. I conclude this section by exploring the possibility that these proto forms may be behind concepts and practices anthropologists have used to describe what are called 'subclans' across the northern side of the *Kula* Ring. To what extent might it be accurate to understand 'subclans' as paths, as sequences?

The Muyuw word is *dal*; the Trobriand, *dala*. This term contrasts with *kum* in Muyuw and *kumila* in the Trobriands, which is usually translated as 'clan'. *Dal/dala* are inside of *kum/kumila*. Conventionally, both are understood as matrilineal units. There is an indeterminate number of *dal/dala*. Trobriand *dala* are ranked. Muyuw *dal* are not ranked, though they may gain or lose stature as they gain or lose resources. There is a fixed number of *kum/kumila*: eight in Muyuw, four in the Trobriands. Everyone west of Muyuw—that is, from Gaw through Iwa and Kitava—proclaims that Muyuw people 'lie' when they assert there are eight.[14]

The container/contained logic employed with these categories allows Muyuw people to sometimes use the category *kum* to invoke what they really mean by *dal*. Possible ambiguities in this usage may be easily disambiguated because, in a formal sense, the clan idea, *kum*, specifies marriage relations—a very specific kind of *ked*—but does not contain property. By contrast, the subclan idea, *dal*, does not specify marriage relations with other like units but they hold property. Similarly, although people may speak of the actors in mortuary rituals as clans, *kum*, in fact the real actors are members of a specific subclan, *dal*, and these are the units that hold the debts or credits created in ritual action and the resources attached to those debts/credits.

Representations in space create the principal ways by which Muyuw *kum* (clan) and *dal* (subclan) ideas are understood. Muyuw gardens must be configured by at least two paths, with the idea of *kum* located at their

---

14 'Lie' (*yaweid*) covers a range of ideas that go from 'mistaken' to 'lie' in English. Muyuw distinguish between the 'old' *kum*, which are the four to the west, and 'new ones', two of which in fact play roles as *dala* on, for example, Iwa. Eastern and central Muyuw tended to become embarrassed when asked why they had eight clans; some muttered about incestuous ancestors. In western Muyuw, a well-known myth tells of people from the Kwasis clan building a tower to the heavens. The tower collapses and the fallen members turn into the new clans.

intersection.[15] Ideally, one path goes 'sunrise/sunset'—from east to west—and the other bisects it, going by what Muyuw call *bomat/yals*, which is more or less 'north/south'.[16] The four 'old clans' are positioned around the garden intersection east (*Malas*), west (*Kubay*), north (*Dawet* or *Kulabut'*) and south (*Kwasis*). These directions stipulate reciprocal marriage relations, which are customarily spoken of as if women are exchanged between the clans/*kum*; people can and do also think of them exchanging men. This construct is a *ked*. In it the genders are separated.

In contrast to *kum*, *dal* (subclans) are distributed over the landscape, including locations far beyond Muyuw, and almost invariably individually rather than as part of a set of relations. These spaces are the antithesis of the organised garden form in which *kum* are set. And although the first emergence points are said to be part of a *dal*'s property,[17] usually they are the opposite of productive resources such as garden land, sago orchards and so on. Among the listed emergence points—which in fact are often very vague—are mountain tops, small islands (some far from Muyuw, others close by), swamps and unspecified beaches. They are called *mumugw*, which is a duplication of the word for 'lead', *mugw*. Very few Muyuw, however, profess to know very much about their 'origin stories' (*taleliu*). Yet everyone presumes that a brother and sister were together under the ground. They came out, emerged (*kapow*) and then separated to be where they are today. As the social relationship in that underground abode is virtually an incestuous, negative reality, so is the property an antithesis. Only when they separate do you find people where they are now, married and with their *dal* possessing real entities, totems, names

---

15 The garden form is the culture's most elaborate formal model, discussed in detail in Damon (1990: Ch.4) and Damon (2017: Ch.1).

16 In 2017, I learned that this coordinate also follows the Milky Way in the early evening darkness of June, running more or less east–west. Correspondingly, the line bisecting it follows, though not as exactly, the swing of the Milky Way in the early evening of, approximately, December, when it is oriented northeast/southwest. This is a significant addition to the ethnography of this region and will require much new research (see Damon 2018). Although east–west–north–south are relatively accurate representations of the Muyuw categories *nuvid–yavat–bomat–yals* as idealisations of wind directions, such an understanding does not prevail in Iwa, to the west, nor in Gaboyin, which is an important island in the *Kula* Ring to Muyuw's south. Mosko (2009: 507n.6) provides Trobriand direction names, some of the terms for which are equivalent to those just listed, but the directions Mosko claims they specify differ.

17 There is pressure to make *dal* origin stories deeds to owned land. Dividing royalties from logging and mining have been principal forces behind this movement. About half of the people in Wabunun came out of the ground at Kavatan, along Muyuw's eastern flank. Some of those people wondered whether they would be moved back there. In 1996, the people who lived in Kavatan—none of whom was a member of that subclan—feared they would be removed from the only land they have ever known.

of significant boats, garden land, sago orchards and, increasingly west across the Muyuw landscape towards the islands of Gaw and Iwa and eventually the Trobriands, sets of personal names. In Muyuw, this real property is a function of the state of (usually pig) debts between subclans.[18] Unlike the intervals between the emergence place and present locations in space, the state of credits and debts between subclans is specifiable and is the primary, though not overtly public, point to the exchange of pigs in the culture's primary mortuary ritual (*sagal* or, more definitively, *anagin tavalam*: literally, 'fruit of our crying').

These facts are consistent with the idea of a subclan as a path through time. Abstractly and vaguely, this path is from the origin point to people's present locations. If the (imaginary) origin spot can be pinpointed, present locations can be very diverse. A dominant subclan in Wabunun thinks it has representatives in Misima, Nasikwabw, Waviay, Kaulay and Kawuway, Gawa, Iwa and, I believe, Sinaketa in the southern Trobriands. In principle, real dots connect those lines; in fact, Muyuw people do not keep tract of such relations. Yet it would not have occurred to me to consider the subclan category *dal* to be related to **zalan* as the Proto-Malayo-Polynesian term and **jalan* as the Proto-Oceanic word for 'path' or the Motu *dala* but for one recently learned set of facts. In Muyuw, distinct varieties of sago are also called *dal*. A unique named sago orchard, for example, will have many different clumps of growing sago, usually with one in each group much taller than the others; the latter bud off the former. People name the different varieties, calling each one a different *dal*. An orchard might, for example, have 20 different clumps, but only two or three or four varieties—that is, *dal*. People insisted this *dal* was the same word used for what I call subclans. One woman, sitting on a step with her daughter perched between her legs, said that just as a sago plant buds off its mother, taking over its position, so does she give birth to her daughter so that the unit continues. They create a sequence. The 'path' here is an abstracted time concretised through birth rather than a finite space, which is much more the case with the *ked* usage. Muyuw do not believe in reincarnation. A deceased person's 'soul' (*kaluan*) goes to Tum and never comes back. By contrast, in the Trobriands, ideas about reincarnation are well formed and, in Mosko's work at least, *dala* are an

---

18   I have touched on these procedures in many places (Damon 1983a; 1989; 1990: 94–118; 2017: 152–53).

elaborated construct running the course between Boyowa, this land, and the after and before-life in Tuma. The idea is profound and is much more road-like.[19]

On origin myths

A central component of Western cosmology is that Western societies developed from an original primitive and, in Durkheimian terms, mechanical form to the organic, highly differentiated form they have today.[20] Muyuw origin mythology is different. They understand the form of their culture being defined by a creator called Geliu. She— he to some—comes to the island by boat, organises the local practices and then goes on to the west. I was told I had to go to those places to understand what Geliu did there. For a long time, it was convenient to take that information as a limit; over there was another social system. Only in the course of doing research realised in my ethnobotanical study (Damon 2017) was I forced to take such data as the reciprocal of an essentially organic view of the world. In 1996, I was shocked to discover that people on Iwa Island did not know the names of much of the taro and yam they were planting; somewhat huffily, I was told that if I wanted to know that information I should go to Muyuw. Only much later did I realise that this was a division of labour created around the expected consequences of El Niño–Southern Oscillation (ENSO) events, called 'big suns' in the region. People know that Iwa's circumstances—as a small uplifted island with a meagre underground water lens easily exhausted by drought—mean it will lose its root crops during an ENSO event. Consequently, it falls to others to know the details of these means of production. People on other islands keep Iwa supplied with yam and taro seeds in exchange for its services—the nuts from several tree species that survive the droughts. The same conditions prevail on nearby Gawa and Kweywata islands—islands sculpted to produce the trees needed for large outrigger canoes.

---

19 So, also, are the 'stories' (*leliu*) Trobriand people know about the intervals between the origin point and the present. Muyuw complain about how little they know compared with Trobriand people, sometimes coming back from an encounter with a Trobriand person filled with stories ostensibly about their own identities.

20 In complex ways, 'exchange theory' in anthropology and its single-site long-term fieldwork methodology contributed to the problem I allude to here.

It is in this context that the idea of paths (*ked*) must be understood as a consideration encompassed by wider totalities just as it becomes clear that formulations in any one place speak at best to part of a set of discontinuous but interlinked structures. I will review this orientation with the exchange of shell-wealth concerned with *kula*; a similar argument could be made with respect to the exchange spheres in the domain of kinship but for reasons of time and space that argument must rest inside the concluding section of this chapter.[21]

Practically every time I started a conversation about the *kula* with a new informant, they broke off my question to make sure I understood the whole institution. They would list all the major social units through which it ran, always defining the customary circle of islands—those depicted on maps since Malinowski's *Argonauts*. The idea of the *kula ked* first entails a holistic view of the valuables circulating around the *Kula* Ring's two circuits: *mwal* (armshells), going from left to right, and *veigun* (Muyuw's generic term for the necklaces), going from right to left. Some of my sources were men who then had little stature in the institution. Significant players readily defined specific important *ked* by name of person and often their spouse and home village. One informant demurred on the last when he got to Dobu because he knew they practised what we understand from Fortune's work as bilocal residence; he did not keep up with those movements from, ideally, one year to the next.

This macroframe of reference is realised in the formal terminology used for specifying acting agents, by the way valuables are discussed and in the way names circulate on the backs of valuables. Inside these general orientations every participant has to know at least two people on his immediate left and right, and successful actors are likely to be able to specify a complete ring of actors in their larger relationships. I turn to these matters shortly.

---

21   Although I have not researched this material intensively since my original time in Muyuw (1973–75), I have made casual inquiries about various matters on each of the 11 times I returned to the island between 1982 and 2017. During these returns, I sought information about the travels of the five large *mwal* that defined most *kula* activities between 1973 and 1975 (Dayay, Nimov, Kunakwan, Mantasop and Tuidaman). In 2017, I rehearsed a manoeuvre I described in Damon (1983c: 332–34) to see whether my understanding still seemed accurate; it did.

This level of knowledge, however painstaking it is to first acquire, gives an incorrect understanding of what *kula ked* are. Synthesising the gift literature in the mid-1990s, Godelier opened up an important level of analysis when he argued:

> [I]n analyzing a gift, whatever it may be, one needs to consider the relationship that existed between the giver and the receiver *before* the former made a gift to the latter. (Godelier 1999: 13; emphasis in original)

What follows from this for the *Kula* Ring concerns the tiers of knowledge people have of the villages and islands around them. This knowledge is both detailed in a particularistic manner and encompassed by means of various cosmological and geographical, almost geological, orientations. This knowledge system approaches in form the likes of that which one may intuit from Chinese materials totalising 'China' from ancient times (Pankenier 2013).[22] The particulars quickly speak to the real or created ecological differences in the region—facets that become organised in subsidiary *kula* exchanges. Well-known ones concern Budibud, to Muyuw's southeast, being planted with coconut trees long before copra plantations were enforced on the region. Budibud's coconut palms were turned into coconut-leaf skirts, coconuts themselves and pigs—all of which, along with the region's high-quality pandanus-leaf sleeping mats, were traded to Muyuw for sago. Although the sago was a matter of daily consumption for its Budibud recipients, Budibud products were often used to capitalise productive relationships in Muyuw. Many Budibud coconuts and pigs went into Muyuw mortuary rituals, all of which had to do with subclan resources noted in the discussion of *dal*. Budibud skirts and sleeping mats often were—and, in the case of mats, remain—shuffled into *kula* relationships, sometimes being exchanged for clay pots from the southeastern corner of the *Kula* Ring. To Muyuw's southwest is the volcanic cone of Yemga, amid an almost classic coral atoll structure. A small sailing community without enough land to support itself by horticultural pursuits, Yemga trades its seaside life for vegetable products from Yanab on the northern side of its atoll structure and virtually all of the villages across Muyuw. Most of that seaside life concerns the outrigger canoes it maintains as one of the principal sailing villages coordinating travel between the northeast and southeast corners of the *Kula* Ring.

---

22   See also Granet (1973: 47) as well as recent explorations of classical texts (Dorofeeva-Litchmann 1995).

But it also concerns a fish, *papis* (perhaps *Siganus argenteus*), that schools right off its sandy beaches. Now and again, hundreds of these fish will be caught, smoked and taken to Muyuw as prestations for vegetables; these exchanges are specifically designed to feed into the *kula*. These are not incidental exchanges, but are rather fixed in the region's social organisation. As noted elsewhere (Damon 2017: 165–74), there is a system using ritual firewood marking differences among and therefore relations between places. In most rituals, only this wood should be burned, and a significant affinal responsibility for women entails knowing which trees should be given in the appropriate context. Although not everyone knows all the wood for every place, most know about the practice. In my published account, I did not list Yemga's wood because I did not then know it. In 2017, I learned it was *mwadog* (mangrove). As in all the other cases, this tree speaks to Yemga's specific situation—nestled along the shoreline as it is. Although individual trees can be harvested for ritual purposes, the grove must be maintained to protect the island from the occasional 'big wave'—presumably, tsunamis. Other villages' trees mark other specific orientations. The tree for several southeastern villages comes from early fallows because those villages use fallows of that age for growing food of a certain quality and generating hundreds of species-specific saplings for outrigger canoes—canoes usually owned and operated by other sailing villages.

If ritual firewood knowledge reflects organised consciousness one level up from the pragmatics of specific exchanges, land names and real or mythical histories entail another level. The identity of Nasikwabw, another sailing village south of Muyuw, is bound up with the idea that part of its heritage derives from Misima, an island east of the southeastern corner of the *Kula* Ring and outside the immediate flow of *kula* valuables, but inside the limits of the current social system. People say that Misima people first came to Nasikwabw to make their living—a time evinced by a scatter of potsherds and chipped stone. But while perched at Nasikwabw's eastern end one day, people saw the Sulog Mountains to the north, so the pot and stone-tool works moved there; Nasikwabw mediates between Misima and the stone-tool industries once located on Sulog. Iwa, the little island dot that stands almost exactly between Muyuw and the Trobriands, has its northeastern/southwestern axis defined by a myth that orients that place exactly to its social connections to those very directions. Liluta is the name of an important Trobriand village and also of a plot of garden ground to the west of the important central Muyuw village of Kaulay. Although

I was surprised by that 'Trobriand' name amid Kaulay's territory, my Kaulay informants were not and added to the seeming coincidence that implanted near the Trobriand Liluta is a piece of igneous stone derived from Mount Kabat, the tall mountain to the south of Kaulay and the source of standing—or fallen—stones that demarcate the travels of the ancestors who created standing stones and stone ruins scattered about the landscapes of Kaulay Gawa, Iwa, Kitava and Kiriwina. Following Strathern's (for example, 1988, 1991) work, Mosko (2017) demonstrates the pertinence of the partible person idea for Trobriand sociality, showing how much Trobriand reality has to do with passing qualities from one person to another. But it is not just people who are understood as composites here; by complementary exchanges, mythical stories and land names, islands are understood in the same way.

One learns about this information as almost incidental, and, in my case at least, as tangents to other questions. However, there is reason to believe they are fundamental, not tangential. In 2017, a Yemga man recounted a myth about the beginning of the *kula*. It concerns a snake on Goodenough Island, beyond the southwestern corner of contemporary *kula* flows. The snake gives birth to a woman, who in turn has a daughter too anxious to see her grandmother. When she does the snake becomes angry and runs away, with a *mwal* on one side of its mouth and a *veigun* on the other. It first goes to Rossel Island at the very southeastern end of Milne Bay. It leaves the *veigun* there as Rossel Island's work. It passes on to Yemga, where, among other things, it makes the fish noted above, *papis*, Yemga's work and, because of another altercation, makes the island of Yalab like a snake. Thence it goes to Kilivil, the Trobriands, where it leaves *mwal* as their work. My source told me that originally Muyuw was not in the *kula*, but because Muyuw had sago it was eventually incorporated.[23]

Myths like this one are, of course, just stories. But the truth they contain is that of an organised consciousness that probably has more layers than usual anthropological knowledge manages to circumscribe. And there is no reason to think that any one point in a social system is going to encompass all of the knowledge necessary for its functioning, just as it is reasonable to assume that the villages lying to the *Kula* Ring's southern borders are going to have cultural openings to regional relations

---

23 I do not recall hearing this myth earlier. In the autumn of 2017, I repeated the story to Professor Maria Lepowsky, who did research in what many people know as Sudest Island, Vanatinai. She recounted a much fuller version. For some, it is a well-known story.

external to the institution. Indeed, over the past decade of my visits to the area, I have become aware of a peculiar geographical model, the full implications of which remain unclear. Many Muyuw people claim that Rossel Island is the highest island in the region while the Trobriands are the lowest. This geographical understanding inverts the social standings of the respective areas: Trobriand hierarchy is legendary, as are the lack of status and indeed apparent isolation of Rossel Island. When I asked people where Muyuw and Goodenough stood in this ordering, I was told they were about the same, between Rossel and the Trobriands. At least some of the people who reported these facts also know that they are not a literal description of reality. Although the Trobriands are among the lowest islands in the region and Rossel's peaks, at about 840 metres are taller than Muyuw's (perhaps 350 metres), Goodenough towers over all of them at more than 2,500 metres. Going along with the precise geographical model of all the islands in the region—on a southeast to northwest axis, geological and social elevation invert one another—is the fact that all islands are conceived to be correlated with, if not under, specific stars. This order of facts has to do with navigational models, but it nevertheless implicates well-formed models about star locations, island locations and relations among these. *Ked* operate within social conventions organised by complex structures.[24]

Conclusion: On the structures

The idea of *ked*—an operation among agencies in the form of people and their places—exists inside a complex of semantic spaces. This complex space is why people speak as if *ked* determine their actions. For different purposes, I have described many of the pertinent details of these forms elsewhere (Damon 1980a, 1980b, 1983a, 1983c 1993, 2002). Here I argue that the idea of a *ked* is a diacritic establishment of a set of relationships manifesting a social field. The idea organises ranked intentionalities. I start with *kula* exchange, illustrate the ordering of relationships in the domain

---

24   In a recent archaeological synthesis of the *kula* region, Irwin et al. (2018) create a picture of, on the one hand, near-Lapita origins for the region and, on the other, the recent emergence of the order we have known from Malinowski over the past several hundred years. The image of chaos in their model fits one of the versions Muyuw have of their own history: until the Europeans arrived, there was nothing but fighting, no villages, gardens, *kula* or anything else. Slightly more detailed versions of that chaos argue that the fighting took place between 'villages' (*ven*) organised into two groups, and in the 1970s, elders easily divided every village I could name, on Muyuw and other islands, into one of these two moiety-like groups (Damon 1990: 70–83).

of kinship and conclude with a description of procedures for asking for things—the order of metonymies in the request forms illustrative of the kinds of totalities that make up this social system. These forms return us to this contribution's East Asian framing.

Each *ked* has its own form. A *kula* relationship could start with innocent exchanges of betel nut for betel pepper between young people who barely know one another. One gives the other nuts to chew; the recipient reciprocates with pepper. The two different things are combined and, as talk flows, they begin to learn about each other. Nobody more need be involved. But time may turn that simple encounter into the exchange of low-ranked *kula* valuables. *Kula* relationships, however, are not dyadic. If the details of a particular valuable are not already known, they are figured out. And the information has a grammar. If C wants a valuable from D, he must know or will ask whose 'hand' it is. D must answer by specifying not his partner's name, E, but the partner of his partner, F: 'F's hand' is the answer to the question 'whose hand is it?'. In Muyuw, immediate partners are called *veiyou-*, which is the same word used to refer to clan/subclan members. Partners of partners are referred to as −*mul*, and all people on a line of transactors beyond immediate partners can be designated by this term. This means the minimal transactional order for a *kula* relationship contains five nodes: two *veiyou-* on either side of ego and two −*mul* on each side of them. Hence −n-A-B-C-D-F-n. *Kula* action is realised in this structure. People participate in the system to make their names rise, to make the name seen. The hand of F that D gives to C makes C's name go up. But when C gives this valuable to B, B's name goes up and C's name goes down—the exact opposite of what is wanted. Only when B gives that valuable on to A does C's name go up and C becomes 'seen' or 'known' (*kakin*, a duplicated form of the verb 'see'; *kin*) or his 'fame/noise' (*bulagan*) is heard. Muyuw claim that control over the use of valuables follows this form. B may get a valuable from C with the stipulation that it go to a particular A_1. Various factors, however, may make B give the valuable to a different person, A_2. In this situation, C may disallow the manoeuvre, force B to retrieve the valuable and do what he was supposed to do or just reclaim it himself, cancelling the initial transaction. People explained this distribution of responsibilities to me in the context of differences that exist in relationships, *ked* and paths held to be subsidiary to *kula* relationships. On large *kula* relationships, for example, pigs often flow back and forth. B might have received the valuable from C in part because he gave C a pig that he, C, needed for a certain ritual. C may decide, however, to use the pig for a different ritual. This is not B's business and he cannot withdraw the pig. C, however, will still owe B a pig as a replacement, and would no matter what he did with the animal. The same relations prevail among all the subsidiary things exchanged beneath *kula* valuables. Their structure is effectively binary, whereas *kula* has the aforementioned five-part structure. The lower-level exchanges correlate with the organic division of labour symbolised by the firewood used for each place. By contrast, the vision of two circulating rings and the five-part form of every *kula ked* correlate with the encompassing structures, mythological and geographical, noted in the previous section.

As noted elsewhere (Damon 2002: 122–23), *kula* valuables are also thought to move up and down, not just left to right (*mwal*) and right to left (*veigun*). So, *veigun*, necklaces, go down from Muyuw to points south. They also go down from central Muyuw to southeastern Muyuw. Both vectors must involve a point of inversion, and one informant located that inversion near Iw, the small island between Muyuw and the Trobriands. I do not know how this spinning model relates to the southeastern–northwestern axis. The region is, however, a complex topological space. And it should be recalled that, by string and other materials, especially as represented in the string figures that are basic cultural activities throughout this region (see Damon 2017: Ch.5), topological transformations are modes of thinking made common by various cultural practices.

The different *ked* of *kula* and its subsidiary spheres entail a reciprocal but asymmetrical ordering. Lower-level exchanges lead into and are usually for the productive order that is the *kula*—a method for producing ranked names. Just the same, some *kula* relationships are designed to gather the resources that are in the lower tiers. Their operation does not usually alter the nature and flow of *kula* valuables on specific paths, but they might. All lower-level spheres are defined, like *kula*, by being able to make or acquire, often, different things, the exchange of which is considered to be the exchange of equivalents. Equivalence here is abstracted into the idea of 'intentions', complementary though they usually are. By giving a partner a bundle of sleeping mats, the giver 'makes' (*-vag*) the intentions of the receiver. Following the giving of some article, the giver might say to the recipient 'you make your mind' (*kuvag nanom*), the clear implication being that the giver created the wherewithal for the receiver to follow his plans. This statement, however, is not often heard in *kula* exchanges because their intentions are usually finely specified before the exchange is made, all the more so when a specific article is a return gift and must follow the course of the initial debt-making item. So, when a receiver returns clay pots for mats he earlier received, he makes the original giver's intentions. This basket of yam tuber seeds is given for that bundle of taro stalks; the seeds for taro. One of the ways villages differentiate themselves is by their relative ability to withstand fluxes that come with El Niño/La Niña dynamics for which yams and taro have complementary strengths and weaknesses.

The primary purpose of the subsidiary exchanges is, overtly or covertly, the exchange of *kula* valuables as *mwal* (armshells) and *veigun* (necklaces). In the classic exchange literature (Bohannan 1955; Bohannan and Dalton 1962), this is two sets of conveyances designed so that the lower one converts into the higher one. Purposefully or not, sometimes a particular agent cannot return what he must. That can result in the creditor being able to claim an armshell or necklace as a *kitoum*, the short definition of which is a personally owned *kula* valuable. This alters the understanding of all the flowing objects but not necessarily the obligations those objects have created. If B can claim a valuable from C as his *kitoum* because of flows on subsidiary paths, C cedes the valuable to B whether or not it was his *kitoum* to begin with. If he takes the valuable as a *kitoum*, B does not owe C anything. However, C still carries the obligations of the valuable he had to give over, to some D and he owes a return to that D. These kinds of intricacies are understood as the rules that go along with the content of these unique but intermingling *ked*. As is the case in many Austronesian societies, degrees of precedence and the recognition of variability flow within and between the ranked exchange spheres (Fox 1999).

As the global understandings of *kula* transactions rest upon important and sometimes determining relationships beneath them, so the idealised exchange of women, or men, depicted in the model of *kum* (clans) in the Muyuw garden contains a series of subsidiary paths. Foremost among these is the exchange of pigs in the primary Muyuw mortuary relationship, *sagall anagin tavalam*. In this ritual, if a man gives his wife's father, mother's brother or brother a live pig for a mortuary ritual when he puts on one of these rituals, it is expected that they will give him a live pig in return. Various other things—such as sticks draped with cloth, tobacco, money and betel nuts, units of sago and baskets of yams and taro—go along with the pig in these exchanges. They, too, are to be returned but, unlike the pigs, they are not counted against the flow of resources—garden land, sago orchards—that pass back and forth in place of missed pig returns. If the exchange of women and men between the clans is largely an ideal that resembles reality only after the fact, the exchange of pigs of identical size and sex is real, counted, measured and has consequences. However, while often phrased in terms of the ritual of the Kubay, Kwasis or Sinawiy *kum*, in fact the unit holding the debt is really a subclan (*dal*) and, within that, usually a more narrowly configured line of people.

Beneath the real exchange of pigs are several other *ked*, which, while analogised with the two above it, in fact carry different names, forms and purposes. Moreover, while they involve exchanges, their point is not the replacement of this with that but the enabling, rewarding or reproducing of productive capacities. They articulate the real relationships marriages define. A generic term for many of these *ked*—and here a translation like 'transferral' is more apt than 'path' or 'road'—is *takon*, of which there are many kinds. I briefly describe two.

When couples are first married, they usually reside with the wife's family. If children result, they are usually kept by the wife's mother and father because in this context the wife is considered the husband and the husband, the woman. To be made a man, the husband's father must take the couple to his house. He then becomes the man, with his wife only implicitly a woman. Formally, this transferral is accomplished by imposing a *kula* relationship over the married couple that runs through the husband's and wife's parents, and they in fact are the active agents in the exchange, though the young couple may take it over and turn it into a significant *kula* relationship. A woman only becomes a real woman, which means formally separated from but tied to her brother, by means of a large *takon*, often three or more years into their marriage. All *takon* entail the exchange of female things for male things. Female things include pigs, vegetables including raw yams and taro and sometimes cooked sago pudding or *munowun*, which is the culture's most prestigious dish.[25] Male things consist of axes, machetes, knives, now money and, in a specific context, *kitoum*. These are not, however, just female and male things. They are means of consumption on the one hand and means of production on the other, hence the gendering. In the specific *takon* that makes a woman a wife, her brother raises a large pig and, at the appointed time, kills it and gives it, partially butchered, with baskets of yams and taro—the corm separated from its stalk, which is kept by the giver—to his sister and through her to her husband, his brother-in-law (*nubou-*). The partially

---

25   Cooked taro is pounded flat then rolled up and recooked in clay pots full of coconut cream.

butchered pig emphasises that the female things given in this context are means of consumption. Were the pig given lives, it might go into some other circuit. Here its use—as with the cooked and raw yams and taro— is only to be eaten. Moreover, a special piece of pork, often a forearm, goes to the sister's husband's father in honour of his having produced the husband. For the brother's female things—means of consumption—he receives tools, which are obviously means of production. This exchange stresses the complementary differences between men and women— organisers of production on the one hand and of consumption on the other. The difference is deeply embedded in the mores of these exchanges. For, after this successful exchange, and only after it, a husband is bound to give a *kitoum* to his wife's subclan mates when she dies. Such *kitoum* might be given to a living brother-in-law or a man's children, both of whom are in the deceased wife's *dal*. One man told me that a subclan is like a bank; I asked him what was in the bank and he said '*kitoum*'. In saying this, he was referring to the process that turns sisters into *kitoum*—male things.

Various kinds of *takon* run the length of what could be called the Muyuw domestic cycle. Earlier I noted that when a woman first marries, she has to deliver appropriate firewood to all of the elder women related to her new husband. Those exchanges are *takon*; for each bundle of firewood (means of consumption), some male thing needs to be given. These are now usually small pieces of monetary currency. As such, these exchanges are context markers. People say that his female relatives will not help a man when he has (mortuary) ritual obligations to his wife if, at the beginning of their marriage, the wife has not delivered firewood to these people. This lower-level *takon* sets up higher-level exchanges. The last *takon* in a marriage comes in a ceremony called a *lo'un*. Its performance is sometimes coupled with an *anagin tavalam*. The latter serves to put a new person in the place of a deceased. In conducting this ritual, a man literally takes over the deceased's debts and credits. The *lo'un* has a different purpose. It pays off the debt the deceased's father created when he made the deceased. With one exception, it operates like all *takon*. Matrilineal kin of the deceased assemble female things and give them to the matrilineal kin of the deceased's father. For those female things, male things are returned. The exception to the standard *takon* is that in at least one large container or stack of food are yams meant to be taken as seeds, not consumables. In one case, the point was emphasised by placing a whole taro—corm and stalk—with one prominent leaf hanging out, on top of the pile of yams. In all other ritual contexts when taro is given, the stalk is kept by the giver as a means of production. In this case, because the exchange is deemed to end the debt derived from the deceased father's productivity, what is returned are the means of production for male capacities. Although the deceased's father's marriage ended from his wife's point of view when she was replaced with a *kitoum*, it only ends with that father when his capacities have been refurnished. Nominally, that vegetable given as food should also have male things returned for it, and I was told that for a big pile of food a *kitoum* would be appropriate. I think, however, that this does not regularly happen and in one specific case for a 1974 *lo'un* the *kitoum* had not been turned over by 1982.

As Muyuw array their *ked* related to marriage practices, *takon* rank below the ideal exchange of same-sex persons in the marriage model and the somewhat more real exchange of pigs for the primary mortuary rites. But more than just ranking is entailed. In the exchange-of-person model, the same things are exchanged: this female, or male, takes the place of that female, or male. The same holds for the exchange of pigs: like genders and sizes are exchanged and the sizes are measured. In both these exchanges, the genders are separated. *Takon* are different. Qualitatively different things are exchanged and they are realised in the differential capacities of the different genders. Effectively, they are not exchanges or transferrals; they are, and effect, transpositions.[26] Such relations are microcosmic instances of the real division of labour that exists among the places in the *Kula* Ring. And removed from the synthetic model of interclan marriages, Muyuw people will readily specify certain kinds of marriages between— or within—villages to take advantage of their differentiated duties.

The lowest-ranking *ked* concerns betel nut and betel pepper; and not just *kula*, but also courting prototypically start with these two. Yet they are not so much exchanged as they entail a complementary combination. And although nuts are considered female while pepper is male, in courting relationships, either gender may have the male or female item. And the encounter works by each person giving some of what they have while receiving the complement from the other person. Customarily, everyone in Muyuw carries their own supply of lime (*pwakau*),[27] so it is added to

---

26   Many thanks to James J. Fox for carefully following through these data and suggesting the idea of 'transposition' for the ultimate translation of *takon*.

27   This word is also used for the colour white. Semen is *pwak* and the slide in meanings here is a matter of everyday consciousness.

the other two so they become red and tangy. The differences are combined to become one entity, and this becomes a metaphor for the idealised relationship between couples moving to a successful marriage.

These spheres constitute a set defined by the idealised exchange of separated males and females at the top, in the depiction of men and women exchanged between clans (*kum*) to not so much the exchange but rather the combination of male and female qualities of betel nuts and pepper at the bottom.

And the characteristics of this set are witnessed in the euphemisms employed when asking somebody for something—in a sense, initiating a particular *ked*. When I asked why these procedures were employed, I was told because you want to avoid 'startling' somebody as well as give them room to manoeuvre around the request. From bottom to top, these references display a movement from far away from to part of a person.[28]

To request betel nut or betel pepper from someone, you ask for a *kapon* or *giyag*. *Kapon* is a half or quarter of a betel nut implicitly so forgotten or lost in the crevices of one's purse that it has rotted. *Giyag* literally means 'withered', but in this case it references a piece of betel pepper leaf or fruit forgotten and dried or rotten in one's purse. The idea in both these cases is that the things are completely out of mind. If yams are requested, one asks for those that were so small they fell through the floor of the yam house when it was being loaded for storage for the next year or that, when dumped out of the basket in which they were put from harvesting, were so small they were never loaded to begin with. Taro reproduce by new plants budding off the corm of the original seed stalk. The original stalk is almost always replanted, because it gets bigger over the years and a new corm will be proportionate to the size of its originating seed. When a plant is harvested, decisions are always made about which buds are large enough to be gathered and used as new seeds. Unless one is emerging from a drought that has drastically reduced one's taro stock (which was the case across much of Muyuw following the ENSO event of 1972–73), some of the new buds are ignored and left in the ground because they are too insignificant to plant. Those are the ones people ask for if they are in need of a resupply of taro seeds. For clay pots, one asks for shards from a broken pot that might still be large enough to use for minor cooking. If one wants a pig, the requests refer to the owner's door (*kokwed*). This follows because

---

28   Leach's (1964) analysis of animal categories inspired this analysis.

people feed their pigs—sometimes every morning and evening—at their doors. In the morning or evening, standing amid anxious pigs, people can be seen prying coconut meat out of split coconut shells. So, 'how is your door?' means 'do you have a pig to give me?'.[29]

Although an inversion characterises it, asking for a *kula* valuable climaxes this sequence. For all of these other items, the suitor asks for something. And although he asks for something metonymically connected to the person receiving the request, he expects to either be refused or be given something substantial. *Kula* requests are different. The suitor does not ask for something; instead, he commands the person holding the desired valuable to 'go think' (*kun kunuway, igau mobaw*: 'you go away, you think, then later I will come to you').

This sequence epitomises many of the ideas carried by the Muyuw understanding of the word *ked*, for the word carries an ethics of appropriate manners and methods. Although the desire for betel nut and betel chewing is ubiquitous, everyone realises that these are insignificant items, at best the beginning of other forms of sociality. Hence the request is for something completely forgotten. It is the same with the miniature yam seeds and unused taro seeds. But having both of these signals the capacity to manage Muyuw gardening practices with all of their overt cosmological orientations. The next step, doors for pigs, is even closer to a moral agent: somebody who has a house (young unmarried people do not and even young married people usually reside with parents or in-laws) and the wherewithal to maintain resources capable of supporting pigs, which are the primary debt-carrying vehicle for *dal* (subclan) resources. Having a 'door' means you have the resources—larger gardens in central Muyuw, coconut trees/plantations most everywhere else or ties to the Budibud pig-production sites—to maintain and produce other significant relations. The last metonym in this sequence intensifies these relations by invoking the human capacity for intentionality, for planning, keeping things straight, being a responsible person and, eventually, an elder. Unlike the betel nut request for something completely forgotten, the *kula*

---

29 The metonym 'door' for 'house' concerning pigs harkens to the symbolism of houses and marriage relations in China. The character for house (*jiā*), 家, comprises two others: one, 宀 (*mián*), which is translatable as 'roof', and the other, 豕 (*shǐ*), as pig. Pigs regularly figured in Chinese marriages as well. I thank Peng Xinyan for discussing these matters.

invocation implicates what should be a part of a responsible person.[30] And those responsible persons add up to other relations, with the signs of that summation being their *kula* valuables, their debts and credits and their names linked by *ked* to the distant places in the complex geography of the *Kula* Ring.

References

Blust, Robert A. 2009. *The Austronesian Languages*. Pacific Linguistics series. Canberra: Research School of Pacific and Asian Studies, The Australian National University.

Bohannan, Paul. 1955. 'Some principles of exchange and investment among the Tiv.' *American Anthropologist* 57: 60–70. doi.org/10.1525/aa.1955.57.1.02a00080.

Bohannan, Paul and George Dalton, eds. 1962. *Markets in Africa*. Evanston, IL: Northwestern University Press.

Damon, Frederick H. 1980a. 'The Kula and generalised exchange: Considering some unconsidered aspects of the elementary structures of kinship.' *MAN* (NS)15(2): 267–93. doi.org/10.2307/2801671.

Damon, Frederick H. 1980b. 'The problem of the Kula on Woodlark Island: Expansion, accumulation, and overproduction.' *Ethnos* 45: 176–201. doi.org/10.1080/00141844.1980.9981198.

Damon, Frederick H. 1983a. 'Muyuw kinship and the metamorphosis of gender labour.' *MAN* (NS)18(2): 305–26. doi.org/10.2307/2801437.

Damon, Frederick H. 1983b. 'The transformation of Muyuw into Woodlark Island: Two minutes in December, 1974.' *The Journal of Pacific History* 18(1): 35–56. doi.org/10.1080/00223348308572457.

Damon, Frederick H. 1983c. 'What moves the Kula: Opening and closing gifts on Woodlark Island.' In J.W. Leach and E.R. Leach, eds, *The Kula: New perspectives on Massim exchange*, pp. 309–42. Cambridge: Cambridge University Press.

---

30 Because animals—pigs, dogs, cats and so on—do not have minds, they commit incest. People who do not behave correctly—prototypically, young people (and small unnamed *kula* valuables)—are said to not have minds (*teivag ninous*).

Damon, Frederick H. 1989. 'The Muyuw Lo'un and the end of marriage.' In Frederick H. Damon and Roy Wagner, eds, *Death Rituals and Life in the Societies of the Kula*, pp. 73–94. DeKalb, IL: Northern Illinois University Press.

Damon, Frederick H. 1990. *From Muyuw to the Trobriands: Transformations along the northern side of the Kula Ring*. Tucson, AZ: University of Arizona Press.

Damon, Frederick H. 1993. 'Representation and experience in kula and western exchange spheres (or billy).' *Research in Economic Anthropology* 14: 235–54.

Damon, Frederick H. 2002. 'Kula valuables, the problem of value and the production of names.' *L'Homme* 162: 107–36. doi.org/10.4000/lhomme.158.

Damon, Frederick H. 2017. *Trees, Knots and Outriggers: Environmental knowledge in the northeast Kula Ring*. Oxford: Berghahn Books. doi.org/10.2307/j.ctvswx6vz.

Damon, Frederick H. 2018. 'Further notes on Kula Ring calendrics and megaliths? Towards an archaeology of Austronesian East Asian connections—Short communication.' *Global Journal of Archaeology & Anthropology* 5(1): 555654. doi.org/10.19080/GJAA.2018.05.555654.

Dorofeeva-Litchmann, Vera. 1995. 'Conception of terrestrial organization in the Shan Hai Jing.' *Bulletin de l'Ecole française d'Extrême-Orient* 82: 57–110. doi.org/10.3406/befeo.1995.2297.

Fox, James J. 1999. 'Precedence in practice among the Atoni Pah Meto of Timor.' In Lorraine V. Aragon and Susan D. Russell, eds, *Structuralism's Transformations: Order and revision in Indonesian and Malaysian societies*, pp. 3–36. Program for Southeast Asian Studies Monograph Series. Tempe, AZ: Arizona State University Press.

Godelier, Maurice. 1999. *The Enigma of Gift*. Trans. by Nora Scott. Chicago: University of Chicago Press.

Granet, Marcel. 1973. 'Right and left in China.' In Rodney Needham, ed., *Right and Left: Essays on dual symbolic classification*, pp. 43–58. Chicago: University of Chicago Press.

Green, Roger and Andrew Pawley. 1998. 'Architectural forms and settlement patterns.' In Malcolm Ross, Andrew Pawley and Meredith Osmond, eds, *The Lexicon of Proto Oceanic: The culture and environment of ancestral Oceanic society. Volume 1: Material culture*, pp. 37–66. Pacific Linguistics series. Canberra: Research School of Pacific and Asian Studies, The Australian National University.

Irwin, Geoffrey, Ben Shaw and Andrew McAlister. 2018. 'The origins of the Kula Ring: Archaeological and maritime perspectives from the southern Massim and Mailu areas of Papua New Guinea.' *Archaeology in Oceania* 54(1): 1–16. doi.org/10.1002/arco.5167.

Leach, Edmund. 1964. 'Anthropological aspects of language: Animal categories and verbal abuse.' In E. Lenneberg, ed., *New Directions in the Study of Language*, pp. 23–63. Cambridge, MA: MIT Press. doi.org/10.1037/e685262012-044.

Lepowsky, Maria. 1994. *Fruit of the Motherland: Gender in an egalitarian society.* New York: Columbia University Press.

Mosko, Mark S. 2009. 'Omarakana revisited, or "do dual organizations exist?" in the Trobriands.' *Journal of the Royal Anthropological Institute* (NS)19: 482–509. doi.org/10.1111/1467-9655.12046.

Mosko, Mark S. 2017. *Ways of Baloma: Rethinking magic and kinship from the Trobriands.* Chicago: Hau Books.

Pankenier, David. 2013. *Astrology and Cosmology in Early China: Conforming earth to heaven.* Cambridge: Cambridge University Press. doi.org/10.1017/CBO9781139017466.

Pawley, Andrew and Malcolm Ross. 1995. 'The prehistory of the Oceanic languages: A current view.' In Peter Bellwood, James J. Fox and Darrell Tryon, eds, *The Austronesians: Historical and Comparative Perspectives*, pp. 39–74. Canberra: Department of Anthropology, Research School of Pacific Studies, The Australian National University.

Piot, Charles D. 1991. 'Of persons and things: Some reflections on African spheres of exchange.' *MAN* (NS)26(3): 405–24. doi.org/10.2307/2803875.

Ross, Malcolm. 2008. 'The integrity of the Austronesian language family: From Taiwan to Oceania.' In Alicia Sanchez-Mazas, Roger Blench, Malcolm Ross, Ilia Peiros and Marie Lin, eds, *Past Human Migrations in East Asia: Matching archaeology, linguistics and genetics*, pp. 161–81. London: Routledge Curzon.

Strathern, Marilyn. 1988. *The Gender of the Gift: Problems with women and problems with society in Melanesia.* Berkeley, CA: University of California Press. doi.org/10.1525/california/9780520064232.001.0001.

Strathern, Marilyn. 1991. *Partial Connections.* Savage, MD: Rowman & Littlefield.

Therik, Tom. 2004. *Wehali: The female land—Traditions of a Timorese ritual centre.* Canberra: Pandanus Books.

11

Walking on the village paths: *Kanaawoq* in Yap and *rarahan* in Yami

Yu-chien Huang[1]

Path, pathway, pathing

The idea of 'paths' or 'pathways' is immensely important to the historical consciousness of people of Southeast Asia, Indonesia and Oceania (Rosaldo 1980; Lutz 1988; Traube 1989; McKinnon 1991, 1995; Tilley 1994; Parmentier 2002). As Tilley noted, paths are understood as 'a way of doing something as method, technique, pattern or strategy'; paths also denote 'fishing techniques, oratorical skills, patterns of exchange and strategies of warfare' in Indonesia and Oceania but fundamentally involve 'establishing and maintaining social linkages and relations' (Tilley 1994: 30) such as the enduring marriage alliance routes (McKinnon 1991, 1995). In different cultural settings, the idea of 'walking on the path' can hold different meanings. For example, walking on the path connotes a sense of improvising and self-decision among the Ilongot in the Philippines (Rosaldo 1980). For the Mambai in Timor-Leste, walking on the path conveys a sense of hierarchical positionality coupled with

---

1   I am deeply grateful to Professor Susan McKinnon for giving me marvellous advice on my first draft, and to Professor James Fox for his warm encouragement and insightful comments.

imagery of a spatiotemporal journey that began at the time of origin—
usually coming from the mountain and resulting in the present position
(Traube 1989). In Yap, walking on the path denotes conformity to the
past and deference to the land (Throop 2010: 132–34).

Referencing Parmentier's study of Belau metaphors of hierarchy, Fox
emphasises the significance across Austronesia of the idea of a path in
local understandings and experiences of hierarchy, and its connection
to the botanical imagery of trunk and tip, origin and issue and centre
and periphery:[2]

> A particularly striking example is evident in narratives of Belau as
> described by Richard Parmentier in *The Sacred Remains* [1987].
> His description of Belau's mythology links the two common
> Austronesian metaphors, that of the 'path' with its 'origin' to the
> botanic image of the growing and spreading 'tree' that extends
> from its base. (Fox 2006: 9)

Using Peirce's theory of signs, Parmentier's series of works begins with
a concern with historical process in Balau and how history has been
systematically registered in the diagrammatic representations to the
Belauans themselves. Those representations include linear paths, balanced
sides, quadripartition and graded series and undergo a four-part analysis:
lexical labels, schematic arrangements, prototypical embodiments
(physical prototypes) and semantic fields (Parmentier 1985, 1987), as
Figure 11.1 shows. He argues that the 'quadripartite ideology' ramifies in
every level: four powerful villages, four chief houses within a large village,
four ranking titles in a council and four satellite houses surrounding
a principal house.[3]

---

2   Fox (2006) further argues for the comparative study of Austronesian 'pathways' to investigate the
representation of relations and their transformations in the Austronesian world.
3   Notably, the quadripartition is marked by the diagram of the four stone corner posts with
a mythical, maternal and foreign origin: they were believed to be transformed from the four children
born to a goddess who landed on Belau after the flood (Parmentier 1987: 4).

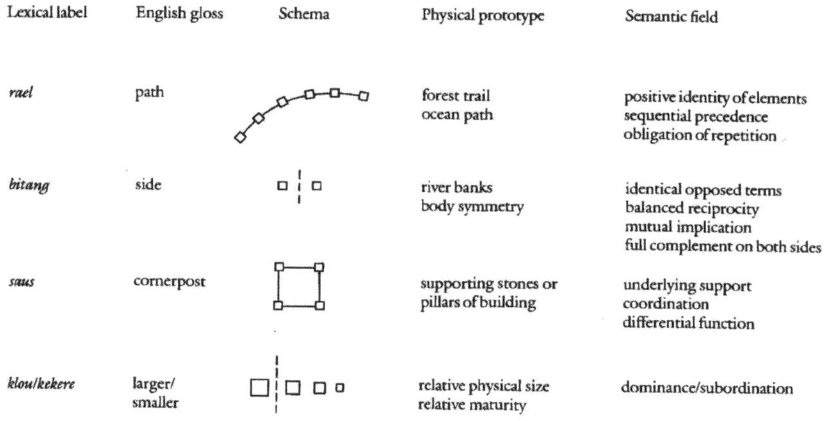

Lexical label	English gloss	Schema	Physical prototype	Semantic field
rael	path		forest trail ocean path	positive identity of elements sequential precedence obligation of repetition
bitang	side	□ ┊ □	river banks body symmetry	identical opposed terms balanced reciprocity mutual implication full complement on both sides
saus	cornerpost		supporting stones or pillars of building	underlying support coordination differential function
kloulkekere	larger/ smaller	□ ┊ □ □ ▫	relative physical size relative maturity	dominance/subordination

Figure 11.1 Diagrammatic icons of Beluan social relations
Source: Parmentier (1987: 110).

Among the four semantic fields, the first, 'path', deserves our attention here. As a semantic field, 'path' includes three features that 'derive from reflection on journeys or migrations along trails' (Parmentier 1987: 109). Those features are 'points' such as sacred stones, trees, valuables, placenames and titles; they are symbolic markers for those locations where 'a god or ancestor stopped on the journey which began the path' (Parmentier 1987: 109). The second feature, sequential precedence, derives from the link connected via those points. The sense of sequential precedence consists of an origin, which implies 'seniority in ceremonial precedence' (Parmentier 1987: 109). The third feature is a linear order, which implies 'the possibility for repeated action with prescribed confines, whether it be retracing a footpath through the forest, pursuing well-attested methods of fishing, or following established social linkages' (Parmentier 1987: 109). Those 'paths' serve as 'sign types' in semiotics or:

> general regularities that impose their template or pattern on 'sign tokens,' so that these individual occurrences are meaningfully categorizable as instances or 'replicas' (to use Peirce's terms) of the general rule. (Parmentier 1987: 109–11)

Parmentier's work foregrounds the significance of the landscape coded with modalities of social relations—for example, the semantic field 'path', consisting of points (ancestors' historical deeds), sequential precedence (linkages) and linear order (repetition). Along with three other semantic fields—balanced sides, corner posts and graded series—'path' signifies historical consciousness. Parmentier's work also represents the profound semiotics of landscape and may coincide with the historicity of Beluan cosmology (Parmentier 1985, 1987). However, his semantics has left very little room for interpersonal interactions and everyday life richness; how those modalities are inscribed into persons, other than through linguistic forms, remains unexplored (Parmentier 1984, 1985, 2002). In this regard, Throop's phenomenological approach demonstrates how 'path is the teacher' and a person's movement over land gradually encodes social values—such as being mindful, vigilant and respectful—into one's body (Throop 2010: 132–34). Tilley's and Harrison's work has also shown how humans, as perceiving and experiencing subjects, read and encode the 'grammar of the space' in their bodily movement across the land (Tilley 1994; Harrison 2004).

As there is vast cultural diversity within the Austronesian world, so, too, is there diversity in the meaning of 'paths' and 'walking on the path'. Here, I use the spectrum of egalitarian–hierarchical to show the contrast. For the egalitarian peoples, such as the Ilongot (Bukalot) living in the highlands of the Philippines, walking on the mountain paths denotes improvisation and self-decision. For them, social order is repeatedly improvising, just as a group of people walking on a path sometimes gather and sometimes disperse. On the contrary, for a hierarchical society, the meaning of improvising is much less emphasised. 'Path' is a metaphor of hierarchy and usually carries some common characteristics, such as the trunk and tip of a tree, the origin and branch, the centre and periphery or the spatial–temporal journey stretching from the ancestors' origin place to the present (Traube 1989). Therefore, 'walking on the path(s)' entails dissimilar meanings in a hierarchical society than in an egalitarian society.

Scope of comparison

This chapter will focus on the diverse configuration of village paths: *kanaawoq* in Yap and *rarahan* in Yami. A *kanaawoq* in Yap is clean, wide, smooth and weed-free. People walking on a *kanaawoq* have to conform to certain decorum: demonstrating respect by walking slowly and mindfully and talking softly. Meanwhile, the *rarahan* in a Yami village is narrow, zigzagging and irregularly sandwiched between individual house compounds, and the villagers' individual walking routes on *rarahan* frequently change for various reasons—such as disputes and feuds, mortuary rituals or when carrying excessive loads of fish. Therefore, the 'path' for the Yami does not denote normative behavioural protocol; it refers to innovation.

Having conducted research on both islands, I believe the difference between village paths in Yap and Yami is not as arbitrary as it appears. Unrelated historically, they seem to occupy two ends of a spectrum between hierarchy and equality within the scope of comparative Austronesian studies. By examining the idea of village paths in two cultures, I hope to discuss the indexicality of 'path' in regard to social order in this comparison, as well as investigate the significance of 'pathing'.

I should note here that among the various meanings and metaphors of 'path', I focus only on the concept of 'village path'. I will discuss how Yapese accommodate their behaviour to the existing village paths, as well as how Yami improvise pathing in the village. I have not included other semantic fields, such as marriage pathways, paths in the wilderness, forests, gardens or paddy fields or paths as methods and techniques. It would be ideal if in the near future I am able to investigate the indexicality/iconicity of the polysemic concept of 'path' and its various forms in Yap and Yami. It might reveal something distinctive in the Austronesian cultures—that is, how humans' signifying practice constantly encodes and transforms cultural indexes that oscillate between hierarchy/equality, collective/individual and normative/improvising.

Yap (path as the teacher)

Yap, called Wa'ab (Uav) by its inhabitants (Müller 1942: 2), is a high volcanic island in the Western Caroline Islands of Micronesia. As an Austronesian language, Yapese probably belongs to the Western Malayo-Polynesian or 'a highly conservative' Oceanic language (Ballantyne 2005; Throop 2005: 99–101, 2010: 18).[4] It has long been known in anthropology for the difficulty of categorising it in any kinship theory classification (Goody 1961; Schneider 1962, 1984) and for its strong hierarchy in this region of the Pacific (Hezel 1983; Bashkow 1991; Throop 2010: 31). In this regard, Throop has carefully argued that the Yapese hesitation to cultural change is mainly attributed to their cultural valuation of careful deliberation, thoughtful action and a morality that emphasises mutuality of being—how the individual internalises community goals as their own

4   Given the extensive borrowing from different language groups, Oceanic and non-Oceanic (Blust 1988: 58–59; Ballantyne 2005: 22; also see Tryon 1995: 28), Yapese is not easily classified within the Austronesian language family.

desires (Throop 2010: 31; Sahlins 2011a, 2011b). In this chapter, I focus on walking on the village paths, which is a demonstration of internalising community values.

Yapese have several terms referring to paths or roads, such as *woq/wol'* ('road', 'way'), *rogon* ('way', 'road', 'method') and *kanaawoq* ('way', 'road', 'path', 'method'). Here, I emphasise *kanaawoq*. It is a special kind of road that existed prior to the colonial period and was usually paved with stones or coral. It connects *tabinaw* ('house estates') within and across villages.[5] Yapese value stone paths greatly, and they are a focus of historical preservation (Krause 2016: Chs 7, 8). There are many regulations for walking on this kind of road.

Kanaawoq refers to 'paths, methods'. The significance can be compared with Paluan *rael*: 'a way of doing something' (Parmentier 1987: 109). Throop points out that 'path is the teacher'—that is, movement across the land has gradually encoded social values, such as being mindful and vigilant (2010: 132–34), into the body. The design of the path is itself normative: individuals walking on the path have to be careful and concentrate on the tasks at hand. For example, walking on a stone path covered with moss, one has to be mindful of one's steps and cannot look around at others' properties, such as gardens, trees and taro-paths. The technique of building the stone path ensures one needs to pay full attention to one's steps: *Daamu changar, mu saap ngaa buut* ('Don't you look around, you look to the ground') (Throop 2005: 295). 'Path as the teacher' keeps reminding those who walk on the pathway to be humble, respectful and mindful of the tasks at hand. Walking on the stone path can be considered as walking meditation (Throop 2010: 133–34):

> In many ways, the path (*kanaawoq*) was characterized as a material reflection of the valuation of reflective action … The very ways in which the rocks are placed on the path serve as a message from the *piiluung*[6] and community to the people walking along it. The path's message is that travelers should always demonstrate respect

5   I was told there are two kinds of *kanaawoq*: *kanaawoq ni gaa* ('big roads' or 'main roads'), connecting villages (sometimes across municipalities), and *kanaawoq ni ichig* ('smaller roads'), connecting villages within a municipality, among *tabinaw*s within a village or between two big roads. Large numbers of *kanaawoq* are paved with stones or coral. Unpaved *kanaawoq* were made from material removed during the Japanese colonial period from roads for motor vehicles.
6   *Piiluung* is usually translated as 'chief'. *Luung or lunguun* means 'voice'; *piiluung* literally means 'many voices'. Thus, *piiluung* is understood as the collective voice of individuals in the village (Throop 2010: 36–37).

(*liyoer*) when traveling in the village. Practically speaking, walking along a Yapese stone path is no simple matter. The rocks are very smooth, often covered with moss, and are, as a result, quite slippery. This is especially so during or after a rainfall. Without careful attention to where you are placing your feet, it is quite easy to fall. When walking on a path it is often necessary to look down to see where you are stepping. In the process, individuals are restricted by the design of the path itself to walk deliberately and slowly, with their heads down. (Throop 2010: 132–33)

In Yap, walking on the village paths means one has to obey the village rules, unlike the Ilongot's improvised walking. Rather, Yapese emphasise following predecessors' rules and respecting the land (Throop 2010: 132–34). Hence, people's lived experience in the landscape is not highly creative and marks the differentiation between generations; the landscape constrains subjects' movements. If we ask how Yapese walk in the village, almost everyone's answer is similar: walk in single file and not side-by-side; men walk in front and women behind; one has to carry a twig in one's hand or under one's armpit. Women usually carry a long basket and men carry a man's basket. One does not look around, but looks at the road, slowly and deliberately, which symbolises respect for the land (*binaw*). Visitors in particular have to obey the rules.

To paraphrase the archaeologist Christopher Tilley (1994: 29), if the 'grammatical system' is inscribed in the cultural space, what is the grammar of space inscribed in Yap? The answer is clear: hierarchy. In Yap, everything—space, crops, land, garments, status—is hierarchical. For Yapese, there are no two things or two persons on the same level; there is always a status difference between one and another person. Anthropologists have used the Dumontian model of Indian hierarchy, distinguishing the Yapese structure of hierarchy between *tabugul* ('pure') and *ta'ay* ('impure'). To quote Labby:

> Like the living area space within the estate, the village was divided into areas that were *tabugul* and *taay*. The estates of high status and the taro patches of the top *yogum* were said to usually be near the center of the village. These areas were generally prohibited to young, fertile women and people of the lower village ranks. The top *tabugul* taro patches were definitely off limits to such people, and only men or women who had ceased to menstruate could work them and collect food from them. Lower estates and taro patches were more and more toward the outskirts of the village, near the

paths for the *rugoth* women and lower villages. The taro patches would furthermore be arranged so that the water flowing through them went into the higher ones first so that it would not pick up contamination. (1976: 83)

Labby has also pointed out that Yapese are cautious to not step into others' territories. Young women would not go to the *tabugul* taro patches; only those of higher status could enter. If a woman accidentally goes into those taro patches, the taro will rot and she will become infertile. If the woman is still very young (very *ta'ay*), she may even die. On the contrary, if 'men of the top *yogum*' ('eating grades') consume food from lower-grade taro patches, they will 'get sores on their throats and become unable to eat … blood would run out of their mouths, and … they could even die' (Labby 1976: 83–84).

Not only do Yapese respect stone paths, as Throop has noted, but also the stone paths are important items of cultural heritage preservation (Krause 2016) and, as such, Yapese would emphasise that, in contrast to other Micronesian islands, Yapese stone paths are relatively unchanging. If a tree grows on the road, other Micronesian islands may let the tree grow and walk around it, but Yapese will almost immediately remove any obstacle on the road to ensure it remains intact and unchanging (Throop 2010: 132). In the village where I stayed, the main path—especially the section lined with stone money—was weeded manually every other month, and every household had to contribute labour (or money) to maintain the road. The weeds had to be pulled by hand, rather than using the weeding machine, to demonstrate respect to the spirit inhabiting the road. The principle that 'the road has to be kept clean' is deeply rooted in Yapese cultural values and practices. In other words, the 'path', as a teacher, remains relatively unchanging, and is taken care of by relatives, ancestors and the persons whom it connects. The paths have to be maintained month by month, generation by generation, carefully and mindfully. Similarly, those walking on the path have to obey the corresponding rules, encoding the grammar of the space into their bodily behaviour through obedience and mindfulness.[7]

---

7   Yapese of different status, gender and age have to walk on different paths. Some are the respected paths, requiring more protocols to walk on them. Young female and low-ranking people should walk on different paths.

To a certain extent, for Yapese, a 'path' is created by people walking on it, but persons are also shaped and made by the 'path', which is loaded with historical and cultural significance.[8]

Thaaq

Another Yapese word, *thaaq* (closely related to paths: *kanaawoq*) also captures the rich meanings of 'path' in Yap society. *Thaaq* refers to strings, threads, connections and relationships.[9] It signifies 'a long line of communication that ties together the various geographical and political units of Yap' (Lingenfelter 1975: 131).[10] Therefore, *thaaq* implies authenticated conduits of communication. Its authenticity is clearly stated by Lingenfelter:

> [A]ny legitimate request or message must follow the channels of communication, or *thaaq*. This is a very serious matter to the Yapese, and if word is passed improperly, regardless of its importance, it may be disregarded. (1975: 131)

Thaaq legitimates almost all perceptible traditional authorities in Yap, from *piiluung* ('chiefs') at all levels to the three paramount seats of power, *Dalip pi Nguchol* ('The Three Paramount Chiefs' or 'three supporting stones of a cooking pot')—the three highest *tabinaw* ('house estates'). Similar to 'eating grades' (*yogum*), which are no longer practised, people may appear oblivious to certain *thaaq* these days. Nevertheless, *thaaq* is still a highly sensitive topic in contemporary Yap.[11] I was forewarned several times that *thaaq* is not supposed to be discussed in public, especially not in front of foreigners.[12]

---

8   The respect Yapese show to *kanaawoq* relates to Yapese sentiment and respect towards the land. For the Yapese, *binaw* ('land') is where identity is tied and where social personhood is marked and cemented by the labour of generations of ancestors. When a Yapese is making a public speech, the opening is always *sirow ko piiluung; sirow ko binaw* ('Excuse me, chiefs; excuse me, the land').

9   A 66-year-old Yapese man described *thaaq* as powerlines: 'Because of power lines, the electricity is able to be carried through.'

10   *Thaaq* can also refer to a type of pandanus (screw palm).

11   The only case I heard where *thaaq* was openly discussed was at men's meetings among the elders of certain *tabinaw* in high-ranking villages, such as Gachpar.

12   The knowledge of political connections is categorised as *machib* ('knowledge within the family' or 'family teachings') and is not easily revealed to outsiders. I admire those predecessors who were able to detail *thaaq*, such as Lingenfelter (1975) and Ushijima (1987). In my experience, *thaaq* is a sensitive issue. People advised me not to investigate *thaaq* too much to protect myself. I consider the ethnographical accounts on *thaaq* as embodiments of mutual trust between the researchers and the Yapese.

Thaaq vividly epitomises the Yapese concept of relations and power. A village community is never a holistic, self-contained social entity. It is penetrated by and constructed through a web of connections. I was reminded from the time of my first visit that not all *tabinaw* ('house estates') in a village share the same rank or status, and there may be several *piiluung* in a village community, each in charge of different spheres of social life.

Ushijima has detailed an example in Gilfith village, Fanif Municipality, to explain how *luungun* ('voice') has to be passed according to appropriate *thaaq* (1987). Briefly, it means only a certain *tabinaw* in the village has the *thaaq* to transmit *luungun*. For example, Gilfith and nearby Rang villages belong to different political alliances (*baan*: 'sides'). If the *piiluung* of Gilfith village wants to convey a message to Rang village, instead of communicating directly, the message has to be passed through a certain *tabinaw*—the 'ears and eyes' of another side. Similarly, if the head *tabinaw* in Rang village has a message for the chief in Gilfith village, it has to be passed through the same *tabinaw* (Ushijima 1987: 193). Nevertheless, for the villages belonging to the same side, the chiefly *tabinaw*s have direct connections with one another; messages do not need to be mediated by the 'ears and eyes' of the other side.

This system seems confusing to outsiders at first glance. It may be easier to comprehend if we imagine it as different telephone companies or computer operating systems in modern life.[13] Ushijima once described the complexity of *thaaq* as follows:

> The particular *tha'* [*thaaq*] employed depends on the nature of the message to be transmitted. One *tha'* is used for the supply of materials and labour for projects such as [the] building of meeting houses. Another *tha'* is used to secure military assistance and communicate battle plans in times of war. Still another *tha'* is used for invitations to ritual exchange. And, apart from these, there is the *tha' ko wolbuw*. *Wolbuw* is the annual ritual exchange of food which is performed at a predetermined time of year. Different

---

13 Nonetheless, the concepts similar to *thaaq* are not unique in Yap. In a non-Austronesian case, in the Arapesh-speaking region (but not restricted to it) of New Guinea, the idea of pathways or roads (*yah* [singular], *yeh/yegwih* [plural]) has become a significant local framework of identity since wartime, persisting even after pacification. Roads served as channels for village units' warfare alliances and as safe passages when intervillage warfare was intense, and they continued to be important in local political manoeuvring when European officials were present in the milieu (Dobrin and Bashkow 2006).

kinds of food, for example, are given as tribute, according to past precedents or in return for assistance received in the past. (1987: 194–95)

I have heard similar descriptions in the field, rendered as 'obligations and privileges', in a simplified version:

One family makes ropes for us; another family replaces the roof for us—now no longer needed because we use tin roofs instead of coconut or napa leaves. But we also provide harvest for other families. So, we work for others while others also work for us. (Male, 60 years old)

In 2014, a large-scale exchange ceremony—*mitmit* ('stuck stuck' or 'stuck again')—was reactivated in Ngolog, Rull. It was a very rare event since *mitmit* had not been held for several decades in Yap. In *mitmit*, *thaaq* is publicly manifested, demonstrated and reconfirmed. Even 'sending word out'—announcing the completion of the men's house in the village, which was an event worthy of *mitmit* celebration—had to follow strict protocols with respect to relative traditional political positions. Krause noted:

In Yap's traditional sociopolitical system, official communications between villages must follow strict protocols that have to do with village rankings and relative positions within the *bulce* and *ulun* political affiliations. As I was told, there are also specific estates that have the roles of messengers for these communications and it is only the specific representatives from those estates who should be carrying the message. And so when word was officially sent out from Ngolog, all of these messengers were called upon to do their duty in notifying the villages. I had learned that this extremely complex network of communications had not been activated in quite some time. In conversations with friends and colleagues after work, *much of the discussion around this time was about who was supposed to contact who[m], and the orders in which the word was supposed to travel as it made its way through all the villages.* (2016: 314; emphasis added)

In one of his dissertation chapters, Krause vividly described people's close attention to this 'extremely complex network of communications'— namely, *thaaq*, which had not been ritually demonstrated for a long time. During the time of my fieldwork (2012–13), anxiety resulting from the confusion of the legitimate *thaaq* was keenly felt. If the messages were not transmitted through the proper channels, the validity would soon be challenged and even nullified.

Thaaq signified Yapese traditional politics, which decided the relative ranking of *tabinaw* ('house estates'), which *tabinaw* is related to which, which would pay respect to which and which should run errands or do service for which. Those *thaaq* rankings are the 'chart' of hierarchy, and Yapese interact with one another according to their respective rankings. It is true that since intervillage warfare was prohibited under the German regime, the dynamism of village ranking has diminished. However, *thaaq* continues to exist and is mobilised whenever necessary.

Thaaq is not unique to Yap. *Va* in Samoa shares the same idea of 'routes'. Pathways or connections suggest a profile or network: a village is a knot of various connections on different scales. For Yap, the symbolism of *thaaq* signifies a certain aspect of sociality: the political alliance. In precolonial times, it meant relative safety, trust, obligations and formal and informal exchanges between the knots on the *thaaq*. For Yapese, administrative territorial boundaries ('municipalities') are designed for governing, but not for the sociality of the locals. As a Yapese man once told me: 'In the past, we had connections rather than boundaries.'[14]

The attitude of seeing the 'path' as the teacher, expecting one to be vigilant and respectful while walking on the path, has demonstrated the Yapese valuation of being humble and respectful—to the environment and to other people. The norms of walking on the path are similar to those of Yapese dancing: mastery of one's own bodily movements is an achievement in self-restraint and self-governance (Throop 2009). Yet the 'lesson' of walking is somehow different. Yapese showing respect to the land, the village and community structures (such as the stone paths) is in fact showing respect to their predecessors' investment of labour; numerous generations have worked on the land where contemporary descendants are living and carrying out daily activities. In fact, the labour investment of previous generations has transformed the environment from unclean, underdeveloped and polluting wilderness to an ordered, clean and inhabitable dwelling space—that is, from *taay* to *tabugul* (Egan 1998: 135). The land in Yap, as well as the historical stone structures, actually epitomise various degrees of labour investment in the past; land embodies and cements hierarchy.[15]

---

14 Roy Wagner's well-known paper 'Are there social groups in the New Guinea Highlands?' (1974) is a continuation of David Schneider's 1965 discussion. The data are based on the above-mentioned 'connections, paths', but he has gone far beyond that and challenged the presumption of the 'unit' or 'group' prevalent in anthropological theory at that time.
15 Unlike caste in South Asia, hierarchy in Yap was not immobile; individuals, houses and villages could alter their ranking through warfare or other historical deeds. Since pacification during the German colonial era, village ranking has become fixed.

In the next section, I will discuss the Yami people in Lanyu (Orchid Island). As an egalitarian society, their concept of 'path(s)' displays a significant contrast with that of the Yapese—in landscaping, in people's movements and the associated etiquettes as well as in the valuations of village paths.

Path(s)/passage(s)/pathing in Yami

The people living on Orchid Island (previously known as Botel Tobago)[16] are named the Yami ('we'), but they call themselves Tao ('person[s]'). The Yami language belongs to the Western Malayo-Polynesian subgroup, as does that of the indigenous people of the Batanes archipelago in the Philippines.[17] In what is characterised as an egalitarian society, the concept of Yami path(s), as for the Ilongot, suggests individual improvisation. Therefore, I use 'pathing' to describe people's movement on the village paths, which constantly varies. To comprehend the Yami's 'individual improvising', I will explain the Yami concept of 'path(s)'.

Unlike Yapese, who have a wide range of words referring to paths and connections, the Yami do not have a rich vocabulary for 'path(s)'. In the Yami language, there is no distinction between 'road' and 'path'. When we ask a Yami about the word referring to paths, roads or passages, *rarahan* comes as the first and most prevalent answer. *Rarahan* stems from *rahan* ('footprints', 'climbing') and refers to paths, roads and trails on which people walk. The cement highway circuiting the island is called *nanad* ('round-island highway').[18] In daily life, *rarahan* is the most common word for physical paths/roads/pathways.

One defining feature of the village path(s) is their publicness: village paths do not belong to any specific persons or individual households, and every villager can walk on them. Being open to everyone has rendered the village path(s) the very few public spaces in a Yami village. In fact, while walking in a Yami village, the first impression one might have is its lack

16 Orchid Island was named Koto-sho (Redhead Island) in Japanese and Lanyu (Orchid Island) in Chinese. The Yami call it Bonsho no Tao (Island of People).
17 It is believed the Yami migrated to the island from the Batanes archipelago.
18 Another word, *onong*, means 'do deal with, forever, paths', relating to *onot* ('stalk, follow'). But *onong* rarely refers to physical pathways or roads; rather, it usually relates to 'walk past', 'forever' or 'decide by oneself' (Rau et al. 2012: 169–70).

of static public space.[19] The *nanad* ('round-island highway'), which ran through the margin of the village communities, is indeed a public space; however, the *nanad* was built by the government, does not belong to anyone and no-one really cares about maintaining its cleanliness. *Rarahan* in the village can be categorised as public and must not be obstructed. Contrary to the village paths in Yap, which are flat, wide and laced with stone money (*rai*), the Yami village *rarahan* around traditional house compounds are zigzagging and rugged like small pathways in a paddy field. Because the sizes of traditional house compounds vary, the passages between and around them zigzag accordingly.[20]

Not only do the passages zigzag and demand that people meander, but also the Yami's walking on the path varies from time to time. For example, when a person dies, people avoid walking around the deceased's household. When one catches a lot of fish (especially flying fish), one should not pass through other people's front yards (*inaorod*). When one is feeding the pigs or carrying crops from the field, one should avoid others' front yards as well. When people are distributing taro and pork from their front yard to reciprocate others' labour contribution (such as in house building), unrelated persons will shun these passages lest they be seen as showing the intention of taking a share. When there is an obstruction on a passage or pathway, or a need to avoid disharmonious relations, the Yami make a detour. Each time—when a burial occurs, when carrying food, when there is an obstacle on the passage—the Yami will find an alternative way to reach their destination, rendering every decision an opportunity (de Certeau 1984: xix). Since the Yami houses are densely concentrated, such events occur very often, and individuals have to choose a suitable itinerary swiftly, resulting in constantly alternating movements within the village. I call the Yami tactical movement 'pathing'—referring to the improvised actions of an experiencing subject to create one's own path.

People pathing denotes this improvisational element. It occurs in the landscape of the paths—the narrow, zigzagging physical space that varies according to the sizes of the nearby houses. To comprehend why the village paths are zigzagged instead of straight, we need to see the Yami

---

19   For the Yami, the spaces that might be considered 'public', such as the elementary school, churches or the playgrounds built by the government, have come later.

20   Even in the cement house areas, where house owners extend their roofs or pavilions unevenly, the paths have to zigzag around them, and a walker must yield to walk around those blocked spaces.

house structure, which entails a lack of public space in the Yami village: the house space grows, therefore, the 'public' spaces become jagged around them.[21]

Yami house compounds and their passages

It is known that the Yami house (and house compound) represents the developmental process of a married couple (Chen 1995: 164). From the time a couple is married and have their first child, they change names (teknonymy), set to work to expand the house and build canoes and hold inauguration ceremonies for achievements in the life course.[22] Therefore, the growth of a *vahay* ('main house') can be thought of as a diachronic objectification of a couple's life cycle (Chiang 1986; Chen 1995). Here, I will focus on the spatial plan of the Yami house compound. We can see that Yami cement houses grow as well, gnawing at the passages between the houses, and the Yami improvise their pathing along these passages.

A complete traditional Yami house is a compound, including three building structures: a main house (*vahay*), a workhouse (*makarang*) and a pavilion (*takagal*).[23] A front yard (*inaorod*), also called an 'extended harbour' (Fang 1984: 81; Kwan 1989: 158),[24] is part of the house compound (see Figure 11.2), and is surrounded by those three structures. In the household compound, sociability is proportional to the height of

---

21   Indeed, whether there is a 'public space' and how such a space is defined would be an interesting point to contrast in hierarchical and egalitarian societies. In my observation, public space is clearly demarcated in hierarchical societies but is fluid and often blurred with private space in egalitarian societies. In an egalitarian society, the places where people gather also shift—depending on relations with leaders or ritual hosts.

22   Getting married is the initial stage of becoming a social person because each significant social action is conducted by a couple, while unmarried people are treated as immature children.

23   The main house is located halfway below ground. The Yami cook, dwell (especially in winter), hold inauguration ceremonies and store inherited treasures here. The workhouse's floor is at ground level. The Yami manufacture artefacts and welcome guests in the workhouse, and also sleep there in summer. The pavilion (*takagal*), built about 60–90 centimetres above the ground, is a place for daily socialising, work and rest.

24   I learned this metaphor—'the extended harbour'—from Fang's Masters thesis (1984: 81), which has been quoted ever since (see Kwan 1989: 158; Tsai 1997: 41; Huang 2005: 116). But Fang did not document the indigenous term. I have asked several Yami people (who have a decent knowledge of local expressions), but they did not know this expression. The only way to find the indigenous term is to verify it with elders on the island. The closest analogy drawn between the front yard and the sea can be found in Liu's documentation of a ritual lyric from a large canoe inauguration ceremony, in which one line states: 'Comparing your front yard to the sea, the canoes never row away from your front yard' (Liu 1982: 193). The genre of this song was called *anohod*—a genre frequently used by the Yami in both ordinary and ceremonial events. *Anohod* lyrics were largely improvised. By contrast, the genre *raod* is only used in ceremonial song-exchange settings and the lyrics are transmitted from the past, and rarely improvised (Chien 2011).

the structure, while privacy is in reverse to its height (Chen 1995: 146). Figure 11.3, the profile of a Yami house, illustrates the differences in sociability and privacy among different structures in the house compound.

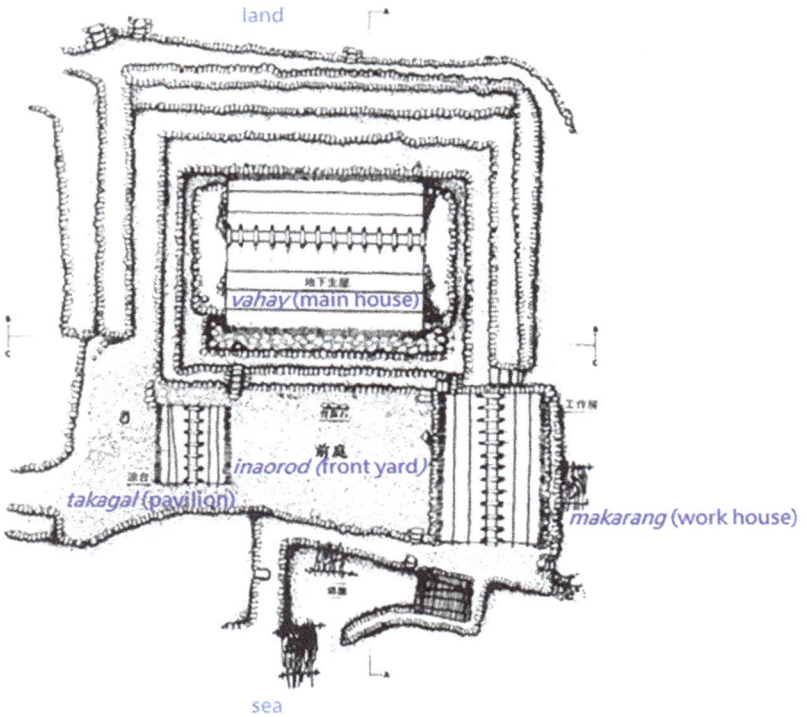

Figure 11.2 The plan of a traditional Yami house

Source: Urban Planning Studio, Department of Civil Engineering, National Taiwan University (1984: 89).

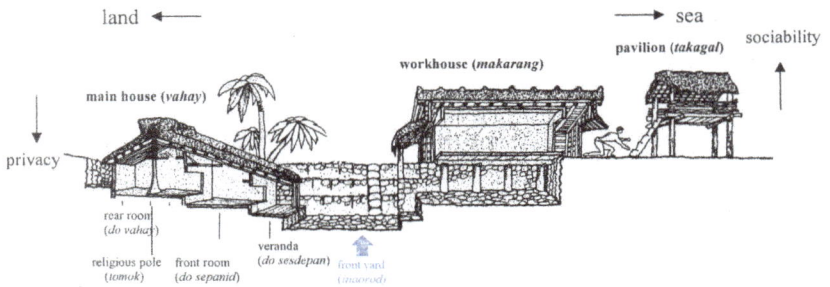

Figure 11.3 The profile of a traditional Yami house compound

Source: Adapted from Huang (1995: Appendix 2).

The front yard (*inaorod*), being surrounded by the three main structures, is a space for receiving guests and for outdoor activities, such as scaling fish, displaying flying fish on a rack and hanging up fishing nets.[25] It is also a ritual space—for example, for welcoming guests to the house inauguration ceremony, for making large canoes, for lifting the large canoes during inauguration ceremonies and for distributing meat and taro during the ceremonies (Kwan 1989: 158; Tsai 1997: 23–24). In fact, Kwan has observed that, within the house compound, the ritual significance of the main house and the front yard was much more salient than for other constructions; while the workhouse and pavilion are used mainly for daily productive and social activities, most rituals are restricted to within the front yard, inside the main house and on the roof of the main house.[26] The roof of the main house, along with the front yard, can be seen as an interface between the spiritual world and daily life (Kwan 1989). Between the houses, there are some narrow passages, called *rarahan nu kuis* ('pigs' ways'),[27] which are usually walled on both sides. When a burial occurs, these passages are the pathways along which the deceased are carried to the graveyard. Traditional houses were situated within compounds, not adjacent to one another, therefore avoiding spirit attacks during burial processions. When a burial occurred, the owners of other houses would fence their compound with bamboo to wall off the spirits of the dead, so the living force of the house would not be endangered (Tsai 1997: 45). During the flying fish ceremony season, if one has caught flying fish, they walk on this passage to avoid passing through those households that have not yet caught their first flying fish.[28]

---

25 While workhouses and pavilions are also places for socialising and outdoor activities, the front yard is a space 'in-between'. It is a space for socialising and greeting guests before inviting them into the main house. It can be a ritual space during ceremonies and an outdoor space for food processing and preparation. None of the buildings in the house compound has such flexibility. The front yard in Figure 11.3 is below ground level. For some Yami houses, the front yard is at ground level, so visibility is increased.

26 For example, the individual cleansing ritual (after a mourning period and at a certain time during a flying fish ceremony) has to be conducted in the front yard. The offering to the ancestral spirits has to be placed on the sunset side (*saray*) of the main house's roof. If a man wants to build a small canoe without patterns, he cannot do it in the front yard for such a canoe is not ceremonial and working in the front yard will provoke the spirits' (and villagers') attention (Kwan 1989: 158–59).

27 Sometimes it is also called *rarahan nu ku rang* ('the path of the spiritual world').

28 It is permissible to pass through households that have already caught and consumed their first catch (usually one fish). I was told the reasons were to avoid showing off and arousing others' jealousy and not infringing on another household's fortune (when those households have not yet caught their first flying fish).

Between 1966 and 1980, the government dismantled most of the traditional Yami houses and built cement dwellings in a checkerboard pattern for the Yami, to modernise them. Traditional houses were only preserved in two of the six villages on Lanyu. Yami were not accustomed to the confined space in the cement dwellings; they chose instead to stay in the traditional house compounds.[29] From the mid-1990s, the government subsidised renovation projects. Yami cement houses have begun to grow in size.[30]

In the village where I was doing fieldwork, the traditional house area was fortunately preserved, with the newly built cement dwelling built adjacent to it (see Map 11.1). From Map 11.1, we can see that, in the traditional living area, the size of each house compound varies and the passages between them are meandering. In the cement house dwelling area, the passages are straight because of the checkerboard design.

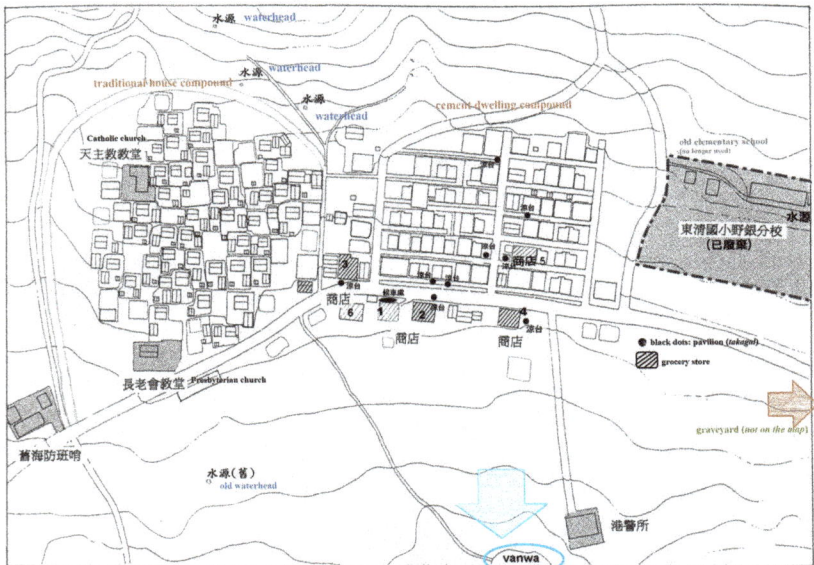

Map 11.1 Map of Ivalinu village

Source: National Taiwan University Building & Planning Foundation (1999: 32).

---

29   For the two villages where the old houses were saved, the villagers had the luxury to choose. For those villages where the traditional houses were gone, villagers slept on the roof or altered the building, adding some wooden structures.

30   The base of the cement dwelling (built between 1966 and 1980) is 39.6 square metres. The renovated house was built on the original foundation. In 1997, the foundation was expanded to 165–98 square metres (Chang 1998: 84), which was 4.1 to 5 times the original.

In contrast to the traditional houses, the cement dwellings do not have a front yard (*inaorod*). The space in front of the house doors has become an in-between liminal space—belonging to the household but also constituting social public space, akin to the front yard. In the daytime, women often make bead necklaces or other similar handicrafts in front of the house. In the afternoon and evening, Yami sit on plastic chairs in this space, chatting with one another and enjoying snacks and drinks. Nevertheless, in the cement house area, the house space is slowly expanding and the front yards often merge with the village passages. The roofs of the cement houses were almost touching one another. Sometimes the space between one house and the next was too narrow to smooth the cement on the walls of the houses. Some people have their *takagal* ('pavilion'), or even the whole second floor, built on top of the passages, rendering the passages corridors with overhangs. Thus, the irregular and crooked pattern of passages of traditional living extends to the cement house area; even though the lanes between rows were designed to be straight, since the houses are expanding, the lanes are shrinking, and people's movements zigzag accordingly.

The growing size of cement houses certainly embodies a Yami idea: the development cycle of a house parallels the life cycle of a couple (see Chen 1995). Similarly, the passages within the cement house area have become crooked; however, they are usually not blocked. Except for some rare cases, there is always a narrow lane: the 'pigs' way'.[31]

Growing cement houses, rugged passages

In 2004–05, when I was doing field research on Lanyu (Orchid Island), the cement houses were expanding in size in every village on the island. Old cement dwellings had certain spatial restrictions designed by the government (no larger than 39.6 square metres). The new cement houses far exceeded the original house area.[32] The observations of a resident Han Chinese, who worked with a nongovernmental organisation and lived in another village, describe this tendency across the whole island at that time:

31 In the rare cases of 'blocking the passage', when houses on the margin of a row use the passages for their own purposes, those passages are less traversed. Thus, the passages might be blocked at the end. But most of the passages in the cement house area are not obstructed.
32 Lin's research showed that the house unit area was expanding and therefore the village paths were narrowing. She investigated 13 renovated house plans in Iraralay village and found that the average area tripled, becoming 3.09 times the minimum. The paths in Iraralay's cement house compounds were formerly 8 metres wide but have now narrowed to between 2.9 and 4.7 metres. The north–south pathway was 5 to 10 metres and now is 4.7 metres (Lin 2004: 3).

> Concerning fire safety, we have had no fire accident here on the island. Once it happens, you see, there is no fire lane between house and house; how can a fire truck come through? It is not only about the fire safety but also concerns landownership. There was no regulation about building coverage ratio and space. Now the houses are expanding and there are no fire lanes.

In the village where I stayed, one renovated cement house had its second floor over the passage and a staircase to the second floor had been built across the path. Therefore, the front yard had been merged with the passage and become part of the house. Sometimes, the house owner would hang up clothes and blankets on a rack over the passage and passers-by would have to make a detour. They would walk on a narrower lane outside the house area. For the villagers, this might be inconvenient, but it was still acceptable for the owner to maintain a lane—the pigs' way (*rarahan no kuis*)—outside the house area.

Traditional Yami main houses face the sea. The main entrances of the cement dwellings also face the sea, and a large number of households have their own ladder at the backdoor. A house owner once pointed to his ladder and explained to me:

> My ladder was made of wood. Why not use cement? [Because, if] there is a burial and people need to carry the deceased to the graveyard, I can take my ladder in [to the house]. This passage is a public passage. They [those who had cement staircases] are breaking the rule. You see, there is no path if we walk up to here [pointing to the aisle behind his backdoor]. (Syaman L., male, aged in his fifties)

What did he mean by 'there is no path'? It derives from the idea that the 'front yard is part of the house', which we have seen in Figures 11.2 and 11.3. During construction and the process of grouting the cement houses, the house can be expanded to such a degree that there is no room for passages, and the front yard and the passage become almost inseparable.

Enlarging the house space requires marking a new boundary for the house. The enclosure and walling off of the household in a cement house area is more prevalent than in the traditional house area. Several houses have cemented their backdoor ladders at the edge of the passage—a phenomenon described as 'breaking the rules', proving that not everyone obeys the consensus about keeping a passage open for pedestrians. However, the narrow pigs' way is saved, although it might be pushed aside. The expansion of individual house space usually results in the shrinking of public space, although the regulations, especially those regarding spiritual beliefs (for carrying a dead body or ceremonial flying fish), still limit individuals' improvisation.

We have seen the expansion of front yards in the cement house area. The front yard is part of the traditional Yami house compound, a place for daily work and socialising, but also a ritual space for welcoming guests in the house inauguration ceremony, lifting large canoes and distributing meat and taro in the canoe inauguration ceremony. In the past, there was no static 'public space' within a Yami village.[33] When there was an inauguration ritual, people gathered at the host's house, being received first in the front yard. The front yard is a space that can be ritual and social, semi-public or totally private. The only places that could always be counted as 'public' were the passages, the 'pigs' ways', which do not belong to any household; everyone is free to walk on them. Those passages run between house compounds and should not be blocked. Today, the checkerboard design of the cement house area does not include a front yard, so people have expanded the space in front of the house, merging it with the passage and therefore infringing on the 'public' space. People have to make detours when they find the front yards are encroaching on these passages. This, however, is not exceptional, since the Yami are always making detours in their daily lives. For example, when they are carrying a heavy load of root crops or bringing flying fish from the sea, they tactically manoeuvre to avoid stepping into another's house area (including the front yard). If they are carrying leftovers to feed the pigs, they also avoid passing through others' front yards.

---

33 Within the village housing area, there were no officially demarcated 'public places' in which the community could gather. When an inauguration ritual takes place, the host's front yard becomes a semi-public place. Thus, 'public space' is fluid in a Yami village (also see Huang 1995: 78–79). In contrast, there are a few public spaces in the Yami world but they are outside the village housing area—for example, *vanwa* (*vanoa*: 'landing place', 'beach', 'small bay', 'harbour') (Rau and Dong 2006: 554)—where men gather for seasonal rituals (in the flying fish season and to worship [*mipazos*]) and for canoe launching ceremonies. The other public space is the graveyard, which everyone avoids. Women look for seaweed/shellfish along the beach (*keysakan*: 'seashore', 'reef', 'intertidal zone'), which might be classified as public, but *keysakan* is not as ceremonial as *vanwa*.

Discussion and comparison

In this section, I discuss the differences between Yap and Yami 'path(s)':
1) the vocabularies about 'path(s)' and their relations with compliance/
improvisation; 2) paths as a landscape, and a relevant idea about the
publicness of the village path(s); and 3) 'pathing' as movement and its
associated etiquette.

First, Yapese have a rich vocabulary describing 'path(s)' and connections,
such as the path (*kanaawoq*), political connections (*thaaq*) and political
alliances (*nug*: 'nets'; and *ban*: 'side'), to name just a few. These words are
endowed with profound meaning and implications, suggesting how one
should behave along those connections. In contrast, Yami do not have
a rich vocabulary for 'path(s)'. In the Yami language, the most common
word for path(s) is *rarahan*, which is derived from *rahan* ('footprints') and
refers to paths, roads and trails on which people walk.[34]

The fact that *rarahan* stems from *rahan* ('footprints') suggests human
actions have created paths for descendants to follow. In fact, village life is
full of innovations and accompanying criticisms.[35] The Yami are typical
bricoleurs in building their own cement houses, repairing scooters and
doing various handyman tasks such as plumbing or electrical work—tasks
that were previously unfamiliar to them. They are cautious about violating
taboos and dread their consequences; therefore sometimes they appear
conservative. Nevertheless, the range of trials and errors in Yami daily life
is far greater than for the Yapese. As Chen (1996) has observed, the Yami
are not hesitant about embracing new materials to reach particular ends
(such as adopting aluminium or plastic food containers or using asphalt
or tin for roofing traditional houses). As long as these alternatives have
safely undergone an initial trial period, others will emulate the innovators
(Miller 1982; Chen 1996). In contrast, in Yapese daily life, the emphasis
is more on being attentive to others' needs and accommodating the
commands from those of higher rank. Yapese highly value demonstrating
one's mindfulness and vigilance in behaviour and showing one's respect

34   Other words, such as *nanad* ('round-island highway') or *onong* ('walk past', 'forever', 'decide by
oneself'), are not as salient as *rarahan*.
35   In this regard, Kao and I have different opinions about improvisation in Yami society. Kao considers
Yami are more cautious in innovating and prefer following their predecessors' footprints. For example,
the elderly would not try an unfamiliar cooked fish and a new architectural design might arouse the
community's gossip (Kao 2014). By contrast, I consider Yami social life to be full of improvisations/
innovations as long as they do not break taboos; taboos delimit the range of innovations.

to the established order (*thaaq*). Improvisations do often occur (Throop 2010: 31–32), but cultural value is placed on deliberation: community goals and needs have to be taken into consideration before one takes action. Compared with Yami, who emphasise that 'men create paths', Yapese take longer to evaluate the possible consequences of any innovations.

There is also a sharp contrast between Yap and Yami when it comes to village paths as a physical landscape and their publicness. Village paths in Yap are flat, wide and kept tidy, while Yami village *rarahan* around traditional house compounds are zigzagging and curved. For Yapese, village paths and the meeting house (*pebay*) beside them are public spaces. Every household has an obligation to weed and maintain the village paths. When outsiders drive cars on village paths or near the meeting house, they must slow to show their respect. If an outsider dares to make noise on the village path, he or she will be severely punished—fined or, sometimes in the past, beaten. For the Yami's traditional dwelling patterns, there was no static or demarcated 'public space' in a village. Any front yard of a house compound could be considered public when the household was holding a ceremony. The only areas that might be classified as strictly public, the village paths or passages, are sandwiched between house compounds (in the traditional house area), even merging with the house front yards (in the cement house area).

Physicality also influences people's pathing. The Yami constantly make detours on their rugged paths, while the Yapese follow the norms of walking manners on their wide, tidy paths. If the Yami were asked, 'How do parents teach their children to walk? Is there any special etiquette to pay attention to?', they would ponder for a while and then respond: 'Not really.' It is not something the Yami elders place particular emphasis on. But they would add that elders (parents) will caution children about avoiding others' house areas. In those cases, people can only walk on the 'public' village passages. Although the Yami do not require specific walking etiquette, they have respect for their fellow villagers. They tactically make detours. For the Yami, loads of labour products, including crops and fish, require zigzag pathing.

I characterise the Yami pathing as 'improvising', partly deriving from their meandering walking routes—constantly making choices and finding detours when there is an obstacle on the path. Yami pathing therefore turns every choice into a new opportunity to form a new trajectory (de Certeau 1984: xix). Improvisation also relates to a Yami ideal: people are born to work (or 'all men are created for labouring'), striving to achieve perfection in life—the accumulation of wealth, power and knowledge (Kao 2014)—and to embody as many relationships as possible (Huang 2005). When one is on one's life course to perfection, improvisations are tolerated and even encouraged as long as one is not violating taboos and imperilling others' wellbeing. Thus, the tactics of Yami pathing in everyday life (*mētis*: 'ways of operating') (de Certeau 1984: xix) are open to a rapidly changing future while also revolving around the limitations imposed by their spiritual beliefs.

In contrasting Yap and Yami, I am not suggesting that when Yapese walk, they never improvise, but rather, when talking about 'walking', Yapese emphasise a stricter protocol: one has to walk in single file; men should be in front of women; one has to look down and at the road; one has to carry a twig or a long basket to display friendliness. Such a walking protocol is absent in Yami society. When I asked the Yapese how people walk and what the regulations or expectations are, almost everyone—male or female, from the north or the south—gave me similar answers. Those answers showed an emphasis on being mindful and attentive to one's walking[36] and paying respect to the village, villagers and the land—the sediment of ancestral labour, history and relationships.

By contrasting Yap and Yami, we can consider collectivity and individuality, compliance and improvisation, past-oriented temporality and future-oriented intentionality. The attitudinal difference in compliance and improvisation has brought us to the next comparisons: labour, temporality and how they relate to path/pathing, as well as to life's trajectory and forms of life.

Labour, temporality and forms of life

At first glance, we might say Yapese value respect and compliance while the Yami admire improvisation. Nevertheless, a deeper investigation would find that both groups value human labour. Yapese value past human labour, which has congealed into the land, whereas the Yami value ongoing human labour, which aligns with the striving for perfection of one's life journey.

---

36   I vividly remember a retired school principal, a Yapese, who nodded when hearing my question: 'It is something the school should have in the curriculum of culture lessons. We should teach our children how to walk, instead of teaching them a fishing skill, which is no longer used.'

Yami believe that humans are born to labour (Kao 2014) and one's life goals have to be achieved via relentless investment in labour, marked by a series of productive activities and inauguration ceremonies. Daily work and its products also largely determine one's pathing routes: one has constantly to make detours because of the requirements for carrying one's own harvest or catch or because of other's growing houses. Improvisations are tolerated and even tacitly encouraged when one is on the course of achieving one's goal: to perfect one's life course. The Yapese also value labour—the human labour of previous generations that has transformed the environment and rendered it inhabitable, ordered and hierarchical (Egan 1998: 134–58). The various degrees of past investment in labour and human deeds have defined the present contours of social hierarchy. Thus, the Yapese demonstrate high respect for order—the hierarchical order epitomised in the land.

Land (*binaw*) in Yap is given a primordial value in every dimension of social interaction, as a repository of Yapese hierarchy (Müller 1942; Schneider 1969; Marksbury 1979; Labby 1976; Egan 1998; Lingenfelter 1975, 1977, 1979; Throop 2010). Land helps to cement 'rank, position, and authority' and the value and power in which successive generations' continuous labour is invested (Throop 2010: 43). It has been emphasised throughout the ethnographic literature that 'land is the chief' and a person is the land's 'vehicle or conduit, its voice' (Labby 1976: 16; Throop 2010: 43). Furthermore, stone constructions on the land, such as stone money (*rai*) and village pathways (*kanaawoq*), index particular modalities of being (see Parmentier 1985, 1987; Throop 2010). *Kanaawoq*, denoting 'path, way, road, method', bears certain semantic meanings akin to the Palauan *rael* ('path')—a sign type referencing the obligation of repetition. For Yapese, the obligation of repetition or of following entails showing reverence to the land and to those who have lived and worked on the land in the past, as well as those who are currently living and working there.

Why is the land so significant in Yap? As Egan and Throop have pointed out, the rank of land—the relative positions on the *tabugul/taay* ('pure/impure') distinction—is, in fact, defined by the labour investment in it by past generations (Egan 1998: 134–35; Throop 2010: 72). Collective human labour has transformed the low-grade, unclean and underdeveloped land into a high-grade and productive land, governed by *yalean* ('customs')[37]

---

37 Yapese often translate *yalean* as 'customs and traditions'. *Yalean nu Wa'ab* is understood as the 'Yapese way' or, as Egan (1998: 135) puts it, 'the prescriptions of Yapese culture'.

that prescribe one's behaviour, roles and obligations in a complex of hierarchical relations (Egan 1998: 135; Throop 2010: 72; Krause 2016: 235–36). This term certainly indicates collectivity and temporality; *yalean* is viewed as something that precedes one's birth by many generations and therefore implies 'largely unquestioned and relatively fixed' ways of doing, thinking and being-in-the-world (Throop 2010: 83). Yapese highly value demonstrating 'respect' (*liyoer*) to *yalean*, to *piiluung* ('chiefs') and to higher-ranked persons or house estates—all of whom are registered in the land. This respect is directed towards predecessors' labour, which has been vested in the land.

The Yapese respect for village paths and stone paths has to be comprehended along with their reverence for the land since land is the embodiment of labour over time. The Yami's improvisation in pathing also relates to their valuation of labour and work: hard work is not only a virtue, but also a defining element of a person.

For the Yami, an ideal life trajectory comprises a series of activities: getting married, bearing children, changing names (teknonymy), building a three-door main house (*vahay*), building canoes, having grandchildren and changing names again, rebuilding the main house into one with four doors and hosting public ceremonies. Every significant life event is accompanied by an inauguration ceremony that requires hard work (clearing fields, rearing taro and pigs). Those activities compose a life course and a traditional form of Yami life (for comparison, see Rosaldo 1980),[38] which could be semantically termed as 'obligations of repetition'. Now, influenced by modern nationalised education and pressed by monetary needs, the Yami have begun to work in Taiwanese cities. It seems there is no longer a clear pattern of life; however, the Yami still highly value labour and hard work, as demonstrated in their expanding houses. We are also reminded of the reason the Yami's daily pathing takes an improvised, zigzagging form: people carrying loads of products of their labour (fish or garden products) avoid passing through others' houses because of respect for others as well as not wanting to arouse others' jealousy or infringe on the fortune of other households. In any case, carrying the products of one's labour matters for one's pathing contour. In the Yami's daily tactical

---

38   This idea of a 'form of life' comes from Rosaldo (1980). The Ilongot's cultural form or pattern could be formulated as 'a number of persons walking single file along paths that shift in direction', 'at times gathering together and at times dispersing' (Rosaldo 1980: 47, 289). This image could also describe the Ilongot's improvised social order, sense of history, social change and social processes (Rosaldo 1980: 54–59).

improvisations, they are still following the obligations of repetition—getting married, bearing children, renovating houses, accumulating relations and, most importantly, working hard—to accomplish the ideal life trajectory.

While the Yami might display a particular form of life—improvising one's path (albeit within the restraints of taboos) in the quest to achieve the ideal personhood throughout one's life journey—do Yapese also have an ideal form of life? I would argue they do. As Ingold (2000: 193) has suggested, the concept of landscape itself emphasises *form*. The Yapese form of life is epitomised in the landscape of village paths (*kanaawoq*). For Yapese, a historical stone path has been made by generations of predecessors and is carefully maintained by their descendants. Yapese pay high respect to the stone path, much as they respect land (*binaw*)—the sediment of history and a symbol of relationships. But Yapese focus more on how humans are shaped by paths. Walking on the paths, one has to follow rules, etiquette and expectations. As a Yapese learns to interiorise these rules, he or she gradually incorporates *yalean nu Wa'ab* and 'becomes Yapese', by experientially embodying the hierarchical order of social relations.

Concluding remarks

Austronesians have various metaphors for social hierarchy: precedence, origin, plants and pathways. I began with the social metaphor of 'paths' and have contrasted the meaning of village paths in two societies. I contend that paths in hierarchical societies such as the Yap are relatively immobile and fixed and endowed with historical depth and multiple metaphors for marriage pathways (McKinnon 1991, 1995), routes of migration, behavioural rules, protocols and etiquette for bodily movement. By contrast, paths and pathways in egalitarian societies such as the Yami are relatively flexible, easily removed and replaced and differ from generation to generation. Their marriage pathways also show a circular pattern over certain generations (three in Yami).[39]

---

39 In this chapter, I have not discussed marriage pathways. Among the Yami, an incest taboo exists among first cousins. For second cousins (*kaposing*), the incest taboo is not so strict. In other words, the third-generation descendants of a couple are marriageable. The third cousin (*kaprongan*) is the preferred pair. The Yami have a circular marriage preference over three generations, which decreases the possibility of creating hierarchy through marriage pathways (Wei and Liu 1962: Ch.5; McKinnon 1991, 1995).

I am concerned with the dynamism of 'making paths' and how people should walk on paths, what needs to be noticed and what rules must be obeyed on the path. In Yap, the path is the teacher. *Kanaawoq* materialise existing connections—the *thaaq*. Those who walk on *kanaawoq* should be mindful and respectful and accommodate themselves to these social relations, which are endowed with temporal and material depth. A *kanaawoq* remains relatively unchanged. While one is walking on a *kanaawoq*, one has to obey a certain behavioural code to show reverence to the village, the land and the people over time. The main village path should be kept clean and unobstructed. Yapese describe the protocol of walking on paths as highly homogeneous—unrelated to the respondents' social ranking or region.

By contrast, the Yami emphasise that paths are made by humans. Landscape physicality can be altered because of human interference (such as the varying size of houses). The individual dynamic of 'pathing' is variable, diverse and improvisational because of different contextual interactions, the purposes of a trip (such as carrying a heavy load of fish or crops or going to feed pigs) and whether ritual matters are involved (such as during a burial or the flying fish ceremony season).

As Mauss (1979) noted several decades ago, bodily techniques—walking, running, dancing, jumping, climbing, descending, swimming—vary from society to society. We have seen the differentiated landscapes of village paths, as well as the divergent attitudes, etiquettes and valuations relating to walking and pathing between the egalitarian Yami and the hierarchical Yap. To simplify: for the Yami, paths are made by humans; improvised pathing takes place on an almost daily basis. For the Yapese, paths shape humans; the village paths and stone paths are carefully maintained and demand people's reverence and behavioural compliance.

Despite the dissimilarities, the attitudinal difference between Yap and Yami reflects an underlying commonality: investment in human labour is highly regarded, despite its disparate manifestations in human constructions (paths in Yap), in products (crops, fish and expanding houses in Yami), in temporalities (past orientation in Yap versus present–future orientation in Yami) and in attitudinal emphasis (compliance and reverence in Yap versus improvisation in Yami). By contrasting the modes of path/pathing, I am not intending to essentialise the two ends of the Austronesian hierarchy–equality spectrum. Rather, I wish to open a window through which we can see the marvellous cultural differences constantly flourishing while ordered around prominent local categories or idioms such as 'path' in the Austronesian-speaking world.

References

Ballantyne, Keira Gebbie. 2005. 'Textual structure and discourse prominence in Yapese narrative.' PhD dissertation, Department of Linguistics, University of Hawai`i, Honolulu.

Bashkow, Ira. 1991. 'The dynamics of rapport in a colonial situation: David Schneider's fieldwork on the islands of Yap.' In George W. Stocking, jr, ed., *Colonial Situations: Essays on the contextualization of ethnographic knowledge*, pp. 170–242. Madison: University of Wisconsin Press.

Blust, Robert. 1988. 'The Austronesian homeland: A linguistic perspective.' *Asian Perspectives* 26(1): 45–67.

Chang, Hsing-Chieh. 1998. 'Restructuring Tao's house in the power of state.' [In Chinese]. MA thesis, Graduate Institute of Building and Planning, National Taiwan University, Taipei City.

Chen, Yu-Mei. 1995. 'Couple, house, and community: The concept of space among the Yami, Lanyu.' [In Chinese]. In Ying-Kuei Huang, ed., *Space, Power and Society*, pp. 133–66. Taipei: Institute of Ethnology, Academia Sinica.

Chen, Yu-Mei. 1996. 'Cultural contact and material culture change: An ethnoarchaeological example from the Yami, Orchid Island, Taiwan.' [In Chinese]. *Bulletin of the Institute of History and Philology, Academia Sinica* 67(2): 415–43.

Chiang, Bien (Daniel). 1986. 'The development, moves and inheritance of Yami residence.' [In Chinese]. *Bulletin of the Institute of Ethnology Academia Sinica* 58: 83–117.

Chien, Shan-hua. 2011. 'On the music of the large canoe inauguration ceremony (*Mapabosbos*) in Iraralay.' [In Chinese]. In Hu Sheng-ling, ed., *2011 Conference on Musical Arts and Pedagogy*, pp. 23–37. Pingtung, Taiwan: Department of Music, National Pingtung University of Education.

de Certeau, Michel. 1984. *The Practice of Everyday Life*. Berkeley, CA: University of California Press.

Dobrin, Lise and Ira Bashkow. 2006. '"Pigs for dance songs": Reo Fortune's empathetic ethnography of the Arapesh roads.' *Histories of Anthropology Annual* 2(1): 123–54. doi.org/10.1353/haa.0.0015.

Egan, James Arthur. 1998. 'Taro, fish, and funerals: Transformations in the Yapese cultural topography of wealth.' PhD dissertation, Department of Anthropology, University of California, Irvine.

Fang, Keng-Shyurng. 1984. 'House and its original study: The Yami tribe, Taiwan aboriginal.' MA thesis, Department of Architecture, Tamkang University, Taipei City.

Fox, James J. 2006. 'Place and landscape in comparative Austronesian perspective.' In James J. Fox, ed., *The Poetic Power of Place: Comparative perspectives on Austronesian ideas of locality*, pp. 1–21. Canberra: ANU E Press. doi.org/10.22459/PPP.09.2006.01.

Goody, Jack. 1961. 'The classification of double descent systems.' *Current Anthropology* (1): 3–25. doi.org/10.1086/200156.

Harrison, Simon. 2004. 'Forgetful and memorious landscapes.' *Social Anthropology* 12(2): 135–51. doi.org/10.1111/j.1469-8676.2004.tb00096.x.

Hezel, Francis X., SJ. 1983. *The First Taint of Civilization: A history of the Caroline and Marshall islands in pre-colonial days, 1521–1885.* Honolulu: University of Hawai`i Press.

Huang, Xu. 1995. *Yami People's Dwelling Culture and Its Transformation.* [In Chinese]. Banciao, Taiwan: Daw Hsiang Publishing.

Huang, Yu-chien. 2005. '"Exchange" and "individualism": A case study of Ivalinu, Lan-yu.' [In Chinese]. MA thesis, Department of Anthropology, National Taiwan University, Taipei City.

Ingold Tim. 2000 [1993]. 'The temporality of the landscape.' In Tim Ingold, *The Perception of the Environment: Essays on livelihood, dwelling and skill*, pp. 189–208. London: Routledge.

Kao, Hsin-chieh. 2014. 'The road to perfection: Personhood and labour in Yami culture.' [In Chinese]. *Taiwan Journal of Anthropology* 12(2): 1–52.

Krause, Stefan Michael. 2016. 'The production of cultural heritage discourses: Political economy and the intersections of public and private heritage in Yap State, Federated States of Micronesia.' PhD dissertation, Department of Anthropology, University of South Florida, Tampa, FL.

Kwan, Hwa-san. 1989. 'The physical environment and religious thought among the Yami.' [In Chinese]. *Bulletin of the Institute of Ethnology Academia Sinica* 67: 143–75.

Labby, David. 1976. *The Demystification of Yap: Dialectics of culture on a Micronesian island.* Chicago: University of Chicago Press.

Lin, Hsi-Chuan. 2004. 'The conflict and adaptation between the house renovation project and the Yami culture in Lanyu: Case studies of building plans.' [In Chinese]. Paper presented to 2004 Conference of Lanyu Research Group, Institute of Ethnology, Academia Sinica, Nankang, Taipei, 20 December.

Lingenfelter, Sherwood Galen. 1975. *Yap: Political leadership and culture change in an island society.* Honolulu: University of Hawai`i Press.

Lingenfelter, Sherwood Galen. 1977. 'Emic structure and decision-making in Yap.' *Ethnology* 16(4): 331–52. doi.org/10.2307/3773261.

Lingenfelter, Sherwood Galen. 1979. 'Yap eating class: A study of culture and communitas.' *Journal of the Polynesian Society* 88: 415–32.

Liu, Pin-Hsiung. 1982. 'Yami text: Boat ceremonial songs.' [In Chinese]. *Bulletin of the Institute of Ethnology Academia Sinica* (54): 147–96.

Lutz, Catherine A. 1988. *Unnatural Emotions: Everyday sentiments on a Micronesian atoll and their challenge to Western theory.* Chicago: University of Chicago Press. doi.org/10.7208/chicago/9780226219783.001.0001.

McKinnon, Susan. 1991. *From a Shattered Sun: Hierarchy, gender, and alliance in the Tanimbar Islands.* Madison: University of Wisconsin Press.

McKinnon, Susan. 1995. 'Houses and hierarchy: The view from a South Moluccan society.' In Janet Carsten and S. Hugh Jones, eds, *About the House: Lévi-Strauss and beyond*, pp. 170–88. Cambridge: Cambridge University Press. doi.org/10.1017/CBO9780511607653.008.

Marksbury, Richard A. 1979. 'Land tenure and modernization in the Yap islands.' PhD dissertation, Department of Anthropology, Tulane University, New Orleans, LA.

Mauss, Marcel. 1979 [1950]. 'Body techniques.' In Marcel Mauss, *Sociology and Psychology: Essays*, pp. 95–123. London: Routledge & Kegan Paul. doi.org/10.2307/3032558.

Miller, Daniel. 1982. 'Structures and strategies: An aspect of the relationship between social hierarchy and cultural change.' In Ian Hodder, ed., *Symbolic and Structural Archaeology*, pp. 89–98. Cambridge: Cambridge University Press. doi.org/10.1017/CBO9780511558252.010.

Müller, Wilhelm. 1942 [1917]. *Yap*. Human Relations Area Files, New Haven, CT.

National Taiwan University Building & Planning Foundation. 1999. *Plan for Ivarinu Settlement Improvement: Improving Lanyu environment. Phase V: Detailed planning*. [In Chinese]. Commissioned by the Council of Aboriginal Affairs, Taiwan Provincial Government, Nantou.

Parmentier, Richard J. 1984. 'House affiliation systems in Belau.' *American Ethnologist* 11: 656–76. doi.org/10.1525/ae.1984.11.4.02a00030.

Parmentier, Richard J. 1985. 'Diagrammatic icons and historical processes in Belau.' *American Anthropologist* 87(4): 840–52. doi.org/10.1525/aa.1985.87.4. 02a00060.

Parmentier, Richard J. 1987. *The Sacred Remains: Myth, history, and polity in Belau*. Chicago: University of Chicago Press.

Parmentier, Richard J. 2002. 'Money walks, people talk: Systemic and transactional dimensions of Palauan exchange.' *L'Homme*: 49–79. doi.org/ 10.4000/lhomme.156.

Rau, Victoria and Maa-Neu Dong. 2006. *Yami Texts with Reference Grammar and Dictionary*. [In Chinese]. Taipei City: Institute of Linguistics, Academia Sinica.

Rau, Victoria, Maa-Neu Dong and Ann Hui-Huan Chang, eds. 2012. *Yami (Tao) Dictionary*. [In Chinese and English]. Taipei: National Taiwan University Press.

Rosaldo, Renato. 1980. *Ilongot Headhunting, 1883–1974: A study in society and history*. Stanford, CA: Stanford University Press.

Sahlins, Marshall D. 2011a. 'What kinship is (part one).' *Journal of the Royal Anthropological Institute* 17(1): 2–19. doi.org/10.1111/j.1467-9655.2010. 01666.x.

Sahlins, Marshall D. 2011b. 'What kinship is (part two).' *Journal of the Royal Anthropological Institute* 17(2): 227–42. doi.org/10.1111/j.1467-9655.2011. 01677.x.

Schneider, David M. 1962. 'Double descent on Yap.' *Journal of the Polynesian Society* 71: 1–24.

Schneider, David M. 1965. 'Some muddles in the models: Or, how the system really works.' In Michael Banton, ed., *The Relevance of Models for Social Anthropology*, pp. 25–85. London: Tavistock Publications.

Schneider, David M. 1969. 'A re-analysis of the kinship system of Yap in the light of Dumont's statement.' Unpublished paper presented at Kinship and Locality: Wenner-Gren Foundation for Anthropological Research—A Burg Wartenstein Symposium, Burg Wartenstein, Austria, 23 August – 1 September.

Schneider, David M. 1984. *A Critique of the Study of Kinship*. Ann Arbor: University of Michigan Press.

Throop, C. Jason. 2005. 'Suffering and sentiment: Exploring the vicissitudes of pain and experience in Yap (Waqab), Federated States of Micronesia.' PhD dissertation, Department of Anthropology, University of California, Los Angeles.

Throop, C. Jason. 2009. '"Becoming beautiful in the dance": On the formation of ethical modalities of being in Yap, Federated States of Micronesia.' *Oceania* 79(2): 179–201. doi.org/10.1002/j.1834-4461.2009.tb00058.x.

Throop, C. Jason. 2010. *Suffering and Sentiment: Exploring the vicissitudes of experience and pain in Yap*. Berkeley, CA: University of California Press.

Tilley, Christopher. 1994. 'Space, place, landscape and perception: Phenomenological perspectives.' In Christopher Tilley, *A Phenomenology of Landscape: Places, paths and monuments*, pp. 7–34. Providence, RI: Berg.

Traube, Elizabeth G. 1989. 'Obligations to the source: Complementarity and hierarchy in an eastern Indonesian society.' In David Maybury-Lewis and Uri Almagor, eds, *The Attraction of Opposites: Thought and society in a dualistic mode*, pp. 321–44. Ann Arbor: University of Michigan Press.

Tryon, Darrell. 1995. 'Proto-Austronesian and the major Austronesian subgroups.' In Peter Bellwood, James J. Fox and Darrell Tryon, eds, *The Austronesians: Historical and comparative perspectives*, pp. 19–41. Canberra: Department of Anthropology, Research School of Pacific Studies, The Australian National University.

Tsai, Hsiao-Chun. 1997. 'The social production of Tao's house.' [In Chinese]. MA thesis, Graduate Institute of Building and Planning, National Taiwan University, Taipei City.

Urban Planning Studio, Department of Civil Engineering, National Taiwan University. 1984. *Commissioned Research Report on the Natural and Human Resources in Lanyu*. [In Chinese]. Taipei City: Department of Civil Affairs, Taiwan Province.

Ushijima, Iwao. 1987. 'Political structure and formation of communication channels on Yap island: A case study of the Fanif District.' *Senri Ethnological Studies* (21): 177–203.

Wagner, Roy. 1974. 'Are there social groups in the New Guinea Highlands?' In Murray J. Leaf, ed., *Frontiers of Anthropology: An introduction to anthropological thinking*, pp. 95–122. New York: Van Nostrand.

Wei, Hwei-lin and Pin-hsiung Liu. 1962. *Social Structure of the Yami, Botel Tobago.* [In Chinese]. Taipei: Institute of Ethnology, Academia Sinica.

Contributors

Frederick H. Damon received his PhD in Anthropology from Princeton University in 1978. He has accumulated over four years of research on Muyuw in the northeast corner of the Kula Ring in Papua New Guinea's Milne Bay Province and close to a year of preliminary research in Fujian Province, southeast China. He published *From Muyuw to the Trobriands: Transformations Along the Northern Side of the Kula Ring* (University of Arizona Press, 1990) and *Trees, Knots and Outriggers: Environmental Knowledge in the Northeast Kula Ring* (Berghahn Books, 2017). With Roy Wagner, he edited *Death Rituals and Life in the Societies of the Kula* (Northern Illinois University Press, 1989) and, with Mark Mosko, *On the Order of 'Chaos': Social Anthropology and the Science of 'Chaos'* (Berghahn Books, 2005). He researches and writes about ritual, exchange and production, environmental relations and Indo-Pacific cultural history. He is Professor of Anthropology at the University of Virginia, where he has been located since 1976.

James J. Fox is an Emeritus Professor at The Australian National University, where he has been Professorial Fellow and Professor since 1975. He was Director of the Research School of Pacific and Asian Studies until his retirement in 2006. He was the initiator of the interdisciplinary Comparative Austronesian Project, which was begun in the late 1980s as a major research focus at The Australian National University, and he has edited many of the volumes in the Comparative Austronesian series published by ANU Press, including the most recent volume, *Expressions of Austronesian Thought and Emotions* (2018). Professor Fox's most recent publications are *Explorations in Semantic Parallelism* (ANU Press, 2014) and *Master Poets, Ritual Masters: The Art of Oral Composition among the Rotenese of Eastern Indonesia* (ANU Press, 2016).

Yu-chien Huang received her MA from National Taiwan University and her PhD from the University of Virginia. Her doctoral fieldwork in Yap, Micronesia, focused on the local responses to a large-scale tourism development in relation to gender, kinship and hierarchy. She has also worked among the Yami people off eastern Taiwan on their forms of exchange and concepts of life. She is currently a postdoctoral scholar at the Institute of Ethnology, Academia Sinica.

Monica Janowski received her PhD in social anthropology from the London School of Economics in 1991. She undertook field research among the Kelabit in Sarawak between 1986 and 1988, 1992 and 1993 and for shorter periods since then. She is currently carrying out research among tribal groups, Chinese and Malays in Sarawak on beliefs relating to water and spirit snakes/dragons. Her publications include *The Forest, Source of Life: The Kelabit of Sarawak* (British Museum and Sarawak Museum, 2003), *Kinship and Food in Southeast Asia* (co-edited with Fiona Kerlogue, NIAS Press, 2007), *Why Cultivate? Anthropological and Archaeological Approaches to Foraging–Farming Transitions in Southeast Asia* (co-edited with Graeme Barker, McDonald Institute for Archaeological Research, 2011), *Imagining Landscapes, Past, Present and Future* (co-edited with Tim Ingold, Ashgate, 2012) and *Tuked Rini, Cosmic Traveller: Life and Legend in the Heart of Borneo* (NIAS Press, 2014). She retired from School of Oriental and African Studies in 2015.

Susanne Kuehling is an Associate Professor at the University of Regina in Canada. She taught for five years at Heidelberg University before moving to Canada in 2008. She received her MA from Göttingen University in Germany. For her doctoral research, she conducted 18 months of fieldwork on Dobu Island in Papua New Guinea. Her PhD thesis, submitted to The Australian National University in 1999, was titled 'The Name of the Gift: Ethics of Exchange on Dobu Island'. She has published a monograph, *Dobu: Ethics of Exchange on a Massim Island* (University of Hawai`i Press, 2005), and journal articles on *kula* exchange, value, personhood, morality, gender, emplacement and teaching methods. Her current project on the revitalisation of *kula* exchange was developed during a number of visits to Dobu Island in 2009, 2012 and 2015 and is funded by the Canadian Social Sciences and Humanities Research Council.

Yi-tze Lee is an Assistant Professor in the Department of Ethnic Relations and Cultures at National Dong Hwa University, Hualien, Taiwan. He received his PhD in Anthropology from the University of Pittsburgh in 2012. He has conducted extended fieldwork on the rituals and traditional ecological knowledge of the Amis in eastern Taiwan. His research interests include environmental humanities, science and technology studies and the ritual practices of the Taiwanese indigenous people. He has published a monograph on the traditional ecological knowledge of the Amis people and several journal articles about Amis contemporary livelihoods in Chinese. He is currently participating in a research project entitled 'Austronesian World: Human–Animal Entanglement in the Pacific Anthropocene'.

Wen-ling Lin is currently an Associate Research Fellow at the Institute of Ethnology, Academia Sinica, Taiwan, and a joint Professor at the Department of Humanities and Social Sciences and the Institute of Social Research and Cultural Studies at the National Chiao Tung University. Lin's main research areas include contemporary indigenous studies (focusing on West Rukai in southern Taiwan), indigenous gendered otherness studies, digital anthropology and visual anthropology. Recent works include *Mediations and Transformations of Indigenous Social Issues: The Contemporary Agenda for Taiwan Indigenous Documentaries* (In press), *The Digital Lives of Indigenous Female Elders in Remote Taiwan* (in Pi-chen Liu, ed., Cultural Heritage, Tourism, Museums and Visual Media: Contemporary Taiwan Indigenous Cultural Performances, SMC Publishing Inc. Southern Press, 2017) and 'From Site to Sight: Embodiment, Repositioning and Challenge of Transgender Corporeality' (*Taiwan Journal of Anthropology*, 15[1], 2017).

Dana Rappoport is a French research fellow at the Centre National de la Recherche Scientifique. She is a member of the French Centre for Southeast Asian Studies (Ecole des Hautes Etudes en Sciences Sociales). After devoting a large part of her work to the ritual musical productions of the Toraja in Sulawesi, Rappoport's research is now focused on small societies of eastern Indonesia and Timor-Leste. She is the author of *Songs from the Thrice-Blooded Land: Ritual Music of the Toraja (Sulawesi, Indonesia)* (Editions de la Maison des Sciences de l'homme, 2009).

Denis Regnier obtained his PhD in social anthropology from the London School of Economics and Political Science in 2012. He has been conducting fieldwork among the Betsileo of Madagascar since 2008 and has recently started new research on family violence in the Pacific. He currently teaches at the University of French Polynesia in Tahiti and is an Associate Researcher at the newly created Maison des Sciences de l'Homme du Pacifique. He has published articles on slavery, marriage, essentialism, funerary practices, ancestral tombs and naming. His first monograph, *Slavery and Essentialism in Highland Madagascar: History, Ethnography, Cognition*, is forthcoming.

Clifford Sather received his PhD in social anthropology from Harvard University in1971. He did field research with the Bajau Laut in Sabah between 1964 and 1979 and with the Iban in Sarawak since 1977. His publications include *The Bajau Laut: Adaptation, History, and Fate in a Maritime Fishing Society of South-Eastern Sabah* (Oxford University Press, 1997), *Seeds of Play, Words of Power: An Ethnographic Study of Iban Shamanic Chants* (Tun Jugah Foundation, 2001) and *A Borneo Healing Romance: Ritual Storytelling and the Sugi Sakit* (Borneo Research Council, 2017). He also co-edited with James J. Fox *Origins, Ancestors and Alliance* (ANU Press, 1996) and, with Timo Kaartinen, *Beyond the Horizon: Essays on Myth, History, Travel and Society* (Finnish Literature Society, 2008). He retired from the University of Helsinki in 2005.

Index

Numbers in bold are illustrations. A number containing 'n.' indicates a reference appearing in a footnote on that page.

www.ingramcontent.com/pod-product-compliance
Lightning Source LLC
Chambersburg PA
CBHW051442270326
41932CB00038B/3396

* 9 7 8 1 7 6 0 4 6 4 3 2 5 *